D0687527

BIOFEEDBACK

Theory and Research

BIOFEEDBACK
Theory and Research

Edited by

GARY E. SCHWARTZ

Department of Psychology
Yale University
New Haven, Connecticut

JACKSON BEATTY

Department of Psychology
University of California
Los Angeles, California

ACADEMIC PRESS New York San Francisco London 1977

A Subsidiary of Harcourt Brace Jovanovich, Publishers

ACADEMIC PRESS, INC.
111 Fifth Avenue, New York, New York 10003

United Kingdom Edition published by
ACADEMIC PRESS, INC. (LONDON) LTD.
24/28 Oval Road, London NW1

Library of Congress Cataloging in Publication Data

Main entry under title:

Biofeedback, theory and research.

Includes bibliographies.
1. Biofeedback training. I. Schwartz, Gary E., Date II. Beatty, Jackson.
BF319.5.B5B573 615′.851 76-30395
ISBN 0-12-632450-6

PRINTED IN THE UNITED STATES OF AMERICA

Contents

II THE AUTONOMIC NERVOUS SYSTEM

III THE CENTRAL NERVOUS SYSTEM

IV THE SKELETAL MUSCULATURE

List of Contributors

Numbers in parentheses indicate the pages on which the authors' contributions begin.

JOHN V. BASMAJIAN (415), Regional Rehabilitation Research and Training Center, Emory University, Atlanta, Georgia

JACKSON BEATTY (1, 351), Department of Psychology, University of California, Los Angeles, California

A. H. BLACK (89), Department of Psychology, McMaster University, Hamilton, Ontario, Canada

JOSEPH V. BRADY (243), Division of Behavioral Biology, The Johns Hopkins University School of Medicine, Baltimore, Maryland

JASPER BRENER (29), Department of Psychology, University of Hull, Hull, England

THOMAS H. BUDZYNSKI (433), University of Colorado Medical Center, and Biofeedback Institute of Denver, Denver, Colorado

A. COTT (89), McMaster University, Hamilton, Ontario, Canada

BARRY R. DWORKIN (129, 221), The Rockefeller University, New York, New York

ALAN H. HARRIS (243), Division of Behavioral Biology, Department of Psychiatry and Behavioral Sciences, The Johns Hopkins University School of Medicine, Baltimore, Maryland

L. C. JOHNSON (163), Psychophysiology Division, Naval Health Research Center, San Diego, California

G. H. LAWRENCE* (163), Human Resources Research Office, Defense Advanced Research Projects Agency, Arlington, Virginia

RICHARD S. LAZARUS (67), Department of Psychology, University of California, Berkeley, California

* Present address: National Academy of Sciences, CPRD/JH315, 2101 Constitution Avenue N.W., Washington, D.C. 20418.

J. ALBERTO MAINARDI (313), Department of Psychiatry, University of California, Los Angeles, California

NEAL E. MILLER (129, 221), The Rockefeller University, New York, New York

THOMAS B. MULHOLLAND (9), Psychophysiology Laboratory, Veterans Administration Hospital, Bedford, Massachusetts

R. PAVLOSKI (89), McMaster University, Hamilton, Ontario, Canada

RAYMOND C. ROSEN (301), Department of Psychiatry, CMDNJ–Rutgers Medical School, Piscataway, New Jersey

J. PETER ROSENFELD (371), Psychology Department, Cresap Laboratory of Neuroscience and Behavior, Northwestern University, Evanston, Illinois

GARY E. SCHWARTZ (1, 183), Department of Psychology, Yale University, New Haven, Connecticut

DAVID SHAPIRO (313), Department of Psychiatry, University of California, Los Angeles, California

M. B. STERMAN (389), Veterans Administration Hospital, Sepulveda, California, and Departments of Anatomy and Psychiatry, University of California, Los Angeles, California

RICHARD S. SURWIT (313), Department of Psychiatry, Harvard Medical School, and Massachusetts Mental Health Center, Boston, Massachusetts

EDWARD TAUB (265), Institute for Behavioral Research, Inc., Silver Spring, Maryland

Preface

Biofeedback: Theory and Research is a volume born in conversation between us at the 1973 American Psychological Association meetings in Montreal. Its purpose is to provide a detailed scholarly and comprehensive treatment of a large series of recent experiments dealing with the learned control of central and autonomic nervous system functions.

It is our firm belief that the body of research often denoted by the term "biofeedback" does not represent a separate or isolated series of investigations. This growing literature has drawn, in some cases extensively, upon the well-developed operational methods of instrumental conditioning. Systems control theory has also been utilized as a theoretical framework by some investigators in the field. Still others have conceived the learned control of autonomic or central nervous system activity as an instance of skill learning, and have employed the theoretical formulations from that literature as appropriate models. Thus, in our view, one primary function of the present volume is to establish firmly such conceptual bridges between the biofeedback experiment and other productive areas of psychological research.

The greater part of this volume is concerned with the substantive study of the autonomic nervous system, the central nervous system, and the skeletal musculature. Given the current state of biofeedback research and the lack of definitive reviews in this area, we felt that the substantive issues could best be treated by providing a mixture of selective reviews and detailed treatments of particular investigations of special importance. This approach provides the reader with both an overview of emerging research areas and a closer acquaintance with projects of a special significance. The present volume is not an exhaustive review of all the major theories and findings involving biofeedback procedures. It is nonetheless a representative one.

Since its inception, the biofeedback literature has concerned itself with clinical problems. Indeed, in his first major review of the subject, Miller[1] discussed the therapeutic possibilities of learned autonomic control. Interest in biofeedback as treatment has continued to rise, despite the fact that current data do not support all of the optimistic predictions of earlier years. Although our major concern is with basic research and theoretical issues, the question of clinical application is sufficiently important to warrant consideration and evaluation in this volume.

Because the field is new, and still relatively undeveloped, it is premature to attempt a fully integrative and definitive treatment of biofeedback and the learned regulation of bodily functions. Many controversies characterize the published literature. This diversity is preserved in this volume through the perspectives of the various contributing authors. We have deliberately refrained from attempting to edit the volume into a more "uniform" or integrated whole, and we acknowledge the individual authors' willingness to present their views in a clear and cogent fashion.

With the endorsement and support of Academic Press, the initial organization of the volume was developed in the winter of 1973–1974 and invitations to authors were sent in the winter and spring of 1974. Many chapters were completed during the 1974–1975 academic year, and final editing was finished in the winter of 1975–1976, while G. E. S. was on leave from Harvard University at the University of British Columbia. The volume could not have been completed without the assistance of a number of talented and able secretaries, notably Sharon Cronan and Joey Fergiola at Harvard University, and Florence Stuart at the University of British Columbia. During the preparation of the volume, both editors received funding from a five-year research program on biofeedback and self-regulation from the Advanced Research Projects Agency of the Department of Defense and monitored by the Office of Naval Research under contract N00014-70-C-0350; this support is gratefully acknowledged.

Finally, each of us would like to express a special thank you: To Jeanne I. and Charlie N. Schwartz, who provided loving support during the hours of stimulation and frustration that are inherent in the production of a volume of this sort, and to Nancy V. Peter, who understands such things.

[1] N. E. Miller, Learning of visceral and glandular responses, *Science,* 1969, *163,* 434–445.

1

Introduction

GARY E. SCHWARTZ
Yale University
JACKSON BEATTY
University of California, Los Angeles

"Biofeedback" is a recently coined term that refers to a group of experimental procedures in which an external sensor is used to provide the organism with an indication of the state of a bodily process, usually in an attempt to effect a change in the measured quantity. That indication has been termed "feedback" (hence, biofeedback) or "reinforcement," depending primarily upon the theoretical perspective of the investigator. The uses to which biofeedback procedures have been applied range from the experimental study of bodily systems, through the investigation of brain–behavior relationships, the study of the nature of learning and behavioral plasticity, and the attempted quantification of conscious experience, to the therapeutic treatment of behavioral and functional disorders. It is not surprising that the result is not a theoretically unified set of findings, an orderly body of knowledge that may be neatly summarized and noncontroversially reviewed. For despite one's wishes to the contrary, the field of biofeedback research is unified not by a single experimental goal, theoretical problem, or substantive concern, but rather by methodological similarity. From this perspective, the substantive contributions of biofeedback research to scientific knowledge are not only varied, but also reflect new integrations of diverse disciplines in the behavioral and biological sciences.

Biofeedback: Theory and Research attempts to define this new body of knowledge through the eyes of investigators who helped create it.

BIOFEEDBACK AS A SCIENTIFIC TOOL

Biofeedback represents a scientific tool for manipulating, and thereby studying, physiological processes. Historically, biofeedback grew out of the behavioristic traditions of operant or instrumental learning paradigms (Kimmel, 1967; Miller, 1969) coupled with the evolving paradigms of feedback in cybernetics and systems analysis (Wiener, 1948; Powers, 1973). Within the restricted S–R learning theory framework, the long-standing distinction between classical and operant conditioning led researchers to shy away from using instrumental procedures for studying visceral and glandular processes. The initial demonstrations from Miller's laboratory (Miller, 1969) cast doubt upon this distinction and induced a number of investigators to begin studying the instrumental control of central and autonomic nervous system functions. An excellent review of the history of biofeedback from the S–R learning theory perspective, including reference to relevant Russian research on feedback and interoception, is provided by Kimmel (1974), one of the original investigators in this area.

As noted by several writers (e.g., Miller, 1969; Shapiro & Schwartz, 1972), a unique property of the operant–feedback procedure as a tool for scientific investigation is its capability to generate highly specific changes between and within different physiological systems. By examining the effects of such changes, it is possible to explore relationships between *(1)* different physiological systems in the intact organism, and *(2)* complex behavioral responses and their underlying biological substrates.

In this respect, biofeedback can be viewed as a powerful research tool, not in the sense of necessarily producing large magnitude changes, but rather as a means of gaining experimental manipulation over specific physiological processes so as to explore the nature of their relationships with other such processes and their association with specific environmental and behavioral conditions. It is this aspect of biofeedback that qualifies it as a general research method for studying problems relating biology and behavior.

An important extension of the idea of specific control of discrete physiological systems is the concept of simultaneous regulation of patterns of response. In this respect, biofeedback procedures provide the investigator with a technique for the induction of complex physiological patterns to investigate the relationships between brain and behavioral events (including the study of consciousness) at a level of complexity that was not previously possible (Schwartz, 1975). A detailed description of this approach is presented by Schwartz in Chapter 8.

For these reasons, it is reasonable to view biofeedback procedures as a scientific tool of some promise and utility, but that promise is not without its limitations. For example, there are technical difficulties in monitoring many of the physiological processes that one would like to control for the purposes of a particular experiment. Somewhat deeper is the problem that not all physiological systems are equally responsive to biofeedback intervention. The features that distinguish modifiable from unresponsive physiological systems are at present far from clear, but the nature of these differences is likely to be a biological distinction of some importance. Finally, the possibility of learned regulation of physiological functions as a research method is not relevant to a large class of scientific problems and, in these areas, biofeedback procedures are of little use. But where feasible and appropriate, biofeedback procedures are likely to contribute increasingly to the conduct of scientific research in future years.

THERAPEUTIC APPLICATIONS OF BIOFEEDBACK

Interest in biofeedback is stimulated in part by its potential contributions to clinical research and therapy. Although the present volume is primarily devoted to basic research on biofeedback and self-regulation, each section concludes with one or two chapters evaluating the status of biofeedback techniques in specific clinical disorders. The range of opinions expressed in this volume regarding the clinical potential of biofeedback goes from pessimism, through caution, to guarded optimism. In the same way that biofeedback is not a research strategy for all problems, it is not a clinical strategy for all disorders or all patients. The complexity of functional disease and its regulation is emphasized in this volume. From this perspective, biofeedback may be viewed as one possible component in a multicomponent treatment approach to specific, selected functional and behavioral disorders.

Biofeedback procedures may play an additional role in clinical research as a method for investigating the etiology and mechanisms underlying specific clinical disorders. This function should be distinguished from the application of biofeedback as a treatment modality for producing clinical correction in physiological dysfunction. Systematic research on the mechanisms of learned regulation of clinically relevant physiological systems, both in normal and pathological conditions, can provide the necessary foundation for determining the potentials and limitations of biofeedback procedures in treatment.

BIOFEEDBACK: OUR CURRENT STATE OF KNOWLEDGE

Our current state of knowledge with regard to biofeedback, the relations between biofeedback phenomena and our understanding of brain events, brain–behavior relationships and the nature of behavioral plasticity, and the clinical utility of such procedures, is best summarized by investigators whose recent work has contributed heavily to our understanding of these things. The result is not tidy and well-integrated, but to some extent disjointed, contradictory, and confusing. However, it is also seminal and exciting, and it is this that gives vitality to the 18 chapters of this volume. This book is organized in the following manner.

In Chapter 2, Mulholland explores the use of control system theory in the analysis of feedback-regulated electroencephalographic activity. This is followed by Brener's experimental analysis of visceral perception, in Chapter 3, in which the sensory information accompanying visceral events is considered. In Chapter 4, Lazarus presents a formulation of biofeedback control from the perspective of cognitive theory. Lazarus' approach may be contrasted with that of Black, Cott, and Pavloski in Chapter 5, which deals with an operant learning theory formulation of biofeedback training.

Clinical issues receive explicit theoretical treatment in Chapter 6 by Miller and Dworkin, who concern themselves with both the research and therapeutic aspects of clinical biofeedback practice. In Chapter 7, Lawrence and Johnson review the literature on the uses of biofeedback as an aid to human performance in a variety of contexts.

Schwartz, in Chapter 8, raises the matter of psychophysiological response patterning and CNS mechanisms underlying visceral self-regulation, with special emphasis on cardiovascular control.

The question of learning in the curarized preparation is treated in detail by Dworkin and Miller in Chapter 9, and the validity of the reports of visceral learning in this preparation are evaluated.

Harris and Brady, in Chapter 10, describe the results of a major experiment showing long-term cardiovascular regulation in monkeys exposed to a cardiovascular reinforcement contingency for prolonged periods.

The question of learned local vasomotor regulation in man is explored in Chapter 11 by Taub, which describes the outcomes of a number of experiments on temperature control.

Learned regulation of sexual response in man is the subject of Chapter 12, in which Rosen reports the results of his initial experiments in this area.

In Chapter 13, Shapiro, Mainardi, and Surwit review and critically examine the large literature on the regulation of cardiovascular activity in man with special reference to the problem of essential hypertension.

In Chapter 14, Beatty presents a summary of a series of experiments on learned regulation of electroencephalographic rhythms with emphasis on the control of alertness in man.

In Chapter 15, Rosenfeld considers the problem of learned control of event-related cortical potentials and presents data that bear upon this issue.

The use of biofeedback regulation in the treatment of epilepsy is examined by Sterman in Chapter 16.

The final two chapters of the volume deal with the question of learned regulation of skeletal muscle events. Chapter 17, by Basmajian, addresses the question of control of single motor units. Chapter 18, by Budzynski, explores the clinical usefulness of training relaxation through electromyographic feedback.

Together these chapters portray the current state of biofeedback research with considerable accuracy. Where consensus is lacking, controversy brings vigor to the research enterprise. No longer is biofeedback a technique that is foreign to the experimental psychologist, physiologist, and physician. We expect that biofeedback methods will continue to serve a restricted but useful role as a research tool and therapeutic procedure in the years ahead.

REFERENCES

Kimmel, H. D. Instrumental conditioning of autonomically mediated behavior. *Psychological Bulletin*, 1967, *67*, 337–345.

Kimmel, H. D. Instrumental conditioning of autonomically mediated responses in human beings. *American Psychologist*, 1974, *29*, 325–335.

Miller, N. E. Learning of visceral and glandular responses. *Science*, 1969, *163*, 434–445.

Powers, W. T. *Behavior: The control of perception.* Chicago: Aldine, 1973.

Schwartz, G. E. Biofeedback, self-regulation, and the patterning of physiological processes. *American Scientist,* 1975, *63,* 314–324.

Shapiro, D., & Schwartz, G. E. Biofeedback and visceral learning: Clinical applications. *Seminars in Psychiatry,* 1972, *4,* 171–184.

Wiener, N. *Cybernetics or control and communication in the animal and machine.* Cambridge: M.I.T. Press, 1948.

I

THEORETICAL AND APPLIED ISSUES IN BIOFEEDBACK

2

Biofeedback as Scientific Method

THOMAS B. MULHOLLAND
Veterans Administration Hospital
Bedford, Massachusetts

Biofeedback usually refers to a method for training a person to control voluntarily a physiological response. Although this is the most familiar application of biofeedback, it is a special case. In my opinion, biofeedback has more general and deeper implications for method in behavioral and biological science than current applications would indicate. In the speculative presentation that follows, I shall advance the thesis that biofeedback offers a method for testing hypotheses concerning unidirectional deterministic links in living but "noisy" systems. In support of this, I shall draw analogies between feedback control systems and schematic general models of experimental methods. Reasoning by analogy is not as rigorous as a deductive proof, yet I believe that these analogies, which point to an extension and elaboration of experimental methods for testing hypotheses, will be shown by logicians and mathematicians to rest upon an intrinsic, formal identity (McFarland, 1971). Some of these ideas have been introduced previously (Mulholland, 1968, 1973; Mulholland & Peper, 1972) and are extended and elaborated here.

The "feedback" effects discussed here refer to those dynamic functions of a system in which there is feedback from the output to the input. These effects are not necessarily due to biofeedback training, though they can be modified by training.

FEEDBACK CONTROL

Feedback control is widely used in industry and electronics to improve the control, i.e., precision, and accuracy of a system, so that whatever it is required to do, it does better with feedback. For instance, radar antennae scan the sky and detect flying objects. To do its job properly, an antenna must be accurately aimed and quickly moved. If the antenna is on a ship, gusts of wind and movement of sea add to the unpredictable inaccuracies already in the system due to imperfect components. When the antenna is "commanded" by electronic messages to point at 30°, it may not go to that position. The wind, sea, and unpredictable variation within the antenna system combine so that it might point wrongly at 40°. The difference between "commanded" position and actual position could be minimized if the "commander" knew where the antenna actually were aimed so that errors of position could be corrected by another command. The solution to this kind of problem is to send back a measurement of the antenna's position to the controller. This feedback in control systems provides a speedy way of *(1)* detecting errors and *(2)* correcting them.

Two kinds of antenna systems are diagramed in Figure 2.1. The first, without feedback, is called "open-loop control"; the second, with feedback, is called "closed-loop" or "feedback control." The diagrams also provide an illustration of the meaning of common terms that describe control systems.

In Figure 2.1a, there is no feedback but only a *feedforward* path from the controller's input, through the system's electronics and machinery, to the output which is the movement and position of the antenna.

As diagram Figure 2.1a shows, the position of the antenna is set by the controller and also by unpredictable disturbances due to winds, waves, and other "noise" in the system. Such variation is undesirable because it reduces the accuracy and precision of the antenna control system. The unpredictable, unwanted variations are called "noisy variation" or "noise," a term that is widely used in engineering and cybernetics. Errors of position are not automatically corrected by this system.

In Figure 2.1b, a feedback system is shown. The position of the antenna is measured, and this measurement is fed back and combined with the command from the controller. If the command was "30° position" and the antenna was measured actually at 40°, the difference between the two would be −10°. The antenna would receive this as a new input and would swing −10° to correct the error. In a linear,

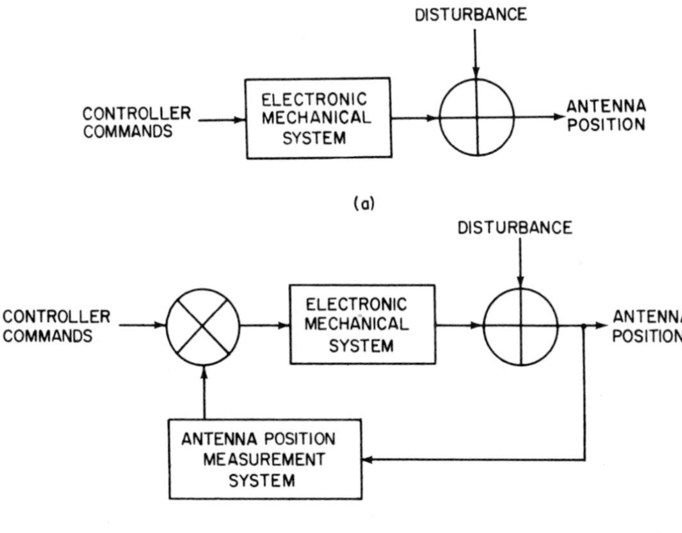

Figure 2.1 (a) Diagram of an open-loop system for controlling the position and movement of an antenna. Unpredictable disturbance is put into the diagram in one place. Actually "noise" is distributed throughout the system, but its ultimate effect is on the antenna position and movement. (b) A closed-loop negative feedback antenna control system. The feedback is subtracted from the controller command. This difference, called an "error signal," is the input to the control system.

negative feedback control system, the actual output is fed back and subtracted from the controller's command position. The difference or "error" actuates the system. (In a linear, *positive* feedback system, the output is fed back and added to the controller's command. Their sum actuates the system.)

Notice that it does not matter why the antenna was at 40°. Whether blown by wind or moved by sea or whether noisy variation in the system was involved, the overall error is detected and a new command issued. This general error-correcting effect is typical of negative feedback systems. Noisy variation of the output is greatly reduced and the output is a predictable function of the controlling signal. With powerful motors to turn the antenna and a speedy detection and feedback of antenna position, an antenna weighing hundreds of pounds can follow the "commands" given to it quickly, smoothly, and accurately. The desired, predictable variation of the response is much more prominent relative to an undesirable, unpredictable, "noisy" variation of the response. In technical jargon, the ratio of the signal to the noise is increased, or the ratio of systematic variation to unsystematic variation is increased.

There are analogies between the control systems shown in Figure 2.1 and many biological systems, and because of them, many control-systems approaches to the study of behavior and to the study of special functions, such as vision and movement, have been presented (Ashby, 1954; Stanley-Jones, 1960; Wiener, 1961; Wiener & Schade, 1964; Milhorn, 1966; Milsum, 1966; Buckley, 1968; Kelly, 1968; Stark, 1968; McFarland, 1971).

These cybernetic interpretations and new models of behavioral and physiological systems are important and powerful ways of schematizing a living system. However, they are not concerned with experimental method so they are not discussed here. For me, they have provided a conceptual framework for new analogies between feedback models and models of experimental methods, which are presented here.

MODELS OF EXPERIMENTAL METHODS

Returning to Figure 2.1a, the *input* to the system are commands from the controller, the *output* is the position of the antenna and the "*noise*" is all the unpredictable variations in any part of the system. The flow of information from input through to output is a *feedforward path*.

In Figure 2.1b, the nomenclature is a little more complicated. The position of the antenna is the output and the path from the input through to output is the feedforward. The path from the measured output back to the controller's commands is called the "feedback path." The combination of the feedback information and the controller's commands is the input. Where they are combined is called the "summing point."

Schematic diagrams of dynamic behavioral systems are analogous to Figure 2.1a. For instance, Figure 2.2 shows the familiar stimulus–organism–response system. Stimulus is input, response is output.

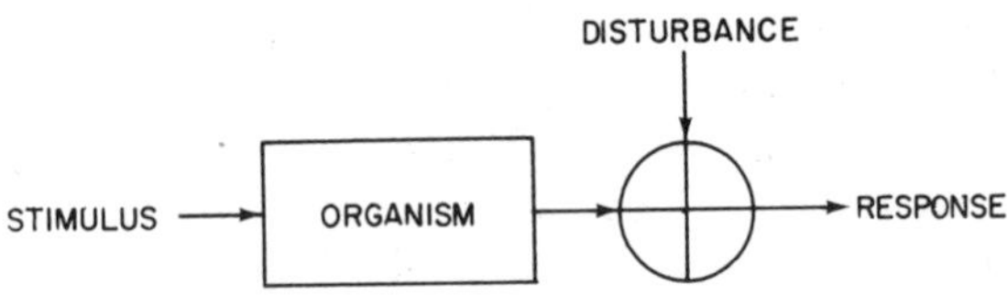

Figure 2.2 Diagram of the control of a response by a stimulus acting on an organism.

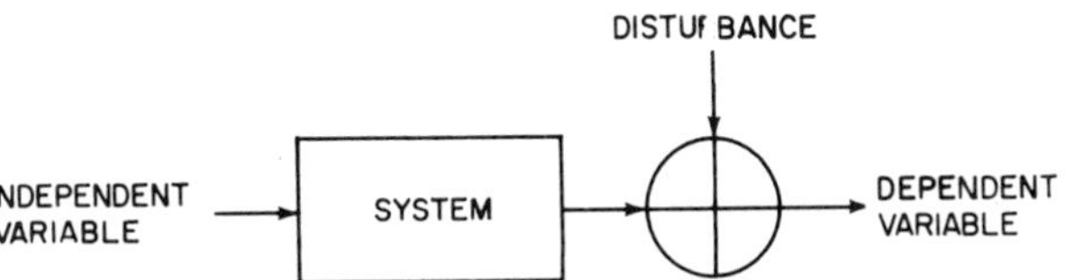

Figure 2.3 Diagram of the "control" of a dependent variable by an independent variable acting on the system under observation.

In behavioral science, Figure 2.3 is often generalized to a form that expresses a more abstract dynamic relation between a stimulus and a response. In Figure 2.3, the independent–dependent variable paradigm is analogous to the model in Figure 2.2 and in Figure 2.1a. It is an open-loop system. In Figure 2.3 and elsewhere in this chapter, the terms independent and dependent *variables* are selected values of the independent and dependent *functions*, values that are actually measured and tested in the experiment.

In Figure 2.4, a diagram of a generalized open-loop control system is presented. It is analogous to those presented before. All of these systems have some unpredictable "noisy" variation. The engineer deals with the problem of noise and output "error" by using feedback control which is schematized in Figure 2.5.

The scientist, using an experimental design as in Figure 2.3, is faced with a similar problem of noisy variation. Values of the independent variable are not perfectly predictably associated with values of the dependent variable. Noisy variation occurs due to the uncontrolled variables in the experiment. Typically, the scientist solves the problem of variation with *(1)* procedures to control the experimental situation, and *(2) statistical summarization* of the measures of the dependent variable. Both of these techniques are important. However, if the analogy between a generalized schema of control systems and schema of experimental methods is valid, then noisy variation in the dependent variable relative to systematic variation can be reduced by feed-

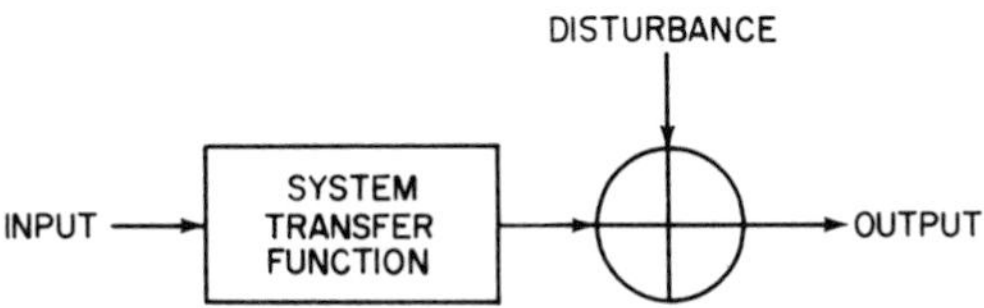

Figure 2.4 Diagram of a generalized open-loop control system. It is assumed that this is the general case of Figures 2.2 and 2.3.

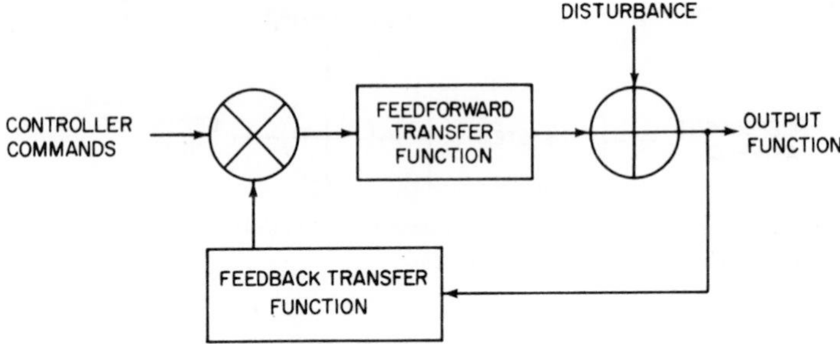

Figure 2.5 Diagram of a generalized feedback control system.

back from the dependent variable back to the independent variable. Such an arrangement, because it is analogous to a feedback control system, should have analogous signal-to-noise enhancement.

The system schematized in Figure 2.6 is analogous to the feedback control system shown in Figure 2.5. Such a system would be a new scientific method and would, in a noisy system, enhance the reliability of the function that relates the dependent variable to the independent variable. This would provide a more powerful test of the hypothesis that the dependent function includes a nonrandom function of the independent function. In short, the experimenter could make as good a test of that hypothesis with fewer observations than he could without feedback. Feedback would also reduce the need for statistical analysis since noisy variation of the dependent variable would be reduced on-line. The feedback method can give the experimenter more control over a "noisy" preparation since a desired range of values of the dependent variable can be maintained more reliably than without feedback.

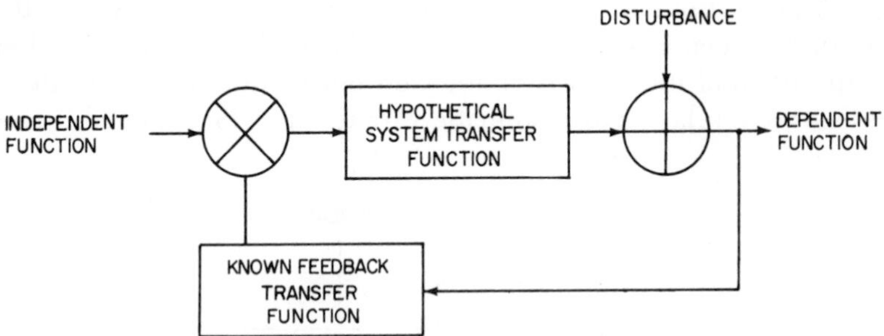

Figure 2.6 Diagram of a speculative scientific method that includes feedforward and feedback relationships between values of the dependent function and values of the independent function acting on a system under observation.

TESTING HYPOTHESES THAT FEEDFORWARD EXISTS

Increased Control

Because feedback effects like those described cannot occur if there is no feedforward, an observation of feedback effects is itself evidence for a feedforward path. Imagine the radar antenna system. If the antenna were buffeted by winds and moved by the pitch and roll of the ship, and its mechanical linkages were quite loose and worn, then conceivably a human controller may wonder if, in fact, the antenna system were connected to the controller. The antenna might be so variable that he could not tell. If he then switched on feedback, the system may stabilize enough for him to prove that the antenna was in fact connected to the controller, that is, that there was a *feedforward* path, because now the antenna would obviously follow the controller's commands. This illustration is silly in terms of *nonliving* systems. Engineers know they have feedforward and they know that feedback improves the precision and accuracy of control. But the scientist often does not know if he has a feedforward path in a noisy system. If there were one, he would better be able to prove that with feedback than without feedback, because feedback would increase the reliability of the relation between independent and dependent variables.

Once a feedback loop has been created, as evidenced by an improvement in the control of the system and a more reliable relation between the input and output or between the independent and dependent variables, then additional feedback effects can be demonstrated which can further test the hypothesis that there is a feedforward path.

Controlled Oscillation of the Dependent Variable

As described before, negative feedback is used to correct errors by subtracting feedback from the controlling function to maintain the output as close as possible to the commanded value. In the case of the antenna, negative feedback would be used. If the feedback is not delayed, then errors are corrected in minimum time but, in all real systems and especially in living systems, there is a delay between the output and the feedback function at the input. In the case of the antenna, if it "overshoots" the correct position and its position is fed back with a long delay, during that time, it could continue to move in the wrong direction and not be corrected. When correction did occur and the antenna reversed its movement, it would go too far the other way and not be corrected soon enough. An oscillation could be set up that would be determined by the system transfer function which now includes a longer feedback time delay. Though such oscillation of the output is to be avoided where accurate error correction is required, it could be useful to the scientist who is trying only to demonstrate that a feedforward exists. If the dependent variable exhibits sustained oscillation as a function of the time delay between the independent variable and feedback from the dependent variable, that would be a convincing demonstration. Sustained oscillation, because it is a recurring, periodic phenomenon, is readily detectable.

Differences in Control with Positive and Negative Feedback

To add even more evidence, the experimenter could reverse the sign of the feedback to see if the output, or dependent variable, is changed. In a nonliving, typical control system this reversal would change the feedback from negative to positive.

The antenna system with positive feedback would be useless. An error of position would be added to the input and it would continue to move in the wrong direction until it reached its mechanical limits. A disturbance to the system would set up a movement that would go to a limit. With powerful motors and heavy parts, the antenna would be wrecked.

Positive feedback increases the gain and responsivity of a system but reduces control. Negative feedback decreases responsivity and increases control. In an idealized simple feedback system shown in Figure 2.5, reversing the sign of the feedback from negative to positive decreases the control of the system.

The researcher can look for changes in the living system when the sign of the electronic biofeedback is reversed. If control greatly increased compared to decreased control in the reverse feedback, a shift from negative to positive feedback would be inferred. The *difference* between these conditions may be more evident than the effects of either alone. This would be evidence for a feedforward path (Peper, 1970; Mulholland & Peper, 1974).

PRAGMATICS

The values of the parameters of the external feedback path for testing hypotheses about the relation between independent and dependent functions are selected by trial and error. The experimenter, guided by whatever information he has about the system, tries various combinations of variables, watching for feedback effects such as increased control or controlled oscillation.

If the relation between independent and dependent functions is already reliable enough, the standard open-loop test of a hypothetical functional relation between them is as good as a feedback method and is likely to be more economical.

If there is no "feedforward" or the system has a very low signal-to-noise ratio, convincing evidence for a link between independent and dependent variables might not be obtained even with a feedback method. From this it would seem that feedback methods would be an improvement over open-loop methods in *some* cases.

Feedback method is not going to prevent the experimenter from drawing invalid conclusions. Feedforward paths may be present but may be organized into a hierarchical feedback system that is very stable and an additional feedback may not make a detectable difference. However, before concluding that there is no evidence for a link between independent and dependent variables, feedback should be tried because it can improve the reliability of the functional link, that is, it could reduce unsystematic variation in the measures of the dependent function relative to systematic variation associated with measures of the independent function.

These practical considerations reflect the current "state of the art" for testing hypotheses with feedback methods. They may seem much too conservative when reviewed a few years hence. Much more research is required to give a proper evaluation of the utility of these suggestions.

FEEDBACK EFFECTS IN A NOISY EEG SYSTEM

The examples I have chosen to illustrate the ideas presented before are taken from my research on the electroencephalographic alpha rhythm. I have used feedback methods to increase the control of the EEG during visual stimulation. Over the course of these studies, other effects, less obvious but reproducible, have been observed which have relevance to the general problem of identifying feedforward paths when the output, dependent variable is excessively noisy under usual laboratory conditions. The feedback method as illustrated here does not eliminate noisy variation—it reduces the noise to manageable levels, making a better method, not a perfect one.

Controlling the Response of the Occipital Alpha Rhythm

The occipital EEG for a typical person sitting quietly in the dark is continually alternating between prominent alpha rhythms and little or no-alpha. The latter is usually low amplitude, higher frequency activity under the conditions of our experiments. This alternation, called the "alpha-attenuation cycle," is the most common feature of the occipital EEG. With eyes closed or open in the dark, the alpha-attentuation cycle is unpredictable. Visual stimulation is normally followed by a disturbance of the alpha-attenuation cycle. In standard EEG terminology, this is called "alpha blocking." However, alpha does not "block" permanently nor completely. Initially, alpha durations become brief, while no-alpha durations increase. Afterward, without further stimulation, the alpha-attenuation cycle recovers erratically to values near baseline.

With repeated visual stimulation, the alpha-attenuation cycle gradually and erratically recovers from the initial disturbance. In classical terminology, this is called "habituation" of alpha blocking. After recovery, the variability of the durations of alpha and no-alpha is relatively large, that is, there is a large unpredictable variation in the alpha-attenuation cycle.

With feedback, the experimenter can control the durations of alpha and no-alpha and minimize the time spent in alpha or no-alpha. When alpha occurs, a visual stimulus is presented. It is followed by alpha attenuation. When alpha is attenuated enough or blocked, the stimulus is removed, which is followed, after a delay, by alpha. The stimulus occurs again and the cycle of alpha–stimulus–no-alpha–no-stimulus repeats. Variability is reduced by feedback from the occurrence of alphas to the visual stimulus. This is shown in Figure 2.7. Visual feedback stimulation begins with the arrow in the top tracings. There are two aspects of the response to feedback: the effect upon alpha durations and the effect upon intervals of little or no-alpha.

Alpha durations immediately exhibit reduced variation as stimulation continues. The change in no-alpha durations is more complex. Initially, no-alpha intervals are longer (disturbance), then gradually become shorter (see Figure 2.7, the first and second set of tracings). After recovery, however (shown in the third set of tracings), the no-alpha intervals are less variable, though still more variable than durations of alpha. When feedback is stopped (arrow in the fourth set of tracings), the EEG rapidly reverts to a less predictable series of alpha and no-alpha intervals.

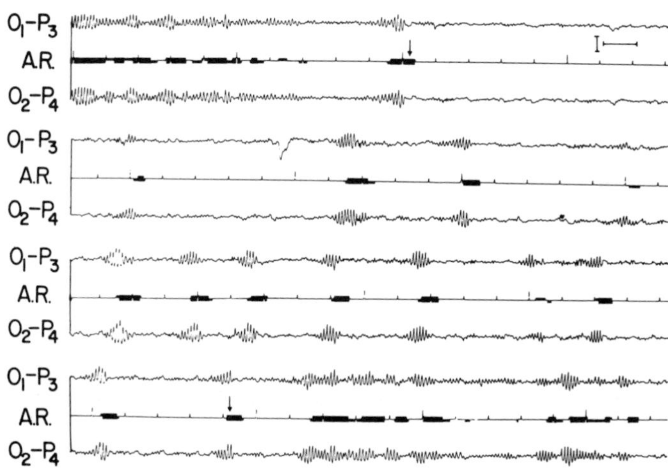

Figure 2.7 Behavior of the EEG alpha rhythms during feedback visual stimulation. Feedback begins with the arrow in the top tracings. The recording is discontinuous at the end of the second set of tracings. The third set shows the effects of feedback after 22 stimulations. The bottom set continues the feedback up to the arrow where feedback stops. The control of the alpha-attenuation cycle is apparent in the third and the beginning of the fourth set of tracings which show the system after recovery from the initial disturbance at onset of feedback.

In Figure 2.7, the effects of feedback seem to be bilaterally identical. They *are* similar but not identical. In fact, I have recently found that the effects of feedback in terms of increased control are significantly greater on the EEG which is physically connected into the feedback system, for example, the left EEG compared to the right EEG which is simultaneously recorded. In the jargon of feedback EEG, the EEG connected into the system is called the "contingent" EEG. Thus, one can have "left contingent" or "right contingent" feedback. In both cases, the EEG is recorded from and measured on both sides.

The visual stimulation is contingent feedback from the EEG that is physically connected into the system; it is not necessarily contingent feedback from the other side. Any contingency for the EEG not physically connected into the system is due to internal correlations between brain processes as represented in the EEG.

The bilateral response of the EEG alpha-attenuation to visual stimulation can be approximated by two simple functions.

$$\Delta t \text{ alpha} = (A \cdot N + B) \pm SE = F_1(N)$$
$$\Delta t \text{ no-alpha} = (C/N + D) \pm SE = F_2(N)$$

where Δt is the duration, N is the serial number of the event, and SE is the standard error of estimate; A, B, C, and D are parameters of the best-fit functions which are used to compute the estimated durations of alpha and no-alpha for each value of N. With feedback stimulation, the scatter (SE) of the actual alpha and no-alpha around the best-fit functions for alpha $(F_1(N))$ and no-alpha $(F_2(N))$ is reduced by a feedback compared to no feedback (Mulholland, 1968, 1973).

I have recently found that the standard error (SE) of alpha and no-alpha durations around the estimated best-fit trend lines described before is significantly less on the contingent side.

The experiment was complicated by the number of variables, the fact that some variables were simultaneous while others were successive, and the necessity to control for habituation. The main variables were:

1. *External path (EP).* There were two physically different electronic paths for detecting, filtering and measuring alpha and no-alpha.
2. *Side (L and R).* These were electrode placements O_1–P_3 and O_2–P_4.
3. *Contingency (C).* This referred to the side physically connected into the feedback system.
4. *Stimuli (W and V).* Two sets of visual stimuli were used, four words and four visual illusions projected onto a screen in front of the subject.

Four combinations of loop variables were tested with words and illusions. These were:

I. EP_1, C, L; EP_2, NoC, R
II. EP_1, C, R; EP_2, NoC, L
III. EP_1, NoC, L; EP_2, C, R
IV. EP_1, NoC, R; EP_2, C, L

These four complex variables were ordered in a Latin Square.

The major result was that the scatter of alpha and of no-alpha durations around the best-fit trend lines computed in each trial were significantly less on the side externally connected to the feedback system compared with the other side, which was simultaneously recorded but not *externally* connected to the feedback system. For alpha durations, the average standard error was .13 seconds on the driving side and .19 seconds on the nondriving side. The F associated with this difference was 70.5, $p < .001$. For no-alpha durations, the SE was 1.83 seconds on the driving side and 2.57 seconds on the nondriving side. The F value was 8.71, $p < .01$. The trend lines were the same for the contingent

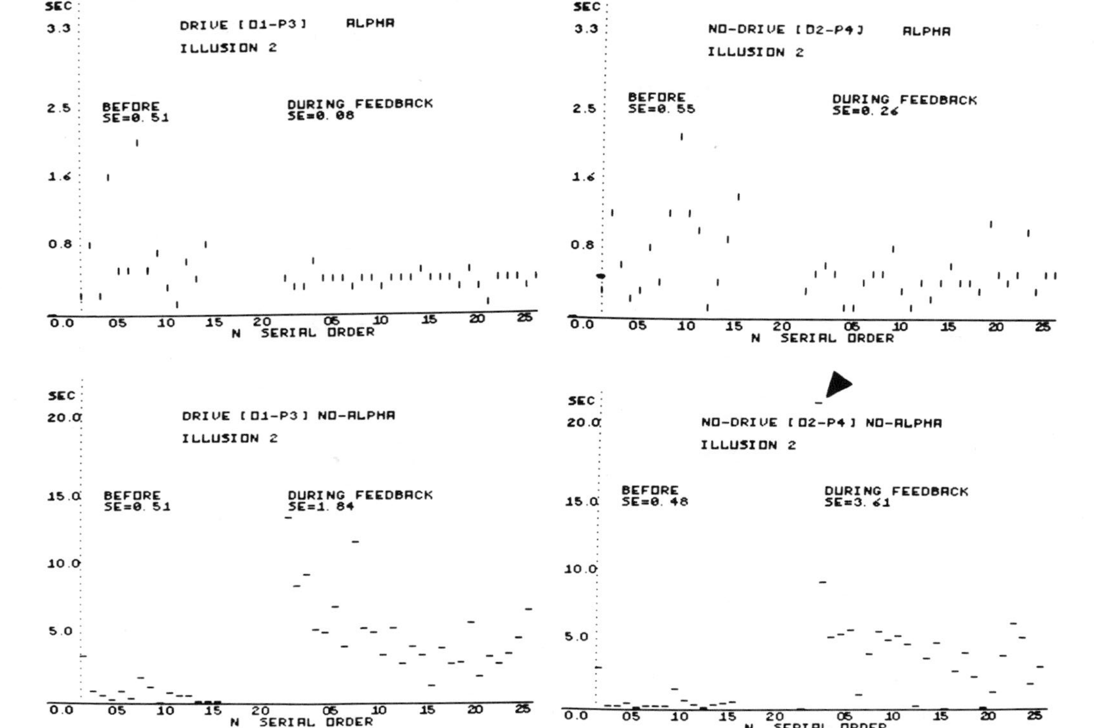

Figure 2.8 Computer display of raw data for a single trial on one subject before and during feedback. Left EEG (O_1–P_3) is connected to the stimulus. The "scatter" of alpha durations (top) and no-alpha durations (bottom) is greater on the right-contingent EEG (O_2–P_4). See text. Numerical values of the Standard Error *(SE)* are also included.

EEG and the other, noncontingent EEG. Small but significant left–right differences were noted. There was no difference between external paths.

The reduced variability of the alpha-attenuation cycle in the contingent EEG is often evident in a single trial (see Figure 2.8). The stimulus is a visual illusion. At the onset of feedback, alpha durations (Δt alpha) show a bilateral decrease. But, alpha durations in the right EEG are more variable than alphas in the contingent left EEG. No-alpha durations are also more variable in the right EEG than in the left. This difference in variance between the contingent and noncontingent EEG's is more reliable for alpha durations compared with no-alpha durations.

This experiment has been reported in more detail elsewhere (Eberlin & Mulholland, 1976). It shows that feedback stimulation is *not* the same as merely intermittent stimulation where no such bilateral differences have ever been observed. Feedback changes the dynamics of the EEG; these feedback effects are more prominent when the relevant electrophysiological response is externally coupled or connected into the loop. Increased control of the series of Δt alpha and Δt no-alpha provides convincing evidence for a feedforward path between the visual stimulus and EEG alpha rhythms. That this particular fact is already known is irrelevant. The evidence is better with feedback.

Controlled Oscillation of Alpha and No-Alpha

The experimenter can generate feedback effects by varying the time delay between the EEG and the stimulus if a feedforward path exists. These effects are usually undesirable, but, for the experimenter, they provide a convincing demonstration that a feedforward path must exist.

In the EEG alpha feedback just described, there is already a time delay between the occurrence of alpha and the occurrence of the stimulus of about .25 seconds. There is a further biological delay (latency) between the occurrence of the stimulus and the attenuation of alpha. A second biological delay occurs between stimulus offset and the return of alpha.

With delayed feedback, the alpha-stimulus system oscillates between on–off modes. The period of oscillation is a function of the delay. Figure 2.9 illustrates this effect (Mulholland, 1973). In the top tracings, there is a brief delay between the detection of alpha and the onset of stimulus. Brief alpha intervals alternate with brief no-alpha intervals. In the middle tracings, the time delay between alpha and

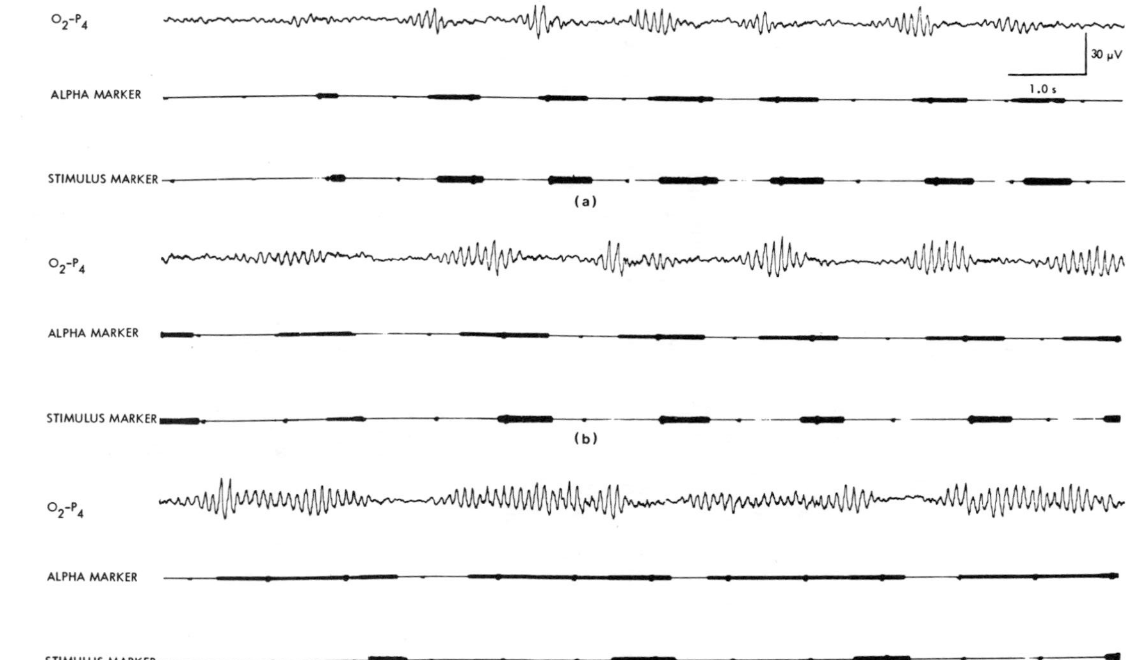

Figure 2.9 By increasing the time delay between the feedback visual stimulus and the occurrence of alpha, stable alternation between alpha and no-alpha occurs. The period of alternation increases with the delay.

stimulation is increased. Alpha durations become longer while no-alpha durations become shorter. In the bottom tracings, there is a long delay between alpha detection and stimulation. Alpha durations are long, while no-alpha durations remain brief. As delay increases, the period of alternation between alpha and no-alpha and between stimulus on and off increases. Such a change in the period of the output response is typical of on–off control systems (Rose, 1967). The production of a controlled oscillation in the dependent variable by time-delayed feedback from the independent variable is readily recognizable and is convincing evidence that a feedforward path exists between the visual stimulus and the alpha-attentuation cycle.

Differences in Control by Reversing the Sign of the Feedback

In a feedback control system, reversing the sign of feedback produces a marked change in the output. For instance, output that is stable with negative feedback may swing erratically between upper and lower limits or go to a limit and stay there with positive feedback. For our purposes here, the contrast between the way the system behaves with feedback compared to its behavior when the feedback is reversed is evidence for a feedforward path in the alpha-stimulus system.

In the alpha feedback system, Loop 1 feedback causes the stimulus to go ON when alpha occurs and to go OFF when it does not; Loop 2 feedback causes the stimulus to go OFF when alpha occurs and ON when it does not. If the stimulus ON produces the opposite effect from stimulus OFF, and if there is a feedforward path, the EEG should be different in Loop 1 compared with Loop 2. In fact, it is (see Figure 2.10). With Loop 1, the EEG alternates between alpha and no-alpha in a fairly regular way. When the system is switched to Loop 2, the EEG becomes unstable and swings erratically between limits of long durations of alpha and long durations of little or no alpha (Mulholland & Peper, 1971).

When both alpha and no-alpha are associated with visual stimulation but with different intensity, reversing the feedback contingency does not always change the alpha-attenuation cycle. In an experiment, alpha was associated with a moderate increase of stimulus intensity from a middle value, and no-alpha, a moderate decrease. This contingency was reversed to test the hypothesis that reversing the contingency was the same as changing the sign of the feedback. There was no difference between the two contingencies. Both directions of stimulus

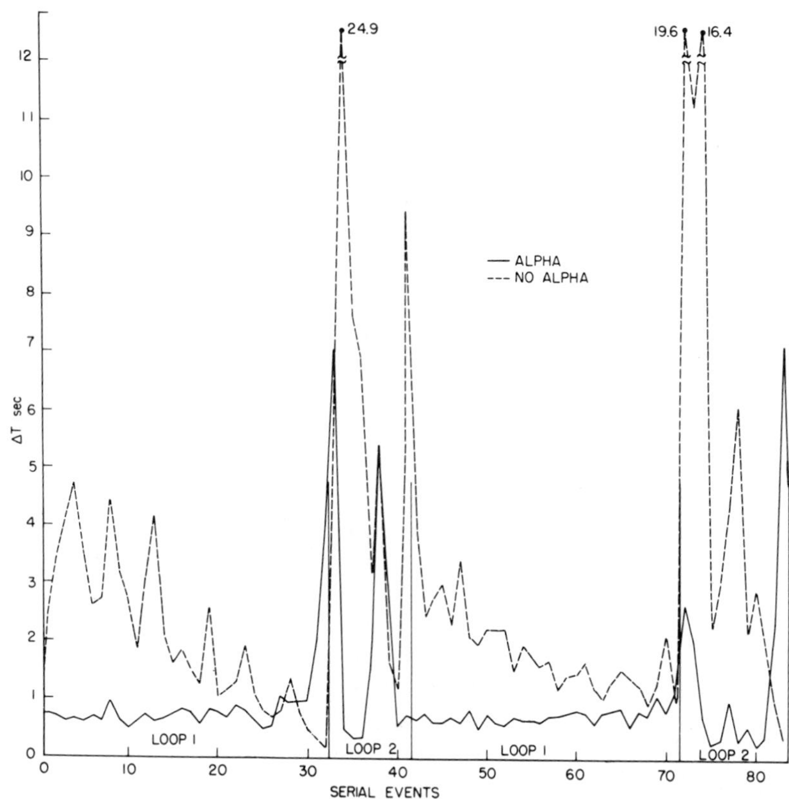

Figure 2.10 Durations of alpha and no-alpha are shorter and less variable with delayed negative feedback (Loop 1) compared with delayed positive feedback (Loop 2). [From "Occipital alpha and accommodative vergence, pursuit tracking and fast eye movements," by T. B. Mulholland and E. Peper, in *Psychophysiology*, 1971, 8, 556–575. Reprinted by permission of the publisher. Copyright © 1971, The Society for Psychophysiological Research.]

change produced a control of alpha and no-alpha durations (Mulholland & Runnals, 1964).

INTERNAL BIOFEEDBACK

In the electronic biofeedback described, the electrodes were placed on the surface of the body and the feedback display was a stimulus for the exteroceptors. In principle, electronic biofeedback could be studied when the electrodes are inside the body, closer to the relevant physiological process so that the feedback is a physiological stimulus applied not to an exteroceptor but to an internal process.

Traczyk *et al.* (1969) connected an external feedback of activity recorded from dorsal hippocampal (rabbits) to an electronic device that controlled a stimulator whose output was inserted into midbrain processes. By changing the parameters of the external path, the animal could be maintained at stable, long-lasting levels of hippocampal activity. Shifts from one kind of activity to another were achieved by changing the feedback path. Although the authors did not mention it, these feedback effects were themselves convincing evidence that a feedforward existed between brainstem processes and the recorded hippocampal activity. There may be a place in electrophysiological methods for biofeedback techniques for testing hypotheses about deterministic links in noisy systems.

BIOFEEDBACK AND LEARNED CONNECTIONS IN THE INTERNAL PATH

The biofeedback effects described before occur because there is a closed-loop system consisting of feedforward and feedback elements. The engineer designs and builds them together. In some cases, the feedforward is designed first but is found to be inadequate, and feedback is added to improve the system. Engineers do not use feedback to build the feedforward path. However, in living systems that learn, an internal feedforward path may be "constructed" *after* new external feedback links are established. The living system can "rebuild" its feedforward and improve its "commands" so that the commands are more accurate and effective. As learning proceeds, the feedforward path is improved (temporary connections) to optimize the control that is possible once feedback is available. To return to the simple radar system, it would be as if the fanciful "controller" did not have a way of commanding the antenna but did have feedback; the controller received accurate information about where the antenna was pointing. Assume that the controller has a way of building a path from command through to antenna position. With feedback, a feedforward path can be developed using a basic plan and modifying it by trial and error until control is optimal: that is, the input error signal would approach zero. This would be a highly adaptive control system.

On the level of speculative analogies, the following is one way of describing the biofeedback training situation. Let us say that a person does not have control over his brain rhythms. For instance, he cannot command them to be alpha or no-alpha. Moreover, he cannot know what EEG changes are occurring from moment to moment. The person is now given biofeedback information about his brain waves. He has a new source of information to guide the "building" of a feedforward path which is evidenced by more reliable detection and control of EEG rhythms.

Learning to control physiological processes means forming new sequences of transfer functions in feedforward paths from controller to output. The feedforward paths that are being formed using feedback already provided: *(1)* will take time to be formed, *(2)* may be revised; and *(3)* if not used, may be dismantled. There would be an acquisition of a feedforward path, an optimized feedforward path, and a "forgotten" feedforward path.

Once a feedforward path has been established and optimized, the controller may adaptively improve its performance. Feedback from the response would be used to guide the controller as it alters its commands to produce an even better system. The controller could reach a level of performance that, with a very reliable feedforward path, would no longer require feedback. That terminal system would have the advantage of a higher speed of operation.

To pursue these speculations here would not be warranted. Obviously, a tremendous amount of experimental research is required to see if these analogies are verifiable and useful.

REFERENCES

Ashby, W. R. The application of cybernetics to psychiatry. *Journal of Mental Science,* 1954, *100,* 114–124.

Buckley, W. (Ed.). *Modern systems research for the behavioral scientist.* Chicago: Aldine, 1968.

Eberlin, P., & Mulholland, T. Bilateral differences in parietal-occipital EEG induced by contingent visual feedback. *Psychophysiology,* 1976, *13,* 212–218.

Kelly, C. R. *Manual and automatic control.* New York: Wiley, 1968.

McFarland, D. J. *Feedback mechanisms in animal behavior.* New York: Academic Press, 1971.

Milsum, J. H. *Biological control systems analysis.* New York: McGraw-Hill, 1966.

Milhorn, H. T. *The application of control theory to physiological systems.* Philadelphia: Saunders, 1966.

Mulholland, T. Feedback electroencephalography. *Activitas Nervosa Superior* (Prague) 1968, *10,* 410–438. (Reprinted in T. X. Barber *et al.* (Eds.), *Biofeedback and self-control reader,* Chicago: Aldine-Atherton, 1969.)

Mulholland, T. Objective EEG methods for studying covert shifts of visual attention. In F. J. McGuigan & R. A. Schoonover (Eds.), *The psychophysiology of thinking.* New York: Academic Press, 1973, pp. 109–151.

Mulholland, T., & Peper, E. Occipital alpha and accomodative vergence, pursuit tracking and fast eye movements. *Psychophysiology*, 1971, *8*, 556–575.

Mulholland, T., & Runnals, S. Cortical activation during steady and changing visual stimulation. *Electroencephalography and Clinical Neurophysiology*, 1964, *17*, 371–375.

Peper, E. Feedback regulation of the alpha electroencephalogram activity through control of internal and external parameters. *Kybernetic*, 1970, *7*, 107–112.

Rose, J. *Automation. Its anatomy and physiology*. Edinburg: Oliver & Boyd, 1967. P. 125.

Stanley-Jones, D. & K. *The kybernetics of natural systems*. New York: Pergamon Press, 1960.

Stark, L. *Neurological control systems, Section IV: The Eye. Studies in Bioengineering*. New York: Plenum Press, 1968.

Traczyk, W. Z., Whitmoyer, D. I., & Sawyer, C. H. EEG feedback control of midbrain electrical stimulation inducing sleep or arousal in rabbits. *Acta Biologiae Experimentalis* (Warszawa) 1969, *29*, 135–152.

Wiener, N. *Cybernetics*. New York: Wiley, 1961.

Wiener, N., & Schade, J. P. (Eds.). *Progress in biocybernetics* (Vols. 1–3). New York: Elsevier, 1964, 1965–1966.

3

Sensory and Perceptual Determinants of Voluntary Visceral Control*

JASPER BRENER
University of Hull, England

INTRODUCTION

A recent and authoritative physiology textbook defines a voluntary response as "one that I believe I could make if I wanted to" (Brobeck, 1973, pp. 9–88). This definition, which has a good deal of face validity and which accords with our intuitive understanding of voluntary behavior, does not provide objective criteria for determining whether a particular response is voluntary or not. It is nevertheless true that the primary reason for the involuntary classification of visceral responses is that most individuals do not believe that they could produce variations in their visceral activity, even if they wanted to. The basis of this common belief and an assessment of its validity form the focus of this chapter.

In order to pursue this issue on a scientific footing, it is necessary to develop some objective means of distinguishing those activities that people believe they could control if they wanted to from those they do

* The preparation of this chapter was supported by MH Grant No. 17061 and MRC Grant No. G974/440/B.

not believe they can control. To this end, we may provisionally agree that a voluntary response is one that is amenable to control via self-instruction. In other words, if I am satisfied that I am able to comply with my own instruction or decision to execute a response, then I shall classify that response as voluntary. In these terms, *compliance with instructions* forms the basis of my belief that I can voluntarily control the response in question. As has been suggested elsewhere (Brener, 1974a,b), compliance with instructions represents a useful definitional criterion for determining the voluntary–nonvoluntary status of a response. To apply this criterion objectively, it is necessary only that the instructions to perform the act be delivered by a third party rather than the subject organism, and that the assessment of compliance with the instruction be measured by objective means. Thus, it is proposed that *a voluntary response is one that is systematically influenced by verbal instructions.* The assumption underlying this definition is that a response that is amenable to control via self-instruction will also be amenable to control via instructions delivered by a third party.

It will be recognized, however, that although an individual may have the capacity to comply with an instruction to perform a response, he may not manifest this capacity because he does not want to. Thus, the simple application of this definitional criterion may lead us to classify as nonvoluntary those certain responses that, under other conditions, may meet the criterion for classification as voluntary. The approach adopted here with respect to this issue is derived from traditional learning theory. In particular, the capacity to comply with an instruction is viewed as the consequence of associative (learning) processes, whereas the manifestation of this capacity is viewed as a performance process and, as such, is determined by the interaction of learning and motivational factors. Quite clearly, there are conditions under which the majority of individuals will comply with instructions with which they have the capacity to comply. Although motivational processes are undoubtedly important in the determination of voluntary behavior and have a special significance in the analysis of voluntary visceral control, they will not be intensively discussed here. The major emphasis here will be in analyzing the associative processes that determine the ability of individuals to comply with instructions to modify their visceral activity.

For reasons that have been elaborated elsewhere (Brener, 1974b,c), the processes underlying operant and voluntary control are considered to be equivalent. It is nevertheless possible to distinguish voluntary from operant responses on the basis of two operational criteria. Firstly, the experimental operations for probing voluntary control consist of presenting the subject with verbal stimuli (instructions), whereas nonverbal (discriminative) stimuli are generally employed for probing operant control. A second distinction lies in the setting operations employed for establishing incentive properties in the response-contingent (feedback or reinforcing) stimuli used respectively in the procedures for establishing voluntary and operant control. In the case of operant conditioning, the incentive properties of reinforcing stimuli are not necessarily based upon associative processes and are determined by experimental operations such as food deprivation or manipulating the intensity of electrical stimulation. Such operations tend to act more directly on the biological substrate than those employed in voluntary control procedures. In the latter procedures, the incentive properties of feedback stimuli are based primarily upon associative processes and are determined by verbal setting operations usually contained within the instructions (e.g., "for every increment in the counter total, you'll receive an extra nickel at the end of the experiment"). Apart from these distinctions, the operations associated with the development and manifestation of operant and voluntary control are considered here to be functionally equivalent. In particular, they both result in the acquisition of response-controlling properties by previously neutral (instructional or discriminative) stimuli as a function of procedures employing response-contingent (feedback or reinforcing) stimulation.

Most of the experimental data to be discussed concern the development of voluntary control over cardiovascular activities. In view of the definitional criterion of voluntary responses that is adopted here, the present analysis will emphasize the nature and function of instructions (the initiating conditions for voluntary responses) and of response feedback (the means by which compliance with the instruction is assessed).

OUTLINE OF THE SYSTEM OF ANALYSIS

In the experimental setting, instructions are a device for transmitting information to the subject. Either implicitly or explicitly, instructions transmit information of a motivational nature. The simple instruction to "raise the arm" implies certain social consequences of complying or not. In other cases, the consequences of compliance may be made explicit by the instruction (e.g., "If you raise your arm, I'll give you a dollar"). More importantly, from the present point of view, instructions serve to designate a particular state of affairs that the subject is required to achieve—instructions describe a *goal* or, in feedback language, a *setpoint*. Thus, the instruction "Raise your arm" informs the subject that he is required to achieve a state of affairs that may be described as "raising his arm."

Instructions may vary in the complexity of the behavioral goals they specify. Simpler instructions tend to designate broad classes of activity as the goal (e.g., "Move" or "Stop"), whereas more complex instructions demand more specific responses (e.g., "Move your right index finger" [while keeping the rest of your fingers immobile]). In this chapter, we shall be concerned primarily with simple instructions that are cast in the form of imperative sentences. They are usually comprised of a verb (e.g., "raise" or "lower") and a noun phrase (e.g., "your heart rate" or "your blood pressure"). The verb describes the direction of the required behavioral adjustment, and the noun phrase, the effector system in which the directional requirement is to be fulfilled.

In order to comply specifically with an instruction to execute an act, a subject must understand the nature of the behavioral requirement specified by the instruction. In particular, he must be able to recognize acts of the class referenced by the instruction (e.g., "increases in heart rate"). This implies an ability to discriminate the sensory state associated with the performance of the act and also the ability to label this sensory state appropriately. Thus, when a subject is instructed to increase his heart rate, he is in effect being instructed to produce the sensory state that he has learned to label as an "increase in heart rate." Since most individuals have not received specific training in the verbal labeling of sensations associated with variations in visceral activity, it is likely that they will interpret instructions to perform visceral responses in idiosyncratic and inaccurate ways. This ambiguity may be reduced by designating the occurrence of an external stimulus as the goal. Thus, instead of instructing individuals to increase their heart rates, they may instead be instructed to "move a meter needle to the right" or to "produce a high-pitched tone," where these external stimuli are programmed to occur when the subject's heart rate increases. Therefore, some instructions specify external stimulus changes as the goal ("produce a tone"), whereas others imply the occurrence of an internal stimulus as the goal ("increase your heart rate"). Instructions that designate external stimulus changes as the goal are often functionally equivalent to instructions that specify a behavioral goal. For example, the instruction "press the key" may produce the same movements as the instruction "produce the tone" where the tone is programmed to occur as the result of a key press.

However, it is generally the case that instructions specifying a behavioral goal require more specific behavioral adjustments than those specifying an external stimulus change as the goal. In instructions of the latter sort, the behavioral means of achieving the goal is unspecified, whereas the behavioral means is the goal specified by instructions of the former sort. The point to be emphasized here, however, is that all instructions to execute acts are reducible to instructions to produce stimulus changes in either some internal[1] or external sensory modality and sometimes in both internal and external modalities.

The instruction establishes the reference or setpoint against which the subject's performance is assessed both by the subject and the experimenter. In other words, the subject is said to have complied with an instruction when his activity leads to a stimulus change (either internal or external) of the sort demanded explicitly or implicitly by the instruction. Where the instruction specifies an external stimulus change as the goal, the subject is provided with an objective (intersubjective) means of assessing his success in complying with the instruction; where it specifies a behavioral goal (an internal stimulus change), the subject's ability to assess his performance is dependent upon his ability to correctly identify and label the interoceptive changes associated with that behavioral goal. By examining the behavioral adjustments produced by instructions that specify a behavioral goal rather than an external stimulus, it is possible to infer what individuals understand by such concepts as "increases in heart rate" or "decreases in blood pressure."

[1] In the present chapter, a sharp distinction is not drawn between proprioception and interoception. Either or both will be implied by the term "internal feedback." Sherrington (1906) and Ádám (1967) amongst others have emphasized the differences between proprioceptors, which provide information about movements of the striated musculature, and interoceptors, which provide information about the visceral field. In terms of the present functional analysis, however, the distinction between these two internal feedback systems is not considered to be crucial: They are both involved in processing information about the activities of the organism and are clearly distinguished from the exteroceptive system which processes information about the organism's external environment. From the present viewpoint, the most important distinction between the proprioceptive and interoceptive afferent systems is that the former system is considerably more elaborate, both peripherally and centrally, than the latter. This structural distinction must be acknowledged as an important factor in determining why the activities of the striated musculature which are served by the proprioceptive system are more easily and more finely discriminable than the activities of the viscera which are served by the interoceptive system. It will be argued that this factor is equally important in determining why the activities of the striate musculature are more finely *controllable* than those of the viscera.

It is assumed then that under appropriate motivational conditions, individuals will comply with instructions they understand. The instruction specifies the sensory goal *to be achieved*, and feedback from the internal and external receptors provides information that permits an assessment of whether or not the required sensory state *has been achieved.* Thus, instructionally produced activity is of a regulatory nature—its "purpose" is to achieve a sensory state similar to that *represented* by the central neural circuits which gave rise to it and were activated by the instructional stimulus. Viewed in the context of a *homeostatic* framework, instructions serve to establish a state of nervous system imbalance that may only be restored by the occurrence of certain stimuli. The unique characteristic of such stimuli is that they are labeled in the same terms as those employed in their instructional designation as the goal of performance. Thus, an individual who is motivated to comply with, for example, an instruction to *decrease* his *blood pressure* will continue his efforts until such time as he achieves a state that he recognizes as a *decrease* in *blood pressure.* Appropriate response feedback terminates the behavioral control process. Von Holst and Mittelstaedt (1950) have provided evidence indicating that a primary function of response-produced feedback (reafference) is to neutralize the central neural state that gave rise to the response producing the feedback. Something that has not been made explicit and that may be acknowledged as a substantial hiatus in our knowledge of learned motor control is how central motor programs for learned movements are formulated and activated.

The point of view adopted here with respect to this issue is derived primarily from the writings of William James (1890). James suggests that the *template* (*response image,* in his terms) for a learned response is constituted by a stored representation (memory) of the sensory consequences of prior occurrences of that response. Thus, it is the *memory* of the sensations produced by prior responses that represents the goal to be achieved by present and future occasions in which that response is demanded by instructions. The instructional stimuli arising from the organism's environment and not directly dependent upon its activity (*exafference* in von Holst's terms) activate the neural circuit which stores the pattern of feedback stimuli produced by prior occurrences of the activity referenced by the instruction. Response feedback is therefore also a precondition to the development of voluntary control.

The ability of a verbal instruction such as "raise your arm" to activate the circuits previously activated by the occurrence of arm raising is assumed to depend upon the formation of an association between the verbal labels employed in the instruction and the sensations that are consequent upon this response. This process of stimulus association has been termed *calibration* or *labeling.* The internal sensory consequences of an act are said to be calibrated in terms of their external sensory consequences. Calibration provides a *dimensionality* to internal sensations—it enables us, for example, to describe the positions of our limbs and the intensity of their movements on the basis of the internal stimulus states associated with variations in their activities and independently of their *immediate* external sensory consequences. If it can be demonstrated that external feedback was necessary for the development of instructional control over a particular response *and* that the control is maintained following the withdrawal of the feedback, it may be inferred that the external feedback has served a calibrating function. The feedback made available during training has enabled the individual to employ internal feedback stimuli to identify the behavioral goal demanded by the instructions. Evidence of calibration, therefore, implies that discriminable internal feedback is associated with the occurrence of the response in question.

It should be noted that instructional control of behavior may develop and be maintained in the absence of discriminable internal feedback. For example, individuals with *tabes dorsalis,* a syphilitic condition resulting in the loss of leg sensation, can comply with instructions to stand and walk *provided that they can see their legs.* When deprived of this external visual feedback, voluntary control of leg movements is eliminated. Where external feedback is necessary for the maintenance of voluntary control, such feedback is said to function as a *performance crutch* (Bilodeau, 1966). It is assumed that, in such cases, the goal of performance is represented by an external stimulus state (e.g., the image of seeing the legs in a particular position) and that the activity in question is regulated by comparing its external sensory consequences with this goal state. Behavior regulated via external feedback lacks the specificity and precision of behavior regulated via its internal sensory consequences.[2]

[2] The demonstration that individuals may not only maintain voluntary control over responses following experimental deafferentation but may actually learn new responses of the deafferented effectors (Taub, Bacon, & Berman, 1965) is in apparent conflict with the hypothesis presented here. In explaining such phenomena, the investigators involved (Taub & Berman, 1968; Festinger, Ono, Burnham, & Bamber, 1967) have made recourse to the ability of organisms to monitor the efferent output of the motor system (central feedback or central efferent monitoring). The present emphasis upon peripheral feedback processes is in no way meant to minimize the importance of central feedback in the development and maintenance of voluntary control. It has been argued elsewhere (Brener, 1974b) that central feedback serves an *enabling* function during the calibration

Thus, it is argued that external feedback is a necessary precondition to the development of instructional control of behavior but not always necessary for the maintenance of such control. The available evidence supports the assumption that instructional control over any response may be developed under appropriate conditions of external feedback. What has not been firmly established is whether, in the case of visceral control in particular, the external feedback serves a calibrating or a crutch function. This question has obvious and important ramifications both for the theoretical analysis of voluntary visceral control and for the application of this phenomenon in the clinical setting.

In terms of the theoretical framework developed in this introduction and more fully described elsewhere (Brener, 1974b,c), it will be appreciated that conscious intentionality does not figure as a factor in voluntary control. Simple introspection confirms that cognitive processes are not involved in the *production* of movement. Although we may decide whether or not to execute a movement, we remain unaware of how we produce even the most rudimentary responses. In other words, the antedating nervous system activities that give rise to movement are not within the conscious domain. As Sherrington (1940) pointed out, the mind is unaware of how it executes any act; it knows but the consequences. Thus, the decision to execute an act, or in James's terms, "to attend to the image of a response," appears to be followed by the response without further intermediate cognitive steps.

The simple hypothesis that derives from this understanding of voluntary control is that, if an individual can learn to appropriately label the sensory consequences of a response, then he will be able to comply with instructions to execute that response.

INSTRUCTIONS

Methods employed for training voluntary visceral control generally contain two procedural elements: instructions and response-contingent stimulation. For reasons of historical bias, the experimental analysis of voluntary visceral control has tended to emphasize the role

process ensuring that only response-contingent stimuli are associated. Such a function has been proposed by Held (1965) and is supported by his data. Following calibration, central feedback is assumed to function in tandem with internal feedback and to serve an equivalent regulatory function. As with internal feedback, however, intermittent recalibration of central feedback is thought to be necessary for the maintenance of this regulatory function.

of feedback and has neglected the influence of instructions. However, it will be recognized that, since instructions are viewed here as the fundamental operation for probing the "voluntariness" of a response, the role of feedback cannot be assessed independently of instructional influences. From the present point of view, effective procedures for training visceral control are those that establish the ability of instructions to reliably influence visceral responses. As the data described below indicate, it is mistaken to assume that instructions are neutral in their effects on visceral activity even prior to training. Although, in 1938, Hilgard and Humphreys drew attention to the profound influence instructions may have in determining the effects of experimental contingencies, researchers in visceral learning have only just begun to examine these influences in a methodical way.

As mentioned earlier, simple instructions are generally comprised of a verb that specifies a *directional requirement* (e.g., "increase" or "decrease") and a noun phrase that designates the effector system in which that directional requirement is to be fulfilled (e.g., "heart rate" or "blood pressure"). Let us call the noun phrase the *effector referent* of the instruction. The available data indicate that each of these components acting independently and in concert with the other exerts a powerful pretraining influence on visceral activity. These influences may be illustrated by reference to experiments on heart-rate control. This response clearly meets the criterion for classification as a voluntary response. A number of investigators have reported that, without any special training and in the absence of any special feedback conditions, naive subjects will reliably comply with instructions to increase and decrease their heart rates (Bergman & Johnson, 1971, 1972; Blanchard, Scott, Young, & Edmundson, 1974; Brener, Kleinman, & Goesling, 1969; Johns, 1970; Ray, 1974).

The reliable influence on heart rate of the "increase" and "decrease" components of instructions has been demonstrated independently in two investigations employing very similar techniques. Brener and Goesling (1968) provided four groups of subjects with exteroceptive feedback of heart rate in the form of a brief high-pitched tone contingent upon each short interheartbeat interval (IBI) and a brief low-pitched tone contingent upon each long IBI. Thus, high-pitched tones signaled the occurrence of high heart rates and low-pitched tones the occurrence of low heart rates. Subjects in two groups were given instructions requiring increases in heart rate, namely, "Produce high-pitched tones" (Group 1) and "Inhibit low-pitched tones" (Group 2). The other two groups were given instructions requiring heart-rate decreases, namely, "Produce low-pitched tones"

(Group 3) and "Inhibit high-pitched tones" (Group 4). No subjects were informed that variations in heart rate controlled the tones. Throughout the experiment, the criterion for distinguishing short from long IBIs was adjusted to approximate the subject's median IBI. This procedure ensured that the groups did not differ in terms of the number of success or failure signals they received during training. Nevertheless, it was observed that subjects who were instructed to *produce* high-pitched tones (Group 1) displayed significantly greater increases in heart rate than subjects instructed to *inhibit* low-pitched tones (Group 2). Conversely, subjects instructed to *inhibit* high-pitched tones (Group 4) displayed significantly greater heart-rate decrements than subjects instructed to *produce* low-pitched tones (Group 3). Since the groups were not differentiated with respect to the informational content of the external feedback, we concluded that the effect was due to the incompatibility of the response sets induced by the "increase" and "decrease" components of the instructions, and the requirements of the task in the cases of Groups 2 and 3. The instruction to produce something implies an increase in activity, and increases in activity are incompatible with decreasing the heart rate (Group 3). Similarly, the instruction to inhibit something implies a reduction in activity, and reductions in activity are incompatible with increasing the heart rate (Group 2).

An almost identical result has been reported by Bouchard and Corson (1976). In this study, subjects in two groups were provided with binary visual feedback whenever their heart rates increased. Subjects in one of these groups received instructions and reinforcement for keeping the light on (INC–POS) and subjects in the other group received instructions and reinforcement for keeping the light off (DEC–NEG). Two other groups of subjects received visual feedback for low heart rates, with subjects in one group receiving instructions and reinforcement for keeping the light on (DEC–POS) and subjects in the other group for keeping the light off (INC–NEG). It will be appreciated that these treatments are directly equivalent to the treatments employed in the Brener and Goesling study. In full agreement with the results of this earlier study, Bouchard and Corson observed significantly greater heart-rate increases in the INC–POS group than in the INC–NEG group, and significantly greater decreases in the DEC–NEG group than in the DEC–POS group. These results again indicate that the "increase" and "decrease" components of verbal instructions have an important influence on heart-rate control. This influence is assumed to operate by establishing response sets in individuals that may vary in terms of their compatibility with the behavioral adjustment required by other aspects of the training procedure.[3]

These experiments contain procedures for investigating the pretreatment influence of the *directional requirement* component of instructions. They control for the influences of specific *effector referents* by designating an external stimulus change as the goal. In the case of heart-rate change, at least, it would appear that the effects of the "increase" and "decrease" components of instructions are more profound than those produced by specific effector referents. Thus, we have observed that instructions to "increase" and "decrease" either heart rate, blood pressure, or respiration reliably lead to equivalent changes in heart rate.

The dominant effect of this instructional component may be attributed to the tendency of individuals to respond in a predictable but nonspecific manner to instructions that incorporate the commands "increase" and "decrease." In particular, they comply with "increase" instructions by increasing striate muscle (somatomotor) activity, manifesting sympathetic-like increases in visceral activity and displaying a desynchronization of the electrical activity of the brain (an arousal pattern). To "decrease" instructions, they tend to display decreases in striate muscle activity, parasympathetic-like decreases in visceral activity, and a synchronization of the electrical activity of the brain. These two types of behavioral adjustment have been termed *ergotropic* and *trophotropic* responses (Hess, 1954) and are of special significance in evaluating the evidence for voluntary *cardiovascular* control. Most importantly, they imply that individuals may meet the requirements of instructions to perform particular responses without being able to detect instances of the activity referenced by the instruction. In other words, comprehension of the *directional requirement* may enable behavioral compliance with an instruction, irrespective of

[3] It will be noted that the groups that displayed the greatest increases in heart rate (INC–POS in the Bouchard and Corson study, and Group 1 in the Brener and Goesling study) were both instructed to *produce* external feedback which was contingent on *heart-rate increases.* The groups that displayed the greatest decreases (DEC–NEG in the Bouchard and Corson study, and Group 4 in the Brener and Goesling study) were instructed to *inhibit* external feedback which was also contingent upon *heart-rate increases.* These results would therefore also support the alternative interpretation that exteroceptive feedback contingent upon heart-rate increases carries more useful information than exteroceptive feedback contingent upon heart-rate decreases. Such an effect is not incompatible with the response-setting functions of instructions which I have emphasized.

the individual's ability to identify and label responses of the exclusive class designated by the *effector referent.* This latter ability is considered here to be a determinant of the specificity of voluntary visceral control rather than a criterion to be employed in assigning responses to the classes of voluntary or nonvoluntary.

Although these data suggest that the heart-rate changes produced in untrained individuals by simple instructions are components of nonspecific voluntary motor adjustments to the commands "increase" and "decrease," more detailed analysis of the data indicates that such a simple interpretation is not wholly satisfactory. For example, Shanks (1973) observed that, although naive subjects display equivalent heart-rate changes when instructed to increase and decrease either their heart rates or blood pressures, the responses to instructions that referenced heart rate as the required response were reliably accompanied by substantial EMG changes, whereas the responses produced by instructions that referenced blood pressure were not accompanied by correlated changes in EMG activity. Thus, the reference to heart rate in the instructions clearly transmitted some specific information to the subjects. This observation suggests to us that naive subjects have learned to label variations in EMG activity as "heart-rate increases and decreases," but not as "blood pressure increases and decreases." Since individuals are usually aware of their cardiac activity only when engaging in strenuous exercise, the basis of this association seems well-founded in common experience.

Additional evidence that reference to heart rate in instructions carries specific information is contained in a report by Blanchard *et al.* (1974). These investigators provided subjects with exteroceptive feedback of variations in heart rate. One group of subjects was instructed simply to produce the appropriate external feedback (uninformed about the effective response: a control for the directional requirement component), another group was told to control the feedback by varying their skin resistance (misinformed about the effective response), and a third group was instructed to control the exteroceptive feedback by varying their heart rates (informed of the effective response). The subjects who were correctly informed of the effective response displayed significantly greater compliance with the instructions than subjects who were misinformed or uninformed. These data again suggest that specific information is transmitted by the effector referent of an instruction. If, as our results suggested, the heart rate referent leads to systematic variations in muscle tension, the differences between Blanchard *et al.*'s three groups may be accounted for in terms of the magnitude of the nonspecific (ergotropic or trophotropic) motoric adjustment induced by the different effector referents employed in the three instructional variations.

It is interesting to note that subjects who were instructed to control their skin resistance displayed significantly worse heart-rate control than subjects who were uninformed of the effective response. This suggests that the activities that subjects have learned to label as "increases and decreases in skin resistance" are antagonistic to the production of systematic variations in heart rate. In certain cases, a specific effector referent may interfere with the performance of the desired behavior in much the same manner as instructions to "increase" or "produce" something interfere with the learning of heart-rate decreases. An example of this type of effect is contained in an experiment by Hefferline, Keenan, and Harford (1959). These investigators attempted to condition the frequency of contraction in a small muscle in the thumb. Some subjects were informed of the effective response ("a tiny twitch of the left thumb"), whereas other groups of subjects were not so informed.[4] Under equivalent feedback conditions, subjects who were informed of the effective response displayed poorer conditioning than subjects who were not informed. Subjects in the informed group "were so busy producing voluntary thumb twitches that the small, reinforcable type of response had little opportunity to occur" (p. 1339). With regard to the findings of Blanchard *et al.*, this observation seems particularly germane since, as Roberts and Young (1971) have shown, electrodermal activity tends to change independently of heart rate and movement. Thus, individuals who were attempting to vary their skin resistance and perhaps even succeeding in doing so should not be expected to display systematic variations in heart rate. The very fact that instructions that referenced skin resistance rather than heart rate had an inhibitory influence on the development of heart-rate control seems to imply that the individuals involved had formulated a correct idea of what variations in skin resistance are. Presumably, individuals learn that clamminess of the palms is, unlike sensations produced by variations in cardiac activity, unassociated with general movement processes. Although the basis of this type of effect is at present rather obscure, it can be positively asserted that the effector referent employed in an instruction may, in and of itself, have a systematic influence on the development of learned visceral control. Such "pure" instructional influences as those described in this section are brought into the experimental situation in the form of the subject's preconceptions of the meaning of such phrases as

[4] It should be noted that the thumb is moved by muscles in the forearm.

"heart-rate increases" and "blood-pressure decreases." As the experimental evidence indicates, the influence on visceral control of such preconceptions is profound and unless they are well controlled for, the interpretation of results in this area of research becomes extremely difficult.

In a sense, the acquisition of meaning by words that are used to describe variations in visceral activity may be viewed as the fundamental process of voluntary visceral control. When an individual acquires the ability to comply reliably and specifically with an instruction to produce a particular variation in visceral activity, it may be asserted that he has learned the meaning of the instruction. In order to determine whether or not our procedures (biofeedback, reinforcement, etc.) have been effective in establishing meaning in a set of instructions, it is necessary to probe the meaning of the instruction prior to and following the training procedure. If we are to investigate precisely what a subject understands by an instruction, it is of little use to measure only one index of his activity. The broader the spectrum of activities that are measured in investigating the influence of instructions, the more precise will be our inferences regarding the subject's interpretation of those instructions.

In terms of this approach, the self-reports of subjects in visceral learning experiments are in themselves of very dubious utility. Such self-reports achieve interpretive significance only when data on the internal events to which the reports refer are also available. Introspections are, after all, descriptions of the internal stimulus state. As is well-known (e.g., Kuntz, 1953), individuals are notoriously bad at describing the sources of visceral sensations. Visceral sensation tends to be of a gross, undifferentiated nature and, in many organ systems, there is a reliable disparity between the actual and subjectively perceived sources of sensation. Consequently, it is not surprising that untrained individuals will tend to employ the vocabulary for describing such sensations in an imprecise and idiosyncratic manner.

In this connection, it is important to note that in addition to their effects upon activity described above, instructions have also been demonstrated to have a profound effect on the self-reports of subjects. In other words, instructions influence not only what subjects will do in the experimental situation, but also what they will say they are doing or experiencing. This has been noted by Beatty (1972) in relation to subjective reports of increased alpha wave states. Subjects tend to report pleasant experiences if the instructions lead them to expect such experiences. More recently, Walsh (1974) has provided data that suggest that instructions influence subjective reports by predisposing subjects to employ certain vocabulary items in describing their experiences. In this experiment, groups of subjects were provided with external feedback either when alpha wave activity was presented in their EEG records or when it was absent. Subjects who received instructions that did not make specific reference to the "pleasantness" of the alpha state reported that affectively neutral mental experiences accompanied external stimuli that were contingent upon either the presence or absence of alpha wave activity. However, subjects who received instructions that specifically referenced the "pleasantness" of the alpha state reported that positive affective experiences accompanied external stimuli contingent upon alpha wave activity and that negative affective experiences accompanied stimuli that were contingent upon nonalpha activity. As Walsh points out, his results are assimilable with hypotheses proposed by Shachter and Singer (1962) regarding self-reports of emotional states. As these investigators demonstrated, environmental contextual factors determine the labels subjects will apply to the description of their internal sensations.

Verplanck (1962) too had demonstrated that what individuals do and what they say they are doing may be concurrently and independently manipulated. Instructions are an instrument of such manipulation. As we have seen, they exhibit reliable pretreatment influences upon somatic and visceral activities. Instructions also serve to determine the descriptions that subjects apply to their activities by biasing them toward the use of certain verbal labels. In view of this, the investigation of instructional setting processes is of fundamental importance to the analysis of voluntary visceral control.

SOMATOMOTOR INVOLVEMENT IN THE DEVELOPMENT OF VOLUNTARY AND OPERANT CARDIOVASCULAR CONTROL

It has been noted that learned variations in cardiovascular activity tend to be reliably associated with variations in somatomotor and "cognitive activities." For example, learned increases and decreases in heart rate are generally correlated with increases and decreases in somatomotor and respiratory activity (Belmaker, Proctor, & Feather, 1972; Wells, 1973). Learned heart-rate changes are also frequently accompanied by subjective reports of particular cognitive activities such as thinking about active processes during heart-rate increases and passive processes during heart-rate decreases (Ray, 1974). The interpretation of these correlational data has provided the focus of a considerable amount of theoretical discussion.

The conventional bipartite view of the organism incorporates a rational entity manifesting its activities through the striate musculature, and a mechanical entity manifesting its vital functions through the visceral system. Influenced by this dualistic conception, many researchers have tended to ascribe causal properties to the somatomotor and cognitive activities that accompany learned visceral responses. Katkin and Murray (1968), for example, have suggested that, in the interests of parsimony, visceral activities should not be classifed as voluntary or operant responses unless it can be shown that they were not elicited in a reflexive or respondent fashion by intermediate somatomotor or cognitive responses. The application of this criterion in the voluntary classification of visceral responses requires that members of this class should occur in the absence of other activities, which by convention fall within the class of voluntary responses. This logically untenable requirement stems from yet another subjectively apparent but objectively unwarranted attribute of voluntary responses. As has been pointed out elsewhere (Brener, 1974a), current convention explicitly defines voluntary and operant responses as activities that occur in the absence of an objectively identifiable cause. If an activity can be ascribed to the influence of a particular antedating agent, then that activity cannot be classed as a voluntary or operant response. In other words, if we cannot specify the events and conditions that give rise to an activity, we tend to classify that activity as a voluntary response. This tendency is consistent with the peculiar human penchant for assigning the highest status and the greatest importance to those phenomena about which least is known.

Our ignorance in these matters, as in others, is sensory in origin. Subjective hypotheses about the modus operandi of organisms are inevitably derived from personal experience and experience in turn derives from the sensory impact of the world. The tendency to believe that the striated muscles are directly controlled and therefore "truly voluntary" is not based upon the absence of processes intervening between the decision to tense a muscle and the execution of that response, but upon our inability to subjectively experience these intervening processes. We can have an idea of tensing a muscle because we have previously experienced the sensation of tensing that muscle; etiologically, the idea is secondary to the response (James, 1890). When we do tense a muscle, our heart rate increases. However, the sensations produced by an increase in heart rate are overshadowed by the concurrent sensations produced by the accompanying striate muscle response and cardiac sensations do not, therefore, become part of our experience. Only vicariously or under extreme conditions of exercise or arousal do we experience cardiac sensations. However, because of the structural and functional characteristics of the internal sensory systems, the subjective experience of somatomotor activities and the ideas that derive therefrom will tend to dominate and provide associative meaning for visceral sensations. Somatomotor activity leads not only to more discriminable internal sensations than does cardiovascular activity (proprioception versus interoception), but in addition, somatomotor activity reliably gives rise to exteroceptive feedback, whereas cardiovascular activity does not. It is not surprising, therefore, that when subjects are asked how they increased their heart rates, they report tensing their muscles or thinking about tensing their muscles; these components of the behavioral adjustments in which heart-rate increases are embedded are more easily experienced and more adequately labeled. In such cases, however, the prevailing subjective impression is one of indirect or mediated control: They appear to involve the active translation of one requirement ("increase heart rate") into another requirement ("increase muscle tension"). The subjective impression of direct or unmediated control, on the other hand, appears to result from instances in which the ideas activated by the instruction and contained in the decision to perform a response are congruent with the experience of sensing that response (e.g., tensing a muscle).

Although the mediation issue is primarily a definitional rather than an empirical problem, it has given rise to a good deal of research. In fact, the curare experiments (Miller, 1969; DiCara, 1970) were designed specifically to demonstrate that visceral learning may occur independently of somatomotor activity. Since curare totally paralyzes the striated (voluntary) musculature while leaving visceral and nervous system functions relatively unimpaired, the curarized subject is prevented from manipulating its visceral activity by engaging in somatomotor or respiratory maneuvers. As Miller and DiCara and their associates, among others (Hothersall & Brener, 1969; Slaughter, Hahn, & Rinaldi, 1970; Thornton & van-Toller, 1973), have demonstrated, reward and punishment procedures are effective in training curarized animals to control a great variety of specific variations in visceral activity. Although the phenomena reported in this literature are not presently replicable (Brener, Eissenberg, & Middaugh, 1974; Hahn, 1974; Miller & Dworkin, 1974), the curare experiments undoubtedly served to legitimize the phenomenon of visceral learning in the eyes of the scientific community. The contribution to knowledge that these experiments provided was that the immediate availability of feedback from the striate musculature is not prerequisite to visceral learning. However, few physiologists believe that the visceral system is *driven* by the peripheral somatomotor system. On the contrary, an overwhelming body of hard evidence supports the view that visceral and somatomotor activities are integrated at a central level (Germana, 1969; Obrist, Lawler, & Gaebelein, 1974; Rushmer & Smith, 1959). As a number of recent experiments have demonstrated, the data derived from the curare experiments are quite assimilable with this view. The primary function of curare appears to have been to foster the illusion of "direct" visceral control by preventing the experimenter from sensing the somatomotor correlates of the visceral responses conditioned in his subjects.

For example, DiCara and Miller (1969) conditioned heart-rate increases in one group of curarized rats and heart-rate decreases in another group. Following successful conditioning of these cardiac responses, the animals were permitted to recover from curare and then were tested again in the noncurarized state. It was observed that the animals that had been taught to increase their heart rates displayed substantially higher activity levels and respiration rates than animals that had been taught to decrease their heart rates. In other words, the conditioning procedure to which these paralyzed animals had been subjected had served to modify those brain processes that regulate the functionally integrated respiratory, cardiac, and somatomotor components of increases and decreases in movement. The possibility that paralyzed animals may learn to modify somatomotor activity that is proximal to the blocked myoneural junction has recently been established by Koslovskaya, Vertes, and Miller (1973). In this experiment, curarized rats were successfully trained to increase and decrease the rate of firing in motor nerves by reinforcement of the appropriate responses with electrical stimulation of the brain.

Another experiment that indicates that somatomotor processes may continue to influence cardiac activity even in the curarized animals has been reported by Goesling and Brener (1972). Using a shock-avoidance procedure, these investigators trained freely moving rats to be either active or immobile. The subjects were then curarized and, by means of a similar shock-avoidance procedure, reinforced for either increasing or decreasing their heart rates. It was found that regardless of these reinforcement contingencies, subjects that were pretrained to be immobile all displayed heart-rate decreases and subjects pretrained to be active all displayed heart-rate increases in the curarized condition. This experiment provides further support for the view that cardiovascular and somatomotor responses are centrally integrated. When the somatomotor component of the learned behavioral adjustment was blocked by curare, the cardiac component was still manifested under the appropriate conditions.

Nevertheless, because these data indicate that the conditioning procedure implemented prior to curare had a more profound influence on heart rate than the procedure implemented when the subjects were curarized, they suggest that peripheral somatomotor processes may play an important part in the development of learned cardiovascular control. This possibility has received consideration by Smith (1967), whose article "Conditioning as an artifact" (Smith, 1954) was instrumental in provoking an earlier rash of curare experiments (Black & Lang, 1964; Smith, 1964a,b). Smith argued that although somatic and cardiac efferent processes were centrally integrated, learning was primarily a somatomotor affair. This hypothesis is based upon the recognition that the internal feedback from the striate muscle effectors (proprioception) is more conspicuously involved in the associative learning process than feedback from the cardiovascular effectors (interoception). In other words, Smith suggested that the activity of the entire learned somatic–cardiac Gestalt is regulated by feedback from the peripheral somatic component. An experimental finding supporting this view comes from a recent study by Obrist, Howard, Lawler, Galosy, Meyers, and Gaebelein (1974). These investigators demonstrated that the magnitude of operantly conditioned heart-rate changes is inversely proportional to the degree of somatomotor restraint imposed upon subjects. Thus, subjects who were instructed not to vary their breathing and to remain immobile throughout conditioning displayed significantly smaller heart-rate increments than subjects who were not so instructed.

Procedures that produce changes in somatomotor activity also lead to correlated changes in cardiac activity. Sutterer and Obrist (1972), for example, observed that a tone that has been paired with a shock acquired the ability to elicit increases in somatomotor activity and heart rate in dogs. However, if the tone–shock pairings were presented while the dog was engaging in food-reinforced operant behavior (conditioned suppression procedure), the tone elicited a decrease in somatomotor activity and heart rate. Similar results in rats have been recorded by Black and de Toledo (1972). In the study by Goesling and Brener (1972), it was found that rats reinforced for increasing their activity displayed increases in heart rate whereas those reinforced for immobility displayed decreases in heart rate.

What is not made clear by these data is whether the close correlation between the cardiac and somatic responses to voluntary and operant control procedures is due to the central efferent integration of these two effector systems or to sensory factors of the sort suggested by Smith. This view suggests that, if two activities are highly correlated and if one of the two activities is more readily discriminable than the other, then the integrated response will be identified and regulated by feedback from the more discriminable component.

In terms of the model presented here, if two responses have sensory consequences that are not discriminable, then the individual will respond similarly to instructions that demand changes in either response. It also follows from the arguments presented that, if an individual were able to discriminate instances of each of two responses independently, differential control over the two responses should be demonstrable. In order to explore more fully the extent to which learned somatomotor and cardiac activities are differentiable, we (Brener, Eissenberg, & Connally, in preparation) have recently undertaken a series of experiments with freely moving rats.

In the first of these experiments, a shock-avoidance procedure was employed to condition heart-rate increases in one group of rats and heart-rate decreases in another group. The conditioning environment in these experiments consisted of a running wheel with an electrifiable grid. Following 5 days of habituation to the experimental environment during which no experimental stimuli were applied, 10 sessions of shock-avoidance training were administered. Each conditioning session consisted of 20 minutes of SΔ, during which the house lights were off and no experimental stimuli presented, and 20 minutes of SD, during which the house lights were on and the reinforcement contingencies were in effect. During SD periods, if the subject failed to achieve the appropriate heart rate, a tone was presented. If in the presence of the tone, the subject continued to display noncriterion heart rates for 20 successive IBIs, it received a brief, inescapable electric shock to the feet; the procedure was then recycled. Throughout the procedure, heart rate, wheel turns, and general activity (sensed with an ultrasonic motion detector) were monitored.

After 10 days of conditioning, the data provided clear evidence of discriminated operant heart-rate increases and decreases. The mean heart rates for subjects reinforced for increasing were approximately 30 beats per minute (bpm) higher during SD than SΔ, whereas they were 80 bpm lower during SD than SΔ for subjects reinforced for heart-rate decreases. Furthermore, the mean SΔ heart rates did not differ between the groups reinforced, respectively, for increasing and decreasing. Although the terminal (tenth conditioning session) effects were symmetrical for the increase and decrease groups, the acquisition curves were substantially different. Subjects that could avoid the electric shock by increasing their heart rates displayed very rapid acquisition, achieving their asymptotic levels by the third session. On the other hand, subjects reinforced for decreasing, displayed a gradual reduction in heart rate more characteristic of a typical learning curve. Of importance to the issue presently under consideration was the observation that all of the heart-rate variations referred to above were highly correlated with accompanying variations in wheel turning and general activity. This observation indicated that a reinforcement contingency, which specified heart-rate change as the effective response, served to identify a complex of functionally interrelated responses in which somatomotor activity figured prominently.

These results led us to ask the question of whether contingencies that specified somatomotor activity as the effective response would lead to a different behavior adjustment from that produced by contingencies that demanded heart-rate changes.

Another group of rats was run under conditions that were identical to those employed for conditioning heart-rate increases except that the shock-avoidance was programmed to be contingent upon increases in wheel turning rather than heart rate. The behavioral adjustment induced by the wheel-turning contingencies proved to be virtually identical to that produced by the heart-rate-increase contingency. During SD periods, the activity levels and heart rates of subjects increased; during SΔ periods, they fell. The shape of the learning curves and the relationships between the three measures (heart rate, wheel trrning, and general activity) were not different between the groups reinforced, respectively, for heart-rate increases or activity increases.

These results indicate that under the conditions prevailing in these experiments, rats are unable to discriminate heart-rate increases from increases in somatomotor activity. Because these two activities are so highly correlated, a stimulus that is made contingent upon a particular variation in one of the responses will almost certainly be contingent upon a correlated variation in the other response. Under these conditions, stimulus contingencies cannot identify instances of either component of the cardiac–somatic Gestalt independently of the other. Perfect efferent integration implies perfect afferent integration. However, although heart rate and somatomotor activities are highly correlated, increases in cardiac activity unaccompanied by somatomotor increases have been noted (Obrist, Lawler, & Gaebelein, 1974). As Obrist's experiments have indicated, this cardiac–somatic dissociation is sympathetic in origin and may be of considerable importance in defining the etiology of essential hypertension. Our interest in this issue has led us to ask the question of whether such sympathetically mediated increases in cardiac activity may be brought under experimental control independently of somatomotor activity. However, as the experimental results described above indicate, this cannot be achieved by the simple application of reinforcement contingencies that identify heart-rate increases as the effective response. We are therefore presently investigating the possibility of inducing independent control of cardiac and somatomotor activities by employing situations that differentially inhibit the somatomotor component of the cardiac–somatic Gestalt. One such procedure involves increasing the energy cost of somatomotor activity during heart rate conditioning in freely moving animals. This is achieved by gradually increasing the force required to rotate the running wheel that forms the conditioning environment and that is an important releasing stimulus for somatomotor activity in the rat (Brener & Goesling, 1970).

Where two responses do not display the same high degree of correlation as heart rate and somatomotor activities, simple contingencies may be employed effectively to produce independent control of either of the activities. In such cases, response-contingent (feedback or reinforcing) stimuli will always be associated with instances of the effective response, but will only sometimes be associated with the occurrence of related responses. This has been demonstrated in the development of control over heart rate and blood pressure (Brener & Kleinman, 1970; Shapiro, Tursky, Gershon, & Stern, 1969), and also in the conditioning of heart rate and gastric activity (Miller & Banuazizi, 1968). Although, under certain conditions, common sources of influence may produce reliable covariation of heart rate, blood pressure, and gastric activity, under other conditions, independent sources of influence may produce differential changes in these responses. Schwartz (1972) has demonstrated that, in the extent to which the latter conditions prevail, differential feedback contingencies may be employed to produce experimental control over convergent and divergent variations in heart rate and systolic blood pressure.

INTEROCEPTIVE DISCRIMINATION

It has been argued that the primary associative function of exteroceptive feedback (including reinforcing) stimuli is to identify or label particular effective states of the organism. When a stimulus is made to occur contingent upon a response, it does, *inter alia,* inform the organism that the response that has just occurred is associated with that variation in the external environment. By way of illustration, it is suggested that if, in an appropriate instructional context, the words "high heart rate" were flashed on a screen whenever a subject's heart rate exceeded its normal level, the subject would learn to identify the internal sensations associated with the occurrence of the visual stimulus and would come to employ the words "high heart rate" to describe those sensations. In support of this suggestion, reference is made to an experiment by Hefferline and Perera (1963) entitled "Proprioceptive discrimination of a covert operant without its observation by the subject." Subjects in this experiment were reinforced for pressing a key whenever they heard a tone. The tone, unknown to the subjects, was contingent upon a small muscle twitch in the thumb. When subjects were reliably pressing the key on the occurrence of the tone, its intensity was gradually decreased until the tone was completely eliminated. Nevertheless, subjects continued reliably to press the key whenever the muscle twitch, which had previously produced the tone, occurred. Of particular relevance to the process under consideration is that the subjects reported detecting the tone even after it had been eliminated. During periods when the tone was being presented at a very low intensity, a subject occasionally reported that he heard two tones. The events that he was apparently discriminating were the muscle twitch itself and the actual tone, which followed the twitch after a brief delay. As these investigators note, "Apparently the two kinds of discriminative stimulus, 'subjective tone' and 'objective tone', were not appreciably different" (p. 835).

In the case of heart-rate variations, however, as we have seen, the sensations that the subject learns to label may not be cardiac in origin. Although cardiac afferentation projects to levels of the brain that should, in principle, permit its discrimination (Chernigovskii, 1967; Ádám, 1967), variations in the cardiac afferent channel are accompanied by variations in other afferent channels (notably respiratory and striate muscle) which are far more easily discriminable. It seems reasonable to assume that, if one stimulus is consistently preceded by a complex stimulus comprised of a number of signals that vary in terms of their discriminability, the strongest association will be formed between that component of the compound stimulus which has the highest signal-to-noise ratio and the second stimulus of the pair.

This point of view is supported by the relevant experimental literature on compound classical conditioning. For example, Pavlov (1927) noted that, if a compound CS is used (one that is comprised of a number of distinct components—e.g., tactile, thermal, auditory, visual), one of the components tends to gain all the associative strength. He referred to this phenomenon as the "overshadowing" of the less intense by the more intense stimulus. What is being proposed here is that, in the development of cardiac control, somatomotor feedback tends to overshadow cardiac feedback, thereby leading the subject to label the somatomotor component of the cardiac–somatic Gestalt at the expense of the cardiac component. However, provided that there is some independence of somatomotor and cardiac activity, it should in principle be possible to label independently the internal stimulus consequences of the cardiac and somatic responses.

At present, very little is known about the psychophysics of interoception. We do not know whether or not individuals have an intrinsic ability to detect normal variations in visceral activity or whether or not they can be trained to do so. If they can be trained to detect the interoceptive consequences of variations in visceral activity, is it possible to determine a just-noticeable difference in visceral sensation? Questions of this sort are clearly important to the analysis of visceral learning that has been proposed here. This model makes a number of specific predictions. In particular, it predicts that, if an individual is able correctly to identify and label a visceral response, then he will be able to comply with instructions to perform that response. Conversely, it predicts that, if an individual is able to comply with instructions to perform a particular response, then he should have a demonstrable ability to detect instances of that response. Furthermore, it is predicted that the specificity with which an individual complies with an instruction to execute a response is determined by the extent to which he can discriminate instances of that response independently of the other activities that form its normal behavioral context. Conversely, it would predict that, if an individual reliably responds to instructions to, for example, increase his heart rate by not only increasing his heart rate but also by increasing his respiration, then he should be demonstrably unable to discriminate increases in heart rate from increases in respiration. Before any of these questions may be answered, a reliable and valid means of measuring interoceptive discrimination is necessary.

The experimental literature on interoceptive conditioning firmly establishes that sensory processes arising in the visceral field may and do participate fully in the intersensory mechanisms of learning. Experiments reported in this literature demonstrate that interoceptive stimuli may acquire respondent-controlling properties when employed as conditional stimuli in a classical conditioning procedure (Bykov, 1957; Razran, 1961). They may also acquire discriminative operant-controlling properties in the appropriate procedural context (Cook, Dairdson, Davis, & Kelleher, 1960; Schechter & Rosencrans, 1972; Slucki, Ádám, & Porter, 1965; Slucki, McCoy, & Porter, 1969). Although these studies establish the feasibility of studying the discriminability of interoceptive processes associated with normal variations in visceral activity, the methods they employ are not directly applicable. The procedures used for stimulating interoceptors in these studies generally involve chemical and surgical intervention of a sort that would be neither ethically tolerable nor methodologically appropriate in the context of human psychophysiology. Furthermore, the method of direct interoceptive stimulation is by its very nature incapable of answering the question of whether or not normal variations in visceral activity produce discriminable sensory consequences.

In view of these considerations, several investigators have evolved less drastic procedures for studying the interoceptive processes normally associated with the regulation of behavior. Using an open-tipped catheter to record intragastric pressures, Griggs and Stunkard (1964) investigated whether human subjects were able to detect stomach contractions. Intermittently, an obese and a nonobese subject were asked to indicate whether or not they were experiencing a stomach contraction and also whether or not they felt hungry. It was observed that, whereas in the nonobese subject, 72% of hunger reports coincided with stomach contractions, in the obese subject, only 10% of hunger reports coincided with stomach contractions. We may infer from this observation that these subjects were employing the term "hunger" to label different sensations. It was also found that, prior to training, the obese subject succeeded in detecting stomach contractions approximately half as well as the nonobese subject, although both subjects detected strong contractions more reliably than weak contractions. By using appropriate contingencies to reward correct discriminations, Griggs and Stunkard succeeded in training the obese subject to detect his stomach contractions as accurately as did the nonobese subject. Also of importance to the analysis undertaken in this chapter was the observation that, when tested 1 year following the termination of this discrimination training, it was found that the obese subject retained the ability to detect stomach contractions. The clear implication of this study is that pathological disturbances in eating may result from the inability of certain individuals to accurately detect and appropriately label the interoceptive preconditions and consequences of food ingestion.

A related observation has been reported by Silverstein, Nathan, and Taylor (1974) in relation to factors associated with chronic alcoholism.

These investigators worked from the assumption that chronic over-ingestion of alcohol is based upon the inability of alcoholics to accurately detect blood alcohol levels (BALs). In this experiment, blood alcohol levels were manipulated by requiring subjects to drink measured amounts of 86-proof whiskey at stipulated intervals. Their ability to detect blood alcohol levels was measured initially by requiring them to rate their levels of intoxication on a 40-point scale, where 0 represented "cold sober" and 40 represented "extremely drunk." By appropriate instruction, subjects were then trained to specify their levels of intoxication by using a BAL scale rather than a "drunkenness" scale. This training involved substituting one set of labels for another (e.g., instead of "cold sober," the subject rated his condition as BAL=0). In all the subjects investigated, it was found that the discrepancy between actual and subjectively reported blood alcohol levels decreased substantially when they were provided with feedback of the accuracy of their estimations. It was also found that, under conditions of feedback, subjects displayed a substantial improvement in their abilities to achieve target BALs by controlling their alcohol intake. Unlike the Griggs and Stunkard results, it was found in this study that, when external feedback was withdrawn, the ability of subjects to detect blood alcohol levels as well as to control alcohol intake tended to decline to pretraining levels. Although this suggests that feedback here was serving a crutch rather than a calibrating role, it will be recognized that the behavioral process in question is subject to influence by powerful motivational factors.

These studies contain procedures for assessing the ability of individuals to detect mechanical and chemical interoceptive processes and for investigating the influence of training procedures upon these abilities. We (Brener & Jones, 1974) have described a noninvasive procedure that may, in principle, be employed to examine interoceptive processes associated with voluntary cardiovascular control in human subjects. This procedure was used in an attempt to determine whether or not normal individuals are capable of detecting internal stimulus events associated with the beating of the heart. It involved instructing subjects to indicate by pressing one of two buttons whether or not variations in an external stimulus were correlated with the beating of their hearts. On half the trials and in a random order, subjects were presented with a sequence of brief vibratory stimuli in which each vibration was triggered by the R-wave of the subject's EKG. On the other trials, the vibratory stimuli occurred at the same rate as the subject's EKG, but were triggered independently of his cardiac activity by a clock pulse generator. Subjects were instructed that following each stimulus sequence, a light would come on. When the light was presented, they were to press buttons with their left hands if they thought that the stimuli in the preceding sequence had been associated with the beating of their hearts, and to press buttons with their right hands if they thought the tones were not contingent on cardiac activity. The performance of the control groups indicated that the two sorts of stimulus sequences (heart-contingent and heart-noncontingent) could not be discriminated in terms of differences in their respective physical attributes. We argued, therefore, that the only way to tell them apart was for the subject to perceive that the heart-contingent stimuli were correlated with internal sensations also arising from the action of the heart, whereas the stimuli that were triggered by the clock pulse generator occurred independently of these internal sensations. The results indicated that, prior to training, subjects were unable to discriminate between the two sorts of stimulus sequences. However, if they were provided discrimination training in the form of a brief buzz every time they pressed the correct button, their discriminative performance rapidly improved. Furthermore, subjects who received training retained the ability to descriminate heart-contingent from heart-noncontingent stimulus sequences when the buzz telling whether or not they were correct was discontinued.

A similar procedure has been used by Stern (1972) in investigating the ability of subjects to detect their own GSR's (galvanic skin responses). Untrained subjects were unable to discriminate external signals that were contingent upon their GSRs from external signals that were noncontingent. However, subjects who were provided with external feedback of GSR activity prior to the discrimination assessment procedure did provide evidence of GSR detection and tended to detect large GSRs more accurately than small GSRs. Although these data indicate that individuals may be trained to detect the occurrence of cardiac and electrodermal activity, they do not serve to isolate the sources of interoception employed by subjects in discriminating contingent from noncontingent external stimuli.

It is possible, for example, that subjects in the Brener and Jones study employed the internal sensations derived from activities that accompanied heart-rate changes to discriminate contingent from noncontingent external stimuli. That such a possibility should be seriously entertained is emphasized by recent data from our laboratory (Shanks, 1973). It was found that under instructions demanding either heart-rate or blood-pressure changes, exteroceptive feedback of heart rate led to more profound and statistically reliable control of respiratory amplitude than of heart rate itself. We interpreted this observation as indicating that exteroceptive stimuli that were contingent upon variations in heart rate served to identify the more discriminable internal sensory consequences of accompanying respiratory activity. This observation suggests that subjects in our discrimination study may have employed respiratory sensations in distinguishing heart-contingent from heart-noncontingent exteroceptive stimuli.

Variations of the basic procedure may, however, be employed to investigate this hypothesis. For example, on half the trials, the external stimulus could be made contingent upon heart-rate changes, and on the other half, it could be made contingent upon variations in the relevant parameter of respiratory activity. If, under adequately controlled conditions, experimental subjects could learn to reliably discriminate between these external stimuli, it could be inferred that they could discriminate cardiac variations independently of the respiratory variations under study. Adequate control in this case would include a demonstration that the cardiac-contingent and respiration-contingent stimuli were not different in terms of their physical attributes. A yoked-control discrimination procedure could be effectively employed to this end. By this process of elimination, the sources of interoception employed by subjects in discriminating response-contingent from response-noncontingent exteroceptive stimuli may be more and more precisely defined. Although somewhat cumbersome, this method has the virtue of requiring experimenters to operationalized their hunches about how individuals discriminate variations ations in visceral activity.

A slightly different means of examining the detectability of cardiac activity has been described by Epstein and Stein (in press). Here, subjects were instructed to press a button either when their heart rates were low or when they were high. Discrimination was assessed prior to, during, and following discrimination training by measuring the coincidence of button presses with the relevant variations in heart rate. As in the Brener and Jones study, training involved providing subjects with feedback following correct discriminative responses. It was found that subjects displayed significant improvements in detecting heart-rate increases and decreases during training, but that their discriminative performance deteriorated following the withdrawal of feedback. Since respiration rates were found not to differ between conditions where high heart rates served as the discriminative stimulus and conditions where low heart rates served as the discriminative stimulus, it was concluded that the internal consequences of variations in this parameter of respiratory activity were not employed in making the discriminations. However, as has been suggested, the internal consequences of variations in respiratory amplitude or volume are more likely to serve as the sensory basis for discriminating high from low heart rates.

The methods of studying interoceptive processes by requiring subjects to discriminate response-contingent from response-noncontingent external stimuli (Brener & Jones, 1974; Griggs & Stunkard, 1964; Stern, 1972) and of requiring subjects to indicate the occurrence of particular sensations (Epstein & Stein, in press; Silverstein *et al.*, 1974) may be employed to answer somewhat different questions. In a sense, these interoceptive discrimination procedures are, respectively, equivalent to instructional control procedures which, on the one hand, specify an external stimulus change as the goal and, on the other, employ a specific effector referrent to designate the goal. Where subjects are required to discriminate response-contingent from response-noncontingent external stimuli, it is unnecessary to make specific reference to the internal source of variation in the contingent stimulus, thereby controlling for the preconceived notions that subjects may have concerning what, for example, heart-rate increases and decreases "feel" like. Where subjects are instructed simply to indicate the occurrence of activities referenced specifically by the instruction, the meaning of that reference for the subject may be inferred by determining which variations in activity most reliably predict the occurrence of a "detection" response. In either case, it will be appreciated that the broader the spectrum of activities measured during experiments on the detection of visceral activities, the more precise will be the inferences that may be drawn regarding the sensory sources of such discriminations. In principle, then, it is possible to provide a sound experimental basis for inferring the discriminative dimensions of interoception. Such a step would appear to be necessary in examining the role of interoceptive processes in the development of voluntary visceral control.

THE DETECTION AND CONTROL OF VISCERAL ACTIVITIES

In this chapter, particular emphasis has been placed upon the interaction of internal and external feedback processes in the development of voluntary visceral control. It has been argued that, before a verbal stimulus may produce a response, it must first of all have acquired the property of labeling that response. This property is assumed to depend upon the formation of an association between the internal sensory consequences of the response and the verbal items used to label it. Two lines of evidence support the inference of such an associative, calibrating processes, being sometimes involved in the development of voluntary visceral control.

The first line of evidence is of a relatively indirect sort. As we have seen, instructional stimuli may acquire the capacity of reliably producing visceral responses when the subject is provided with external feedback of such responses (biofeedback). If the instructions retain this controlling capacity following the withdrawal of the external feedback, it may be inferred that the internal sensory state associated with that response has been calibrated in terms of the verbal labels used in the instructions to reference it. Thus, Brener *et al.* (1969) found that the ability of individuals to comply systematically with instructions demanding increases and decreases in heart rate was retained following the withdrawal of external feedback. Furthermore, the magnitudes of the instructionally produced heart-rate changes were directly proportional to the amount of external feedback provided during training. A similar calibrating effect has also recently been observed in our laboratory (Shanks, 1973) in the development of instructional control over diastolic blood pressure. Prior to feedback training, instructions to increase and decrease blood pressure produced very small and insignificant changes in this parameter of cardiovascular performance. Following feedback training, however, instructions produced substantial and reliable increases and decreases in diastolic blood pressure. A similar result has also been reported by Shapiro, Schwartz, and Tursky (1972). The persistence of cardiac control following the withdrawal of external feedback has been reported in a clinical setting by Engel and Bleecker (1974). It was observed that, following training with external feedback of heart rate, cardiac patients retained the ability to control abnormal variations in the rhythm of the heart for periods of up to 5 years. These investigators also describe an informal observation that is relevant to the other, more direct, line of evidence supporting the calibrating functions of external feedback in the development of voluntary visceral control. In particular, they reported that certain patients acquired the ability to detect instances of their abnormal cardiac rhythms. Similarly, Kamiya (1969) has reported that subjects trained to control their alpha rhythms are subsequently able to detect the occurrence of the alpha rhythm. These observations, among others, are in accord with the results of Stern (1972), indicating that subjects who had received feedback training for GSR control were subsequently better able to detect their GSRs than subjects who did not receive such training.

Given the system of analysis adopted here, it is to be expected that learning to comply with instructions to control a visceral response will lead to a demonstrable improvement in the ability of the individual to detect instances of that response. In a recent experiment specifically designed to examine the effects of interpolated feedback training of heart-rate control on the discrimination of cardiac activity, Clemens and MacDonald (in preparation) obtained inconclusive results suggesting the need for more intensive investigations in this area. In this experiment, one group of subjects was pretested for heart-rate discrimination employing a procedure similar to that described by Brener and Jones (1974). They were then tested for heart-rate control under conditions of exteroceptive heart rate feedback. Following the heart-rate control procedure, subjects were retested on heart beat discrimination. It was found that the initial heart beat discrimination performance predicted success in increasing the heart rate but not in decreasing it. However, the discrimination performance that followed the heart-rate control phase correlated significantly with success in decreasing the heart rate but not in increasing it. The tentative explanation of this effect offered by Clemens and MacDonald is that among some of these experimentally naive subjects, the initial discrimination performance and the control of heart rate increases was based upon internal feedback from the somatic correlates of cardiac activity. Subjects who could effectively control the external feedback by relying upon somatic feedback were led away from using cardiac feedback. Subjects who did not employ this strategy did not perform as well either on the initial discrimination test or subsequently in increasing their heart rates. This accounts for the significant correlation between the precontrol discrimination scores and success in increasing heart rate. Subjects who did not achieve success in controlling their heart rates by relying on somatomotor feedback were led to rely on sources of internal feedback that were more cardiac-specific during the control phase of the experiment and manifested this learning by exhibiting good control over heart-rate decreases (which have less discriminable somatomotor correlates) and also by performing well on the subsequent discrimination test. This interpretation of the data is supported by the observation that success in increasing the heart rate was negatively (nonsignificantly) correlated with success in decreasing. It also finds support in recent data (Ray, 1974) on differences in heart-rate control between individuals classified as either internal or external *locus of control* subjects using Rotter's (1966) scale. Internal locus of control (ILC) subjects complied significantly better with instructions to increase the heart rate than external locus of control (ELC) subjects. However, compliance with instructions to decrease the heart rate was substantially better in ELC than in ILC subjects. Interestingly, although exteroceptive feedback of heart rate augmented the compliance of ELC subjects to "decrease" instructions, it had only a marginal influence on their compliance with "increase" instructions. In the case of ILC subjects, exteroceptive feedback actually impaired compliance with "decrease" instructions while augmenting compliance with "increase" instructions. These findings not only support the conclusion reached by many investigators (e.g., Engel & Gottlieb, 1972; Lang, 1974) that different mechanisms are involved, respectively, in the learning of heart-rate increases and decreases, but they also suggest that there may be substantial individual differences in the sensitivity of these mechanisms. In terms of the present analysis, individuals who are more sensitive to external stimuli (ELC subjects) will be more amenable to the calibrating functions of exteroceptive feedback. Where such functions are realized, it is assumed that feedback training will, in parallel, augment the abilities of individuals to comply with instructions to control particular visceral responses and also to detect instances of those responses.

By the same principles, it is to be expected that, if an individual is trained to detect instances of a particular visceral response, then he should display a demonstrable improvement in his ability to comply with instructions to control that response. Here again, the available evidence is very scanty and does not permit a firm evaluation of the hypothesis. Donelson (1966) employed Mandler, Mandler, and Uviller's (1958) Autonomic Perception Questionnaire (APQ) and also a stimulus matching procedure to investigate heart-rate discrimination in humans. Although she found significant correlations between her behavioral and paper-and-pencil tests, both the methods she employed are subject to serious criticism as objective measures of interoceptive discrimination. Donelson did not find a significant correlation between autonomic perception as measured by the APQ and heart-rate control. Blanchard, Young, and McLeod (1972) have, however, reported that individuals who scored high on the APQ were significantly worse at controlling their heart rates than individuals who scored low on this test. Although such findings appear to contradict a basic assumption of the model developed here, it must be borne in mind that the APQ is a paper-and-pencil test of visceral perception. As such, it is a test of the extent to which individuals employ words that denote visceral sensations in describing their emotional ("happiness" and "anxiety") reactions. As was pointed out earlier, it cannot be assumed that untrained individuals employ such verbal labels accurately. These results suggest, in fact, that subjects who score high on the APQ and therefore employ the vocabulary of visceral sensation in describing their reactions are not applying the labels appropriately. They appear to employ the verbal items in question to describe the sensory consequences of activities that are antagonistic to the behavioral goal designated by the instructions. In this respect, their performance is similar to that of the "informed" subjects in the Hefferline *et al.* (1959) study referred to earlier.

Evidence in support of the predicted relationship between visceral discrimination and control was, however, obtained in an experiment by Kleinman (1970) which was designed specifically to investigate the effects of training in heart-beat discrimination upon subsequent control of heart rate. This investigator used a signal detection method for assessing discrimination. Subjects were instructed to press a button whenever and as soon as they sensed a heart beat during discrimination assessment trials. Interspersed among these trials were trials on which the subject was provided with auditory feedback of the beating of his heart. Subjects who received such feedback displayed an improvement in their heart-beat discrimination as measured by the distribution of latencies from heart beats to button presses, whereas subjects who received false feedback did not show improvement. Furthermore, in subsequent heart-rate control trials, Kleinman found that subjects who had received discrimination training displayed significantly better heart-rate control both with and without external feedback of heart rate than subjects who had not received discrimination training.

CONCLUSIONS

The model of voluntary visceral control that has been described in the present chapter has emphasized the mutual interdependence of the sensory and motor components of the behavioral control process. It has been proposed that the fundamental prerequisite to voluntary visceral control is the acquisition of internal sensory associations by the verbal components of instructional stimuli. Internal stimuli that are the normal consequences of variations in activity become the denotative referents of words. Implicit in the acquisition of these associations, words acquire the capacity to designate specific behavioral goals and thereby to initiate and direct activity. As a by-product of this associative process, words may come to be employed accurately by the subject in describing his activity.

Because this system of analysis views the acquisition of voluntary visceral control as being dependent upon perceptual learning (sensory labeling), it suggests that the understanding of visceral control may be facilitated by the study of visceral sensation and perception. The structural characteristics of internal afferent systems and the functional interdependence of visceral and somatomotor efferent processes tend to militate against the acquisition of response-specific visceral control. Visceral and somatomotor activities generally occur in concert, thereby leading to visceral sensations which are overshadowed by accompanying and more discriminable somatomotor sensations. Despite these impediments, however, specific control of visceral activities may be produced by appropriate training procedures. It has been argued that the primary function of procedures that are effective in establishing response-specific visceral control is to teach the subject to discriminate the internal consequences of the response in question from the internal consequences of its normal behavioral correlates. Since it is implied that the limits of specificity in voluntary visceral control are determined by such discriminative processes, these limits may be more directly assessed by experimentally examining the ability of individuals to detect and label specific variations in visceral activity.

REFERENCES

Ádám, G. *Interoception and Behavior.* Budapest: Akademiai Kiado, 1967.

Beatty, J. Similar effects of feedback signals and instructional information on EEG activity. *Physiology and Behavior,* 1972, *9,* 151–154.

Belmaker, R., Proctor, E., & Feather, B. W. Muscle tension in human operant heart rate conditioning. *Cond. Refl.,* 1972, *7,* 97–106.

Bergman, J. S., & Johnson, H. J. The effects of instructional set and autonomic perception on cardiac control. *Psychophysiology,* 1971, *8,* 180–190.

Bergman, J. S., & Johnson, H. J. Sources of information which affect training and raising of heart rate. *Psychophysiology,* 1972, *9,* 30–39.

Bilodeau, E. A. *Acquisition of skill.* New York: Academic Press, 1966.

Black, A. H., & de Toledo, L. The relationship among classically conditioned responses: Heart rate and skeletal behavior. In A. H. Black & W. F. Prokasy (Eds.), *Classical conditioning II: Current theory and research.* New York: Appleton, 1972. Pp. 290–311.

Black, A. H. & Lang, W. M. Cardiac conditioning and skeletal responding in curarized dogs. *Psychological Review,* 1964, *71,* 80–85.

Blanchard, E. B., Scott, R. W., Young, L. D., & Edmundson, E. D. Effect of knowledge of response on the self-control of heart rate. *Psychophysiology,* 1974, *11*(3), 251–264.

Blanchard, E. B., Young, L. D., & McLeod, P. Awareness of heart activity and self-control of heart rate. *Psychophysiology,* 1972, *9,* 63–68.

Bouchard, C., & Corson, J. A. Heart rate regulation with success and failure signals. *Psychophysiology,* 1976, *13,* 69–74.

Brener, J. Learned control of cardiovascular processes: Feedback mechanisms and therapeutic applications. In K. S. Calhoun, H. E. Adams, & K. M. Mitchell (Eds.), *Innovative treatment methods in psychophysiology.* New York: Wiley, 1974. Pp. 245–272. (a)

Brener, J. A general model of voluntary control applied to the phenomena of learned cardiovascular change. In P. A. Obrist, A. H. Black, J. Brener, & L. V. DiCara (Eds.), *Cardiovascular psychophysiology.* Chicago: Aldine, 1974. Pp. 365–391 (b)

Brener, J. Factors influencing the specificity of voluntary cardiovascular control. In L. V. DiCara (Ed.), *Limbic and autonomic nervous systems research.* New York: Plenum, 1974. Pp. 335–368. (c)

Brener, J., Eissenberg, E., & Connally, S. R. The relationship between operantly conditioned changes in heart rate and somatomotor activity. In preparation.

Brener, J., Eissenberg, E., & Middaugh, S. Respiratory and Somatomotor factors associated with operant conditioning of cardiovascular responses in curarized rats. In P. A. Obrist, A. H. Black, J. Brener, & L. V. DiCara (Eds.), *Cardiovascular psychophysiology.* Chicago: Aldine, 1974. Pp. 251–275.

Brener, J., & Goesling, W. J. Heart rate and conditioned activity. Paper read at Society for Psychophysiological Research Meeting, Washington, D.C., October, 1968.

Brener, J., & Goesling, W. J. Avoidance conditioning of activity and immobility in rats. *Journal of Comparative and Physiological Psychology,* 1970, *70,* 276–280.

Brener, J., & Jones, J. M. Interoceptive discrimination in intact humans: Detection of cardiac activity. *Physiology and Behavior,* 1974, *13,* 763–767.

Brener, J., & Kleinman, R. A. Learned control of decreases in systolic blood pressure. *Nature,* 1970, *226,* 1063–1064.

Brener, J., Kleinman, R. A., & Goesling, W. J. The effects of different exposures to augmented sensory feedback on the control of heart rate. *Psychophysiology,* 1969, *5,* 510–516.

Brobeck, J. R. *Best and Taylor's physiological basis of medical practice* (9th ed). Baltimore: Williams & Wilkins, 1973.

Bykov, K. M. *The cerebral cortex and the internal organs.* New York: Chemical Publishing, 1957.

Chernigovskii, V. N. *Interoceptors.* Washington, D. C.: American Psychological Association, 1967.

Clemens, W. J., & MacDonald, D. F. The relationship between heart beat discrimination and heart rate control. In preparation.

Cook, L. A., Davidson, D. J., Davis, D. J., & Kelleher, R. T. Epinephrine, norepinephrine, and acetylcholine as conditioned stimuli for avoidance behavior. *Science,* 1960, *131,* 990–991.

DiCara, L. V. Learning in the autonomic nervous system. *Scientific American,* 1970, *222,* 30–39.

DiCara, L. V., & Miller, N. E. Transfer of instrumentally learned heart-rate changes from curarized to noncurarized state: Implications for a mediational hypothesis. *Journal of Comparative and Physiological Psychology,* 1969, *68,* 159–162.

Donelson, F. E. Discrimination and control of human heart rate. Unpublished doctoral dissertation, Cornell University, 1966.

Engel, B. T., & Bleecker, E. R. Application of operant conditioning techniques to the control of cardiac arrhythmias. In P. A. Obrist, A. H. Black, J. Brener, & L. V. DiCara (Eds.), *Cardiovascular psychophysiology.* Chicago: Aldine, 1974. Pp. 456–476.

Engel, B. T., & Gottlieb, S. H. Differential operant conditioning of heart rate in the restricted monkey. *Journal of Comparative and Physiological Psychology,* 1972, *73,* 217–225.

Epstein, L. H., & Stein, D. B. Feedback-influenced heart rate discrimination. *Journal of Abnormal Psychology,* in press.

Festinger, L., Ono, H., Burnham, C. A., & Bamber, D. Efference and the conscious experience of perception. *Journal of Experimental Psychology,* 1967, *74* (4, pr.2).

Germana, J. Central efferent processes and autonomic behavioral integration. *Psychophysiology,* 1969, *6,* 78–90.

Goesling, W. J., & Brener, J. Effects of activity and immobility conditioning upon subsequent heart-rate conditioning in curarized rats. *Journal of Comparative and Physiological Psychology,* 1972, *81,* 311–317.

Griggs, R. C., & Stunkard, A. The interpretation of gastric motility: Sensitivity and bias in the perception of gastric motility. *Archives of General Psychiatry,* 1964, *11,* 82–89.

Hahn, W. W. The learning of autonomic responses by curarized animals. In P. A. Obrist, A. H. Black, J. Brener, & L. V. DiCara (Eds.), *Cardiovascular psychophysiology.* Chicago: Aldine, 1974. Pp. 295–311.

Hefferline, R. F., Keenan, B., & Harford, R. A. Escape and avoidance conditioning in human subjects without their observation of the response. *Science,* 1959, *130,* 1338–1339.

Hefferline, R. F., & Perera, T. B. Proprioceptive discrimination of a covert operant without its observation by the subject. *Science,* 1963, *139,* 834–835.

Held, R. Plasticity in sensory–motor systems. *Scientific American,* 1965, *213,* 84–94.

Hess, W. R. *Diencephalon: Autonomic and extrapyramidal functions.* New York: Grune and Stratton, 1954.

Hilgard, E. R., & Humphreys, L. G. The effect of supporting an antagonistic voluntary instruction on conditioned discrimination. *Journal of Experimental Psychology,* 1938, *22,* 291–304.

Hothersall, D., & Brener, J. Operant conditioning of changes in heart rate in curarized rats. *Journal of Comparative and Physiological Psychology,* 1969, *68,* 338–342.

James, W. *Principles of psychology.* New York: Holt, 1890.

Johns, T. R. Heart rate control in humans under paced respiration and restricted movement: The effect of instructions and exteroceptive feedback. *Dissertation Abstracts International,* 1970, *30,* 5712–5713.

Kamiya, J. Operant control of the EEG alpha rhythm and some of its reported effects on consciousness. In C. Tart (Ed.), *Altered states of consciousness.* New York: Wiley, 1969.

Katkin, E. S., & Murray, E. N. Instrumental conditioning of autonomically mediated behavior: Theoretical and methodological issues. *Psychological Bulletin,* 1968, *70*(1), 52–68.

Kleinman, R. A. The development of voluntary cardiovascular control. Unpublished doctoral dissertation, University of Tennessee, 1970.

Koslovskaya, I. B., Vertes, R. P., & Miller, N. E. Instrumental learning without proprioceptive feedback. *Physiology and Behavior,* 1973, *10,* 101–107.

Kuntz, A. *The autonomic nervous system* (4th ed.). Philadelphia: Lea and Febiger, 1953.

Lang, P. J. Learned control of human heart rate in a computer directed environment. In P. A. Obrist, A. H. Black, J. Brener, & L. V. DiCara (Eds.), *Cardiovascular psychophysiology.* Chicago: Aldine, 1974. Pp. 392–405.

Mandler, G., Mandler, J. M., & Uviller, E. T. Autonomic feedback: The perception of autonomic activity. *Journal of Abnormal and Social Psychology,* 1958, *56,* 367–373.

Miller, N. E. Learning of visceral and glandular responses. *Science*, 1969, *163*, 434–445.
Miller, N. E., & Banuazizi, A. Instrumental learning by curarized rats of a specific visceral response, intestinal or cardiac. *Journal of Comparative and Physiological Psychology*, 1968, *65*, 1–7.
Miller, N. E., & Dworkin, B. R. Visceral learning: Recent difficulties with curarized rats and significant problems for human research. In P. A. Obrist, A. H. Black, J. Brener, & L. V. DiCara (Eds.), *Cardiovascular psychophysiology*. Chicago: Aldine, 1974. Pp. 312–331.
Obrist, P. A., Howard, J. L., Lawler, J. E., Galosy, R. A., Meyers, K. A., & Gaebelein, C. J. The cardiac–somatic interaction. In P. A. Obrist, A. H. Black, J. Brener, & L. V. DiCara (Eds.), *Cardiovascular psychophysiology*. Chicago: Aldine, 1974. Pp. 136–162.
Obrist, P. A., Lawler, J. E., & Gaebelein, C. J. A psychobiological perspective on the cardiovascular system. In L. V. DiCara (Ed.), *Limbic and autonomic nervous systems research*. New York: Plenum, 1974. Pp. 311–334.
Pavlov, I. P. *Conditioned reflexes*. Oxford: Oxford University Press, 1927.
Ray, W. J. The relationship of locus of control, self-report measures, and feedback to the voluntary control of heart rate. *Psychophysiology*, 1974, *11*, 527–534.
Razran, G. The observable unconscious and the inferable conscious in current Soviet psychophysiology: Interoceptive conditioning, semantic conditioning, and the orienting reflex. *Psychological Review*, 1961, *68*, 81–147.
Roberts, L. E., & Young, R. Electrodermal responses are independent of movement during aversive conditioning in rats but heart rate is not. *Journal of Comparative and Physiological Psychology*, 1971, *77*, 495–512.
Rotter, J. B. Generalized expectancies for internal versus external control of reinforcement. *Psychological Monographs*, 1966, *80* (Whole No. 609), 1–28.
Rushmer, R. F., & Smith, O. A. Cardiac control. *Physiological Review*, 1959, *39*, 41–68.
Schachter, S., & Singer, J. E. Cognitive, social and physiological determinants of emotional state. *Psychological Review*, 1962, *69*, 379–399.
Schechter, M. D., & Rosencrans, J. A. Atropine antagonism of acetylcholine-cued behavior in the rat. *Life Sciences*, 1972, *11*, 517–532.
Schwartz, G. Voluntary control of human cardiovascular integration and differentiation through feedback and reward. *Science*, 1972, *175*, 90–93.
Shanks, E. The interaction between instructions and augmented sensory feedback in the training of cardiovascular control. Unpublished doctoral dissertation, University of Tennessee, 1973.
Shapiro, D., Schwartz, G. E., & Tursky, B. Control of diastolic blood pressure in man by feedback and reinforcement. *Psychophysiology*, 1972, *9*, 296–304.
Shapiro, D., Tursky, B., Gershon, E., & Stern, M. Effects of feedback and reinforcement on the control of human systolic blood pressure. *Science*, 1969, *163*, 588–590.
Sherrington, C. S. *The integrative action of the nervous system*. Cambridge: Cambridge University Press, 1906.
Sherrington, C. S. *Man on his nature*. London: Penguin Books, 1940.
Silverstein, S. J., Nathan, P. E., & Taylor, H. A. Blood alcohol level estimation and controlled drinking by chronic alcoholics. *Behavior Therapy*, 1974, *5*, 1–15.
Slaughter, J., Hahn, W., & Rinaldi, P. Instrumental conditioning of heart rate in the curarized rat with varied amounts of pretraining. *Journal of Comparative and Physiological Psychology*, 1970, *72*, 356–359.
Slucki, H., Ádám, G., & Porter, R. W. Operant discrimination of an interoceptive stimulus in Rhesus monkeys. *Journal of the Experimental Analysis of Behavior*, 1965, *8*(6), 405–414.

Slucki, H., McCoy, F. B., & Porter, R. W. Interoceptive S^D of the large intestine established by mechanical stimulation. *Psychological Reports,* 1969, *24,* 35–42.

Smith, K. Conditioning as an artifact. *Psychological Review,* 1954, *61,* 217–225.

Smith, K. Curare drugs and total paralysis. *Psychological Review,* 1964, *71,* 77–79. (a)

Smith, K. Comment of paper by Black and Lang. *Psychological Review,* 1964, *71,* 86. (b)

Smith, K. Conditioning as an artefact. In G. A. Kimble (Ed.), *Foundations of conditioning and learning.* New York: Appleton, 1967. Pp. 100–111.

Stern, R. M. Detection of one's own spontaneous GSR's. *Psychonomic Science,* 1972, *29,* 354–356.

Sutterer, J. R., & Obrist, P. A. Heart rate and general activity alterations in dogs during several aversive conditioning procedures. *Journal of Comparative and Physiological Psychology,* 1972, *80,* 314–326.

Taub, E., Bacon, R. C., & Berman, A. J. Acquisition of a trace-conditioned avoidance response after deafferentation of the responding limb. *Journal of Comparative and Physiological Psychology,* 1965, *59,* 275–279.

Taub, E., & Berman, A. J. Movement and learning in the avsence of sensory feedback. In S. J. Freedman (Ed.), *The neuropsychology of spatially oriented behavior.* Homewood, Ill.: Dorsey Press, 1968. Pp. 173–192.

Thornton, E. W., & van-Toller, C. Effects of immunosympathectomy on operant heart rate conditioning in the curarized rat. *Physiology and Behavior,* 1973, *10,* 197–201.

Verplanck, W. S. Unaware of where's awareness: Some verbal operants. In C. W. Erikson (Ed.), *Behavior and awareness.* Durham, N. C.: Duke University Press, 1962. Pp. 130–158.

Von Holst, E., & Mittelstaedt, H. Das Reafferenzprincip. *Naturwissenschaften,* 1950, *37,* 464–476.

Walsh, D. H. Interactive effects of alpha feedback and instructional set on subjective states. *Psychophysiology,* 1974, *11,* 428–435.

Wells, D. T. Large magnitude voluntary heart rate changes. *Psychophysiology,* 1973, *10,* 260–269.

4

A Cognitive Analysis of Biofeedback Control*

RICHARD S. LAZARUS
University of California, Berkeley

Feedback is, without a doubt, one of the most profound and unifying concepts in all the behavioral sciences. It is fundamental in biological adaptation, being the basis of natural selection and evolution. Feedback from the environment about the consequences of one's acts provides the rewards and punishments that are in part responsible for learning. Maintenance of homeostasis and the neurohumoral regulation of behavior also operate through feedback loops; the brain is, among other things, a great feedback or servomechanism system. Social psychology too makes use of feedback principles in viewing the interaction of persons—social reactions feed back and modify the behavior of each party of a social interaction. Biofeedback is a special case, referring to information the person is provided technically about his bodily processes. Whether and how this information may be used to regulate such processes is not yet fully understood.

Current research in biofeedback brings together under a single rubric a group of psychologists with very diverse objectives and interests. For some, the fundamental issue of such research is whether or not visceral reactions can be controlled through a "pure" process of

* This article is an expanded and modified version of a paper entitled "A cognitively-oriented psychologist looks at biofeedback," which appeared in *American Psychologist*, 1975, *30*, 553–561.

operant conditioning, pure in the sense that it is said not to depend on any of several types of mediation, including, for example, extraneous cues, perceptual or cognitive processes, and internal muscular or respiratory ones. I have in mind here the debate between Katkin and Murray (1968) and Crider, Schwartz, and Shnidmen (1969). For still others, a key feature of biofeedback consists of the practical possibilities afforded for the amelioration of diseases of adaptation—for example, tension headaches, hypertension, and so on (Schwartz, 1973). There is still some uncertainty about the practical potential of biofeedback procedures in the control of autonomic end-organ responses, as evidenced by Blanchard and Young's (1973) review of such work with cardiovascular measures, and a paper by Miller in this volume. However, my purpose is not to rehash such issues, or to review biofeedback research or its use in clinical practice. Rather, I want to embed biofeedback research and clinical practice in what I see as a larger context—namely, adaptation and emotion. Many of the points I will make here accord closely with the valuable comments and analyses made by Schwartz (1973).

Biofeedback processes are important for three main reasons: First, the recognition that bodily processes can be volitionally regulated, even if only to a small extent, corrects the partially erroneous classical position in which voluntary regulation is opposed to involuntary or autonomic regulation (Schwartz, 1973). This classical tendency to separate voluntary from involuntary regulation went hand in glove with the view that the emotions belonged to the evolutionarily primitive, animal side of human nature, while rational thought processes represented the advanced, human side. Thus, the physiology of emotion has largely been focused on lower nervous centers and the viscera, and little progress has been made in understanding the role of the cerebral cortex in emotions compared with the role of lower and midbrain centers. To this day, the neural signaling systems determining whether an event signifies danger or harm rather than being benign occupy virtually no role in physiological research on stress and emotion, although much has been learned about the bodily consequences of stress once it has been aroused (cf. Selye, 1956). Second, biofeedback seems to offer an informational aid to the person in his quest for control of his bodily processes, particularly those that get in the way of successful behavioral adaptation or result in "diseases of adaptation." Third, biofeedback research could throw light on important theoretical and practical questions about the diverse psychological processes by which people regulate their emotional life and how well these processes work.

In this paper, there are three main, interrelated themes: *(1)* the somatic reactions with which biofeedback deals are really part of a much broader set of issues, namely, those related to the stress emotions and their role in human adaptation: *(2)* emotional processes and their self-regulation are products of mediating cognitive appraisals about the significance of an event for a person's well-being; and *(3)* the control of somatic processes is an integral aspect of emotional states and their self-regulation. Indeed, this self-regulation is going on all the time in day-to-day living and is accomplished through a variety of mechanisms whose workings, determinants, and consequences are badly in need of understanding. The first theme is a fairly obvious assertion that I will not elaborate further, while the second and third have to do with the nature of emotions and their regulation, and form the crux of the argument throughout the remainder of the paper.

COGNITIVE PROCESSES AND EMOTION

If, indeed, the somatic reactions dealt with in biofeedback research and therapy are aspects of emotion and adaptation, then we must consider what an emotional state is and how it is brought about and regulated. From my theoretical perspective (Lazarus, 1966, 1968; Lazarus, Averill, & Opton, 1970), the various emotions arise from and reflect the nature of a person's or animal's ongoing adaptive commerce or transactions with his environment. Each of us has special personality attributes (e.g., motives, belief systems, and competencies to cope with environmental pressures) that shape reactions and the way he/she interprets and arranges these transactions.

Emotions are complex disturbances having three loosely related main components: subjective affect; physiological changes that are linked to species-specific forms of mobilization for adaptive action; and action impulses having both instrumental and expressive qualities. The somatic disturbance arises from the impulse to act that, in part, defines biologically the particular emotion. Were these somatic disturbances always in accord with the subjective and behavioral responses, emotions would represent a far simpler problem for scientific study and analysis. We could make do with a single-dimensional process to describe its intensity as in the concept of activation or arousal. However, the three components correlate very poorly with each other: An individual might report no distress, yet exhibit strong physiological reactions, or the behavioral responses signifying anger or fear might be inhibited as a result of social or internal pressures—this is why it is necessary to speak of an impulse to act rather than actions themselves. In short, the somatic changes connected with an emotion usually appear in a complex pattern of end-organ responses rather than in a simple, highly correlated one (cf. Lacey, 1967). And for this reason, Shapiro, Tursky, and Schwartz (1970) were able to show in a biofeedback study that subjects rewarded only for increases or decreases in systolic blood pressure were able to raise or lower their blood pressure while their heart rates remained unchanged.

The problem is that each somatic change and, for that matter, each of the three main components of an emotion marches to its own drummer, so to speak; each is responsive to influences other than the body's mobilization for adaptive action. This creates very difficult analytic and research problems for anyone who takes seriously the idea that there are distinct emotional states such as anxiety, sadness, guilt, and anger. Since an emotion is an amalgam of so many differentiated elements, we can know about it only by inference from the complex patterning of its various component responses, in a way very much like medical inferences are made about disease syndromes (Lazarus *et al.*, 1970).

The quality and intensity of the emotion and its action impulse all depend on a particular kind of *cognitive appraisal* of the present or anticipated significance of the transaction for the person's well-being. At least four kinds of appraisal are critical to the emotional response: *(1)* harm–loss; *(2)* threat; *(3)* challenge (accent on the positive rather than the negative or harm aspect); and *(4)* benign–positive. In lower animals, such as those studied by Tinbergen, the evaluative or appraisal feature of the emotion-eliciting perception is very concrete and simple and is built into the nervous system. In higher animals, such as man, symbolic thought processes and learning play a predominant role.

This viewpoint is, of course, a version of numerous earlier and current attempts to develop a metatheory of psychological activity and behavior in cognitive–phenomenological terms. It contains recognizable elements of the work of William James, for whom emotion involved an evaluative perception, the field theoretical approach of Lewin, and the more recent cognitive outlooks of theoreticians such as Tolman, Heider, Murray, Rotter, and a current group of attribution-oriented researchers such as Weiner (1972, 1974a). Cognitive approaches are certainly not new. In summarizing historical trends Bolles (1974) points out that psychology has always been more or less cognitive in outlook. It has only rather recently turned to mechanistic philosophy, at that for only a brief interlude in the overall history of the field. Psychology seems to have begun to turn around from its brief flirtation with a mechanistic approach to behavior, and to return to a cognitive orientation.

In regard specifically to emotion, the cognitive–phenomenological outlook was evident in the earlier writings on stress of Grinker and Spiegel (1945) in which the term "appraisal" appears, though somewhat unsystematically, and in the more recent writings of Arnold (1960), who uses the term quite self-consciously in her analysis of emotion. A book by Mandler (1975) is also highly relevant. The resurgence of cognitive approaches to emotion is also illustrated by the Loyola Symposium on Feelings and Emotion (Arnold, 1970) following up two earlier ones, the Wittenberg Symposium in 1927 and the Mooseheart Symposium in 1948, which were clearly dominated by a mechanistic orientation. Likewise, a recent symposium by Weiner (1974b) has cognitive views of motivation as its theme.

One way to highlight the importance of cognitive appraisal in the mediation of emotional states is to point to a contrast between Hans Selye, on the one hand, and John Mason and me on the other. Selye argues that the "General Adaption Syndrome" (GAS) is a universal biological defensive reaction aroused by any physically noxious agent. Mason (1971), also an endocrinologist, points out, however, that the endocrine response to stressor conditions is constantly being affected by cognitive processes. To express this mediation of the physiological response, Mason uses the compound term "psychoendocrinology." Mason and I go even further, however, suggesting that the *essential* mediator of the GAS may indeed be cognitive (Lazarus, 1966; Mason, 1971). In effect, the pituitary–adrenal cortical response to disturbed commerce with the environment may require that the animal or person somehow *recognize* his plight. Any animal that has sustained an injury is apt to sense that he is in trouble; and if he does not, there will be no GAS. In research on the GAS, cognitive mediation has almost never been ruled out. Thus, one could argue with some justification that this cognitive appraisal of harm via cerebrally controlled processes is necessary to initiate the body's defensive adrenal cortical response.

An animal that is unconscious can sustain bodily harm without the psychoendocrine mechanisms of the "general adaptation syndrome" becoming active. Data from Symington, Currie, Curran, and Davidson (1955), for example, suggest that unconsciousness and anesthesia eliminate the adrenal effects of physiological stress. It was observed that patients who were dying from injury or disease show a normal adrenal cortical condition as assessed during autopsy as long as they have remained unconscious during the period of the fatal condition. In contrast, patients who were conscious during the periods of the fatal disease process and died did show adrenal cortical changes. Gray, Ramsey, Villarreal, and Krakaner (1956) have also shown that general anesthesia, by itself, does not produce a significant adrenal reaction. These studies raise the question of whether it is the *psychological significance of the injury* rather than the physiologically noxious effects of that injury which produces the adrenal cortical changes associated with stress.

In a book entitled *Stress without distress,* Selye (1974) now seems to have changed his generalist, noncognitive position somewhat by suggesting that only certain kinds of stress, for example, the stress of frustration or failure, are harmful, while other kinds of stress such as the joyful pursuit of one's occupation are benign or even beneficial. This seems to limit the GAS, or at least its damaging features, to certain kinds of transactions, and gives an essential role to mediating psychological processes. Similarly, Rahe (1974), who had once emphasized that all life changes demanding adaptive effort contributed to illness regardless of whether they were regarded as positive or negative by the person, now considers it important to consider psychological defenses and coping activities as mediators of somatic illness. There seems to be a widespread movement toward the position that cognitive processes intervening between the person's adaptive transactions with the environment and the emotional reaction (including its somatic consequences) are important determinants (see for example, Dohrenwend & Dohrenwend, 1974), though the empirical case for this position still remains somewhat limited.

Incidentally, the debate between generalists such as Selye and Rahe and those who argue that cognitive mediators are of major importance touches upon a distinction I made earlier between challenge and threat. It is an assumption, though I think a good one, that the outlook of threat versus challenge affects how one goes about dealing with the situation, one's morale, and one's state of mental and physical health during a long-term adaptive transaction. I see the distinction mainly as a matter of positive versus negative tone, that is, whether one emphasizes the harm, actual or potential, in a transaction, or the possibilities of positive mastery and gain in the face of circumstances that tax one's resources. We should look for the determinants of such appraisals in the situation itself and in personality characteristics forged from past experience, such as confidence or lack of confidence in own's coping resources. We continually observe persons who, under essentially similar situations, react with a sense of challenge and others who react with a sense of threat.

In moving toward the biofeedback context, let me take a somewhat different tack and consider the point made recently by Janis (unpublished manuscript) that the *interpersonal features* of biofeedback research and therapy situations are primary sources of the mediating psychological processes responsible for successful training in the control of bodily reactions, in contrast with the conditioning paradigm variables that some biofeedback researchers think are sufficient (see also Morris & Suckerman, 1974a, b). Janis quotes (Jonas, 1972) a young woman who had undergone an arduous 10-week training period during which she succeeded temporarily in lowering her diastolic blood pressure from 97 to about 80. She stated: "I always depend very heavily on Barry Dworkin's [her trainer] encouragement and on his personality. I think he could be an Olympic Coach. He not only seems aware of my general condition but he is never satisfied with less than my best, and I can't fool him. I feel we are friends and allies—it's really as though *we* were lowering my pressure."

Here one mediator of the self-control processes appears to be the quality and significance to the subject of the relationship with the therapist, a relationship that sustains her in the arduous training program and without which the self-control might have been impossible. If we can accept the statements of the young woman at face value, we must look at the components of this relationship and their determinants to understand adequately the way biofeedback procedures work, and perhaps to arrange for something to take their place outside the laboratory situation so that generalization can occur. I am saying two things here: First, we cannot in our thinking isolate the somatic disturbances and their self-regulation in biofeedback from the larger context of the person's adaptive commerce with his environment. Second, this adaptive commerce is constantly being mediated by social and psychological processes.

A comparable point is implied in Marston and Feldman's (1972) analysis of the concept of self-control in the context of behavior modification. Although seeming to identify themselves as behavior modifiers, they make use of mediating psychological processes in discussing the acquisition of self-control as a two-stage process. Initially there is the development of a general "cognitive set" in which the person comes to value the inhibition of the impulse and commits himself to the effort. The authors use the expression *executive response* in referring to this cognitive set. The person is described as making a commitment and evaluating the chances of success and the relative importance of the desired change as against the effort required. There are surely individual differences in the motivation to do this, and in the relative costs and benefits as evaluated by the person. There follow attempts by the person, with or without therapeutic guidance, to arrange the environmental contingencies that presumably will aid in overcoming the bad habit or impulse. Why not recognize at the outset that, in the biofeedback situation, just as in any other situation of learning and performing, there is an active, striving, evaluating person at the helm struggling to do something for which information about his/her own success can be enormously useful in increasing the chances of ultimate mastery or self-control?

From this standpoint, we have a great need for an adequate transactional language to describe individual differences in the way a person relates psychologically to the environment. I have constructed a simple hypothetical example. Consider two different persons who perceive that they are facing a demand, or the juxtaposition of several demands, which seems to them to be at the borderline or beyond their capacity to master—too much is expected of them. As a result of their individual histories and particular personalities, Person A feels that failure of mastery reflects his own inadequacy, while Person B, by contrast, feels the same inadequacy, but interprets the situation as one in which people are constantly trying to use or abuse him/her. Both experience similar degrees of anticipatory stress and are mobilized to cope with the problem. Prior to the confrontation that will reveal the success or failure of mastery, both experience anxiety, an anticipatory emotion in the context of appraised threat. In Person A, the anxiety is mixed, perhaps, with anticipatory depression, while in Person B, the anxiety is mixed with external blaming and anger. Following confrontation in which, let us say, both perform badly, Person A experiences mainly loss and depression, while Person B experiences mainly anger and resentment. A similar set of overwhelming demands has been construed or appraised quite differently because of different personality dispositions. If these persons do well in the confrontation, both may experience elation because they have overcome the difficulty, depending on whether the explanation of the success is luck or their own perseverance and skill (see, for example, Weiner's, 1974a, attribution theory approach to achievement motivation).

Thus, what I am speaking of as a transactional language refers not to objective commerce with the environment as it is seen by the observer, but commerce from the perspective of the person, that is, as he/she appraises the situation. Certain characteristics of personality in a given individual make a variety of situational patterns "functionally equivalent" in their capacity to produce threat, say, or to elicit any given type of coping process. This is what we should mean when we say an individual is vulnerable or has the disposition to deny or intellectualize potential threats. Personality traits are not operative in all situations necessarily, but only in a class of situations in which the trait has the capacity to produce the same reaction, say, by eliciting threat appraisal or a particular coping process. This class of functionally equivalent situations may be broad or narrow. Thus, some individuals are threatened by virtually any strange interpersonal situation while others react with threat only when they are criticized. Part of the task of describing and understanding individual differences in emotional and coping reactions is to specify the personality characteristics that lead to threat appraisal in a given class of situations, or that lead to the use of a given type of coping process when the person is threatened. The transactional language we need to seek is one that takes into account the properties of the person, determining the way he/she construes environmental pressures and how he/she tries to cope. We are a long way from this assessment goal although it clearly must be a programmatic feature of the study of psychological stress and coping.

In any case, subtle differences in appraisal of a stressful commerce with the environment underlie variations among individuals in the severity (and possibly the pattern) of bodily reactions, the intensity and chronicity of the accompanying emotion, the quality of the affects experienced, and the types of solutions for which they opt, including seeking, accepting, and using clinical help. I do not think such personality-based variations can be ignored in biofeedback therapy or in research on how such therapy works. As Schwartz (1973, p. 670) puts it, "biofeedback should be viewed as but one approach to the treatment of the 'total person', realizing that to 'cure' a problem such as hypertension will require more than just the patient consciously attempting to lower his pressure."

THE SELF-REGULATION OF EMOTION

Emotion is not a constant thing, but it ebbs and flows and changes over time, as the nature of the adaptive commerce and the information about it changes. Anger suddenly melts and changes to guilt, depression, love; anxiety changes to euphoria; guilt changes to anger. Rarely are strong emotional states so simple that they have only one quality; more often, emotions involve complex combinations of affect, each deriving from multiple elements of cognitive appraisal—some even ambivalent—to be found in any complex human transaction with the environment. These shifts in intensity and quality over time reflect perceived and appraised changes in the person's relationship with the environment, based in part on feedback from the situation and from his/her own reactions. In the stress emotions, the changes reflect, in part, the person's constant efforts to cope with and master the interchange by overcoming the damage, by postponing or preventing the danger, or by tolerating it. Thus, expectations and discoveries about one's power to cope with the environment and master danger are a constantly changing factor in whether he/she will feel threatened, say, or challenged by what happens.

Although the above analysis emphasizes flux, there is of course also stability in emotional life. One individual experiences intense episodes of emotion frequently, another lives more or less blandly. Some persons are easily threatened and chronically or repeatedly anxious, while others react typically with anger or depression, and still others with exhilaration and joy. Some periods of an individual's life are filled with depression, although at other periods he/she may have felt quite positively. It is important to understand how such stability comes about.

When an individual reacts consistently with, say, anxiety, cognitive theory provides us with two basic kinds of explanation. On the one hand, we may be dealing with a person who views the environment as dangerous and who believes that he/she lacks the resources to master it. We speak of such individuals in many similar ways, for example, as lacking in self-esteem, or as not having confidence in themselves. When the range of situations in which they feel inadequate is large, they will often feel threatened—perhaps by any new situation into which they are placed—and we say they have the trait of anxiety, that is, they carry the disposition to react with anxiety. This trait or disposition is a feature of personality.

On the other hand, stability of an emotional pattern also can occur because a person must continuously operate in repeated environmental settings that produce threats to which he/she are vulnerable. In this case, it is the environment that is stable, though its capacity to produce threat is commonly engendered as much by the person's areas of vulnerability as by any external property, and part of the problem is that the person stays in the situation that is threatening. Thus, although stability in emotional pattern can be the logical result of either personality or environmental characteristics, in most instances both are likely to be involved. By the same token, somatic illnesses that have emotional processes as determinants can come into being only when troubled commerce with the environment occurs repeatedly or chronically to a person. The wear and tear of stress implies not occasional, short-lived emotional episodes but emotional states that continue long enough for tissue damage or dysfunction to occur.

The theme of self-regulation is especially important for an understanding of emotional processes, and for the link between biofeedback and the study of emotion. It places emphasis on *coping processes* as a central feature of the emotional state. We are, of course, sometimes accidentally confronted by a situation having major relevance for our welfare; but we also do a great deal of active regulating of our emotional reactions. To some extent, the person selects the environment to which he/she must respond; shapes his/her commerce with it; plans, chooses, avoids, tolerates, postpones, escapes, demolishes, manipulates his/her attention; and he/she also deceives him/herself about what is happening, as much as possible casting the relationship in ways that fit his/her needs and premises about him/herself in the world. In regulating one's emotional life, a person is also thereby affecting the bodily reactions that are an integral part of any emotional state.

The idea of coping is hardly new. It has a considerable recent history, largely clinical in focus, although, as will be seen shortly, coping processes have usually been treated as consequences of an emotion rather than playing the causal role I give to them. The Freudian conception of anxiety, for example, emphasized not only its drive and cue functions, but its control by ego-defensive operations, and it helped establish the study of coping processes in adaptive functioning. It would not be fruitful here to try to summarize this history of ideas about the relationships between coping processes and emotional states. Suffice it to say that my basic position is that we cannot hope to understand the emotions unless we also take into account the coping activities that affect them.

Coping and the Control of Emotion

There are countless observations of the important role coping or self-regulatory processes play. In a previous discussion of these (Lazarus, 1975), I cited everyday life anecdotal examples, such as the management of grief, the escalation or discouragement of a love relationship, being a good loser, and formal research examples, such as field studies of combat stress, the psychoendocrine research of the Bethesda group on parents of children dying of leukemia, and research from my own laboratory (Koriat, Melkman, Averill, & Lazarus, 1972) dealing with the self-control of emotional states. It will be useful to illustrate with some examples below.

There would be little argument that people are capable of inhibiting emotional behaviors such as avoidance and agression, or the behavioral expression of emotions such as grief, love, depression, and joy. I am saying, of course, more than this, namely, that intrapsychic forms of coping such as detachment and denial are also capable of modifying, eliminating, or changing the emotion itself, including its subjective affect and bodily changes. When successful, these mechanisms not only affect the visible signs of emotion, but they dampen or eliminate the entire emotional syndrome. Thus, in the well-known Bethesda studies of parents with children dying of leukemia (Wolff, Friedman, Hofer, & Mason, 1964), by denying the fatal significance of their child's illness the Bethesda parents no longer felt as threatened, and, in consequence, they exhibited lower levels of adrenal cortical stress hormones prior to the death of the child than those parents who engaged in anticipatory grief.

Consider another example. Lief and Fox (1963) have done extensive interviews with medical students witnessing for the first time a medical autopsy. Most such students, who are probably self-selected to a high degree, achieve detachment from the experience, though there are some failures too. Certain features of the procedure itself and of the institutionalized behavior of the participants probably evolved out of the wisdom of long professional experience and provide great help to the student in the process of achieving detachment. For example, during the autopsy, the room is immaculate and brightly lit, and the task is approached with seriousness, skill, and a professional air facilitating a clinical and impersonal attitude toward death. Certain parts of the body are kept covered, particularly the face and genitalia; and the hands, which are so strongly connected with human, personal qualities, are usually not dissected. Once the vital organs are removed, the body is taken from the room, bringing the autopsy down to isolated tissues which are more easily depersonalized. Students avoid talking about the autopsy; and when they do, the discussion is impersonal and stylized. Finally, whereas in laboratory dissection, humor appears to be a widespread and effective emotional control device, it is absent in the autopsy room, perhaps because the death has been too recent and joking would appear too insensitive. One senses here the process of struggling to achieve a proper balance between feeling things and looking at them objectively; in short, there is an effort to regulate a common and expected emotional reaction in which detachment or distancing is the mode of coping. We also recognize that some individuals in medicine and nursing overdo the coping strategy of detachment or dehumanization and appear to their patients to be cold and indifferent.

Studies such as these, and quite a few others in which somatic changes normally associated with stress were reduced by coping processes (cf. Lazarus, 1966), are important because they demonstrate that coping is indeed a causal factor in stress states. Such studies are often imperfect and the measures of coping are sometimes confounded with the measures of stress reaction. For example, in the Wolff *et al.* (1964) study, denial was in part indexed by evidence of lowered levels of subjective emotional distress as well as by denial statements, rather than being meticulously separated from subjective distress in the assessments. Nevertheless, the concatenation of much evidence does indeed suggest that coping, when successful, does affect subjective, behavioral, and physiological stress reactions. Clinicians are also familiar with the use of defenses such as denial or intellectualized detachment which are unsuccessful in their aim, that is, the person expressing denial is not able to sustain the conviction that all is well, or he/she is unable to achieve successful detachment though he/she appears to try. In such instances, we would expect to find that the denial or detachment is not associated with lowered stress levels; there will be, in effect, a contradiction between what one infers at the psychological level and what is observed at the physiological level.

Behaviorally, it is very difficult to distinguish between successful and unsuccessful defenses, and often we see the individual struggling with varying success to achieve a workable defensive interpretation of his/her plight. In their work with terminal cancer patients, for example, Hackett and Weisman (1964) use the expression "middle knowledge" to refer to the patient's dim sense of the truth that he/she is dying, though he/she appears mostly to manifest a denial of the terminal nature of the illness (see also Weisman, 1972). Intrapsychic coping processes are not usually static traits, but constantly reflect changes in the person's situation and how it is interpreted, presumably with concomitant changes in the level of stress reaction. Traditionally, clinicians have spoken of consolidated defenses in referring to such forms of coping when they are stable implying, of course, that often defenses are in flux. Sometimes people are unsuccessful in creating a believable and benign fiction about the true nature of things.

The issue is far from trivial if we wish to understand the control of bodily reactions via intrapsychic processes. The fact that, sometimes, defenses successfully reduce the somatic correlates of stress and, at other times, the same defenses fail greatly complicates research because we must find ways of differentiating between the two independently of the somatic indicators. To the extent that similar processes are involved in the biofeedback context, resolving this question in general might throw some light on why biofeedback procedures work sometimes and not others.

Moreover, much coping activity is anticipatory; that is, the person expects a future harmful confrontation, such as failing an examination, performing in public, or confronting a flood, tornado, or a personal criticism, and this leads him/her to prepare against the future possibility of harm. To the extent that he/she prepares effectively, overcoming or avoiding the danger before it materializes, or being better able to function adequately in the anticipated confrontation, the nature of the ultimate transaction is thereby changed, along with the emotions that might have been experienced. Overcoming the danger before it materializes can lead to exhilaration rather than fear, grief, depression, or whatever, depending upon the nature of the harm or loss that might have been experienced and the appraisal of the reasons for success.

You will note that this analysis *reverses* the usual wisdom that coping always follows emotion (or is caused by it), and suggests that coping can precede emotion and influence its form or intensity. In fact, my general position requires the assertion that *coping never follows emotion in anything but a temporal sense,* a stance in direct opposition to the longstanding and traditional view that emotions (such as anxiety) serve as drives or motives for adaptive behavior. The exception to this is when the person is trying to regulate the bodily state directly; but more about this in a moment.

Unfortunately, the psychology of coping is largely descriptive in nature, rather than systematic and predictive. People use a wide variety of coping processes, depending on their personal characteristics, the nature of the environmental demands and contingencies, and how these are appraised. They engage in a variety of preparatory activities. For example, they may worry without taking adequate steps to increase their effectiveness in confrontation; they reduce intense arousal by periodic disengagements from stressful transactions; they take tranquilizers to lower excessive levels of arousal; they use antispasmodics to quiet their bowels; they practice positive mental attitudes; they try to tell themselves that the problem will work itself out or that there is really no problem; they seek support from loved ones or those they trust; they try this or that stress-preventive fad or fashion, such as transcendental meditation, psychotherapy, relaxation, hypnosis, or yoga; they direct their attention away from the source of threat and toward benign or escapist literature or movies; they cope with loss ultimately by giving up what was previously a central portion of their psychological domain. However, we still know extremely little about the conditions, both within the person and in the stimulus configuration, that lead to one or another coping process, about the relative effectiveness of such diverse coping processes in regulating emotional states, or about the comparative costs or maladaptive consequences of each form of coping.

A Typology of Coping and Self-Regulative Processes

My earlier comment about attempts directly to regulate bodily reactions draws an implicit distinction between two kinds of emotion-regulatory or coping processes, a distinction others, too, have made (cf. Mechanic, 1962). One type, which might properly be called *direct action*, concerns efforts by the person to deal with the problem generating the stress emotion in the first place. Whether the person takes direct action, say, by planning for a future danger, attacking or escaping the harmful agency, the focus of the coping effort is on the plight in which the person finds himself.

For example, if a student who is facing an important and very threatening examination spends the anticipatory interval reading relevant books and articles, rehearsing understanding of the subject matter with other students or teachers, trying to guess or find out the questions that will be asked, and so on, he/she is engaged in direct actions to master the problem whether this is done effectively or ineffectively. Such a person is attempting to alter his/her basic relationship with the environment, or, put differently, to change the nature of his/her troubled commerce with it. To the extent that such activity leads to a more benign appraisal of the potential outcome of the examination—for example, by giving him/her a sense of preparedness and mastery—the emotional reaction attendant on the threatening character of the situation is to some extent short-circuited. Anxiety is also reduced, along with its bodily concomitants, and the person is better able to sleep, think, and draw upon knowledge in the examination.

The other type of coping, which might be called *palliation*, is focused on reducing the affective distress or the visceral motor disturbances that are features of stress emotions. There are two subtypes of palliation, both primarily oriented to making the person feel better rather than to solving the adaptational problem per se. *(a)* The person can engage in *intrapsychic* or defensive maneuvers. We have long recognized a large variety of such modes of coping; denial, intellectualized detachment, and attention deployment (trying not to think of the threat or focusing attention on nonthreatening features or tasks) are among the most common and widely researched. *(b)* The person can, alternatively, make use of a number of procedures directed entirely at the disturbed bodily state. We might call these *somatic-oriented* modes of palliation. Thus, if the student mentioned above in connection with direct action uses tranquilizers, drinks to control his/her disturbed bodily state, takes sleeping pills, engages in muscle relaxation, diverts attention for a time, or tries other techniques designed to quiet the heightened arousal, he/she is seeking directly to control the emotional response itself rather than to alter the environmental transaction that generated the arousal in the first place. He/she is dealing with the somatic reaction rather than its cause. In all likelihood, the rules by which these two divergent kinds of processes operate are also quite different.

I do not intend any derogation of this latter, "sympton"-oriented or peripheral approach. We all use a variety of coping devices, including palliative ones, in a complex mixture in any personal crisis, and this often helps greatly. Sometimes palliation is the only relief available to the person, perhaps because the source of threat is unknown and hence fairly refractory to change. In the case of inevitable harms such as death or imminent surgery, there is little concrete that can be done to alter one's plight. Moreover, as in the handling of test anxiety, sometimes effective direct action in the problem-oriented sense is severely impaired by the emotion itself, as when the person finds he/she cannot think clearly about the problem and prepare adequately in the face of the interfering effects. Under such conditions, reducing the anxiety or the correlates of anxiety by *any* means available may serve to facilitate adaptive coping.

Moreover, in chronic or repeated situations of threat, even merely lowering debilitating arousal may swing the balance of the approach–avoidance conflict in favor of approach and commitment and away from avoidance and disengagement, and this may make possible the attainment of goals of great importance. For example, a professional person who fears to fly in jets and yet wants to attend a conference in a distant city has four choices: He/she can try to tolerate the psychological and bodily distress and fly anyway; he/she can avoid flying and eschew such professional activity at obvious professional disadvantage; therapy can be sought to reduce or eliminate the problem, hopefully with positive results but no guarantees; or he/she can take drugs to limit the disturbance. Though less than ideal, using the palliative at least prevents total avoidance with its high social costs.

The form of control which I have called "somatic-oriented palliation" is the arena in which biofeedback research and its use in therapy falls. I would argue that those who want to rule out a complex assortment of active mediators in biofeedback research miss the central point in the self-regulation of emotion. Not only does such an effort greatly narrow the basis and scope of such self-regulation, but it minimizes the complexity of the problem and the diverse patterns by which it typically operates in all our lives. We need to have more knowledge of the myriad forms of self-regulation that are available and serviceable to given kinds of people and in given types of situations in managing their emotional lives (see also Schwartz, 1973). As my opening statements suggest, a major virtue of the biofeedback movement lies in the opportunity it provides to test as well as to take advantage of some of our ideas about the coping processes that are capable of influencing the emotional response.

What actually mediates biofeedback effects themselves is still an open question. One possibility is that the relaxation process could serve as a means of attention deployment (Budzynski, Stoyva, Adler, & Mullaney, 1973). The person learns to focus attention on relaxing his/her muscles, while the attention is turned away from the stress-producing sources of the tension from which the headaches are indirectly derived. Or, alternatively, such training might induce a relaxed psychological state that is incompatible with the tension, a mechanism that has been suggested by Wolpe (1958) and by Mendelsohn (1962). Or it might merely create a physiological state (muscle relaxation) that is itself incompatible with the physiological headache mechanism. None of these are mutually exclusive in any biofeedback situation, and these plus others well could be operating. If these processes could be shown to generalize to situations outside the laboratory, they might provide powerful tools of therapy as well as research into the efficacy of the various self-regulatory processes.

Some of my own research (Koriat *et al.*, 1972), in fact, has emphasized the cognitive mediators regulating autonomic nervous system activity while subjects watched a stressful movie. We asked subjects to watch the film while adopting two different attitudes, one to involve themselves more fully in the stressful episodes, the other to detach or distance themselves. Evidence that our subjects were capable of such self-control of emotional states came from autonomic as well as self-report measures. This research was also designed to discover the cognitive processes producing altered emotional arousal, though it well might have been improved by the use of biofeedback procedures to aid subjects in assessing how well they were succeeding in involving themselves in or detaching from the stressful scenes. We found that certain strategies were reportedly widely used to achieve detachment, while others predominated in the effort to create emotional involvement; but we could not adequately test the effectiveness of these strategies.

Coping–Environmental Interactions

An important qualification should also be stated here. We should not expect any given self-regulating strategy to be effective in every context of adaptive commerce. Rather, depending on the environmental demands and options open to the person, some strategies should be serviceable and others not. Cohen and Lazarus (1973) found that patients who approached surgery with avoidant strategies, that is, those who did not want to know about their illness and the nature of the surgery, showed a more rapid and smoother postsurgical recovery than did patients adopting a vigilant strategy. It was speculated that vigilance might actually be a handicap for the surgical patient because there was nothing constructive to do in the postoperative recuperation period except simply to ignore or deny the sources of threat and pain. Trying postoperatively to pay attention vigilantly to every possible cue of danger or sign of discomfort resulted in a longer and more complicated recovery, and this appeared to be maladaptive in this situation.

However, a very different strategy seems called for in the stressful context studied by Gal (1973)—namely, seasickness among Israeli navy personnel. Holding constant the degree of seasickness, it was found that sailors who had the trait or disposition to cope in an active, purposive, and vigilant fashion despite being sick, functioned much better at their normal jobs. Forgetting for a moment several possible sources of confounding in comparing these two studies, such as the measures of coping (trait versus state) and the type of population, their juxtaposition points up the potential interaction that might exist between type of coping and the nature of the environmental demands. Moreover, such research also points up another one of the major gaps in theory and research in the biofeedback arena, namely, the absence of evident interest in individual differences. Biofeedback procedures, even when oriented to therapy, seem generally to be approached normatively rather than ipsatively to assess the contribution of situations and individual differences in personality to the results. Depending on preferred coping styles and patterns of belief and expectations, and on the nature of the situational demands, individuals should differ greatly in their capacity to profit from particular biofeedback procedures, particular kinds of coping processes, and to acquire control over their bodily reactions (see also Schwartz, 1973, p. 672).

CONCLUDING COMMENT

I started in this paper with three interrelated themes: *(1)* that biofeedback deals with psychosomatic processes falling within a larger, central area of psychology having to do with the stress emotions and their role in adaptation; *(2)* that emotion and its regulation depend on cognitive processes mediating between the environment and the person interacting with it; and (3) that what happens in biofeedback must be parallel with what goes on in the routine self-regulation of emotional states occurring constantly, with more or less success, in the day-to-day affairs of all humans.

These themes, I believe, all converge into one final main point, namely, that the biofeedback laboratory seems to offer excellent opportunities to add to our knowledge of the mechanisms of self-regulation, especially the intrapsychic ones, and, indeed, this constitutes one of psychology's most important difficult issues. What we know about coping or self-regulation is, as I said, mostly descriptive, and in spite of widespread and long–term recognition of the importance of this topic, we still do not have a solid body of knowledge at the behavioral or psychological level about how in the normal course of events we manage to keep our emotions and their somatic consequences under control, or why we fail. We need to know the conditions under which this or that form of coping is selected, and this requires that we address not only external stimulus conditions but those within the person as well. We need to know something about the successes and failures of given forms of coping in specific contexts, and the cost–benefit involved. The problem extends clinically to human distress and somatic illness, both major health and morale issues.

In the biofeedback laboratory or clinic, the person is given information about the activities of his visceral systems and asked to regulate these. How he/she does this, what works and what does not work, the limits of the effects in magnitude of control, over time—all such information is capable of contributing something of immeasurable value to our knowledge. Research using biofeedback procedures could help us discover much more than we now know about the psychological mechanisms of self-regulation, particularly the intrapsychic ones.

If the problem is approached only in a parochial way, or as merely a gimmick limited to the biofeedback laboratory, then we are likely to advance little in spite of the evident potential. Biofeedback research will go much farther and rapidly become an integral part of psychology if it is seen and approached within the larger context in which it belongs. I hope it will avail itself of the rich variety of question and hypothesis presently available in the psychology of stress, emotion, and coping in everyday life as well as in situations of crisis.

REFERENCES

Arnold, M. B. *Emotion and personality.* New York: Columbia University Press, 1960.

Arnold, M. B. (Ed.). *Feelings and emotions.* New York: Academic Press, 1970.

Blanchard, E. B., & Young, L. D. Self-control and cardiac functioning: A promise yet unfulfilled. *Psychological Bulletin,* 1973, *79,* 145–163.

Bolles, R. C. Cognition and motivation: Some historical trends. In B. Weiner (Ed.), *Cognitive views of motivation.* New York: Academic Press, 1974. Pp. 1–20.

Budzynski, T. H., Stoyva, J. M., Adler, C. S., & Mullaney, D. J. EMG biofeedback and tension headache: A controlled outcome study. *Psychosomatic Medicine,* 1973, *35,* 484–496.

Cohen, F., & Lazarus, R. S. Active coping processes, coping dispositions, and recovery from surgery. *Psychosomatic Medicine,* 1973, *35,* 375–389.

Crider, A., Schwartz, G., & Shnidman, S. On the criteria for instrumental autonomic conditioning: A reply to Katkin and Murray. *Psychological Bulletin,* 1969, *71,* 455–461.

Dohrenwend, B. S., & Dohrenwend, B. P. *Stressful life events.* New York: Wiley, 1974.

Gal, R. Coping processes under seasickness conditions. Unpublished research, 1973.

Gray, S. J., Ramsey, C. S., Villarreal, R., & Krakaner, L. J. Adrenal influence upon the stomach and the gastric response to stress. In H. Selye & G. Hansen (Eds.), *Fifth annual report on stress, 1955–1956.* New York: MD Publications, 1956. P. 138.

Grinker, R. R., & Spiegel, J. P. *Men under stress.* New York: McGraw-Hill, 1945.

Hackett, T. P., & Weisman, A. D. Reactions to the imminence of death. In G. H. Grosser, H. Wechsler, & M. Greenblatt (Eds.), *The threat of impending disaster.* Cambridge: M.I.T. Press, 1964. Pp. 300–311.

Janis, I. L. Preventing dehumanization: Some comments on Howard Leventhal's analysis. Unpublished manuscript.

Jonas, G. Profiles: Visceral learning I. (On Neal E. Miller.) *New Yorker,* August 19, 1972.

Katkin, E. S., & Murray, E. N. Instrumental conditioning of autonomically mediated behavior: Theoretical and methodological issues. *Psychological Bulletin,* 1968, *70,* 52–68.

Koriat, A., Melkman, R., Averill, J. R., & Lazarus, R. S. The self-control of emotional reactions to a stressful film. *Journal of Personality,* 1972, *40,* 601–619.

Lacey, J. I. Somatic response patterning and stress: Some revisions of activation theory. In M. H. Appley & R. Trumbull (Eds.), *Psychological stress.* New York: Appleton, 1967. Pp. 14–37.

Lazarus, R. S. *Psychological stress and the coping process.* New York: McGraw-Hill, 1966.

Lazarus, R. S. Emotions and adaptation: Conceptual and empirical relations. In E. J. Arnold (Ed.), *Nebraska Symposium on Motivation.* Lincoln, Neb.: University of Nebraska Press, 1968. Pp. 175–266.

Lazarus, R. S. The self-regulation of emotion. In L. Levi (Ed.), *Emotions: Their parameters and measurement.* New York: Raven Press, 1975. Pp. 47–67.

Lazarus, R. S., Averill, J. R., & Opton, E. M., Jr. Towards a cognitive theory of emotion. In Magda B. Arnold (Ed.), *Feelings and emotions.* New York: Academic Press, 1970. Pp. 207–232.

Lief, H. I., & Fox, R. S. Training for "detached concern" in medical students. In H. I. Lief, V. F. Leif, & N. R. Lief (Eds.), *The psychological basis of medical practice.* New York: Harper & Row, 1963. Pp. 12–35.

Mandler, G. *Mind and emotion.* New York: Wiley, 1975.

Marston, A. R., & Feldman, S. E. Toward the use of self-control in behavior modification. *Journal of Consulting and Clinical Psychology,* 1972, *39,* 429–433.

Mason, J. W. A re-evaluation of the concept of "non-specificity" in stress theory. *Journal of Psychiatric Research,* 1971, *8,* 323–333.

Mechanic, D. *Students under stress.* New York: Free Press of Glencoe, 1962.

Mendelsohn, G. A. The competition of affective response in human subjects. *Journal of Abnormal and Social Psychology,* 1962, *65,* 26–31.

Morris, R. J., & Suckerman, K. R. The importance of the therapeutic relationship in systematic desensitization. *Journal of Consulting and Clinical Psychology,* 1974, *42,* 148. (a)

Morris, R. J., & Suckerman, K. R. Therapist warmth as a factor in automated systematic desensitization. *Journal of Consulting and Clinical Psychology,* 1974, *42,* 244–250. (b)

Rahe, R. H. The pathway between subjects' recent life changes and their near-future illness reports: Representative results and methodological issues. In B. S. Dohrenwend and B. P. Dohrenwend (Eds.), *Stressful life events: Their nature and effects.* New York: Wiley, 1974. Pp. 73–86.

Schwartz, G. E. Biofeedback as therapy: Some theoretical and practical issues. *American Psychologist,* 1973, *28,* 666–673.

Selye, H. *The stress of life.* New York: McGraw-Hill, 1956.

Selye, H. *Stress without distress.* Philadelphia: Lippincott, 1974.

Shapiro, D., Tursky, B., & Schwartz, G. E. Differentiation of heart rate and blood pressure in man by operant conditioning. *Psychosomatic Medicine,* 1970, *32,* 417–423.

Symington, T., Currie, A. R., Curran, R. S., & Davidson, J. N. The reaction of the adrenal cortex in conditions of stress. In *Ciba Foundations Colloquia on Endocrinology.* Vol. 8. *The human adrenal cortex.* Boston: Little, Brown, 1955. Pp. 70–91.

Weiner, B. *Theories of motivation.* Chicago: Markham, 1972.

Weiner, B. An attributional interpretation of expectancy-value theory. In B. Weiner (Ed.), *Cognitive views of motivation.* New York: Academic Press, 1974. Pp. 21–32. (a)

Weiner, B. (Ed.), *Cognitive views of motivation.* New York: Academic Press, 1974. (b)

Weisman, A. D. *On dying and denying.* New York: Behavioral Publications, 1972.

Wolff, C. T., Friedman, S. B., Hofer, M. A., & Mason, J. W. Relationship between psychological defenses and mean urinary 17-hydroxychoticosteroid excretion rates: Parts I and II. *Psychosomatic Medicine,* 1964, *26,* 576–609.

Wolpe, J. *Psychotherapy by reciprocal inhibition.* Stanford, Ca.: Stanford University Press, 1958.

5

The Operant Learning Theory Approach to Biofeedback Training*

A. H. BLACK, A. COTT, R. PAVLOSKI
McMaster University, Hamilton, Ontario, Canada

INTRODUCTION

"Biofeedback" is a term that is employed to describe procedures for training subjects to control responses governed by the autonomic nervous system (AS responses) and responses of the central nervous system (CNS responses).[1] Perhaps the easiest way to communicate the essential features of these training procedures would be first to describe and then to discuss some examples.

Example 1. The subjects are food-deprived rats at 80% of their normal body weight. The response to be trained is an elevated heart rate.

* The research described in this chapter was supported by Research Grant 258 from the Ontario Mental Health Foundation, and by Research Grant A0042 from the National Research Council of Canada to A. H. Black. In addition, Dr. A. Cott was supported by an Ontario Mental Health Foundation Scholarship. We would like to thank E. Ball, B. Osborne, and W. Ristow, who collaborated in the research that is described in this chapter.

[1] In this chapter, we shall discuss only AS and CNS responses. Electromyographic responses, which are often grouped with these two types of responses, are omitted because of their close relationship to skeletal responses, which are, of course, the standard object of operant control.

Each rat is placed in the experimental situation, and a tone is sounded periodically. The mean heart rate level during and between tone presentations is measured and found to be 470 beats per minute (b/m). Then training begins. Whenever the animal's heart rate rises above 510 b/m in the presence of the tone, the experimenter gives the rat a small amount of food. After a number of such occurrences, the mean heart rate rises to 510 b/m in the presence of the tone, and remains at 470 b/m in the absence of the tone.

Example 2. The subjects are humans. The response to be trained is occipital alpha electroencephalographic activity (EEG) recorded from scalp electrodes. The subjects are instructed to sit quietly in a room with their eyes closed. They are also instructed to rest during periods in which white noise is present and to produce occipital alpha activity during periods in which the white noise is absent. In addition, they are informed that when the white noise is absent, a tone will be presented when they successfully produce the required pattern of brain electrical activity, and that their task is to keep the tone on as long as possible. Before training begins, alpha activity is measured during a baseline period and found to be present 20% of the time. Then training is carried out for 80 minutes. At the end of training, alpha activity is present only 20% of the time during a 2-minute rest period in the presence of the white noise, and is present 80% of the time during a 2-minute period when the white noise is absent.

Even a superficial reading of these examples brings to mind a number of questions: *(1)* Why have responses as apparently disparate as heart rate and EEG activity been grouped together? *(2)* What features of these training procedures are necessary and sufficient for establishing control over the response? *(3)* What are the mechanisms underlying this control? *(4)* Are the mechanisms essentially the same in both of the above and in other, similar examples?

One clearly formulated theoretical position that has proved to be fruitful in dealing with such questions is instrumental or operant learning theory.[2] In fact, with one or two exceptions (Brener, 1974, for example), there is no other well-formulated theory that deals with these questions. It is clear, however, that certain beliefs about the nature of biofeedback training that are inconsistent with the principles of operant learning theory are shared by many researchers, particularly

[2] It is not our intention that "the operant learning theory approach" be equated with the approach taken by Skinner (1938). We employ the term much more broadly. Perhaps the label "instrumental learning approach" or "learning theory approach" would be more accurate. We have used the term "operant," however, because it tends to be employed in such a broad sense by researchers in the biofeedback field.

those who work with human subjects. The main principle underlying these beliefs is, we think that one establishes control over a response by making a subject aware of the sensations that are produced by the occurrence of the response. Because of the central role of the notion, we have labeled this account "the awareness view" of biofeedback training (Black, 1974b).

The purpose of this chapter is to describe and evaluate the operant approach to the biofeedback area. In addition, we will attempt to determine the validity of the main principles of the awareness view. Because the awareness view has not been articulated into a consistent theory, we have attempted to organize its assumptions and principles into a testable theoretical account which, we hope, accurately reflects the position of those who hold it. In this introductory section, we shall first describe the relevant features of operant conditioning theory, and then attempt to formulate more explicitly the other approach.

The first question asks why heart rate and EEG activity are classified together. Operant learning theory provides a straightforward answer: These responses have not been employed as instrumental or operant responses in the past. There are several plausible reasons for this. First, because these responses are internal, they have not been amenable to the continuous monitoring and accurate measurement required for external reinforcers to be made contingent on their occurrence. More generally, it is possible that these responses have not been operantly conditioned because no one has attempted to condition them. An alternative reason is that these responses are by nature refractory to operant control; this position has been maintained most vigorously with respect to AS responses. (See Black, 1971a, for a review of this position.) There may be other reasons. The main points, however, are that these responses are grouped together because they have not been operantly conditioned and that the only way to determine whether or not a particular response can be brought under operant control is by attempting to condition that response. It may be that certain responses can be operantly conditioned, that others cannot be operantly conditioned, while still others can be conditioned only within certain limits; that is, there might be some constraint on the changes that can be produced by means of operant conditioning.

The second question that was posed above concerns training procedures. Operant learning theory focuses on three main elements in its description of such procedures: *(1)* discriminative stimuli (SDs), *(2)* responses, and *(3)* reinforcers. The basic principle of operant conditioning can be stated quite simply. The probability of an operant response is increased when a reinforcing stimulus follows that response. In the first example, the reinforcer was food, and the reinforced response was a high heart rate. In the second example, the reinforcer was the tone, and the response was a high alpha EEG density. (In the latter case, the tone was a reinforcer as a consequence of the particular instructions that were given.) While this principle of reinforcement deals with the increase in the probability of high heart rates and high alpha EEG densities, it does not specify the operations that led to an increase in probability of each response in the presence of a particular stimulus—the tone in Example 1 or the absence of the white noise in Example 2. For this, we have to employ the principle of discriminative stimulus control. When we reinforce the response in the presence of one SD and do not reinforce the response in the presence of other SDs, the changes in response probability will occur only in the presence of the first SD. In the first example, the response was reinforced only in the presence of the tone. In the second example, the response was reinforced only in the absence of the white noise.

Little is known about the basic mechanisms underlying these principles of operant conditioning. There is perhaps more information at the behavioral level than at the neurophysiological level, but, even at the former level, much remains to be learned. Consider, for example, the obviously important relationship between response and reinforcer. There is still some question concerning the role of *contingency* between response and reinforcer versus the role of the *temporal contiguity* between the response and the reinforcer. Contingency refers here to the conditional probabilities of reinforcement given a response and given a failure to respond, and temporal contiguity refers to the time interval between response and reinforcement. Similar questions exist with respect to the nature of reinforcement. Probably the most prevalent theoretical position relates reinforcement to some change in motivational level—drive reduction, a satisfying state of affairs, and so on. But this position is not considered by many to be adequate, and no generally acceptable alternative characterization of reinforcers has been proposed (Tapp, 1969).

We have, therefore, much to learn about the fundamental mechanisms underlying the principles of operant conditioning. We can say, however, that these mechanisms must apply to the two examples we have been considering as well as to other, similar examples, since all of these represent instances of operant conditioning.[3]

This operant conditioning analysis can be contrasted with the awareness view. In the latter case, high heart-rate level and high alpha EEG densities are grouped together because the subject is not nor-

[3] The position that the principles of instrumental or operant learning (along with the related principles of classical conditioning) are adequate to describe motor skills learn-

mally aware of them, in the sense that he cannot discriminate their occurrence from their absence. The basic principle of this approach as far as we can ascertain is this: If we provide information about a response, the subject becomes aware of the response, and this leads to voluntary control over that response. In short, becoming aware of a response is a necessary condition for achieving voluntary control over that response.[4] Either of two training regimens might, in principle, be successfully utilized to establish awareness. In one procedure, the response could be employed as a discriminative stimulus so that the

---

ing, concept formation, problem solving, and language learning is held by many (Berlyne, 1975). Although we would not agree that this is a fruitful position, we do think that these principles do handle motor skills training, a form of training that, some researchers have argued, provides a prototypic model for biofeedback training. One of the main variables in motor skills training is knowledge of results. Knowledge of results is usually provided by response-contingent stimuli. Such stimuli are assumed to have two functions—providing information and reinforcement (Deese & Hulse, 1967). The feedback stimuli that occur in simple operant conditioning can, of course, be described in the same manner. For example, when lever pressing is reinforced by presenting a rat with food after every response, the food can be conceived of as providing information that a correct response has occurred, as well as increasing the probability of lever pressing. From an operant point of view, information can be treated as an SD for the next response. The SD in the case of motor skills learning is complex, and usually of the type that is seen in a matching problem, that is, the subject must match some property of his response with a value of the SD. For example, one might provide information about the amount of error between performance and some target level of performance. In this case, the subject must modify his response so that the error between the response and the target is reduced to zero. Thus, knowledge of results can function to reinforce the previous response and provide an SD for subsequent responses. This may account for the fact that increasing the interval between the response and the giving of knowledge of results has less of a deleterious effect than increasing the interval between the giving of results and the next trial (Welford, 1968, pp. 304–305). In the former condition, the subject is helped by having the temporal interval between SD and response reduced.

One other point: There is another way in which the concept of information can be employed in analyzing the effects of knowledge of results. One might argue that the provision of information is the feature that makes a stimulus reinforcing. Gibson (1970), for example, has argued that information that leads to "the reduction of uncertainty" is reinforcing. This attempt to explain why reinforcers work in terms of information transmission is different from our separation of the SD function and the reinforcing function of response-contingent stimuli.

[4] Should awareness of a response be considered not simply necessary but also sufficient for establishing voluntary control? This notion of sufficiency is somewhat more complex in that there may exist a subclass of responses over which one will not obtain voluntary control even though the subject can be made aware of them. For responses *not* in this subclass, the position seems to be that making a subject aware of a response is sufficient. From an experimental point of view, this is equivalent to the following: If one method for producing awareness leads to voluntary control, any other method for producing awareness should do so.

subject learns to identify either sensory stimuli produced by the occurrence of a response or sensory stimuli produced by naturally occurring causes, concomitants, or consequences of the response. In the other procedure, some salient exteroceptive stimulus could be made contingent on the response. In the examples given above, the food and tone that followed each occurrence of the response presumably made the subjects aware of the response and resulted in voluntary control, while food deprivation and the instructions provided the motivation for performing the appropriate response.

This account employs two concepts, awareness of a response and voluntary control, neither of which has been defined adequately (except perhaps by Brener, 1974) to our knowledge. We have, therefore, attempted to provide definitions that are in accord with our reading of the literature. We shall define awareness in this section and voluntary control in the section beginning on p. 104, where it is discussed in detail.

A subject can be said to be aware of some response if that response can be employed as a discriminative stimulus (Kamiya, 1969; Beninger, Kendall, & Vanderwolf, 1974; Rosenfeld & Hetzler, 1973). For example, suppose a human subject has a choice of two levers that he can press for reinforcement. The discriminative stimuli are his EEG patterns. In the presence of a desynchronized cortical EEG, pressing the first lever is the response that is reinforced; in the presence of alpha cortical EEG, pressing the second lever is the reinforced response. If the subject presses the appropriate lever in the presence of the appropriate EEG pattern, he can be said to be aware of, that is, capable of discriminating between, the EEG patterns. It is important to note that this operational definition does not distinguish between awareness as based on sensations of some feature of the EEG response itself, and awareness as perception of some direct, internal cause, concomitant, or consequence of the response.

As in the case of the operant paradigm, the neurophysiological mechanisms involved in the acquisition of control are not known. This point will be discussed in more detail in the section beginning on p. 104. Also, it is not clear whether voluntary control is thought to occur in both human and infrahuman subjects. We suspect that many who accept the awareness approach would argue that voluntary control applies only to human subjects.

The remainder of this chapter will be divided into two sections. The first is a discussion of operant learning theory in which we note that the most fruitful of the operant conditioning research methods have not, as yet, been exploited adequately in biofeedback research. The second is a comparison of the learning and awareness approaches, including an experimental evaluation of the latter which leads to the conclusion that the awareness approach in not particularly useful and that the phrase "voluntary control" could be dropped from the vocabulary of biofeedback researchers.

THE OPERANT LEARNING THEORY APPROACH

In the introductory section, we discussed two basic principles of operant conditioning—the principles of reinforcement and stimulus control. Operant conditioning theory obviously involves a great deal more that is relevant to research on the control of AS and CNS responses.

First, methodological rigor and sophisticated designs have resulted from the great amount of research concerned with the operant conditioning of observable responses. These are particularly useful in determining specifically which variables result in a given effect. The bidirectional research design, for example, in which subjects are trained to produce or inhibit a response, or to increase or decrease the rate of a response, was introduced originally as a means for determining whether control could be attributed to the effect of reinforcement or to such processes as sensitization and classical conditioning.[5]

Second, there exists a fund of information on methods for controlling behavior (Honig, 1966; Hulse, Deese, & Egeth, 1975; Mackintosh, 1975). There is no need to refer to the vast literature on variables such as magnitude of reinforcement, delay of reinforcement, schedules of reinforcement, informational feedback accompanying reinforcement,

[5] Two further points should be made about the bidirectional design. First, it can be criticized on the grounds that the bidirectional procedure alone is not sufficient for concluding that both increases and decreases have, in fact, been conditioned. It is clearly necessary to include a condition in which discriminative stimuli and reinforcers are presented randomly in order to provide a proper baseline for determining whether both increases and decreases were conditioned. An example of research in which this random procedure is employed is given later in the chapter. Second, the within-subject bidirectional design is identical to the design that has been employed to determine operationally whether voluntary control has been achieved. (See the discussion of the operational definition of voluntary control in the section beginning on p. 104). The only difference between these two uses of this design is that the demonstration of voluntary control requires a within-subjects design, whereas the demonstration of operant control requires either a within-subjects or a between-subjects design. It is clear that the inclusion of the random control is also necessary in order to conclude that voluntary control has been established.

and motivation to see that this issue has received a great deal of attention. The purpose of this research has been to determine the effects of manipulating these variables on simple measures of changes in behavior; for example, the probability of occurrence, the vigor, or the latency of a response such as lever pressing. Procedures required for more subtle types of behavior modification have been investigated in research on "shaping"—changing the form or topography of a response or even producing a new response by reinforcing successive approximations to some previously chosen target response. Another well-researched procedure is "chaining"—the construction of sequences of responses. Finally, research on motor skills is concerned with manipulations that improve the accuracy or precision of responses. In each of the above examples, procedures have been developed that can be employed to modify various features of behavior—probability, magnitude, latency, topography, sequential organization, and precision.

Third, there is a wealth of knowledge concerning stimulus control (Mostofsky, 1965; Sutherland & Mackintosh, 1971). Information is available on discrimination training procedures and on related phenomena such as generalization and contrast. At a more complex level, data on discrimination training with SDs that are formed by compounds of individual stimuli have permitted the analysis of phenomena such as overshadowing and blocking. Of particular interest to researchers in the biofeedback field is the analysis of interoceptive discriminative stimuli as contrasted with exteroceptive discriminative stimuli (e.g., Beninger, Kendall, & Vanderwolf, 1974; Kamiya, 1969; Mandler & Kahn, 1960). This comparison is important for an analysis of the terms, "self-control" and "voluntary control," which we will discuss later in the chapter.

Finally, there are the applications and extensions of operant learning theory in research on behavior modification (Kanfer & Phillips, 1970), in particular, self-control (Goldfried & Merbaum, 1973). Obvious methods of self control are *(a)* self-reinforcement and *(b)* management of the external discriminative and eliciting stimuli that control one's own behavior.

It is astonishing that so little of the theoretical and experimental armementarium of operant conditioning has been mobilized in research on the development of control over AS and CNS responses. Beyond the application of simple reinforcement contingencies and discriminative control procedures, only two of the topics that were mentioned above have received serious attention until relatively recently.

The first of these topics concerns an analysis of the relative effectiveness on the acquisition of control over the response of: *(1)* different qualities of response-contingent stimuli (e.g., different modalities, and various physical properties such as frequency and amplitude); and *(2)* different functional relationships between the response system and the feedback stimulus. For example, in studies of alpha density conditioning in human subjects, visual and auditory feedback stimuli have been compared (Lynch, Paskewitz, & Orne, 1974; Travis, Kondo, & Knott, 1975). In addition, comparisons have been made, in studies using human subjects, between binary and proportional or continuous feedback (Blanchard, Scott, Young, & Haynes, 1974; Kinsman, O'Banion, Robinson, & Staudenmayer, 1975; Lang & Twentyman, 1974; Travis, Kondo, & Knott, 1974, 1975).

This latter question regarding the functional relationship between response system and feedback stimulus is complicated by the fact that, when human subjects are employed, instructions about which feature of the feedback stimulus indicates success have two functions from the point of view of the experimenter. In addition to defining the aspect of the response-contingent stimulus that is the reinforcer, they define the aspect of the response system that is being reinforced. For example, in a situation in which the frequency of a tone varies linearly with heart rate, instructions to "increase the pitch of the tone beyond a certain point" define the response as an absolute heart rate, whereas instructions to "increase the pitch of the tone" define the response as a heart rate acceleration. We should point out that the conspicuous lack of data on the effectiveness of different functional relationships between response system and feedback stimulus is unfortunate since the response–reinforcer relation is fundamental to an operant analysis.

The second topic that has received attention in the biofeedback literature is shaping. Many studies have employed informal shaping procedures at the beginning of the experiment in order to produce responses with a particular topography (Babb & Chase, 1974; Harris, Gilliam, Findley, & Brady, 1973; Howe & Sterman, 1973; Wyrwicka & Sterman, 1968). More complex procedures involve the shaping of response patterns. In dissociative conditioning, for example, one measures two correlated responses and attempts to break the correlation by shaping changes in one while requiring the other response to be maintained in a steady state (Black, 1971a; Fetz, 1974; Fetz & Finocchio, 1971; Linnsteadter & Perachio, 1974). An identical procedure is utilized in the reinforcement of response patterns (Schwartz, 1975), in which the attempt is not to break the correlation between responses but rather to condition certain response profiles. These shaping procedures provide a powerful analytical technique for studying the relationships and dependencies among AS, CNS, and skeletal responses. The shaping of response patterns is particularly interesting because it is in large part a contribution by biofeedback researchers rather than an import from the major stream of operant conditioning research.

Why have so few of the principles and procedures that have been developed over the years of research on the operant conditioning of observable responses been taken over, utilized, and developed further by biofeedback researchers? There are, we think, two major reasons. First, many researchers, especially those who work with human subjects, assume that what we have termed the "awareness" view of biofeedback training is correct. They believe that control over AS and CNS responses is achieved by making a subject aware of some feature of the response to be controlled, or of some immediate internal cause, correlate, or consequence of that response (e.g., Brown, 1970, 1971; Kamiya, 1969). It is not surprising, therefore, that these researchers did not borrow very extensively from the operant conditioning literature; from their point of view, it is not particularly relevant. The second reason concerns those who did assume that biofeedback training is a form of operant conditioning. We think that these researchers failed to employ the available knowledge fully because they did not think it necessary to do so. The early research on the operant conditioning of AS and CNS responses employed simple procedures and produced striking and powerful results. The work of Miller, DiCara, and their associates was outstanding in this respect (Miller, 1969; Miller & Banuazizi, 1968; Miller & DiCara, 1967). Why carry out research using sophisticated techniques when relatively simple ones will do? Consequently, very little of the available information on operant conditioning procedures and principles has been employed.

This failure to employ the full range of operant conditioning principles and techniques for manipulating behavior has had at least two serious consequences. First, it has left us with too few scientifically sound data on the operant conditioning of AS responses.[6] The early

[6] The problem is less serious for CNS responses. There are many well-controlled studies on both animal and human subjects in which relatively sophisticated procedures have been utilized to condition operantly a variety of CNS responses. (See Black, 1972, for a review of that literature.)

If a question were to be raised about this literature, it would not concern the procedures that have been employed but, rather, the types of responses that have been conditioned. In most cases, the CNS activity that has been conditioned is a component of, or is related to, some motor control circuit (Black, 1972). The only apparent exceptions are provided by the work of Fox and his associates (Fox & Rudell, 1968, 1970) and, more recently, Rosenfeld (1974). The operant conditioning of CNS activity that is re-

results of Miller, DiCara, and their colleagues on the curarized rat have not been replicated (Obrist, Black, Brener, & DiCara, 1974), and there are not many other studies on infrahuman AS operant conditioning. For example, clear-cut conditioning of low and high heart rates has been reported in subjects that were incompletely curarized only by Black (1967, 1971a) and in normal subjects only by Engel (1974) and Engel and Gottlieb (1970). This work can be criticized: For example, in no cases were random controls utilized; the subjects in the Black studies appeared to employ simple skeletal mediation to change heart rates. The operant conditioning of increased blood pressures has been successful (Harris *et al.*, 1973). Furthermore, although the data on human subjects tend to be more satisfactory (e.g., Blanchard *et al.*, 1974; Gatchel, 1974; Lang & Twentyman, 1974; Schwartz, 1975), the effects of biofeedback training have been small and the research designs often inadequate (Blanchard & Young, 1973, 1974).[7]

Even if one accepts the above conclusion that autonomic operant conditioning has been demonstrated in some cases, we still lack data that we must have if we are to say anything sensible about the amenability of autonomic responses to operant conditioning. We still do not know how many and which AS responses are amenable to operant control. Until we have this information, it is unwise to draw any conclusions about AS responses as a class. Furthermore, we need to know more about the amount of change and type of change that can be produced on a given AS or CNS response. Homeostatic and what we have called "systems" constraints (Black, 1974a; Black & Young, 1972)

---

lated to motor control circuits is both interesting and useful. But, the operant conditioning of central components of nonmotor neural control systems is an area that we think is even more interesting. For example, can we condition components of sensory or perceptual circuits, and does such conditioning affect psychological information processing (Rosenfeld, Hetzler, Birkel, & Kowatch, 1975)? Unfortunately, there are very few data on this topic. It is necessary therefore, to map which areas of the brain emit responses amenable to operant conditioning, and to determine which nonmotor CNS events can be conditioned, and the consequences of such conditioning.

[7] The decision as to what is a small change and what is a large change is a difficult one. One could define magnitude or a change in conditioning relative to the normal range of the responses or to the magnitude of changes that occur in pathology. Regardless of which position were taken, one would still have to determine whether the production of the change that was produced by a given procedure was therapeutically useful. The second position has a certain intuitive appeal, but may run into trouble if the factors that control changes differ in the normal and pathological conditions. For our purposes, it is not necessary to deal with this issue. Our point is only that the current biofeedback procedures seem to be limited in their power to change the magnitude of autonomic responses in normal human subjects.

surely limit the extent to which certain AS responses can be brought under operant control.

A second problem that arises from the failure to exploit adequately the full range of operant techniques concerns the interpretation of existing data. When a small effect or no effect of operant conditioning has been demonstrated, we cannot say whether such results are due to some intrinsic constraint on the extent to which the response can be altered, or to an ignorance of the most effective conditioning procedures. Had a wider range of operant conditioning procedures been explored earlier in the development of the field, we might have been able to choose at least a little more confidently between these alternatives.

We have attempted to deal with some of the issues mentioned above in our current research. The main purpose of this research is to compare different shaping procedures with respect to their efficacy in changing heart rate. We hoped that this would provide some information on the degree to which heart rate could be modified by biofeedback procedures in the normal rat, and on the most effective procedures for producing such changes. In addition, we added a random reinforcement control procedure to the usual biofeedback design in order to provide more information on the baseline heart levels. This study is being carried out by B. Osborne, W. Ristow, and A. H. Black.

In this experiment, we employed rats as subjects and attempted to produce high and low heart rates. Our purpose was to compare the effectiveness of different shaping procedures. The reinforcement was brain stimulation of the lateral hypothalamus. Each rat was trained in a running wheel for 20 100-second trials per day over a period of 5 days. A PDP-8 computer was employed to present stimuli and reinforcements and to record and analyze heart rate. An Electorcraft activity recorder and a Sony 3600 videorecorder were employed to measure skeletal activity.

The shaping procedure that has been most frequently employed in biofeedback research can be labeled a *reinforcement density procedure.* In this case, the target response is either an interbeat interval (IBI) of very short duration (i.e., fast heart rate) or an IBI of relatively long duration (i.e., slow heart rate). Reinforcement is given for successive approximations to these responses, that is, IBIs of successively decreasing duration or IBIs of successively increasing duration. In this case, one sets some criterion level to define the first approximation to the response and reinforcement is presented if the criterion is met or exceeded. The criterion is made more difficult when the reinforcement density becomes high or, to put it another way, the latency of response becomes short. The criterion is made easier when reinforcement density falls below some minimum level, that is, long response latency. In this procedure, there are really two criteria, the first for determining when reinforcement is to be given, and the second for determining when the response criterion in effect will be changed.

We employed the following version of this procedure to train a group of four rats (two for producing high heart rates and two for producing low heart rates). The experimenter selected a criterion heart rate level, and any four consecutive IBIs that equalled the criterion or exceeded it in the proper direction were reinforced. The criterion was made more difficult when more than 10 reinforcements were administered on each of the previous five trials. The criterion was made easier when fewer than four reinforcements were delivered on each of the previous five trials. When such an automatic criterion change occurred, it was always by some fixed amount. Whenever the criterion became easier, it was always by 1 millisecond, and whenever it became more difficult, it was always by 2 milliseconds.

A second group of eight subjects was trained (four for high and four for low heart rates) using a *percentile reinforcement procedure* (Platt, 1973). A procedure similar to this has been employed on curarized rats (Fields, 1970; Roberts, Lacroix, & Wright, 1974). In this procedure, the criterion for defining the response that will be reinforced is determined on the basis of a continuously updated frequency distribution of response values, and this criterion is automatically adjusted so that the probability of reinforcement remains constant. We reinforced sets of four consecutive IBIs in the following way. Just prior to the first trial on each day, IBIs were sampled until a total of 50 were collected, and these were used to construct a frequency distribution of IBI values. The four IBIs occurring next were sampled: If all four IBIs equalled or exceeded in the proper direction the shortest IBI in the distribution (for producing fast heart rates), or the longest IBI in the distribution (for producing slow heart rates), a reinforcement was delivered. Regardless of whether a reinforcement was delivered, the IBI among the four that was "worst" with respect to the criterion was added to the distribution of 50, and the IBI that was temporally first to be placed in the distribution of 50 was deleted. Another set of four successive IBIs was then sampled, the above procedure repeated, and so on. This procedure guaranteed that each response of four IBIs had to equal or exceed 2% of the previous 50 responses in order to be reinforced.

In addition to the groups that were subjected to these two shaping procedures, a third group of four rats were trained with a random reinforcement procedure. Reinforcements were not contingent on any

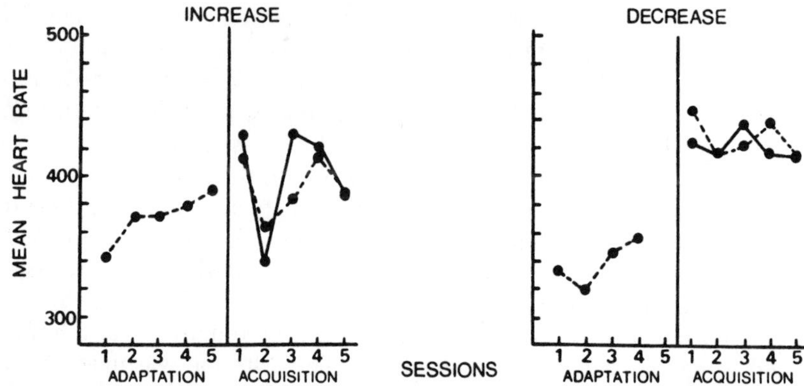

Figure 5.1 Heart rate as a function of days of training (sessions). A reinforcement density training procedure was employed during acquisition. (See text for more details on this procedure.) For rats in the "increase" group, reinforcement was delivered when the heart rate was equal to or greater than a criterion level. For rats in the "decrease" group, reinforcement was delivered when the heart rate fell below a criterion level. Solid lines—SD; dashed lines—SΔ.

aspect of the rats' behavior and the density of reinforcement was approximately equal to that delivered to animals on the percentile reinforcement schedule.

Rats trained on the reinforcement density schedule displayed neither significantly elevated heart rates nor significantly lowered heart rates. Three out of four rats displayed fast heart rate with respect to the pretraining baseline on Day 1 of training, and then all decreased or remained constant over days. An example of data for two rats is shown in Figure 5.1. We had planned to train more animals employing this procedure, but a detailed analysis of the results suggested that it was subject to a serious flaw, which is revealed most clearly when one employs reinforcers such as brain stimulation whose omission leads to rapid extinction.

The problem is this. For those rats in which fast heart rates were shaped, few reinforcements were administered when the criterion became very difficult. When this happened, the animals became quiet and the heart rate dropped; this moved the heart rate farther below the criterion level, and made the occurrence of reinforcement even less probable. In short, a positive feedback loop was established that interfered with conditioning. For those rats in which slow heart rates were shaped, the opposite condition held. When the criterion reached a point at which few reinforcements were obtained, the animals would become quiet, the heart rate would drop, and the frequency of reinforcement would increase. In this case, a feedback loop was established

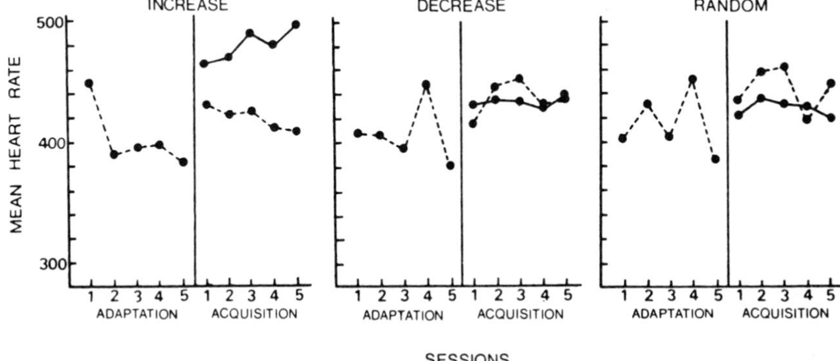

Figure 5.2 Heart rate as a function of days of training (sessions). A percentile reinforcement training procedure was employed during acquisition. (See text for more details on this procedure.) Cardiac accelerations were reinforced in the "increase" group, and cardiac decelerations were reinforced in the "decrease" group. For the "random" group, reinforcement was not contingent on behavior. Solid lines—SD; dashed lines—SΔ.

which facilitated conditioning. This asymmetry between the groups being trained to produce fast and slow heart rates favored slowing of heart rate in both groups. It led, we think, to a failure to find group differences with this shaping procedure. The same flaw may account for the failure of others to find large groups differences in previous experiments on heart rate conditioning in normal rats. In any case, we concluded that this procedure is not particularly useful and so abandoned it.

The data on the percentile reinforcement schedule were more encouraging. Data for animals run in this group and for the rats run in the random reinforcement group are shown in Figure 5.2. At the end of training, there were significant differences between groups reinforced for increasing and decreasing heart rates. The average difference in heart rate was 57.0 beats per minute. Also there were no significant between-group differences in baseline heart rate. A comparison with the random control group showed a significant difference between fast groups and the random group but not between slow groups and the random group. At first glance, this could be taken to mean that the slow group showed no effect of conditioning. A more detailed analysis of the videotapes revealed that the behaviors of the slow and random groups were different. The animals in the group in which decreasing heart rates were reinforced displayed alteration between higher heart rates accompanied by much skeletal activity and lower heart rates paralled by relative inactivity, while the animals in the random group displayed a more random distribution of heart rate and level of activity.[8] Brener (in this volume) has obtained data on heart rate very similar to ours using a shock-avoidance procedure. The main difference is that he carried out training for 10 days rather than 5 and found a more marked decrease in the groups reinforced for slow heart rates by the tenth day.

In summary, the percentile reinforcement procedure was more powerful than the reinforcement density procedure in the operant conditioning of heart rates using brain stimulation reinforcement. This result illustrates the importance of attempting to exploit more fully operant conditioning research designs, procedures, and principles in biofeedback studies. One hopes that such attempts will shortly make available more information about which AS and CNS responses can be controlled, and to what extent they can be controlled. This information will permit us to determine the constraints on the conditioning of different AS- and CNS-response systems and, therefore, the limits to which biofeedback training can be carried. Only then will we be able to evaluate the overblown claims about the power of biofeedback training with which we have been inundated.

A COMPARISON OF THE OPERANT AND AWARENESS APPROACHES TO BIOFEEDBACK TRAINING

In this section, we shall compare the operant and awareness approaches to the control of AS and CNS responses. Both views are similar in postulating that control over a response will result from making certain stimuli contingent on the response. They differ, however, with respect to the critical operations that are presumed to be necessary for establishing control, the description of the control that is established, and, consequently, the mechanisms that are presumed to underlie the establishment of control. According to operant conditioning theory, the contingency and/or contiguity between response and reinforcer lead to a change in behavior, but the theory does not specify the mechanism through which this change is produced; the result of training is described as discriminative stimulus control. According to the awareness view, the contingency and/or contiguity between response and reinforcer is effective because the subject is made aware of

[8] An analysis of the videotapes showed a significant correlation between skeletal activity level and heart rate. The rats in the group for which reinforcement was contingent on high heart rates ran significantly more in the running wheel that the rats in the other two groups. These results will be discussed in detail elsewhere.

the internal response; once the subject is aware, voluntary control follows necessarily. Hence, the result of biofeedback training is described as "voluntary control."

On the basis of this brief comparison, it might appear that the awareness view is superior because it specifies the underlying psychological mechanism through which response-contingent stimuli have their effect, that is, through producing awareness of the response. As we pointed out in our introduction, operant theory has not as yet been successful in specifying the neurophysiological or psychological mechanisms that underlie the effects of reinforcement (Tapp, 1969). This advantage, however, is more apparent than real. The awareness view is incomplete in that little effort has been made, even on the empirical level, to explain the manner in which response-contingent stimuli lead to awareness of response-produced sensations, or to explain how awareness results in control. In fact, we believe that the awareness view is still with us not because of strong evidence in its support, but because it has not been put to the empirical test in the same way as have operant attempts to account for underlying mechanisms. On the basis of data to be presented later in this section, we shall argue that the awareness view is inadequate, and also that the operant view, because of its rigorous methodology and empirically based principles and concepts, can provide the base for further research on biofeedback training.

In order to amplify and substantiate the arguments presented above, it is necessary to analyze the awareness position in more detail. The central concept of this approach is "voluntary control." We shall, therefore, begin our analysis with a discussion of this concept.

Most psychologists have avoided the concepts of volition and voluntary control, particularly as these concepts are applied to human behavior. Among the few behavioral scientists who have considered these concepts, there is little agreement with respect to their definition, theoretical status, or usefulness (Irwin, 1969; Kimble & Perlmuter, 1970). One reason for this lack of agreement is that the concepts that are employed in the definition of voluntary behavior (notions such as "consciousness," "awareness," "intent," and "will") are extraordinarily complex, are not easily defined operationally and are, in some cases, inconsistent with the basic deterministic assumption of the scientific approach to psychology, that is, that the causes of behavior can be specified. Furthermore, the separation and classification of behavior into "respondents" and "operants," and learning into "classical conditioning" and "operant conditioning" has permitted many behavioral scientists to avoid these relatively complex notions.

We shall not give an exhaustive analysis of the usual meanings of "voluntary," but there are three common meanings of the term that must be spelled out. (See Alston, 1974; Kimble & Perlmuter, 1970; Miller, 1942; and Verhave, 1966, for a more detailed discussion.)

1. There is the notion that the occurrence of a voluntary response is not caused by some external agent; that is, the occurrence of the response does not depend on coercion, nor does it depend reflexively on some eliciting stimulus.

2. There is the notion that the response is produced directly by some internal process that reflects our wants, purposes, and intentions; it occurs because we will it to occur, or want it to occur, or intend it to occur, and it ceases because we will, want, or intend its termination.

3. There is the related notion that we are aware of the desire or intention to respond, and/or of the response itself, and/or of the outcome of its occurrence.

A definition of voluntary that includes the meanings listed above is unsatisfactory to those who are interested in a scientific understanding of the concept because it does not permit one to specify empirically the causes of voluntary behavior. (The first describes what is *not* a cause of voluntary behavior; the second and third suggest that will, intentions, and awareness may be part of the cause but provide no means for operationally defining these terms.) Therefore, for those who believe that the concept of voluntary control is amenable to scientific analysis, the problem is to define the term operationally and to specify the causes of voluntary behavior.

It is relatively easy to define operationally the first of the meanings listed above. One should be able to exclude those cases in which the response is elicited reflexively without too much trouble. Similarly, by defining awareness of the response as the ability to employ the response as an SD, one can operationally define the relevant aspect of the third meaning. The second meaning is more difficult. Actually, two related notions are involved in this case. One is the idea that control must be direct. The other is the idea that voluntary behavior is produced by action of the will, and so on. With respect to direct control, the basic point is that other responses must not mediate the occurrence of the response under consideration. Would, for example, hitting oneself on the patellar tendon with a hammer be labeled as voluntary control of the knee-jerk in the sense that we are using the term?[9] It is

[9] It is interesting to note at this point that in the application of learning theory to human behavior (i.e., Behavior Modification) the emphasis in teaching people "self-control" or "voluntary control" is the management of critical environmental variables such as discriminative stimuli, contingencies, and outcomes. In other words, the method

relatively easy to test for several types of mediation, such as mediation by observable responses and mediation by central components of motor control circuits. Other types of mediation, however, are more difficult to test; for example, cognitive mediation. The question as to whether mediation by nonmotor cognitive control events should be classified with the mediators listed above or with those causal factors that produce direct control is purely academic at this time; we do not think that this issue can be resolved until we understand more thoroughly the neurophysiology of motor control.

The notion that voluntary behavior is caused by will, intention, and so on is also difficult to deal with. As an interim measure, most researchers deal with this issue experimentally in terms of the effects of instructions. If we ask a subject to produce a response, and he does so, and if we ask him to withhold the response, and he does so, we say there is voluntary control. This definition does not apply to infrahuman subjects. One could, however, modify or at least reword the definition to state that a subject has voluntary control if it can produce the response to one SD and withhold it to another SD. This modification would permit us to apply the concept to infrahuman subjects.

This operational definition of voluntary control is not fully satisfactory, particularly with respect to the second of the three meanings in our original list. It does, nevertheless, allow us to deal with the main question: How is voluntary control established? One proposed answer to this question concerning the acquisition of voluntary control is what Kimble and Perlmuter have called the "classical theory of volition." The basic feature of the "classical" (in the sense of classical music, not classical conditioning) theory is that voluntary control is learned and that the association of response-produced sensations to events that precede the response plays an important role in such learning. James (1890), for example, argued that we develop voluntary control when we have learned to associate the "image" produced by the occurrence of a response with the stimulus situation that normally sets the occasion for the occurrence of the response. Brener's model of voluntary control (Brener, 1974, and in this volume) seems to fall into this category.

The awareness view, as we have characterized it, is closely related

---

for achieving "voluntary control" over behavior is not by focusing one's attention directly on behavior but, rather, by determining or becoming "aware" of the environmental stimuli that control or affect behavior and then by directly controlling these stimuli—that is, by the management of one's own environment. In this case, indirect control is accepted.

to the "classical" view but differs fundamentally in one respect. The awareness view assumes that the subject learns to become aware of response-produced sensations, and that this results in voluntary control (see Footnote 4). The classical theorists, on the other hand, assume that not only must one become aware of response-produced stimuli, but one must also associate response-produced stimuli with events that precede the response in order to establish voluntary control.

The operant learning theory approach to voluntary control is difficult to characterize because the term "voluntary" has been employed within operant learning theory in so many different ways. Many learning theorists quite sensibly refuse to employ the term at all. Others employ the term simply as a synonym for "operant" (Skinner, 1938). Also, the term is often used to describe any behavior that is not involuntary (e.g., Diamond, Balvin, & Diamond, 1963; Welch, 1955). Still others define voluntary control in much the way that we have, and argue that it is a form of discriminative control that results from a step-by-step series of discrimination training procedures (Black, 1974b). So little work has been carried out on the nature of voluntary control and on the conditions for establishing it that the most we can say at this point is that operant learning theory provides a program for solving the problem, rather than a solution.

What is the role of the awareness of the response in an operant analysis of voluntary behavior? If one employs "voluntary" simply as a synonym for "operant," then awareness is not necessary for voluntary control because the data indicate that awareness is not necessary for operant control. It has been clearly demonstrated that, although disruption or elimination of sensory feedback (kinesthetic, proprioceptive, visual, and so on), presumably necessary for awareness of the response, does have a profound but temporary effect on skeletal responses, such feedback is not necessary for the operant conditioning of what we normally consider to be voluntary acts (Taub & Berman, 1963, 1968). Also, there is the voluminous literature on learning without awareness (see Saltz, 1971, for a review of this work). This research deals with a variety of topics—awareness of the reinforcer, of the reinforcer–response contingency, and of the reinforced response itself. Data on awareness of the response indicate that while such awareness facilitates learning, operant conditioning of responses does occur in subjects who were unaware of the response that had been conditioned and, in fact, were unaware that any response had been conditioned. (In this research, the definition of awareness is different from that given in the introduction. It is simply the ability to verbalize what the relevant feature of the learning situation was after operant conditioning had taken place.)

If one accepts the more complex definition of voluntary that we outlined at the beginning of this discussion, one would, we think, still be compelled to maintain that awareness is neither a necessary nor sufficient condition for establishing voluntary control; when it occurs, it might simply be the end result of the operant training procedures required to produce control. One could, of course, agree that awareness of the response might play a role in the learning of voluntary control because response-produced interoceptive stimuli could act as SDs for the occurrence of subsequent responses. Such awareness would not be essential, however, because either interoceptive or exteroceptive stimuli could act as SDs in this situation. In short, all of these operant positions that employ the term "voluntary" treat the role of awareness differently from the awareness position. The latter maintains that awareness is essential; the former could assign some role to awareness, but in no case claims it to be sufficient or even necessary in establishing voluntary control.[10]

In summary, the main distinction between the operant and awareness views concerns the role of awareness in establishing voluntary control. From an operant learning theory standpoint, awareness is unnecessary for establishing operant or voluntary control over skeletal, AS, and CNS responses. Those who accept the awareness view, on the other hand, assume that response-contingent stimuli do not act as reinforcers in the simple operant sense. They assume that the feedback stimulus, by providing information about a response of which a subject is normally unaware, allows the subject to become aware of the response and thereby achieve direct voluntary control over that response. There are really three assumptions made by these researchers:

1. It is assumed that awareness of the response is both a necessary condition and a prerequisite for voluntary control (i.e., precedes it).
2. It is assumed that awareness of the response is not only necessary

[10] We have omitted from this discussion a consideration of a number of theories of voluntary control. For example, the hypothesis has been made that voluntary movements are simply responses that have been conditioned to stimuli that are produced by other responses, especially language (Hudgins, 1933; Hull, 1933; Hunter, 1934; see Irwin, 1969, pp. 119–122, for a critical analysis of this hypothesis). More recently, it has been suggested that voluntary control is characterized by a comparison between corollary output from the command to perform a response and the outcome of the performance (Von Holst, 1954; Teuber, 1960). We have also neglected physiological hypotheses about the usage of voluntary control (Hebb, 1949; Vanderwolf, 1971). We have omitted these theories because our purpose was not to present a comprehensive analysis of theories of voluntary control, but only to discuss those views that are relevant to the learning of voluntary control as it is conceived in the biofeedback literature.

but is sufficient for achieving voluntary control over the response, in those cases in which voluntary control can be achieved (see Footnote 4).

3. It is assumed that it is possible to become aware of AS and CNS responses and it follows that there must exist direct sensory concomitants of these responses.

Unfortunately, most of the research in this area can be interpreted from either the point of view described above which we have called the "awareness" approach, or from a traditional operant approach. Most experimental procedures involve the presentation of stimuli following a response, and this meets the requirements of both approaches; that is, in such procedures, one could attribute a change in behavior either to reinforcement or to the establishment of awareness of some feature of the response. There is one procedure, however, in which the two approaches do lead to different predictions. This procedure was first described by Kamiya (1969). In it, the internal response is used as an SD; that is, the subject is trained to identify the response. From an operant point of view, ability to discriminate the response would not necessarily lead to control over the response; from the awareness point of view, this ability would necessarily result in control.

Of those researchers who have employed this procedure to study the relationship between awareness of sensations produced by AS and CNS responses and control of those responses (e.g., Blanchard, Young, & McLeod, 1972; Brener & Jones, 1974; Donelson, 1966; Engel & Bleecker, 1974; Stern, 1972), only Kamiya (1969) has reported that a trained ability to discriminate leads directly to voluntary control.

In our first experiment, we attempted to replicate Kamiya's experiment (Kamiya, personal communications). Each subject was told that his EEG was being recorded and examined for two "brain wave states" (corresponding to alpha and nonalpha EEG patterns), and that he was to reply upon hearing a tone whether he thought he was in State A or State B. The subject was also told after each trial whether he was correct. In this experiment, the probability of alpha and nonalpha trials varied widely. The data presented in Figure 5.3 show how one representative subject used this information to do well in the discrimination task. This figure shows several trial and response probabilities as a function of blocks of 20 trials. When the probability of an alpha trial, shown by the solid line on the right, was very high, so was the probability of an alpha response, shown by the broken line. That is, the subjects seemed to match their responses to the more probable

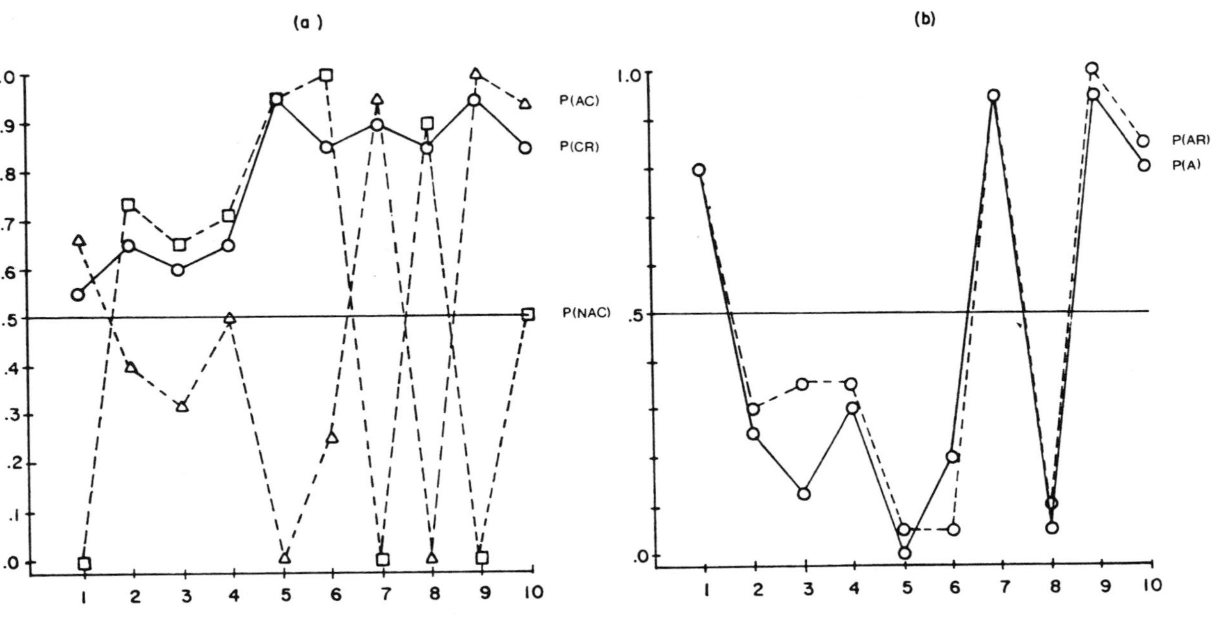

Figure 5.3 Data from one representative subject in our first experiment, illustrating the confounding of responses made on the basis of EEG patterns and responses made on the basis of trial probabilities. As the probability of an alpha trial (P(A)) approaches 1.00, the probability of a correct alpha response (P(AC)) also approaches 1.00, and the probability of a correct nonalpha response (P(NAC)) approaches zero. As P(A) approaches zero, P(AC) and P(NAC) diverge toward zero and 1.00, respectively; P(AC) and P(NAC) are never both above .50 for any given block of 20 trials—Graph (a)—but oscillate between zero and 1.00 as P(A) varies. The close correspondence of P(A) and alpha response probability (P(AR)) is also illustrated, in Graph (b).

type of trial. Some subjects eventually came to make, on every trial, the response that was most often correct for that block of trials. This led to a high probability of a correct response, as illustrated by the solid line on the left. But, since responses made to trial probability were completely confounded with responses made to EEG patterns, we could not tell whether these subjects were responding to trial probability or to EEG patterns. In other words, we could not conclude that the subjects had, in fact, learned to discriminate the EEG patterns. One way to avoid this confounding is to hold alpha and nonalpha trial probabilities near .50. If learning curves are then obtained, we know they cannot be due to the subject's employing high or low trial probabilities as the SD.

In our next experiment, we attempted to keep the probabilities of alpha and nonalpha trial presentations near .50. In this experiment, none of the eight subjects showed any learning after 400 discrimination trials. Thus, when the possibility of probability matching was controlled, subjects did not seem capable of discriminating alpha from nonalpha activity.

This second experiment also showed that there were several cues other than EEG activity to which subjects might be responding. First, we found a strong statistical relationship between a subject's response on a given trial and the correctness of his response on the previous trial. That is, when we informed a subject that his response on a given trial was correct, he was about four times more likely to give the same response on the next trial than he was to switch to the other response. Similarly, if a subject responded incorrectly, he was about twice as likely to switch to the other response on the following trial than he was to make the same response again. Rosenfeld and Hetzler (1973) reported similar confoundings in the discrimination of conditioned and normally occurring components of evoked potentials in rats.

Second, subjects often reported that they tested "hypotheses" about the two EEG patterns by actively putting themselves into a particular state and then determining on the basis of the outcome of their response which EEG pattern corresponded to that state. The manipulations involved ranged from eye movement and visual imagery to problem solving and highly emotional thoughts.

In summary, the results of these two studies were clear-cut. When we failed to control for confounding cues, we obtained results similar to Kamiya's (1969). When we controlled trial probabilities, we obtained negative results. Now, one can always criticize experiments in which negative results are obtained by arguing that the methods were inadequate. We recognized that our two experiments were open to this criticism, and took into consideration two of the most obvious arguments of this sort in the next experiment. First, it is possible that our situation was in some general way inadequate and that our subjects would not have learned anything about their EEG, regardless of the training procedure employed. In order to deal with this possibility, we included, in addition to the discrimination task, a condition in the next experiment in which standard feedback procedures were employed to train subjects to control EEG activity. If the subjects could learn to control their EEG activity as a result of these procedures, it could not be argued that our experimental situation was generally inadequate.

Second, in the studies that were just described, we employed subjects who were naive with respect to biofeedback and the nature of brain electrical activity. One could argue that subjects who knew more about the apparent behavioral and psychological concomitants of CNS electrical activity would more easily develop a discrimination. In order to deal with this issue, faculty members and graduate students knowledgeable in this research area were selected as subjects. Since we could easily communicate with these subjects, and because they were all highly motivated to succeed in the experiment, we thought that this maneuver would also minimize EEG manipulation and the use of previous trial information in the discrimination task. None of the 16 subjects who volunteered for the experiment had previously participated in a study concerned with control or discrimination of EEG activity. This experiment was designed to answer several questions. First, we wanted to determine whether or not subjects could discriminate alpha from nonalpha activity. If this were the case, we wanted to know if this ability to discriminate produces voluntary control over the presence and absence of alpha. Third, we wished to determine if there is any transfer from learned control of alpha activity to discrimination performance.

The left occipital-parietal EEG was quantified in the following way. The raw EEG was amplified, filtered between 8 and 13 Hz, and fed to a Grass Model 7P3 integrator, so that the integrator's output voltage increased as EEG activity entered the alpha frequency range and also varied directly with the amplitude of alpha activity. Each time this voltage exceeded preset criteria, logic levels representing alpha and nonalpha activity were set. These criteria were valid indicators of the presence and absence of alpha activity, and were used in computer analysis of the percentage of the time that subjects produced alpha and nonalpha activity. It is important to note that, because two criteria were used, percent-time alpha and percent-time nonalpha do not sum to 100%. Zero-crossings of the EEG were also processed by a digital filter. This filter had logic outputs that indicated when an EEG in the alpha frequency range or outside the alpha frequency range was present.

Subjects were tested with their eyes closed. Discrimination trials were administered in blocks of 20 on a variable-interval 10-second schedule of trial presentation. The onset of a trial delivered a tone to the subject when the integrator and digital filter agreed that one-half second of alpha or nonalpha activity had just occurred. The subject responded by depressing one of two microswitches mounted on either arm of his chair, and was immediately informed whether he was correct.

Feedback trials were 2 minutes long and were run in blocks of 10 on a variable-interval 10-second schedule of trial presentation. There were two classes of feedback trials. During discrete feedback trials, either a tone or a click stimulus was contingent on the presence of alpha or nonalpha activity. During continuous feedback trials, subjects heard a tone, the frequency of which varied inversely with the integrator's output voltage. That is, as the subject's EEG entered the alpha frequency range and as the amplitude of alpha activity increased, the pitch of the tone decreased. Conversely, as the amplitude of alpha activity decreased and as EEG activity passed out of the alpha frequency range, the pitch of the tone increased. Each subject was given one 10-trial block of each of the following: discrete alpha feedback, discrete nonalpha feedback, continuous alpha feedback, and continuous nonalpha feedback.

Eight subjects received a block of 200 discrimination trials, followed by 20 alpha feedback trials and 20 nonalpha feedback trials, followed by an additional block of 200 discrimination trials. The remaining eight subjects did not receive any discrimination trials preceding feedback, but were otherwise treated identically. Discrete feedback trial blocks were always run before continuous feedback blocks. The discrete feedback stimuli contingent on alpha and nonalpha activity were counterbalanced over subjects, as were the left and right discrimination response switches indicating alpha and nonalpha responses. Probabilities of alpha and nonalpha discrimination trials were held near .50.

In addition, we tested the ability to control alpha activity in the absence of feedback stimulation, immediately before and after each block of discrimination and feedback trials. Each of these stimulus-control tests consisted of four 2-minute units: a baseline in which the subject was asked to relax without attempting to do anything in particular; a unit in which alpha production without feedback was requested; a unit in which nonalpha production without feedback was requested; and a final baseline.

The data from our alpha and nonalpha feedback procedures are in agreement with findings reported by other investigators. We obtained significant increases in percent-time nonalpha from baseline levels to the final minutes of nonalpha feedback. Percent-time nonalpha during the baseline periods immediately preceding continuous feedback sessions, and during alpha and nonalpha feedback trials, is presented in Figure 5.4. While this measure clearly increases over nonalpha feedback trials, it does not change during alpha feedback. As can be seen from Figure 5.5, we also found a significant decrease in percent-time

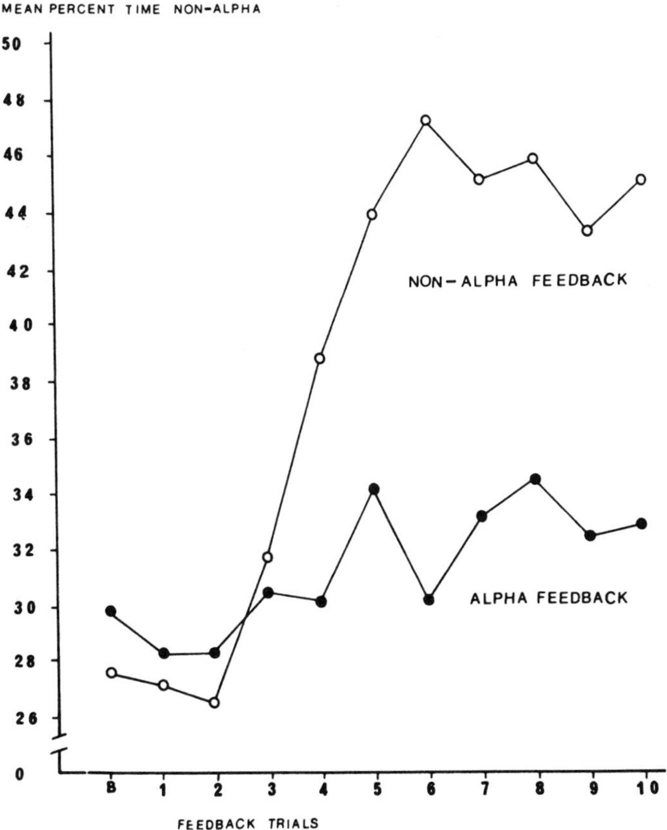

Figure 5.4 Mean percent-time nonalpha for 16 subjects during continuous alpha and nonalpha feedback trials and during baselines immediately preceding each continuous feedback session.

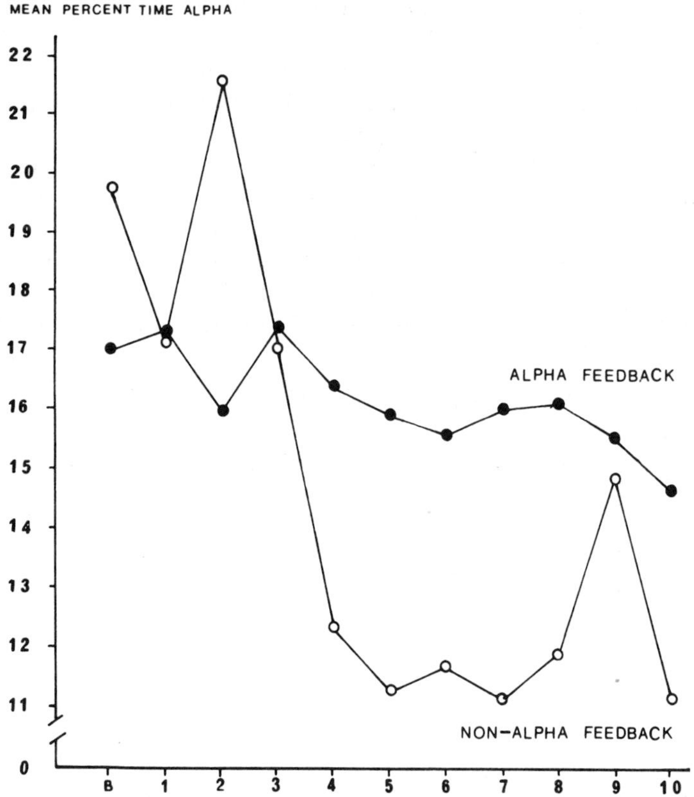

Figure 5.5 Mean percent-time alpha for 16 subjects during continuous alpha and nonalpha feedback trials and during baselines immediately preceding each continuous feedback session.

alpha over nonalpha feedback trials. This is a replication of the general finding that subjects given alpha and nonalpha contingent feedback are capable of increasing percent-time nonalpha, but not percent-time alpha above baseline levels recorded under conditions optimal for the appearance of alpha (Lynch *et al.*, 1974; Paskewitz, Lynch, Orne, & Costello, 1970).

Furthermore, a limited ability to control EEG activity was retained in the absence of feedback stimulation. Subjects displayed no control of alpha activity prior to feedback training. Following feedback training, however, there was significant suppression of alpha when subjects were asked to produce nonalpha activity. That is, the percent-time alpha observed when subjects were asked to produce nonalpha was significantly lower than the percent-time alpha recorded during the other units of the test.

The results of discrimination training were, however, entirely negative. First, no learning curves were obtained over either pre- or postfeedback blocks of discrimination trials for the group of subjects receiving discrimination training prior to feedback, or over postfeedback trial blocks for the subjects not receiving prefeedback discrimination training. Second, although some subjects reported that they were sometimes able to originate an alpha or a nonalpha trial by using various strategies in an attempt to manipulate their EEGs, and could therefore respond correctly on those trials, all subjects felt that the discrimination task seemed impossible if such manipulations were not allowed. There was, of course, no transfer from discrimination training to alpha control, or from control to discrimination.

We conclude from these data that subjects cannot learn to discriminate the presence or absence of occipital alpha activity. Therefore, the contention that awareness of the alpha rhythm leads to the ability to control this response voluntarily has no empirical support. Because we did not establish awareness, the present experiment does not provide data on the assumption that the establishment of awareness is sufficient for voluntary control. The present experiment does, however, demonstrate that the other two assumptions characterizing the awareness view of voluntary control do not hold for control of alpha activity. First, voluntary control of a CNS response can be achieved without the ability to discriminate that response, that is, without awareness of the response. In short, awareness is not necessary for voluntary control. Second, it appears highly unlikely that there exist direct sensory concomitants of occipital alpha and nonalpha activity.

A similar situation exists with respect to control and discrimination of heart rate in human subjects. It is clear that subjects can be trained to achieve voluntary control over their heart rates; that is, to follow instructions to produce high and low heart rates (e.g., Brener, 1974; Lang, 1974; Schwartz, 1975). Nevertheless, it has not been demonstrated that an ability to discriminate high and low heart rates leads to voluntary control. In fact, it is not clear whether or not subjects can discriminate high and low heart rates. Mandler and Kahn (1960) have reported an unsuccessful attempt to train subjects to discriminate between high and low heart rates after confounding variables (i.e., respiratory sinus arrhythmia) were controlled. Brener and his colleagues (Brener, 1974; Brener & Jones, 1974) have shown that subjects can learn both to press a button following each heart beat, and to discriminate stimuli contingent on their pulses from stimuli produced by a multivibrator firing at a frequency equivalent to their mean heart rate; however, control and discrimination are completely confounded in each of these tasks, since the SD is not under the experimenter's control.

There are a number of further problems arising from the awareness view. First, as we pointed out above, none of these data bear on the assumption concerning the sufficiency of awareness for establishing voluntary control. In order to test this assumption, we would have to establish awareness of a response (which we did not do in this experiment), and then determine whether voluntary control over that response followed automatically. If control did not follow, we would reject the assumption. If it did follow, we would still have to demonstrate that the procedure for establishing awareness did not produce control by means of some alternative mechanism. This latter requirement could not be fulfilled, in fact, unless we could enumerate all of the variables involved in the acquisition of voluntary control, which of course is unlikely. It may be, therefore, that the sufficiency of awareness cannot be determined.

Second, the basic procedure of the awareness view lacks plausibility. It seems to follow, from the assumptions concerning the relation between awareness of a response and voluntary control over that response, that an experimenter should attempt to establish discriminative control over some other response in order to establish voluntary control over the AS or CNS response of primary interest (e.g., using alpha and nonalpha activity as SDs for button pressing in order to achieve voluntary control over the presence and absence of alpha activity). This seems to be a rather odd notion; it seems more reasonable to establish SD control over the response of primary interest.[11] Also, this procedure of attempting to use one response to establish discriminative control over another response involves using SDs which might very well be ineffectual; that is, the procedure would not work if the first response could not be discriminated.

It should be clear from this discussion that the awareness view of

[11] However, there is a much more plausible way in which an internal response could act as an SD and be important in the control over the same response. The internal response could act as an SD for some other observable response that is already well learned and that has an effect on that internal response. For example, epileptiform activity (an internal CNS response) could act as an SD for a skeletal response (change in posture, isometric muscle tension, or even self-administration of an aversive stimulus such as shock) which acts to arrest the epileptiform activity and thus to avoid a frank seizure. There may be other examples of this sort, many of which could prove to be very important. However, this does not imply that the ability to discriminate leads to direct voluntary control over the internal response that is discriminated.

voluntary control does not have empirical support, and is inadequate both logically and procedurally. Furthermore, it should also be obvious that the concept of voluntary control is a global term which makes no distinction between the variety of types of discriminative stimulus control recognized by operant learning theory. In fact, the adoption of the term for describing control over skeletal, AS, and CNS responses can lead scientists away from the discovery of variables causally related to control. Skinner made this point with respect to skeletal responses in 1938, and we would argue that it applies equally to AS and CNS responses. "Voluntary" is probably a term that describes the beliefs of subjects about the causal relations between their behavior and environmental events. As we have pointed out earlier in this section of the chapter, most attempts to deal with voluntary control have begun with operational definitions of the most common meanings or connotations of the term "voluntary"; that is, with those notions that lead an individual to believe he is exercising voluntary control. Since these meanings describe not so much the nature of control either physiologically or behaviorally, but rather something about the beliefs of the subject, they are more properly a topic of study by social psychologists than a starting point for a scientific analysis of control over behavior.

CONCLUSION

In the preceding sections of this chapter, we described the operant approach to biofeedback research and argued for more effort in applying and developing procedures for establishing operant control over AS and CNS responses. We also pointed out that there is no compelling evidence to support the alternative approach to biofeedback training which we have labeled the "awareness view." We dealt with the awareness view as a single unitary position, but it is possible to make finer distinctions.

1. The critical feature of the strongest version of the awareness view—the one that we have discussed—is that the ability to discriminate between two internal responses, such as alpha and nonalpha, is both sufficient and necessary for obtaining control over the internal responses. Therefore, teaching subjects to discriminate between the occurrence and nonoccurrence of a response should establish the ability to produce the response on command. It is obvious that this position would not be supported if either *(a)* discrimination learning occurs but does not lead to the ability to produce the response, or *(b)*

subjects can learn to produce the response without being able to discriminate it. Our data indicate that the latter holds; therefore, we reject this particular version of the awareness hypothesis for the particular responses that we have considered.

2. The awareness view could be modified to account for our data as follows. Suppose that there is a many-to-one correlation between a number of different responses and alpha, and/or between a number of different responses and nonalpha. Suppose further that each of these responses has a specifiable probability of occurrence when a subject is at rest. Finally, suppose subjects learn to produce alpha by adopting the strategy of performing one particular correlated response, and learn to produce nonalpha by performing one other correlated response. For example, one might be able to learn to produce nonalpha by one of the following—thinking emotionally, tensing muscles, moving the eyes, and so on. According to this position, the subjects in our experiment fail to discriminate alpha and nonalpha because these internal states are correlated with a variety of responses when they are resting. It is as though we were trying to establish a discrimination while constantly changing the discriminative stimulus. The subjects learn to discriminate and to produce alpha and nonalpha during operant conditioning because the subjects employ only one response for alpha and one for nonalpha. Discrimination training with respect to the two responses that the subjects were actually using to produce alpha and nonalpha, respectively, would result in control over alpha and nonalpha.

This analysis would account for our data as well as other data revealing successful control without the ability to discriminate. It would not, however, account for data that demonstrate successful discrimination without resulting control (e.g., Reynolds, 1966). Furthermore, even if data could be obtained to support this version of the awareness view, it is much weaker than the first version. It does not support the position that the subject must be able to discriminate alpha and nonalpha or feedback from these states in order to develop control over these states. It is the response that is correlated with alpha and the response that is correlated with nonalpha that must be discriminated according to this second version—not alpha and nonalpha and their sensory concomitants or consequences.

3. A third version of the awareness view is similar to the operant conditioning view. This version differs from the two others in that discrimination of internal responses is not thought to be sufficient for establishing control over those responses. There is a variety of reasons for arguing that discrimination training is not sufficient. For example, if one accepts "classical" theory of voluntary control, it is necessary that

the antecedents of attempting to perform a response be associated with consequences of the response; the discrimination training procedure does not lead to the establishment of such associations. At the same time, this view holds that operant conditioning (or production training) is required, and that the subject has to learn to discriminate the response during such conditioning if control is to be established.

This argument that discrimination of the response is necessary for successful operant conditioning can be challenged on two counts. First, this position can be questioned on the basis of the data on operant conditioning without awareness, which we mentioned earlier in the chapter. It does seem that some operant conditioning can occur without awareness of the response being conditioned. Second, data on the removal of exteroceptive feedback could lead to serious problems for this third version of the awareness position. In some cases, subjects can learn to perform a response when an exteroceptive stimulus is made contingent on that response but lose the ability to control the response when the exteroceptive stimulus is removed (Alexander, Holland, & Wallace, 1975). It seems to us that such a result casts very serious doubt on the notion that the addition of an external feedback stimulus acts to make the subject aware of internal responses during operant conditioning. For these who accept this position, the loss of control suggests that either *(1)* the subject was not aware of the internal response, and control was achieved nevertheless, or *(2)* the subject was aware of the internal response, but that awareness was not sufficient to maintain control. Both conclusions are inconsistent with this version of the awareness view.[12]

We would like to propose an alternative to these positions. The main point of this alternative is that the stimuli that are made contingent on a response can have a number of functions. One of those functions has been labeled a "reinforcing function"; that is, the stimulus increases the probability of responses that it follows. The other function we have labeled an "informational function"; that is, the stimulus provides information about the reinforced response. The problem, of course, is how to deal with the reinforcing and informational functions separately. One way of doing so would be to operationalize these functions in terms of temporal relationships. The reinforcing function is based on the temporal relationship of the response and the stimulus that is

[12] In either case, the awareness view would be in trouble. One could avoid all of these problems by stating that the label "operant conditioning" will be employed when the subject is not aware of the response, and the label "voluntary control" will be employed when the subject is aware of the response. One cannot, of course, argue with this position because the decision to define a term in a particular way is quite arbitrary.

contingent on that response; the informational function is based on the temporal relationship between the stimulus and the response on the next trial (i.e., the response-contingent stimulus acts as a discriminative stimulus for the next occurrence of the response). This analysis would lead one to predict that learning might be facilitated by breaking up the reinforcing and informational functions of response-contingent stimuli. In a discrete trial situation, one might present a reinforcing stimulus (some statement such as "very good" or "excellent") immediately after a response, and delay information about the degree to which the previous response was correct until the beginning of the next trial when the discriminative stimulus might be most useful.

It is important to emphasize that this position does not imply that the discrimination of internal responses is unimportant. As we pointed out earlier, it can provide information that is useful in guiding the next performance of the response. (Exteroceptive stimuli could, of course, play the same role as interoceptive response-produced stimuli; in this sense, we assign no special virtue to internal feedback from internal responses as discriminative stimuli). Also, as was pointed out in Footnote 11, internal responses can act as discriminative stimuli for other, "more standard" observable voluntary responses. In short, we would accept the view that the discrimination of response-correlated stimuli may play an important role in facilitating the establishment of control. What we do not agree with is the notion that such discriminations are necessary and sufficient, or even simply necessary, for establishing control. We believe that we know very little about the mechanisms of voluntary control and how it is established, and think that we would be farther ahead if we admitted our lack of knowledge.

We think that the operant approach is more adequate than the awareness views that we have discussed. However, we do not want to give the impression that we believe it to be without problems. Some of these were mentioned in the introduction. We also think that it does not deal adequately with the cognitive aspects of learning in human subjects. The main problem with the operant approach (and the awareness view, for that matter) is that we do not have a theory of the neurophysiological mechanisms involved in establishing control over a response. This is true, of course, for skeletal responses as well as for AS and CNS responses. We do not know any more about the mechanisms involved in training someone to wiggle his ears, for example, than we do about those involved in establishing control over skin temperature. The concern with the problem of mediation in much theorizing about biofeedback and the loose use of terms such as "voluntary" stem in large part from the absence of such a theory.

But whatever its difficulties, the operant view seems to be the most fruitful at present if for no other reason than that there is currently no alternative view whose concepts and methodology are as empirically rigorous and whose theoretical potentials are as rich. This point can be illustrated by the operant analysis of stimulus control over the response. As we noted in the previous section, most of the researchers who accept the awareness view deal with this problem vaguely by talking about voluntary control. If we turn to the operant approach, it becomes obvious immediately that there is a variety of precisely defined types of stimulus control that can be established. We may, for example, want to produce a general change in response level when a subject is placed in a given situation. Or, we may want to produce a change in the level of response that generalizes over a wide variety of situations. Or, we may want to produce a change only when a particular exteroceptive discriminative stimulus is presented, and so on. It seems to us that this operant analysis of types of stimulus control is more rigorous and richer than the alternatives that are available at present, as well as more useful in therapeutic settings. For example, we may not want to establish "voluntary" control over a response in the sense that the subject can increase or decrease the rate of response when he chooses to do so. Perhaps we would prefer to produce a low operant level of response that generalizes across a wide variety of situations. An obvious case is provided by blood pressure in labile hypertensives. It might be preferable to employ a training procedure that leads to a general lowering of blood pressure in labile hypertensives rather than the ability to raise or lower blood pressure to particular stimuli when desired.

One final point: One might argue that we have created a straw man (or, perhaps more accurately, straw approach) in our characterization of the awareness approach. We do not think that this is so. But, even if it is, we believe that a discussion of the awareness view was necessary, because many who would reject it in the explicit and bald form that we have stated it have, nevertheless, accepted it implicitly. The basic principle of the awareness view is, at best, a speculative hypothesis without much empirical support; it is not a self-evident axiom. If our discussion has no other function than to make such people "aware" of the inadequacy of this often implicitly accepted approach, it will have performed a useful function.

REFERENCES

Alexander, A. B., Holland, P. W., & Wallace, H. M. Training and transfer of training effects in EMG biofeedback assisted muscular relaxation. Proceedings of the Soci-

ety for Psychophysiological Research, Fifteenth Annual Meeting, Toronto, Canada, 1975 (Abstract).
Alston, W. P. Conceptual prolegomena to a psychological theory of intentional action. In S. C. Brown (Ed.), *Philosophy of psychology.* London: Macmillan, 1974.
Babb, M. I., & Chase, M. H. Masseteric and digastric reflex activity during conditioned sensorimotor rhythm. *Electroencephalography and Clinical Neurophysiology,* 1974, *36,* 357–365.
Beninger, R. J., Kendall, S. B., & Vanderwolf, C. H. The ability of rats to discriminate their own behaviors. *Canadian Journal of Psychology,* 1974, *28,* 79–91.
Berlyne, D. E. Behaviorism? Cognitive theory? Humanistic psychology?—To Hull with them all! *Canadian Psychological Review,* 1975, *16,* 69–80.
Black, A. H. Operant conditioning of heart rate under curare (Technical Report No. 12). Hamilton, Ontario: Department of Psychology, McMaster University, October 1967.
Black, A. H. Autonomic aversive conditioning in infrahuman subjects. In F. R. Brush (Ed.), *Aversive conditioning and learning.* New York: Academic Press, 1971. Pp. 3–104. (a)
Black, A. H. The direct control of neural processes by reward and punishment. *American Scientist,* 1971, *59,* 236–245. (b)
Black, A. H. The operant conditioning of central nervous system electrical activity. In G. H. Bower (Ed.), *The psychology of learning and motivation.* Vol. 6. New York: Academic Press, 1972. Pp. 35–68.
Black, A. H. Operant autonomic conditioning: The analysis of response mechanisms. In P. A. Obrist, A. H. Black, J. Brener, & L. V. DiCára (Eds.), *Cardiovascular psychophysiology: Current issues in response mechanisms, biofeedback and methodology.* Chicago: Aldine, 1974. Pp. 229–250. (a)
Black, A. H. Summary comments. In P. A. Obrist, A. H. Black, J. Brener, & L. V. DiCara (Eds.), *Cardiovascular psychophysiology.* Chicago: Aldine, 1974. Pp. 565–592. (b)
Black, A. H., & Young, G. A. Constraints on the operant conditioning of drinking. In R. M. Gilbert & J. R. Millenson (Eds.), *Reinforcement: Behavioral analyses.* New York: Academic Press, 1972. Pp. 35–50.
Blanchard, E. B., Scott, R. W., Young, L. D., & Haynes, M. R. The effects of feedback signal information content on the long-term self-control of heart rate. *Journal of General Psychology,* 1974, *91,* 175–187.
Blanchard, E. B., & Young, L. B. Self-control of cardiac functioning: A promise as yet unfulfilled. *Psychological Bulletin,* 1973, *79,* 145–163.
Blanchard, E. B., & Young, L. D. Clinical applications of biofeedback training: A review of evidence. *Archives of General Psychiatry,* 1974, *30,* 573–589.
Blanchard, E. B., Young, L. D., & McLeod, P. Awareness of heart activity and self-control of heart rate. *Psychophysiology,* 1972, *9*(1), 63–68.
Brener, J. A general model of voluntary control applied to the phenomena of learned cardiovascular change. In P. A. Obrist, A. H. Black, J. Brener, & L. V. DiCara (Eds.), *Cardiovascular psychophysiology.* Chicago: Aldine, 1974. Pp. 365–391.
Brener, J., & Jones, J. M. Interoceptive discrimination in intact humans: Detection of cardiac activity. *Physiology and Behavior,* 1974, *13,* 763–767.
Brown, B. B. Recognition of aspects of consciousness through association with EEG alpha activity represented by a light signal. *Psychophysiology,* 1970, *6*(4), 442–452.
Brown, B. B. Awareness of EEG-subjective activity relationships detected within a closed feedback system. *Psychophysiology,* 1971, *7*(3), 451–464.
Deese, J. & Hulse, S. H. *The psychology of learning.* New York: McGraw-Hill, 1967.

Diamond, S., Balvin, R. S., & Diamond, R. F. *Inhibition and choice.* New York: Harp and Row, 1963.

Donelson, F. E. Discrimination and control of human heart rate. Unpublished doctora dissertation, Cornell University, 1966.

Engel, B. T. Operant conditioning of cardiac function: A status report. *Psychophysiology,* 1972, *9,* 161–177.

Engel, B. T. Electroencephalographic and blood pressure correlates of operantly conditioned heart rate in the restrained monkey. *Pavlovian Journal of Biological Science,* 1974, *9,* 222–232.

Engel, B. T., & Bleecker, E. R. Application of operant conditioning techniques to the control of the cardiac arrhythmias. In P. A. Obrist, A. H. Black, J. Brener, & L. V. DiCara (Eds.), *Cardiovascular psychophysiology.* Chicago: Aldine, 1974. Pp. 456–476.

Engel, B. T., & Gottlieb, S. H. Differential operant conditioning of heart rate in the restrained monkey. *Journal of Comparative and Physiological Psychology,* 1970, *78*(2), 217–225.

Fetz, E. D. Operant control of single unit activity and correlated motor responses. In M. H. Chase (Ed.), *Perspectives in the brain sciences.* Vol. 2. *Operant control of brain activity.* Los Angeles: Brain Information Service/Brain Research Institute, 1974, Pp. 61–90.

Fetz, E. D., & Finocchio, D. V., Operant conditioning of specific patterns of neural and muscular activity. *Science,* 1971, *174,* 431–435.

Fields, C. I. Instrumental conditioning of the rat cardiac control systems. *Proceedings of the National Academy of Sciences,* 1970, *65,* 293–299.

Fox, S. S., & Rudell, A. P. Operant controlled neural event: Formal and systematic approach to electrical coding of behavior in brain. *Science,* 1968, *162,* 1299–1302.

Fox, S. S., & Rudell, A. P. Operant controlled neural event: Functional independence in behavioral coding by early and late components of the visual cortical evoked response in cats. *Journal of Neurophysiology,* 1970, *33,* 548–561.

Gaarder, K. Control of states of consciousness. *Archives of General Psychiatry,* 1971, *25,* 429–447.

Gatchel, R. J. Frequency of feedback and learned heart rate control. *Journal of Experimental Psychology,* 1974, *103*(2), 274–283.

Gibson, E. J. The development of perception as an adaptive process. *American Scientist,* 1970, *58,* 98–107.

Goldfried, M. R., & Merbaum, M. *Behavior change through self-control.* New York: Holt, 1973.

Harris, A. H., Gilliam, W. J., Findley, J. D., & Brady, J. V. Instrumental conditioning of large magnitude, daily, 12-hour blood pressure elevations in the baboon. *Science,* 1973, *182,* 175–177.

Hebb, D. O. *The organization of behavior: A neuropsychological theory.* New York: Wiley, 1949.

Honig, W. K. (Ed.). *Operant behavior: Areas of research and application.* New York: Appleton, 1966.

Howe, R. C., & Sterman, M. B. Somatosensory system evoked potentials during waking behavior and sleep in the cat. *Electroencephalography and Clinical Neurophysiology,* 1973, *34,* 605–618.

Hudgins, C. V. Conditioning and the voluntary control of the pupillary light reflex. *Journal of General Psychology,* 1933, *8,* 3–51.

Hull, C. L. *Hypnosis and suggestibility.* New York: Appleton, 1933.

e, J., & Egeth, H. *The psychology of learning.* New York: McGraw-

earning: IV. Experimental studies of learning. In C. Murchison (Ed.), *of general experimental psychology.* Worcester, Mass.: Clark University 34. Pp. 497–570.

The concept of volition in experimental psychology. In F. P. Clarke & M. C. (Eds.), *Philosophical essays in honor of Edgar Arthur Singer, Jr.* Freeport, Books for Libraries Press, 1969. Pp. 115–137.

/. *Principles of psychology.* New York: Holt, 1890.

, J. Operant control of the EEG alpha rhythm and some of its reported effects on onsciousness. In C. Tart (Ed.), *Altered states of consciousness.* New York: Wiley, 1969.

fer, F. H., & Phillips, J. S. *Learning foundations of behavior therapy.* New York: Wiley, 1970.

imble, G. A., & Perlmuter, L. C. The problem of volition. *Psychological Review,* 1970, *77,* 361–384.

Kinsman, R. A., O'Banion, K., Robinson, S., & Staudenmayer, H. Continuous biofeedback and discrete posttrial verbal feedback in *frontalis* muscle relaxation training. *Psychophysiology,* 1975, *12*(1), 30–35.

Lang, P. J. Learned control of human heart rate in a computer directed environment. In P. A. Obrist, A. H. Black, J. Brener, & L. V. DiCara (Eds.), *Cardiovascular psychophysiology.* Chicago: Aldine, 1974. Pp. 392–405.

Lang, P. J., & Twentyman, C. T. Learning to control heart rate: Binary vs analogue feedback. *Psychophysiology,* 1974, *11*(6), 616–629.

Linnstaedter, L., & Perachio, A. A. Operant control and the functional significance of lateral geniculate spikes. In M. H. Chase (Ed.), *Operant control of brain activity; Perspectives in the brain sciences.* Vol. 2. Los Angeles: Brain Information Service/Brain Research Institute, 1974. Pp. 91–104.

Lynch, J. J., Paskewitz, D. A., & Orne, M. T. Some factors in the feedback control of human alpha rhythm. *Psychosomatic Medicine,* 1974, *36*(5), 399–410.

Mackintosh, H. J. *The psychology of animal learning.* London: Academic Press, 1975.

Mandler, G., & Kahn, M. Discrimination of changes in heart rate: Two unsuccessful attempts. *Journal of the Experimental Analysis of Behavior,* 1960, *3,* 21–25.

Miller, J. G. *Unconsciousness.* New York: Wiley, 1942.

Miller, N. E. Learning of visceral and glandular responses. *Science,* 1969, *163,* 434–445.

Miller, N. E., & Banuazizi, A. Instrumental learning by curarized rats of a specific visceral response, intestinal or cardiac. *Journal of Comparative and Physiological Psychology,* 1968, *65,* 1–7.

Miller, N. E., & DiCara, L. V. Instrumental learning of heart rate changes in curarized rats: Shaping and specificity to discriminative stimulus. *Journal of Comparative and Physiological Psychology,* 1967, *63,* 12–19.

Mostofsky, D. I. (Ed.). *Stimulus generalization.* Stanford, Cal.: Stanford University Press, 1965.

Obrist, P. A., Black, A. H., Brener, J., & DiCara, L. V. (Eds.). *Cardiovascular psychophysiology.* Chicago: Aldine, 1974.

Paskewitz, D., Lynch, J., Orne, M., & Costello, J. The feedback control of alpha activity: Conditioning or disinhibition? *Psychophysiology,* 1970, *6,* 637–638 (Abstract).

Platt, J. R. Percentile reinforcement: Paradigms for experimental analysis of response shaping. In G. H. Bower (Ed.), *The psychology of learning and motivation.* Vol. 7. New York: Academic Press, 1973.

Reynolds, G. S., Discrimination and emission of temporal interval, by pigeons. *Journal of the Experimental Analysis of Behavior,* 1966, *9,* 65–68.

Roberts, L. E., Lacroix, J. M., & Wright, M. Comparative studies of operant electrodermal and heart rate conditioning in curarized rats. In P. A. Obrist, A. H. Black, J. Brener, & L. V. DiCara (Eds.), *Cardiovascular psychophysiology.* Chicago: Aldine, 1974.

Rosenfeld, J. P. Evoked potential conditioning in neuroscience research. In M. H. Chase (Eds.), *Operant control of brain activity; Perspectives in the Brain Sciences.* Vol. 2. Los Angeles: Brain Information Service/Brain Research Institute, 1974. Pp. 105–144.

Rosenfeld, J. P., & Hetzler, B. E. Operant-controlled evoked responses: Discrimination of conditioned and normally occurring components. *Science,* 1973, *181,* 767–769.

Rosenfeld, J. P., Hetzler, B. E., Birkel, P. A., & Kowatch, R. A. Operant conditioned potentials, centrally evoked at random intervals. Xeroxed manuscript, 1975.

Saltz, E. *The cognitive bases of human learning.* Homewood, Ill.: Dorsey Press, 1971.

Schwartz, G. E. Biofeedback, self-regulation, and the patterning of physiological processes. *American Scientist,* 1975, *63,* 314–324.

Skinner, B. F. *The behavior of organisms: An experimental analysis.* New York: Appleton, 1938.

Stern, R. M. Detection of one's own spontaneous GSRs. *Psychonomic Science,* 1972, *29,* 354–356.

Sutherland, N. S., & Mackintosh, N. J. *Mechanisms of animal discrimination learning.* New York: Academic Press, 1971.

Tapp, J. T. (Ed.). *Reinforcement and behavior.* New York: Academic Press, 1969.

Taub, E., & Berman, A. J. Avoidance conditioning in the absence of relevant proprioceptive and exteroceptive feedback. *Journal of Comparative and Physiological Psychology,* 1963, *56,* 1012–1016.

Taub, E., & Berman, A. J. Movement and learning. In S. J. Freeman (Ed.), *The neurophysiology of spatially oriented behavior.* Homewood, Ill.: Dorsey Press, 1968.

Teuber, H. L. Perception. In J. Field, H. W. Magoun, & V. E. Hall (Eds.), *Handbook of physiology, neurophysiology III.* Washington, D.C.: American Physiological Society, 1960. Pp. 1595–1668.

Travis, T. A., Kondo, C. Y., & Knott, J. R. Parameters of eyes-closed alpha enhancement. *Psychophysiology,* 1974, *11*(6), 674–681.

Travis, T. A., Kondo, C. Y., & Knott, J. R. Alpha enhancement research: A review. *Biological Psychiatry,* 1975, *10*(1), 69–89.

Vanderwolf, C. H. Limbic-diencephalic mechanisms of voluntary movement. *Psychological Review,* 1971, *78,* 83–113.

Verhave, T. On the nature of voluntary behavior. Unpublished manuscript, 1966.

Von Holst, E. Relations between the central nervous system and the peripheral organs. *British Journal of Animal Behaviour,* 1954, *2,* 89–94.

Welch, L. The relationship between conditioning and higher learning. *Journal of General Psychology,* 1955, *53,* 221–229.

Welford, A. T. *Fundamentals of skill.* London: Methuen, 1968.

Wyrwicka, E., & Sterman, M. B. Instrumental conditioning of sensorimotor cortex EEG spindles in the waking cat. *Physiology and Behavior,* 1968, *3,* 703–707.

6

Critical Issues in Therapeutic Applications of Biofeedback*

NEAL E. MILLER
BARRY R. DWORKIN
The Rockefeller University

This chapter will begin with a theoretical analysis of how the acquisition and reinforcement of symptoms are related to strategies for their therapy. As an example of the kind of specific hypothesis that is needed to guide further investigations on both prevention and therapy, we shall advance a tentative one about how the symptom of essential hypertension might be reinforced. The rest of the chapter will deal with what we consider to be the highest priority needs in the development of therapeutic applications of biofeedback. The first of these is a more rigorous evaluation of those applications that seem to have been most successful. While a number of the new applications of biofeedback have yielded preliminary results promising enough to merit a more rigorous evaluation, none of them has been tested in the ways that are necessary to prove scientifically that they have any specific therapeutic value (Blanchard & Young, 1974). We shall discuss the most important factors that can produce a false impression of therapeutic value and hence must be dealt with in order to prove the therapeutic efficacy of an application of biofeedback. Finally, we shall deal with the need to learn the laws that will allow us to design the

* Work described from this laboratory was supported by U.S. Public Health Service research grant MH 13189 awarded to the senior author.

most effective methods of training and shall suggest what we believe are some of the most profitable variables to investigate in determining these laws.

THEORETICAL GUIDES TO PRACTICE

Biofeedback is an aid to learning but, paradoxically, the symptoms that are most suitable for treatment by this method may not always be those that are learned.

Symptoms That Are Primarily Learned

At one extreme of a continuum of learned versus organic symptoms are those that are entirely functional or, in other words, learned because they are instrumental in producing a reward. The learning of such symptoms has been discussed in greater detail by Dollard and Miller (1950). Such symptoms are learned on the basis of the rewards that they produce. Rewards are sometimes called *reinforcements* by learning theorists, and *secondary gains* by psychiatrists. A reduction in a strong drive such as fear (or anxiety, as it is called when its source is vague) functions as a reward. Success in achieving a goal, or receiving sympathetic attention when one is lonely, also function as rewards. The problem of defining rewards is discussed in more detail elsewhere (Miller, 1959, 1963).

Because rewards may function automatically, the patient often is completely unaware of the connection between the reward and his symptom. Furthermore, even though the symptom is rewarded, its net result may be to increase, rather than to alleviate, the patient's misery. This is because immediate reinforcements are stronger than delayed ones, so that an immediate transient reduction in misery may have more of an effect in maintaining a symptom than does a delayed increase in misery in eliminating it. An example is the problem drinker who is reinforced by an immediate reduction in anxiety that is not canceled out by the delayed effects of a hangover and various socioeconomic problems the next day.

Need to Deal with Underlying Motivation

Theoretically, it should take relatively strong drive and reward to motivate the learning and prolonged performance of an extremely troublesome symptom. Thus, it is easy to see how the relatively weak rewards at the therapist's disposal might not be sufficient to produce the learning and performance of a response strong enough to prevent the occurrence of such a symptom. In such a case, one also can see that, if the therapist is able by his personal relationship to the patient to produce motivation strong enough to suppress the symptom, the drive motivating the symptom will remain so that the patient may learn a second symptom to deal with this drive or may relapse to the old symptom once the direct rewards from favorable attention by the therapist are removed. Frequently, the foregoing types of failures do occur; one should not expect the use of biofeedback to be any exception to such a possibility.

Theoretically, the solution to the foregoing difficulty is to discover the drive or social need that is the basis for the reward that is maintaining the symptom and to teach the patient a more adaptive response to that drive. If the drive is an unrealistic fear, it may be reduced by the related methods of extinction, counterconditioning, and learning an improved discrimination between what is dangerous and what is safe. With a fear that is realistic, the patient may be taught some coping response that is more effective than the symptom (Miller, 1975). If the drive is a social need, the patient can be taught alternate means of achieving that need. A combination of weakening the drive and learning alternative means of dealing with it is used to reward responses strong enough to compete with the symptom. Where biofeedback can be applied, it is useful because it provides immediate reinforcement for the response that competes with the symptom.

In practice, therapists have found that a procedure analogous to the foregoing theoretical description often is required. Thus, Freud early learned that merely suppressing a symptom by a hypnotic command was not an effective way of dealing with it. As behavior therapists have advanced to the treatment of more difficult cases, they also are finding that it is necessary to discover and deal with the real phobia, which may be different from the presenting symptom, and/or to teach the patient alternative means of solving his problem, such as reasonable self-assertiveness (Porter, 1968). There is no reason to believe that therapists using biofeedback should not run into similar problems and have to adopt similar strategies.

Use of Instrumentation to Monitor Responses

In cases in which the symptom involves a physiologically measurable psychosomatic response, such as muscle tension, elevated blood pressure, changes in heart rate, or galvanic skin responses, the recording of such responses may be useful to help both the therapist and the patient to locate more exactly the circumstances under which such responses occur and to monitor the progress of the therapy. Feedback from such a symptom while the patient reports different aspects of his current situation, or attempts to relive certain experiences, may help to convince him that the symptom really is related to specific emotions, desires, or conflicts.

Symptoms That Are Primarily Organic

The fact that the etiology of a symptom is organic does not mean that a response to control that symptom cannot be learned. For example, some cases of paroxysmal tachycardia (i.e., when the heart suddenly starts beating very rapidly) can be arrested by suddenly taking a deep breath. In this case, the visceral consequence of a learned skeletal response arrests a visceral symptom of organic origin.

Control of Premature Ventricular Contractions

To give another example, certain types of premature ventricular contractions (PVCs), commonly described as the heart skipping a beat, are caused by the presence of a second and delayed conduction path from the pacemaker in the atrium to the ventricle, or by a second pacemaker in the ventricle. If the abnormal signal arrives after the ventricle has recovered from the refractory period following its normal contraction, it causes a second contraction. This PVC is of purely organic origin. But if the heart is speeded up so that the second normal beat occurs before the abnormal impulse, the latter will occur during the refractory period of the second beat and hence cannot cause an abnormal contraction. Patients with this kind of PVC can be taught to stop a condition called "bigeminy," in which a normal beat alternates with an abnormal one, by speeding up the heart through exercise. But sometimes an attack of paroxysmal bigeminy makes a patient feel weak, so that he does not feel like exercise, or the social situation may make vigorous exercise inappropriate.

In one such case, Thomas Pickering in our laboratory trained a patient to speed up his heart rate voluntarily without the obvious use of exercise, changes in breathing, or other gross skeletal maneuvers. In this training, the reward was a signal indicating that the subject had succeeded in producing the desired change. First the signal was a light that flashed when the change had occurred; during later trials, the patient watched the needle on a meter that indicated heart rate. Whether because of his high motivation or some innate talent, conceivably related to his symptom, this patient showed unusual ability to learn voluntary control of heart rate, becoming able to produce differences of 40 beats per minute between trials in which he was trying to decrease and those in which he was trying to increase his heart rate. He also became able to arrest most of his attacks of bigeminy by producing voluntary increases in heart rate (Pickering & Miller, in press).

In another patient who learned voluntary control over bigeminy, Pickering used the trace of the ECG on an oscilloscope to inform the patient whether or not his heart was beating normally. Although, in this case, the abnormal rhythm also could be stopped by exercise, the patient had to increase to a higher level when he stopped it in this way than he did when he used the response he had learned by feedback. This result suggests that there are more learnable responses that can affect PVCs. The earlier pioneering work by Weiss and Engel (1971) and Engel and Bleecker (1974) also indicates that there are a number of learnable responses that can control different types of PVCs. Pharmacological tests showed that, in one case, the voluntary control of PVCs involved an increase in sympathetic activity, whereas, in another case, it involved an increase in vagal activity.

Why Certain Organic Symptoms Can Be Easier to Treat Than Functional Ones

If a symptom is primarily organic, it does not need to be motivated by a strong drive and reinforced by a strong reward. In this case, the removal of the symptom will not cause any problems for the patient. So there will be no motivation to oppose learning, to produce a relapse, or to reward the learning of a new symptom. Thus, if a learnable response that can suppress the symptom is available in the patient's innate repertoire (and, of course, such a response may *not* be available for many organic conditions), the treatment can be permanently successful.

But if there is nothing to oppose learning a response that will suppress the symptom, why do the patients not learn such a response by themselves? One answer is that more patients than we realize may learn to control symptoms, but physicians are less likely to become aware of such patients because they do not need treatment. Certainly some such learning does occur. Thus, Hughlings Jackson (1958) reports cases in which patients with epilepsy had discovered various ways of reacting to an aura in such a way as to prevent the attack that it predicted. For example, one man whose convulsion started with twitching in the toe learned that he could avert the full attack by having his son straighten and rub his leg.

Cardiac Arrhythmias as an Example. One reason a patient may fail to learn a response that could inhibit his symptom is that such a response may be extremely unlikely to occur spontaneously; it may have to be shaped by careful training. For example, a heart rate change large enough to stop an attack of paroxysmal bigeminy is unlikely to occur spontaneously; in the case of the patient described above, such a change had to be shaped by rewarding first smaller and then progressively larger increases.

There are a number of other reasons for which one will not expect a patient to learn without aid to control his PVCs by voluntarily speeding the heart without obvious physical exercise. In the first place, he will not know that speeding his heart rate can interrupt the PVCs, nor will he know it is possible for him to learn to speed his heart. Furthermore, his untrained perception of small changes in heart rate is so poor that he cannot shape himself without initial help from instrumentally augmented feedback. Conditions in which the failure to learn is caused by factors like the foregoing, rather than by a strong motivation and reward for the symptom, are those for which training by biofeedback may be expected to be of especial therapeutic value. And, indeed, some of the apparently most successful applications of biofeedback to date have been in treating responses that appear to be primarily of organic etiology. Similarly, Orne (1974) reports that hypnosis is more effective in treating pain that is primarily of organic origin than pain that is functional in achieving a goal.

Torticollis and Certain Paralyses. Spasmodic torticollis, as treated by Brudny, Grynbaum, and Korein (1974) and somewhat differently by Cleeland (1973), appears to be another condition, presumably organic, that meets the foregoing specifications. Apparently, these patients need to be shaped to produce the relaxation of the spastic muscles and the contraction of the atrophied ones that will enable them to hold their heads in a normal position. They are not highly sensitive to slight spontaneous variations in muscle tension so that, without augmentation of feedback by use of electromyographic recording they are unlikely to learn by themselves.

According to reports by Basmajian, Kukulka, Narayan, and Takebe (1975), by Brudny, Korein, Grynbaum, Weinstein, and Frankel (1974), by Bechtereva, Kambarova, Smirnov, Tchernigovskaya, and Shandurina (1976), and by Inglis, Campbell, and McDonald (1976), certain cases of spastic and other forms of paralysis after cerebral vascular accidents may be treated by procedures similar to those used for torticollis. Their reports are challenging and merit rigorous replication.

In this case, an additional factor could be involved. In recording from the sciatic nerves of animals paralyzed by curare, Koslovskaya, Vertes, and Miller (1976) found that a classically conditioned response to painful electrical stimulation of the rear paws was transient while eventually even the unconditioned response to the painful stimulation gradually disappeared. This result contrasted with the persistence of the conditioned and unconditioned responses if they were rewarded by escape from and/or avoidance of the electric shock, or even if the depth of curarization was reduced so that slight muscular contractions, which would be expected to produce some proprioceptive feedback, could be observed in the EMG. Perhaps the procedure of eliciting central commands without any peripheral response produces a profound inhibition. If such a habit of profound inhibition should be established during a transient period of complete paralysis of a muscle group after a stroke, it could interfere with the use of that group after some of the physical causes of paralysis were removed in the process of recovery.

Correcting Interference with Interoceptive Feedback. If the lesion or other organic condition has its main effect by removing, or confusing, the interoceptive feedback for the desired response, replacing that feedback by instrumentation should be especially effective in shaping that response. The possibilities for learning are increased greatly by the fact that the new feedback does not have to resemble the normal type; prompt rewards, escape from punishment, or signals for the avoidance of punishment can be effective. As Koslovskaya, Vertes, and Miller (1973) have shown, when all normal types of feedback, such as proprioception, have been completely eliminated by paralysis by curare, a rat can still learn to fire his sciatic nerve if he is reinforced promptly by a reward or by escape from and/or avoidance of punishment.

The foregoing theoretical analysis suggests that it will be especially profitable for therapists interested in using instrumentally augmented feedback to search for symptoms produced by an interference with the patient's normal feedback mechanisms.

Symptoms That Are Both Organic and Functional

Many symptoms will be expected to fall in between the two extremes described above. In fact, even the symptoms with the purest functional etiology have some organic basis in that the responses that are learned must be within the repertoire of the species. And the responses in that repertoire are organized into an innate hierarchy of those that are more or less likely to occur (Miller & Dollard, 1941). This hierarchy will have an effect on which symptom is most likely to be learned.

On the other hand, symptoms that initially were purely organic may become consolidated by the new learning that is necessary in order to adjust to the symptom. The profound inhibition that may possibly be learned during an initial state of complete paralysis could be an example of this type. Bechtereva *et al.* (1976) have called this process "stabilization."

In other cases, an organic symptom may become instrumental to achieving some additional goal and hence be strongly reinforced. For example, a headache initially arising from the innate tendency of a stressful situation to cause tension in muscles of the forehead and neck may be used as a weapon to force the other members of the family to keep quiet. Success in achieving this goal may be a strong reward that increases the tendency to have headaches. Then any therapeutic success in using feedback from the EMG to train the patient to relax will interfere with the goal achieved by the headaches, punish the relaxation, and create conditions more strongly motivating the tension. In this case, if the therapist wants to avoid a relapse, he will have to give his patient an alternative and better way to achieve his goal; for example, to insist, without using the excuse of a headache, on a reasonable amount of quiet or to go to a quieter part of the house.

Shift from Organic to Functional

When a symptom produced by a *transient* organic cause produces a strong secondary gain, there is a theoretical possibility that it can persist as a primarily functional symptom after the organic cause has disappeared. Thus, a transient infection or injury might induce a headache, stomach ache, backache, or other symptom which could be maintained by the strong reward of any one of a number of secondary gains after the initial organic cause had disappeared.

Shift from Functional to Organic

Finally, there is the converse possibility that a symptom can start out as being primarily instrumental in achieving a goal and end up by producing an organic change that perpetuates the symptom. An obvious example is the preadolescent girl who learns to stoop to avoid being conspicuously tall until the bones in her spinal colunn develop a curved pattern that can be corrected only by surgery. Similarly, it is thought that some cases of essential hypertension may initially be primarily functional but eventually produce enough kidney damage to produce an irreversible organic hypertension.

When Symptomatic Treatment Is Sufficient

From the foregoing analysis, it should be clear that the more important a symptom is in solving an urgent problem for the patient, the more necessary it will be for the therapist to teach the patient other solutions to that problem. Some symptoms that are primarily functional, however, may have been learned under strong motivations and rewards that were present during an earlier set of circumstances in the patient's life (e.g., infancy) but are largely absent during his present conditions of living. As the original strong reinforcement is phased out, such symptoms may be maintained by producing weaker reinforcements or even, as a superstitious response, maintained by occasional chance reinforcements. In yet other cases, an overlearned but outdated symptom could persist because its regular occurrence in a given situation prevents the occurrence of, and hence the chance to learn, other responses that would be more strongly rewarded. Finally, there may be a vicious circle in which, for example, a psychosomatic symptom causes anxiety which, in turn, maintains that symptom. In cases of the foregoing kinds, we would not expect the removal of the symptom to create problems for the patient. Thus, in such cases, a direct attempt to use biofeedback or other techniques to eliminate the symptom should succeed without the necessity to work on any strong underlying motivation.

Where the conditions are clear-cut and known to the therapist, he can be guided by the foregoing theoretical analysis. In the initial stages of the therapy of many patients, the conditions are likely to be unknown. In this case, it is hoped that the theoretical analysis will be able to help the therapist to understand and to cope with the difficulties he is encountering. In many such cases, the problem of whether or not a direct attack on the symptom can succeed or whether or not an underlying motivation will have to be discovered and dealt with will be a problem to be settled by empirical test. For example, in one such empirical test, Baker (1969) has found that treating enuresis by a device that sounded a warning buzzer at the first sign of moisture did not result in any symptom substitution but had the opposite effect of producing a general reduction in symptoms of emotional strain. Incidentally, this type of treatment of enuresis (Mowrer & Mowrer, 1938) is one of the earliest examples of a therapeutic device using instrumentation to augment feedback.

A Hypothesis about the Reinforcement of Essential Hypertension

The foregoing theoretical analysis has, of necessity, been rather general. It is hoped that such a general analysis will be of some aid in guiding therapy and prevention and in stimulating the research that will lead to its refinement or rejection. What we really need, however, is additional specific and experimentally testable hypotheses dealing with specific conditions. As a start in that direction, the following hypothesis is advanced about how the learning of hypertension might be reinforced in certain cases.

There is considerable evidence from physiological experiments showing that baroreceptor stimulation has an inhibitory effect on the reticular formation and on cortical arousal. Koch (1932) observed that stimulating baroreceptors by inflating a balloon in a chronic carotid stump caused dogs to become less active and more relaxed; strong stimulation caused them to go to sleep. Bonvallet, Dell, and Hiebel (1953, 1954) showed that stimulation of the nerves from the baroreceptors inhibited the reticular formation and reversed the EEG signs of cortical arousal. This phenomenon was so robust that Dell (personal communication) now routinely uses it to produce delta-wave sleep for further research on sleep. An effect great enough to put an animal to sleep certainly is strong enough to be of major functional significance. Furthermore, Bartorelli, Bizzi, Libretti, and Zanchetti (1960) have observed that reducing baroreceptor stimulation in decerebrate cats elicits sham rage while increasing such stimulation inhibits it. In the light of such evidence, Lacey, Kagan, Lacey, and Moss (1963, p. 173) have advanced the hypothesis that, by stimulating the carotid sinus, elevated heart rate and blood pressure can lead to decreased sensory sensitivity. A considerable amount of evidence congruent with the application of this hypothesis to human subjects has been summarized in this and subsequent articles (Lacey & Lacey, 1970, 1974). It is known that, under great stress, which would be expected to increase blood pressure—for example, a mother saving her child from fire—people may be oblivious to pain. When life itself is at stake, there probably is a survival advantage in not being reactive to pain. Perhaps the baroreceptor effect on the reticular formation is one of the ways in which a reduced responsiveness to pain is achieved.

Meanwhile, another, different type of evidence has been accumulating to show that changes in blood pressure can be instrumentally learned in animals (Benson, Herd, Morse, & Kelleher, 1969; DiCara &

Miller, 1968; Harris, Gilliam, Findley, & Brady, 1973; Pappas, DiCara, & Miller, 1970) and in man (Benson, Shapiro, Tursky, & Schwartz, 1971; Miller, DiCara, Solomon, Weiss, & Dworkin, 1970; Miller, 1972a; Shapiro, Tursky, & Schwartz, 1970; Schwartz, 1972).

Dworkin has brought these two types of evidence together to advance a hypothesis about how, in some cases, the learning of human hypertension might be reinforced. His line of reasoning is that, in a situation in which a person is suffering from aversive stimulation, an increase in blood pressure will stimulate the carotid sinus and produce an inhibition of the reticular formation which, in turn, should decrease the strength of the aversiveness. Then this decrease in the strength of aversiveness should serve as a reward to reinforce the learning of the increase in blood pressure.

In this connection, it is interesting to note that barbiturates have effects that are similar to those of increased baroreceptor stimulation; these drugs produce a similar inhibition of the reticular formation and a similar inhibition of sham rage (Bartorelli *et al.*, 1960). In the presence of aversive stimulation, the injection of barbiturates is known to have a rewarding effect (Davis, Lulenski, & Miller, 1968) similar to that which, it is assumed, baroreceptor stimulation will have. In short, the hypothesis is that, when suffering from aversive stimulation, certain people may increase their blood pressure to calm down their reticular formation in the same way that others take a barbiturate to achieve the same effect.

While each link in the chain of logic in Dworkin's hypothesis seems theoretically possible, the practical problem is whether or not a reduction in aversiveness produced by carotid sinus stimulation is great enough to produce a strong enough reward for the learning and maintenance of the appreciable increases in blood pressure involved in essential hypertension. The schedules of reinforcement used by Harris *et al.* (1973) did cause baboons to learn and maintain elevations of blood pressure 30 mm Hg or more for long periods of time. Can the reduction in the aversiveness caused by stimulation of the carotid sinus produce similar results?

Not everybody develops essential hypertension. Theoretically, a person should be more likely to develop essential hypertension to the extent that he is genetically endowed with *(a)* unusual sensitivity to aversive stimulation, *(b)* unusually strong inhibition of the reticular formation from a given increase in blood pressure, and *(c)* unusual ability to learn increases in blood pressure. The vulnerability of such an individual would be further increased by *(d)* the degree to which his environment has subjected him to levels of aversive stimulation that can be reduced via inhibition of the reticular formation but not in other ways. In our present state of ignorance, it seems reasonable to suspect that the most effective level of aversive stimulation might be some intermediate one. With a level too low, there will not be enough aversiveness to reduce; while with a level too high, the proportion that can be reduced by increased carotid stimulation may be a fraction of the total too small to serve as an effective reward. On the other hand, its ability to put animals to sleep shows that baroreceptor stimulation can produce a strong effect.

The attractiveness of Dworkin's hypothesis is that it is possible to subject it, step by step, to rigorous experimental tests in order to determine whether or not it is worthy of clinical research. Such tests are under way in our laboratory. Furthermore, if true, it suggests strategies for prevention and therapy. For prevention, young people could theoretically be screened for lability in blood pressure, which presumably would be related to factors *(a)* and *(c)* and, for the factor *(b)*, the degree to which an increase in blood pressure produces an inhibition of cortical activation measured by the EEG.

Dworkin's hypothesis suggests that young people predicted to be especially vulnerable, or patients in the early stages of hypertension, should be specially trained in other methods of coping with aversive stimulation. For example, instead of suppressing the effects of a distracting noise by an increase in blood pressure, they should be trained to shut the door or seek a quieter environment; instead of suppressing anger by an increase in blood pressure, they should be trained in reasonable self-assertion. As one part of such training, used either for prevention or for therapy, the patient might try either to recall or to rehearse in role playing, various concrete experiences from his current life while recently developed devices (Pickering, Brucker, Frankel, Mathias, Dworkin, & Miller, 1976; Tursky, Shapiro, & Schwartz, 1972) are used to provide moment-to-moment measures of blood pressure. Such a procedure clearly showed one of our patients that incidents arousing anger elicited large increases in her blood pressure; it also may have helped her to learn how to vividly relive such incidents but without increases in blood pressure. It also would be extremely desirable to try, if possible, to use recording devices to teach the vulnerable person to increase the accuracy of his perception of changes in blood pressure (Miller, 1972b) in order to know when he should find some other way of reducing aversive stimulation and how well he is succeeding.

URGENCY OF MORE RIGOROUS EVALUATIONS OF THERAPEUTIC EFFECTIVENESS

A number of therapeutic applications of biofeedback have produced preliminary results that are promising enough to merit attempts at replication with more rigorous controls (Miller, 1974a). Such replication is essential because of the various factors, to be described below, that may well be producing spuriously encouraging results. To date, the therapeutic applications of biofeedback have had an exorbitantly high ratio of enthusiastic claims to evaluated fact. Thus, there is a real danger that this new approach will follow the cycle all too characteristic of new forms of treatment from overoptimistic enthusiasm to overpessimistic rejection. Such a course will endanger the support required for the hard work necessary to determine what value the therapy may have and how to improve it. Therefore, there is a greater need now for the careful evaluation of the most promising of the applications that already have been made than for the more glamorous task of pioneering pilot studies of new applications. It is hoped that journal editors and granting agencies will be responsive to this need (Miller, 1974b).

Blanchard and Young (1974) have reviewed in careful detail the current status of the evidence for the therapeutic effectiveness of various applications of biofeedback and have come to conclusions quite similar to those expressed in this chapter, namely, that the evidence is strong enough to justify, but weak enough to require, the performance of more rigorously controlled studies.

Some of the factors to be considered in evaluating the therapeutic effectiveness of biofeedback and other therapeutic techniques are discussed below.

Natural Recovery

The human body, including the brain, has a wonderful capacity to recover from a great variety of infections, physical injuries, and psychological trauma. Therefore the effectiveness of any treatment has to be compared with the rate of spontaneous remission and/or of recovery during a competing type of treatment.

Regression to the Mean

Many of the chronic conditions, such as headaches, to which biofeedback has been applied are subject to spontaneous fluctuations with periods of exacerbation followed by periods of relative remission. But the tendency for patients to come for treatment is far from random; they are much more likely to come when they feel considerably worse. Therefore, their next fluctuation is likely to be a regression toward the mean of feeling better. Such a regression is illustrated by a study in which Johnson, Karunas, and Epstein (1973) found that 62% of patients diagnosed as hypertensive showed a decline in systolic pressure without any treatment.

Furthermore, the termination of treatment is not random but is more likely to occur when the patient appears to have been cured. The double-selection factor exerts a strong bias in the direction of improvement between the beginning and end of treatment. This is one of the reasons it is important to follow up patients for an adequate period of time in order to see whether or not the apparently therapeutic effects persist. If the improvement has been an artifact of the double-selection factor, periods of exacerbation eventually should occur.

For any given patient, a number of previous treatments may have gone through the foregoing cycle and hence be described retrospectively as failures. If one is to contrast the success of a new treatment with the failure of previous ones, it is necessary to ascertain that the previous treatments did not produce transient successes and that the new treatment does produce a more long-lasting one.

Another selective error in the evaluation of new forms of treatment is the fact that there is a much greater probability that a study that shows a promising outcome will get published than will one that does not. By chance, 1 of every 20 studies will produce results reliable at the 5% level, and 1 of every 100 results reliable at the 1% level.

The foregoing considerations alone should make clear the need to repeat, with more rigorous controls, those studies that appear to have produced promising results. But there is another, and even more powerful, type of effect that can produce a misleading appearance of a therapeutic result.

Placebo Effects

The power that purely psychological factors can have on the physical well-being of the patient is shown by clinical observations on the effects of a placebo or, in other words, a pill containing a therapeutically inert substance, such as sugar, or a type of treatment that has no specific effect on the particular illness involved. The ubiquity and potency of placebo effects have been discussed in excellent reviews by Shapiro (1960, 1971). In order to avoid the placebo effect in evaluating the therapeutic action of drugs, pharmacologists have developed a double-blind procedure. In it, the patient is "blind" because he does not know whether he is receiving a presumably active agent or an inert placebo. But, because the placebo effect is known to vary with the enthusiasm of the physician, it is necessary that he be "blind" also. The foregoing model should be followed as closely as possible in studies evaluating the therapeutic effects of biofeedback. And where it is impossible to follow the model, an attempt should be made to achieve the same goal.

Unfortunately, placebo effects are particularly prominent with some of the symptoms that have been involved in biofeedback treatment. Thus, Shapiro (1960) reports that headaches respond flagrantly to placebo medication.

The importance of the placebo effect, even for a physiologically measured factor such as blood pressure, is illustrated by a study in which Grenfell, Briggs, and Holland (1963) found that, in 48 patients, a placebo pill produced a decrease in blood pressure that averaged 25 mm Hg for systolic and 12 mm Hg for diastolic pressure. Furthermore, the decrease was progressive, the maximum effect not being reached until at least 7 weeks.

Another double-blind study of hypertension, by Shapiro, Myers, Reiser, and Ferris (1954), illustrates the clinically well-established fact that the therapist's enthusiasm is an important factor in the results. Toward the latter part of this study, the enthusiasm of the young physician administering the drug was greatly reduced when he learned that he would be inducted into the army in 2 months and that, although the drug being tested was effective, it was not going to be superior to other drugs already on the market, as the investigators had hoped that it would be. The effects of his reduction in enthusiasm showed up in a sharp increase of the blood pressure of the patients under *both* the drug and the placebo conditions.

The impressiveness of the treatment also is an important factor in determining the size of the placebo effect. Because of the effects of impressiveness and of the therapist's enthusiasm, stable baseline measurements before a treatment begins cannot be used to rule out placebo effects unless neither the patient nor the therapist knows when the shift from baseline to active training begins. Similarly, a regression after treatment stops can be merely the termination of a placebo effect. Thus, the experimental design of treatment, followed by discontinuance of treatment, followed by resumption of treatment is not a good control for the placebo effect.

In some cases, it should be possible to design experiments in which neither the patient nor the therapist knows when the "feedback" is shifted from a tape recording to a genuine measurement of the patient's own responses. In other cases, such as recording of the EMG from the frontalis muscles, it may be possible for the subject to discover that the feedback is not genuine by the simple procedure of knitting his brows. But as a paper by Adler and Adler (1975) suggests, it may be possible to avoid this difficulty by letting the patients know that an electronic switch is being used that shuts off all feedback whenever a sudden large change occurs.

Specific Voluntary Control

One way to show that training has produced a specific effect, rather than merely having yielded a general placebo effect, is to test for the patient's ability to turn the symptom on and off upon request. Such a test is illustrated by a patient who had his spinal cord severed by a lesion at T4 and who had suffered from postural hypotension that prevented him from learning to walk with crutches and braces because he tended to faint whenever he was helped into an upright position. At first, this patient had little ability to control his blood pressure but, after training by Bernard Brucker at Goldwater Memorial Hospital, he exhibited the response recorded by Thomas Pickering in Figure 6.1. It seems unlikely that this prompt, specific, 24-mm Hg increase in diastolic pressure, which he could show consistently in response to requests, could have been a mere placebo effect. Furthermore, this patient reported deliberately using his ability voluntarily to raise his blood pressure to fight off postural hypotension as he subsequently learned to walk with crutches and braces. Occasionally, he

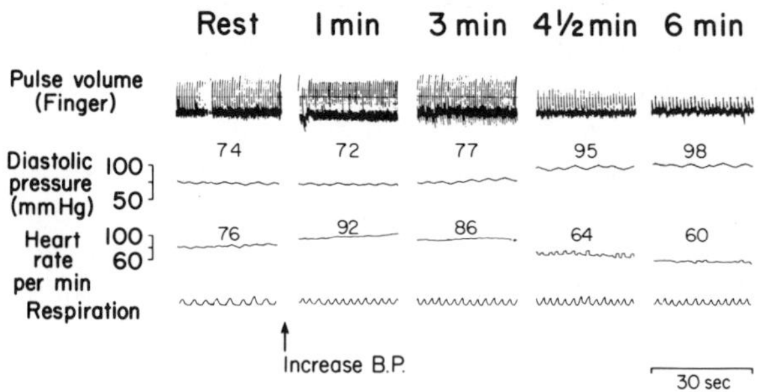

Figure 6.1 Pattern of responses involved in learned voluntary control of blood pressure by patient with spinal cord severed at T4. The patient was trained by Bernard Brucker at Goldwater Memorial Hospital and recorded by Thomas Pickering in the senior author's laboratory.

would feel his blood pressure fall and have to stop to raise it. Simila Engel and Bleecker (1974) report that patients who have learned control their PVCs can turn them on and off upon request. It see unlikely that this type of specific voluntary control could be a me placebo effect. Incidentally, these authors believe that practice i turning a symptom on as well as off aids in achieving voluntary con trol. Pickering and Miller (in press) have replicated training patients with PVCs to turn these symptoms on and off.

Patient Doing Something for Himself

One of the significant features of biofeedback training is that it gives the patient the opportunity—indeed, demands of him—to do something for himself rather than being the passive recipient of a therapeutic procedure of a physician. But learning to perform a coping response, if it is simple and effective enough, will be expected to reduce the patient's feeling of helplessness and anxiety (Weiss, 1971). Thus, there may be an important general therapeutic effect in addition to the specific value of the learned control. This effect is somewhat analogous to that of a placebo, but perhaps should be differentiated from it to the extent that it has a realistic foundation in the acquisition of a specific, useful degree of voluntary control.

Placebo Effect Merits More Research

From a scientific point of view, it is important to be able to distinguish the specific effects of a given treatment from the general, nonspecific placebo effects. This is because an increased understanding of the mechanism of a new type of treatment often leads to highly effective improvements in that type of treatment. It is a waste of time and effort, however, to mount a research program on the assumption that the specific features of a new treatment are producing specific effects when nothing more than a general placebo effect is involved. Furthermore, there is no need to use expensive, sophisticated equipment if flashing lights or a sugar pill can achieve the same results.

The very power of the nonspecific placebo effect that makes it such a nuisance in trying to determine the value of a specific type of treatment means that it is medically important. We do not yet understand enough about the variables affecting it and how these variables act to produce therapeutic changes. Thus, it is important to stop regarding it as a mere nuisance and to design studies to understand it in its own right.

...est Available Alternatives

...ediate, practical point of view, the most important ... whether or not a new form of treatment is more effec- ...est available alternative. Thus, now that there is pro- ...ence that biofeedback may be successful in some appli- ... important next step is to design studies to evaluate its ...ss in each case in comparison with that of the best alterna- ... of treatment. Often new treatments are administered with ...usiasm and hence produce larger placebo effects. All too ...oth the enthusiasm and the effects decline. In comparing ...lback with other forms of treatment, one should be as clever as ...le in seeing that both are administered with equal enthusiasm. ... studies that include long-term follow-up, and some of the other ...ects to be discussed below, show that a particular application of ...ofeedback is indeed superior to other available alternatives, the ...ractical implication is clear. If the alternative is superior, it may still ...be worthwhile to see whether or not the particular application of the new technique of biofeedback can be improved enough to reverse the verdict. But, in this latter case, it will be important to be sure that the therapeutic effects of the biofeedback are not mere placebo effects.

Comparison of Effects of Different Parameters

Somewhat analogous to the comparison of a new treatment with the best possible alternative is a comparison of different versions of that treatment. For example, in evaluating the effectiveness of training epileptic patients to respond with a specific brain rhythm, the sensorimotor one (Sterman, 1973), it will be useful to determine the effectiveness of training them to respond to rhythms somewhat slower or faster than that one. Such a comparison will have two merits: It may discover a better rhythm for the purpose of inhibiting epilepsy and, if indeed some rhythms do turn out to be better than others, the effect will have been shown to be specific to the training, rather than a mere placebo one. Furthermore, it may be possible to design such a study, determining the most effective value of a parameter, so that it can be conducted by a double-blind procedure. In view of Kaplan's (1975) observations, it would be desirable to add to the foregoing type of study another group that is rewarded specifically for relaxation as measured by the EMG.

As a further example, it should be possible to design a study in which one group of patients is selected as relatively pure migraine cases and another group as relatively pure tension-headache ones. Then half of each group should be trained with Sargent, Green, and Walters' (1972) hand-warming technique and the other half with Budzynski, Stoyva, Adler, and Mullaney's (1973) procedure of using the EMG from the frontalis muscles to teach the patient to relax. But in view of widespread publicity, it may be difficult to secure naive patients who do not know which type of treatment is supposed to be effective for their type of headache.

Adequate Follow-up

Placebo effects are often transient. Thus, Trousseau is credited with the admonition: "You should treat as many patients as possible with the new drugs while they still have the power to heal" (Shapiro, 1960). It is possible for a flashy new technique administered by an impressive therapist to produce a transient placebo effect that at first appears to be greater than the genuine specific effect of another form of treatment which will have more lasting beneficial effects. Since the overall effects over the long term are what count, it is important to follow up the effects of the treatment for a sufficient period of time. Such follow-ups, of course, will eliminate the selective errors involved in initiating the treatment when a person is in a worse phase of a fluctuating disorder and terminating it when he is in a better one.

Transfer to Life

While observations in the laboratory can be highly suggestive, the real therapeutic effect must be robust enough to survive under the conditions of the daily life of the patient. For example, suppose one has trained a patient to reduce his blood pressure in the laboratory. It is possible that the patient has learned voluntary control over his blood pressure so that he reduces it whenever it is measured. As a result of these measurements, his physician may take him off antihypertensive drugs. But it is conceivable that, under the stressful conditions of life, his blood pressure still is dangerously high so that the net effect of his transient voluntary control is the adverse one of fooling his physician into stopping the drugs that are needed. Presumably, long-term follow-ups of such patients would eventually detect any such adverse effects. A more direct approach would be to measure blood pressure frequently and unobtrusively in the life situation. Unfortunately, the only technique available for continuous, unobtrusive monitoring of blood pressure is a portable tape recorder that demands a catheter into an artery (Bevan, Honour, & Stott, 1961). While this procedure is not dangerous, it is not trivial. Thus far, our results in trying to train patients to lower their blood pressure have not averaged enough better than what might be expected from a placebo effect to justify the invasive measure. A noninvasive and unobtrusive portable device for measuring blood pressure would be highly desirable for many different applications.

One of the advantages of work on cardiac arrhythmias is the availability of a portable tape recorder for the ECG. This makes it possible to secure adequate data on the performance of the patient's heart in the life situation both before and after training. Engel and Bleecker (1974) have used this device to secure some follow-up data on two patients.

Possible Harmful Effects

We have just mentioned one conceivable harmful effect of biofeedback, namely, learning to voluntarily reduce blood pressure whenever it is taken, but not being able to do this in stressful situations of life so that the doctor is fooled into taking the patient off the drugs that he needs. One of the attractive features of biofeedback training is the fact that it appears to be benign in comparison with drugs, which usually have side effects. Nevertheless, investigators should be on the lookout for possible adverse effects, and report them if they occur. For example, although there have been glowing testimonials for a wide variety of beneficial effects of alpha training (singularly unsupported by systematic studies), Sterman (1973) says that some subjects report undesirable effects, such as being out of control. Training in producing theta waves in the EEG can produce hypnogogic imagery which some psychiatrists believe could be dangerous for certain types of patients predisposed to psychoses. When some subjects achieve deep relaxation, either by EMG or by hand-warming training, terrifying thoughts may occur. These and the Makyo (manifestations of devils) which can occur in certain stages of meditation may be related to the negative therapeutic effect (Miller, 1975). It is conceivable that visceral training might cause certain patients to pay too much attention to, and be overly concerned with, visceral phenomena, or, in other words, produce a visceral neurosis. On the other hand, no such production of visceral neurosis has been reported to date, and it is conceivable that training patients in a more accurate discrimination of their visceral symptoms may have the opposite effect, that of alleviating a visceral neurosis. Another possibility is that, by suppressing a symptom without treating its cause, biofeedback procedures might lead to the substitution of a worse symptom. As we have pointed out in an earlier section, whether or not such substitution occurs is a matter to be settled by empirical test.

RESEARCH TO IMPROVE EFFECTIVENESS OF TRAINING

While biofeedback has shown promising success in helping some patients to extend the range of their voluntary control over certain responses they had not previously been able to control, the procedure often is time consuming and frequently produces only small effects. If larger effects could be produced more quickly, they would be therapeutically more valuable; it also would be much easier unequivocally to demonstrate their value. Therefore, one of the important tasks for research is to try to improve our training techniques by discovering more about the laws that govern the learning of responses that are not usually under voluntary control. Contributions toward this goal can be made by research on animal subjects, on normal human subjects, and on patients suffering from specific symptoms. Some of the approaches that merit further investigation are discussed below.

Effects of Traditional Parameters

Our current knowledge of how various parameters of the training procedure affect learning should be useful in clinical applications. On the other hand, it is entirely possible that strong interactions occur so that the optimal value of these parameters is considerably different in an especially difficult type of learning, such as that involved in the acquisition of control over visceral responses or in relearning after paralysis. It is even possible that new and as yet undiscovered laws are involved. Therefore, we need to investigate in these new types of learning situations the effects of traditional parameters, such as spacing of trials, length of training sessions, strength of drive, delay of reward, and effects of instructions. In addition, there are some new variables to be investigated, such as the rate, type, and modality of feedback. Lang (1974) has made a promising start in this direction and shown that, while some of the traditional parameters seem to have the expected effect on learning to increase heart rate, they do not seem to have as much of an effect on learning to decrease it. Much more work of this kind remains to be done.

Type of Drive and Reinforcement

Many learning theorists make the implicit assumption that, provided no strong, conflicting, unconditioned response is involved and the magnitudes are comparable, one drive and reinforcement may be substituted for another. Miller (1959, p. 241) has made this assumption explicit but has pointed out that it has not been subjected to any systematic tests. Recent work by investigators such as Garcia and Koelling (1966) and Garcia, Ervin, and Koelling (1966) is questioning this assumption by showing that the reinforcement of nausea is more effective in training animals to avoid food with a particular flavor than to avoid a particular place, whereas reinforcement by electric shock is more effective in training the animal to avoid the place than the food.

Most of the reinforcements used in human work on biofeedback have been signals that tell the subject that he is succeeding or failing. Such signals derive their reinforcing value from the cognitive process that determines their meaning. Will a more primitive type of reinforcement, such as the avoidance of or escape from mild pain be more effective than a cognitively derived one in the therapeutic applications of biofeedback, especially those involving visceral responses?

It is also possible that a more relevant type of drive and reward would be more effective. For example, in trying to produce a learned change in a cardiovascular function, it might be useful to use mild peripheral ischemia produced by a pressure cuff as the drive, and relief from it as the reward. We believe that, in many cases, instrumental learning plays an important role in refining the homeostatic regulation of a specific function and in adjusting the priorities among the different functions being regulated (Miller, 1969). If this hypothesis is correct, it may be advantageous to discover and use the reinforcements that are involved in normal regulation in order to correct instances of maladaptive regulation.

Which Parameter of the Response to Reinforce

In dealing with these new types of learning, we frequently do not yet know what is the relevant parameter of the response to reward. Since we do not know what types of change are learnable responses, we may be choosing a criterion that is affected by changes that are not learnable and that reduce the correlation between the changes that are learnable and the reward. For example, heart rate varies during the breathing cycle in what is called a "sinus arrhythmia." If we set the criterion to reward an interval between the individual heart beats that is somewhat longer than normal, the reward may always occur while the subject is in the slowest phase of this cyclic change. If the changes in heart rate that are produced by the sinus arrhythmia are learnable, then we shall have used this arrhythmia to elicit the response to be learned. This will be effective. On the other hand, if the changes in the interbeat interval that occur as part of the sinus arrhythmia are not subject to learning, such changes will be merely noise, and, in many subjects, this noise may prevent the learnable type of changes from being rewarded. One way around this would be to cancel out the changes produced by the sinus arrhythmia by measuring the number of heart beats in a complete breathing cycle and using this as the unit to activate the reinforcement circuit. However, if a sudden change in a single interbeat interval were the most important learnable response, the averaging procedure might produce too long a delay in reinforcement. In that case, it would be necessary to use a computer to calculate the expected interbeat interval at each moment in the breathing cycle and to reward deviations in the proper direction from that expectation. Finally, it is barely conceivable that the clinically significant learnable changes occur on a longer time scale, so that one might need to average together the heart beats during several breathing cycles in order to reward the appropriate type of change.[1]

To make the problem still more complex, it is possible that a specific absolute heart rate is a learnable response, in which case, one would want to have reinforcements contingent on a specified rate; on the other hand, it is possible that the learnable responses are either increases or decreases in rate rather than any absolute rate. In the latter case, one would want to design the criterion device to detect a change in a specific direction rather than a specific rate.

Similarly, with blood pressure, should one reward an absolute level or a relative change? Should one reward changes that occur as a part of each pulse wave, that occur as part of the sinus arrhythmia, or that occur as part of the longer Traube–Hering rhythm, or should one try to cancel out these rhythms? Are the relevant learnable responses only very brief deviations from those to be expected as part of the foregoing rhythms or are they slower, longer-lasting deviations?

[1] In short, considering the tachograph record as a repetitive signal, the problem is determining which Fourier component is subject to learning.

Getting the Desired Response to Occur

Shaping

A response must occur before it can be rewarded and learned. One way of producing an otherwise improbable response is by "shaping" (Skinner, 1938). In this procedure, the trainer immediately rewards any response that does occur that remotely approximates, contains some elements of, or otherwise increases the probability that the desired response eventually will occur. By progressively rewarding better approximations of the desired response, it eventually is shaped into occurring. As already has been pointed out, one of the advantages of instrumentally augmented feedback is that small spontaneous changes in responses such as heart rate and blood pressure can be detected so that they may possibly be shaped into larger ones.

Because we do not have any exact scientific description of the interrelationships among families of skeletal responses, shaping often is something of an art with such responses. And when we are dealing with the less well understood learning of visceral responses, we are faced with difficulties analogous to those discussed in the preceding section. For example, in shaping an individual to make ever larger decreases in blood pressure, we do not know whether it is better to reward immediately each relatively frequent small decrease or to wait longer for the rarer, larger decreases. In other words, we do not know how large a change must be to function as a learnable response.

Induction by Skeletal Responses

Because of the close functional relationships between skeletal and cardiovascular responses, one of the easiest ways to elicit the latter is through the former. We already have seen that taking a sudden deep breath will stop certain attacks of paroxysmal tachycardia, and that increasing the heart rate by exercise is one way of stopping certain types of premature ventricular contractions. Since there is evidence that the strong contraction of even a single muscle group can produce an elevation in both heart rate and blood pressure (Pickering *et al.*, 1976), teaching a patient with such muscle tension to relax it should be one way of reducing heart rate and blood pressure. Other ways of changing these functions are via breathing, but one would not want to alter breathing far enough to seriously disturb the pCO_2 or pO_2 of the blood. It will be worthwhile to continue research on the possibilities of altering cardiovascular, and possibly other visceral, responses by using the skeletal responses that either mediate visceral changes or are part of a more general pattern involving them. In cases in which performing the skeletal response is inconvenient, it will be worthwhile to investigate the possibility of gradually phasing out the skeletal component while maintaining the visceral one so that the effect becomes more specific.

Eliminating "Noise" from Skeletal Responses: Paralysis by Curare

To explore an approach opposite to the one just discussed, it is quite conceivable that, when a visceral response mediated by a skeletal one is reinforced, little or none of the effect transfers to increase the probability of the direct occurrence of the visceral response without skeletal mediation. In that case, if the ultimate goal is to learn an independent visceral response, producing the visceral change via a skeletal response would be going down a blind alley. As the mediating skeletal responses are rewarded and learned, they will account for an increasingly larger proportion of the total variance in the visceral response, so that the possibility of an independent visceral response's being rewarded will become vanishingly small. In this case, the best strategy will be to try to eliminate the interfering skeletal responses.

The elimination of interfering skeletal responses was part of the strategy of using rats paralyzed by curare, a drug that prevents skeletal responses without appreciably affecting autonomic ones (Miller, 1969). This drug eliminates completely those visceral changes that are mediated by the actual occurrence of skeletal responses; for example, the mechanical effects of movement of the diaphragm and of the abdominal muscles on the intestines, the similar effects of the Valsalva maneuver on the heart rate and blood pressure, the effects of hyper- or hypoventilation on heart rate and blood pressure (primarily via changes in blood pCO_2), and the effects of the heat and metabolites created by muscular exertion. The foregoing effects, of course, are those that are least likely to facilitate the learning of the visceral response and are most likely to function as interfering "noise." Furthermore, the paralysis will eliminate distracting stimuli from skeletal responses.

The strategy of trying to eliminate interfering skeletal responses seemed to be supported by results indicating that rats paralyzed by curare could learn faster than nonparalyzed ones, but, more recently, it has not been possible to replicate these experiments on paralyzed rats (Miller & Dworkin, 1974).[2] Furthermore, patients who had most, but

[2] However, the experiments in our laboratory on animals not paralyzed by curare have been replicated. Miller and Carmona (1967) on the instrumental learning of saliva-

not all, of their skeletal responses paralyzed by polio or by muscular dystrophy, diseases that leave the autonomic nervous system relatively unaffected, did not show any unusual ability to learn to control their blood pressure (Pickering *et al.*, 1975). Nevertheless, the paralysis of these patients was most useful in helping to rule out certain of the changes in blood pressure that can be produced by the occurrence of skeletal responses. If the vastly improved technique of maintaining rats paralyzed by curare described by Dworkin and Miller in Chapter 8 (of this volume) does produce consistently replicable visceral learning, this preparation may be highly useful for ruling out the extremely troublesome mechanical and other effects of the occurrence of skeletal responses. The immobilization may also allow the use of sophisticated neurophysiological techniques, such as single-cell recording, that will increase our knowledge of the mechanisms involved in visceral learning and ultimately may lead to a considerable increase in our power to produce it.

Elicitation by Imagery

Luria (1968) describes a subject with unusually vivid imagery, who could speed up his heart from a normal rate of 70–72 to 80–96, and finally to 100 beats per minutes, by imagining that he was running after a train, or could produce a difference of 3.5°C between the two hands by imagining that his right hand was on a hot stove while his left was squeezing a piece of ice. Autogenic therapy (Luthe, 1963) is based on practicing the use of imagery to produce muscular relaxation and increases in the peripheral blood flow. As a control for the effects of concentrating on an image, Blizard, Cowings, and Miller (1975) showed that while autogenic imagery—hands warm and heavy—tended to slow the heart rate, antiautogenic imagery—hands cold and light—had an opposite effect. Finally, some actors who have learned to cry on cue have reported to the authors that they first became able to secrete real tears by vividly remembering all of the details of an extremely sad situation. Later, they became able to omit more of the details, eliciting the tears merely by concentrating on the sensations produced around the eyes when they were crying.

The foregoing observations suggest that it will be worthwhile to conduct more research on the possibility of using imagery to gain

---

tion by dogs has been confirmed by Shapiro and Herendeen (1975), DiCara and Miller (1969) on heart-rate learning in rats has been supported by Engel and Gottlieb (1970) on heart rate in the monkey. A number of experiments (Benson *et al.*, 1969; Pappas *et al.*, 1970; Harris *et al.*, 1973) have demonstrated changes in blood pressure produced by instrumental training.

control over previously involuntary responses. They fit in with the old ideomotor hypothesis of voluntary movement (James, 1950 [1890]).

Training in Visceral Perception

The ideomotor theory cited above predicts that training in the improved identification of the sensations of a specific visceral response should aid in the voluntary control of that response. Brener (1974) confirms this prediction by showing that training in correctly identifying the heart rate yields somewhat better control over it.

Work summarized by Ádám (1967) shows that both animal and human subjects can be trained to improve their discriminative responses to visceral sensations. Miller (1972a,b) has pointed out that such improved discrimination could be useful in helping patients to free themselves from the need for instrumentally augmented feedback; it could permit them to be rewarded by their own perception of a visceral change in the appropriate direction. Eventually, their control might become automatic, like the movements that a skilled bicycle rider makes to correct his balance. If patients can learn a more accurate discrimination of their blood pressure, they could at the very least use this improved perception to help them to avoid situations that induce a large increase.

Counteracting Constraints of Servo-Control

Bechtereva *et al.* (1976) have used electrical stimulation of certain points in the brain, via chronically implanted fine-wire electrodes, to help certain patients suffering from severe spastic paralysis to use EMG feedback to learn to relax the spastic muscles. They report that the most useful stimulation for this purpose is not at a point that elicits relaxation, but rather at one that increases the variability of the strength of contraction. They have called such an effect a *destabilizing* one. Their results suggest that the electrically stimulated complete relaxation is not a learnable response, but that the fluctuations released by appropriate stimulation are learnable. They report that, after the patients have learned to relax their spastic muscles, the destabilizing electrical stimulation of the brain can be phased out; the patients can continue to control their spasticity without it.

Patients with severed spinal cords show much greater variability in blood pressure than do normal subjects. This observation suggests that this lesion has a destabilizing or, as we would call it, an *antihomeostatic* effect (Miller & Dworkin, 1974). As the work on such patients by Bernard Brucker (described earlier on page 144) indicates, they seem to have an unusual ability to learn to produce voluntary increases in blood pressure.

The foregoing observations suggest that it will be worthwhile to make a systematic search for additional antihomeostatic treatments or agents. These may greatly facilitate the early stages of therapeutic learning in situations in which a strong servo-control mechanism is holding a visceral or skeletal response at an undesirable level. A drug that had an antihomeostatic effect on blood pressure would manifest this effect by producing large fluctuations in that pressure. Unfortunately, in the current screening programs of pharmaceutical companies, such an effect on a vital sign would appear to be undesirable and probably would cause that type of compound promptly to be discarded. It may be worthwhile for some drug company to reverse this practice and, instead, to search for antihomeostatic compounds.

GLIMPSES INTO THE FUTURE

If future clinical research should indeed show that psychosomatic symptoms can be learned as responses instrumental to achieving a goal, the diffusion of this knowledge as part of the general culture might make such symptoms less acceptable for this purpose so that their frequency might decline much as that of hysterical symptoms seems to have declined with the wider recognition of the functions they serve. In some cases, this outcome might force the patients into learning more adaptive solutions to their problems; in others, it might lead to a need to discover new types of symptoms. As the use of instrumentation to record moment-to-moment changes in visceral responses is developed further, the use of such instrumentation will increase the general public's awareness of the psychosomatic consequences of environmental stress. This same instrumentation can be used to detect those aspects of the physical, occupational, or social environment that expose people to the greatest stress. This and other increased knowledge may lead to action to reduce such stress and hence help to produce a healthier environment.

SUMMARY

A general theoretical analysis suggests that, when biofeedback is used in an attempt to eliminate a symptom that is functional, or, in other words, instrumental in achieving some goal, the therapist may have to teach the patient other means of achieving his goal. In order to understand how to deal with them better, we need more detailed clinical investigations of how various psychosomatic symptoms may be reinforced and learned. One tentative hypothesis about the learning of functional hypertension is described. The natural mechanisms that cause the body to heal itself, a selective error that causes patients to seek treatments when they are feeling worse and to be discharged when they are feeling better, and powerful placebo effects can cause the therapeutic value of any new form of treatment to be grossly overestimated. While some of the therapeutic applications of biofeedback have yielded promising preliminary results, none of them has been evaluated rigorously enough to rule out conclusively the effects of the foregoing factors, which can produce a spurious impression of therapeutic effectiveness. One of the greatest needs is for a rigorous evaluation of those applications that seem to be most promising. And a number of the applications are promising enough, to justify such evaluation. Another need is for basic research to improve the effectiveness of therapeutic training. The effects of many variables remain to be investigated. Some of these have been discussed. We also need to study the neural mechanisms involved in using learning to modify visceral responses and the possible role of such learning in normal homeostasis as well as in the etiology of psychosomatic symptoms. Much challenging work remains to be done to determine how much we can improve the effectiveness of therapeutic training.

REFERENCES

Ádám, G. *Interoception and behaviour.* Budapest: Akadémiai Kiadó, 1967.

Adler, C. S., & Adler, S. M. Biofeedback-psychotherapy for the treatment of headaches, a 5-year follow-up. Paper presented at the joint meeting of the American Association for the Study of Headache and the Scandinavian Migraine Society, Bergen, Norway, 1975.

Baker, B. L. Symptom treatment and symptom substitution in enuresis. *Journal of Abnormal Psychology,* 1969, *74,* 42–49.

Bartorelli, C., Bizzi, E., Libretti, A., & Zanchetti, A. Inhibitory control of sinocarotid pressoceptive afferents on hypothalamic autonomic activity and sham rage behavior. *Archives Italiennes de Biologie,* 1960, *98,* 308–326

Basmajian, J. V., Kukulka, C. G., Narayan, M. G., & Takebe, K. Biofeedback treatment of foot-drop after stroke compared with standard rehabilitation technique: Effects on voluntary control and strength. *Archives of Physical Medicine and Rehabilitation,* 1975, *56,* 231–236.

Bechtereva, N. P., Kambarova, D. K., Smirnov, V. M., Tchernigovskaya, N. V., & Shandurina, A. N. Methods and principles of using the brain's latent abilities for therapy. Manuscript submitted for publication, 1976.

Benson, H., Herd, A. J., Morse, W. H., & Kelleher, R. T. Behavioral induction of arterial hypertension and its reversal. *American Journal of Physiology,* 1969, *217,* 30–34.

Benson, H., Shapiro, D., Tursky, B., & Schwartz, G. E. Decreased systolic blood pressure through operant conditioning techniques in patients with essential hypertension. *Science* 1971, *173,* 740–742.

Bevan, A. T., Honour, A. J., & Stott, F. H. Direct arterial pressure recording in unrestricted man. *Clinical Science,* 1961, *36,* 329–344.

Blanchard, E. B., & Young, L. D. Clinical application of biofeedback training. *Archives of General Psychiatry,* 1974, *30,* 573–589.

Blizard, D. A., Cowings, P., & Miller, N. E. Visceral responses to opposite types of autogenic-training imagery. *Biological Psychology,* 1975, *3,* 49–55.

Bonvallet, M., Dell, P., & Hiebel, G. Sinus carotidien et activité électrique cérébrale. *Conte rendu des Séances de la Societé de Biologie* (Paris), 1953, *147,* 1166–1169.

Bonvallet, M., Dell, P., & Hiebel, G. Tonus sympathique et activité électrique corticale. *Electroencephalography and Clinical Neurophysiology,* 1954, *6,* 119–144.

Brener, J. A general model of voluntary control applied to the phenomena of learned cardiovascular change. In P. A. Obrist, A. H. Black, J. Brener, & L. V. DiCara (Eds.), *Cardiovascular psychophysiology.* Chicago: Aldine, 1974. Pp. 365–391.

Brudny, J., Grynbaum, B. B., & Korein, J. Spasmodic torticollis: Treatment by feedback display of the EMG. *Archives of Physical Medicine and Rehabilitation,* 1974, *55,* 403–408.

Brudny, J., Korein, J., Grynbaum, B. B., Weinstein, S., & Frankel, G. Therapeutic applications of electromyography in the practice of rehabilitation medicine. *Archives of Physical Medicine and Rehabilitation,* 1974, *55,* 564 (abstract).

Budzynski, T. H., Stoyva, J. M., Adler, C. S., & Mullaney, D. J. EMG biofeedback and tension headache: A controlled outcome study. *Psychosomatic Medicine,* 1973, *35,* 484–496.

Cleeland, C. S. Behavior techniques in the modification of spasmodic torticollis. *Neurology,* 1973, *23,* 1241–1247.

Davis, J. D., Lulenski, G. C., & Miller, N. E. Comparative studies of barbiturate self-administration. *International Journal of Addictions,* 1968, *3,* 207–214.

DiCara, L. V., & Miller, N. E. Instrumental learning of systolic blood pressure responses by curarized rats: Dissociation of cardiac and vascular changes. *Psychosomatic Medicine,* 1968, *30,* 489–494.

DiCara, L. V., & Miller, N. E. Heart-rate learning in the noncurarized state, transfer to the curarized state, and subsequent retraining in the noncurarized state. *Physiology and Behavior,* 1969, *4,* 621–624.

Dollard, J., & Miller, N. E. *Personality and psychotherapy.* New York: McGraw-Hill, 1950.

Engel, B. T., & Bleecker, E. R. Application of operant conditioning techniques to the control of the cardiac arrhythmias. In P. A. Obrist, A. H. Black, J. Brener, & L. V. DiCara (Eds.), *Cardiovascular psychophysiology.* Chicago: Aldine, 1974. Pp. 456–476.

Engel, B. T., & Gottlieb, S. H. Differential operant conditioning of heart rate in the restrained monkey. *Journal of Comparative and Physiological Psychology,* 1970, *73,* 217–225.

Garcia, J., Ervin, F. R., & Koelling, R. A. Learning with prolonged delay of reinforcement. *Psychonomic Science,* 1966, *5,* 121–122.

Garcia, J., & Koelling, R. A. Relation of cue to consequence in avoidance learning. *Psychonomic Science,* 1966, *4,* 123–124.

Grenfell, R. F., Briggs, A. H., & Holland, W. C. Antihypertensive drugs evaluated in a controlled double-blind study. *Southern Medical Journal,* 1963, *56,* 1410–1415.

Harris, A. H., Gilliam, W. J., Findley, J. D., & Brady, J. V. Instrumental conditioning of large-magnitude, daily, 12-hour blood pressure elevations in the baboon. *Science*, 1973, *184*, 175–177.

Inglis, J., Campbell, D., & McDonald, M. W. Electromyographic biofeedback and neuromuscular rehabilitation. *Canadian Journal of Behavioural Science*, 1976, *8*, 299–323.

Jackson, J. H. *Selected writings* (J. Taylor, Ed.). Vol. 1. New York: Basic Books, 1958. Pp. 6, 7.

James, W. *Principles of psychology* (new ed.). Vol. 2. New York: Dover, 1950. Chap. 26. Originally published 1890.

Johnson, B. C., Karunas, T. M., & Epstein, F. H. Longitudinal change in blood pressure in individuals, families and social groups. *Clinical Science and Molecular Medicine*, 1973, *45*, 35s–45s.

Kaplan, B. Biofeedback in epileptics: Equivocal relationship of reinforced EEG frequency to seizure reduction. *Epilepsia*, 1975, *16*, 447–485.

Koch, E. B. Die Irridation der pressoreceptorischen Kreislaufreflexe. *Klinische Wochenschrift*, 1932, *11*, 225–227.

Koslovskaya, I. B., Vertes, R. P., & Miller, N. E. Instrumental learning without proprioceptive feedback. *Physiology and Behavior*, 1973, *10*, 101–107.

Koslovskaya, I. B., Vertes, R. P., & Miller, N. E. Effects of absence of proprioceptive feedback on classical and on avoidance conditioning. In preparation, 1976.

Lacey, B. C., & Lacey, J. I. Studies of heart rate and other bodily processes in sensorimotor behavior. In P. A. Obrist, A. H. Black, J. Brener, & L. V. DiCara (Eds.), *Cardiovascular psychophysiology*. Chicago: Aldine, 1974. Pp. 538–564.

Lacey, J. I., Kagan, J., Lacey, B. C., & Moss, H. A. The visceral level: Situational determinants and behavioral correlates of autonomic response patterns. In P. H. Knapp (Ed.), *Expression of the emotions in man*. New York: International Universities Press, 1963. Pp. 161–196.

Lacey, J. I., & Lacey, B. C. Some autonomic–central nervous system interrelationships. In P. Black (Ed.), *Physiological correlates of emotion*. New York: Academic Press, 1970. Pp. 205–227.

Lang, P. J. Learned control of human heart rate in a computer directed environment. In P. A. Obrist, A. H. Black, J. Brener, & L. V. DiCara (Eds.), *Cardiovascular psychophysiology*. Chicago: Aldine, 1974. Pp. 392–405.

Luria, A. R. *The mind of a mnemonist* (L. Solotaroff, trans.). New York: Basic Books, 1968. Pp. 138–143.

Luthe, W. Autogenic training: Method, research, and application in medicine. *American Journal of Psychotherapy*, 1963, *17*, 174–195.

Miller, N. E. Liberalization of basic S–R concepts: Extensions to conflict behavior, motivation and social learning. In S. Koch (Ed.), *Psychology: A study of a science*. Study 1, Vol. 2. New York: McGraw-Hill, 1959. Pp. 196–292.

Miller, N. E. Some reflections on the law of effect produce a new alternative to drive reduction. In M. R. Jones (Ed.), *Nebraska Symposium on Motivation*. Lincoln, Nebr.: University of Nebraska Press, 1963. Pp. 65–112.

Miller, N. E. Learning of visceral and glandular responses. *Science*, 1969, *163*, 434–445.

Miller, N. E. Learning of visceral and glandular responses: Postscript. In D. Singh & C. T. Morgan (Eds.), *Current status of physiological psychology: Readings*. Monterey: Brooks/Cole, 1972. Pp. 245–250. (a)

Miller, N. E. A psychologist's perspective on neural and psychological mechanisms in cardiovascular disease. In A. Zanchetti (Ed.), *Neural and psychological mecha-*

nisms in cardiovascular disease. Milan: Casa Editrice "Il Ponte," 1972. Pp. 345–360. (b)

Miller, N. E. Biofeedback: Evaluation of a new technic. *New England Journal of Medicine,* 1974, *290,* 684–685. (a)

Miller, N. E. Introduction: Current issues and key problems. In N. E. Miller, T. X. Barber, L. V. DiCara, J. Kamiya, D. Shapiro, & J. Stoyva (Eds.), *Biofeedback and self-control 1973.* Chicago: Aldine, 1974. Pp. xi–xx. (b)

Miller, N. E. Applications of learning and biofeedback to psychiatry and medicine. In A. M. Friedman, H. I. Kaplan, & B. J. Sadock (Eds.), *Comprehensive textbook of psychiatry–II.* Baltimore: Williams and Wilkins, 1975. Pp. 349–365.

Miller, N. E., & Carmona, A. Modification of a visceral response, salivation in thirsty dogs, by instrumental training with water reward. *Journal of Comparative and Physiological Psychology,* 1967, *63,* 1–6.

Miller, N. E., DiCara, L. V., Solomon, H., Weiss, J. M., & Dworkin, B. Learned modifications to autonomic functions: A review and some new data. *Circulation Research,* 1970, *26, 27* (Suppl. I), 1–11.

Miller, N. E., & Dollard, J. *Social learning and imitation.* New Haven: Yale University Press, 1941.

Miller, N. E., & Dworkin, B. R. Visceral learning: Recent difficulties with curarized rats and significant problems for human research. In P. A. Obrist, A. H. Black, J. Brener, & L. V. DiCara (Eds.), *Cardiovascular psychophysiology.* Chicago: Aldine, 1974. Pp. 312–331.

Mowrer, O. H., & Mowrer, W. M. Enuresis—a method for its study and treatment. *American Journal of Orthopsychiatry,* 1938, *8,* 436–459.

Orne, M. T. Pain suppression by hypnosis and related phenomena. *Advances in Neurology,* 1974, *4,* 562–563.

Pappas, B. A., DiCara, L. V., & Miller, N. E. Learning of blood pressure responses in the noncurarized rat: Transfer to the curarized state. *Physiology and Behavior,* 1970, *5,* 1029–1032.

Pickering, T. G., & Miller, N. E. Learned voluntary control of heart rate and rhythm in two subjects with premature ventricular contractions. *British Heart Journal,* in press.

Pickering, T. G., Brucker, B., Frankel, H. L., Mathias, C. J., Dworkin, B. R., & Miller, N. E. Mechanism of learned voluntary control of blood pressure in patients with generalised bodily paralysis. In *Proceedings, NATO Symposium on Biofeedback and Behavior,* Munich, 28–30 July 1976. Pp. 153–162.

Porter, R. (Ed.). *The role of learning in psychotherapy.* London: Churchill, 1968.

Sargent, J. D., Green, E. E., & Walters, E. D. The use of autogenic feedback training in a pilot study of migraine and tension headaches. *Headache,* 1972, *12,* 120–124.

Schwartz, G. E. Voluntary control of human cardiovascular integration and differentiation through feedback and reward. *Science,* 1972, *175,* 90–93.

Shapiro, A. K. A contribution to a history of the placebo effect. *Behavioral Science,* 1960, *5,* 109–135.

Shapiro, A. K. Placebo effects in medicine, psychotherapy, and psychoanalysis. In A. E. Bergin & S. L. Garfield (Eds.), *Handbook of psychotherapy and behavior change: Empirical analysis.* New York: Wiley, 1971. Pp. 439–473.

Shapiro, A. P., Myers, T., Reiser, M. F., & Ferris, E. B. Comparison of blood pressure response to Veriloid and to the doctor. *Psychosomatic Medicine,* 1954, *16,* 478–488.

Shapiro, D., Tursky, B., & Schwartz, G. E. Control of blood pressure in man by operant conditioning. *Circulation Research,* 1970, *26,27* (Suppl. I), 27–32.

Shapiro, M. M., & Herendeen, D. L. Food-reinforced inhibition of conditioned salivation in dogs. *Journal of Comparative and Physiological Psychology*, 1975, *88*, 628–632.

Skinner, B. F. *The behavior of organisms.* New York: Appleton, 1938.

Sterman, M. B. Neurophysiological and clinical studies of sensorimotor EEG biofeedback training: Some effects on epilepsy. *Seminars in Psychiatry*, 1973, *5*, 507–525.

Tursky, B., Shapiro, D., & Schwartz, G. E. Automated constant cuff-pressure system for measuring average systolic and diastolic blood pressure in man. *IEEE Transactions in Biomedical Engineering*, 1972, *19*, 271.

Weiss, J. M. Effects of coping behavior in different warning signal conditions on stress pathology in rats. *Journal of Comparative and Physiological Psychology*, 1971, *77*, 1–13.

Weiss, T., & Engel, B. T. Operant conditioning of heart rate in patients with premature ventricular contractions. *Psychosomatic Medicine*, 1971, *33*, 301–321.

7

Biofeedback and Performance*

G. H. LAWRENCE
Defense Advanced Research Projects Agency

L. C. JOHNSON
Naval Health Research Center

INTRODUCTION

In 1970, a program of research was begun under support from the Defense Advanced Research Projects Agency (ARPA) and monitored by the Office of Naval Research (ONR) to investigate whether or not teaching individuals to control physiological variables could enhance performance and whether or not self-regulation could reduce the performance decrement frequently observed in highly stressful situations. The general experimental plan was *(1)* to offer subjects control over various cardiovascular, EMG, and brainwave events via biofeedback, *(2)* to observe correlations between one or more of these physiological variables and performance, *(3)* to induce stress and observe the performance decrement, and *(4)* to determine whether, through self-

* This work is based on a 5-year research program concerned with self-regulation as an aid to enhance human performance. This research was supported by the Defense Advanced Research Projects Agency through a grant monitored by the Office of Naval Research and administered by the San Diego State University Foundation. The views presented in this paper are those of the authors. No endorsement by the Defense Advanced Research Projects Agency or by the Department of the Navy has been given or should be inferred.

regulation, the stress-related performance decrement could be ameliorated. Generally, the proposition to be tested held that individuals who gain control over their internal physiology concomitant with behavioral events or affective states will perform better and have more control over the behaviors or states.

Consider the case of a pilot whose airplane has been damaged and is in danger of crashing, and who is in a state of near panic. Suppose he voluntarily lowers his heart rate, reduces his blood pressure, and partially relaxes his temporalis muscles. Will he then feel and behave in a more calm and effective manner? Or, if a trainee is taught to emit a particular pattern of brain waves associated with receptivity to new information, will he, by voluntarily emitting this EEG configuration, be able to make more efficient use of the information a computer-assisted instruction system can offer him? Biofeedback appeared to offer a way to allow subjects to vary heart rate or other physiological responses without the use of drugs (which may have direct effects on feeling-states via CNS action) or external stimuli such as electric shock (which obviously does affect feeling-states). The ability to control specific autonomic responses would provide a test of their relation to subjective emotional states and to cognitive and motor performance.

Brain Activity

Perhaps because of its preeminence in biofeedback research circa 1970, self-regulation of alpha activity initially received most attention. Work by Paskewitz and Orne (1973), however, quickly raised questions as to the generally accepted simplicity of the alpha feedback process. In their work, it soon became clear that eyes-open alpha feedback training led to an enhancement of alpha density only in the presence of ambient light. In total darkness, no alpha enhancement over baselines was observed in numerous training sessions. While Paskewitz and Orne's subjects did, with feedback, increase alpha density in the presence of ambient light, they never exceeded resting, nondrowsy alpha baselines obtained in total darkness. Paskewitz and Orne postulated that, by feedback training, subjects were able to overcome partially the inhibitory effects of ambient light on alpha activity. In other individuals, they hypothesized that feedback might overcome the alpha-inhibiting influence of anxiety, concentration, and so on. They further speculated that the subjective effect of alpha enhancement would be directly related to the inhibitory influence that was overcome. Such reasoning, they felt, would explain the varying subjective experiences reported by the subjects while experiencing alpha enhancement.

Kamiya (1969) had suggested that pleasant feelings of relaxation accompany increases in alpha. Nowlis and Kamiya (1970) implied that alpha enhancement aided task performance, and Green, Green, and Walters (1970) asserted that alpha enhancement improved delayed recall. Enhanced alpha appeared to raise the pain threshold (Gannon & Sternbach, 1971), facilitate extrasensory perception (ESP) (Honorton, Davidson, & Bindler, 1971), and lead to a decreased need for sleep (Regestein, Buckland, & Pegram, 1973). For some scientists, as for many laymen, further research was unnecessary; it was a proven scientific fact that high alpha universally enhanced both work and play.

Unfortunately, results from the laboratories of Kamiya (University of California, San Francisco), Beatty (UCLA), and the Naval Health Research Center (San Diego) have not supported this view of alpha as a panacea. The findings of Paskewitz and Orne constitute an important caveat! Self-regulation of alpha activity is not a substitute for sleep, nor can the deleterious effects of acute sleep loss on performance and mood thus be ameliorated (Hord, Tracy, Lubin, & Johnson, 1975; Hord, Lubin, Tracy, Jensma, & Johnson, in press).

Beatty (1973) found no relationship between occipital alpha feedback and two measures of information processing capacity: short-term memory for digits and choice–reaction times. In this study, Beatty selected his five best alpha-producing subjects. An on-line computer was employed to scan the subjects' EEG and to deliver task information to the subject on each trial. Each trial was begun by an instruction that the subject produce either a high alpha state or a beta state. When the desired EEG pattern was maintained for 3 seconds, the digits were presented by the computer-controlled display apparatus.

The data indicated that there was essentially no detectable difference in the efficiency with which most of the subjects processed symbol strings when those strings were presented in periods of occipital alpha or beta frequency activity.

In the choice–reaction paradigm, the subject watched for a signal on a screen and, when it appeared, he was to depress a button indicating its identity as quickly and as accurately as possible. Beatty felt that, if cortical synchrony is related to information processing efficiency, then it should show its effect in the choice–reaction task. This study was again under computer control, and when the necessary EEG state had been maintained for 2 seconds, the stimulus was presented. Three of five subjects showed consistently shorter reaction times when the stimulus occurred during desynchrony than during synchrony.

Kamiya, like Beatty, found EEG activity unrelated to both memory for words and a simple reaction-time test. In another study, Kamiya (1972) attempted to determine whether or not subjects trained to control alpha amplitude would show improvement in performance tasks if break periods from the tasks were used to maintain high alpha amplitude. The reasoning underlying this hypothesis was that alpha is often regarded as indicative of a resting or idling condition, which may be characteristic of rest periods from performance tasks. Five young male adults were given a battery of performance tasks with 4-minute break periods between each task. The control group was told merely to wait for 4 minutes between tasks while the experimental group was trained to produce alpha, and received 4 minutes of alpha feedback between tasks. The tasks were verbal auditory vigilance, rod and frame, Guilford creative intelligence, visual memory, mental arithmetic, digit memory span, and tone tracking. The results were negative. Kamiya concluded that the self-regulated high alpha break period did not facilitate task performance.

Orne, Evans, Wilson, and Paskewitz (1975) explored the ability of subjects to maintain a high alpha state while performing cognitive tasks. Nine well-trained subjects were able to maintain the alpha activity while counting backward by one, but counting backward by seven significantly blocked alpha when compared to nontask trials. Complexity of the task, the subject's ability to perform the task, and level of effort by the subject all were related to the degree of alpha blocking during the tasks. In a series of related studies. Orne *et al.* (1975) were unable to find a relationship between alpha training and performance on various other cognitive tasks. Further, Orne and Paskewitz (1974) concluded, from an unsuccessful attempt to discover a relationship between alpha and anxiety induced by threat of painful electric shock, that their data "not only raise theoretical questions about the meaning of alpha density, but also challenge the widely accepted rationale for using alpha feedback training as a means of teaching individuals control over their own levels of anxiety" (p. 460).

Thus, enhanced alpha activity does not prevent sleep-loss effects or substitute for sleep (Hord, Tracy, Lubin, & Johnson, 1975, and Hord, Lubin, Tracy, Jensma, & Johnson, in press), is not related to memory or choice–reaction performance (Beatty, 1973), does not provide a recuperative break period (Kamiya, 1972), and is incompatible with cognitive tasks requiring any degree of effort (Orne *et al.*, 1975). With respect to self-regulated alpha and pain, Melzack and Perry (1975) used alpha feedback and hypnotic training for the control of chronic pain. They report that the combined procedures produce a substantial decrease in pain (by 33% or greater) in 58% of the patients during the training sessions. They conclude, however, that since alpha alone had no significant effect on pain reduction, the contribution of the alpha training procedure to pain relief, when combined with hypnosis, was "not due to increased EEG alpha as such but, rather, to the distraction of attention, suggestion, relaxation, and sense of control over pain which are an integral part of the procedure" (Melzack & Perry, 1975, p. 452).

In contrast to these findings related to alpha activity, occipital theta (3–7 Hz), and, in particular, the absence of theta, was reported to be significantly associated with ability to maintain vigilance (Beatty, Greenberg, Deibler, & O'Hanlon, 1974). This work will be mentioned only briefly here and presented in more detail by Beatty in another chapter. In the initial paper, it was reported that suppression of theta by operant methods enhanced monitoring efficiency, whereas theta augmentation led to further degradation over a 2-hour watch period. Beatty *et al.* (1974) were encouraged by their theta-suppression results and stated, "This is the first demonstration, to our knowledge, of a lawful relationship between operantly regulated cortical phenomena and performance in man" (p. 873).

The nature of this relation, however, turned out to be influenced by both task and subject. In a 1-hour vigilance task, subjects trained to suppress theta performed no better than a nonfeedback group, though the theta-suppressing subjects did detect signals more rapidly than did subjects trained to augment theta. Because the ultimate goal of the ARPA program was to utilize laboratory findings in an operational environment on tasks of varying duration, Beatty and O'Hanlon shifted from college students to trained radar observers in their UCLA laboratory. The level of self-regulated theta suppression was less with the 11 radar observers than with college students though, like the college students, the naval subjects required significantly fewer sweeps for target detection when theta-suppression feedback was provided (Beatty & O'Hanlon, 1975). But more troublesome was the finding that, in an operational test at a nearby naval air station involving 14 naval petty officers trained as air controllers or radarmen, operant control of theta had no significant effect during a 3-hour vigilance task (O'Hanlon & Beatty, 1975).

As a further test of theta suppression, Hord, Wilson, Townsend, and Johnson (1975) studied 19 naval subjects in a 3-hour sonar task. One group of seven subjects used biofeedback to suppress theta activity, seven subjects were yoked controls (each yoked control received the same tones as those of a feedback subject but had no control over the tone), and five subjects received no theta feedback or tones. There were no significant differences among the three groups in the time to detect sonar signals or in the number correctly detected.

Beatty and O'Hanlon felt that the theta feedback procedures provided a subject with new information concerning his state of nervous system arousal, permitting him to maintain alertness in a manner not otherwise possible. In situations in which there is no lowering in the level of alertness, there should be little performance decrement, and theta suppression would have little impact on performance. Such was the case in the short, 1-hour, vigilance task. Absence of a baseline decrement also may have been a factor in the negative results in the two naval laboratory settings. O'Hanlon and Beatty noted that their two subjects who showed a performance decrement during an initial 3-hour vigilance task without contingent theta feedback showed no decrement during the second 3-hour task when contingent theta feedback was provided (O'Hanlon & Beatty, 1975).

To test further the arousal hypothesis, Morgan and Coates (1975) investigated the extent to which self-regulation of theta activity might be used to enhance performance, or at least reduce the expected performance decrement, during 48 hours of continuous performance and sleep loss. Prior to the 48-hour vigil, nine subjects were trained to suppress theta activity and increase heart rate (HR) concurrently. The tasks were from the Multiple Task Performance Battery (MTPB) used in several studies by this group (Alluisi, 1967, 1972; Morgan & Alluisi, 1972). While the subjects were able to self-regulate theta activity and HR at the beginning of the continuous-performance period, the operant suppression of theta was less effective toward the end of the 48-hour period (Hord *et al.*, in press, have also found that self-regulation of alpha and nonalpha activity deteriorates after one night of sleep loss). Operant control of HR showed less decrement.

Comparison of the performance of these self-regulating subjects with comparable data from an earlier group run on the MTPB showed no statistical difference in level of performance. MTPB performance was not significantly enhanced by the use of self-regulation prior to, during, or subsequent to 48 hours of continuous work and sleep loss.

In summary, whereas alpha enhancement or suppression have not been found to affect performance, theta suppression may prevent or lessen the performance decrements that are typically found in vigilance tasks of long duration. A performance decrement may be a necessary condition for the observance of any theta effect, and there are no data to suggest that theta suppression can lead to performance enhancement above initial levels.

As Beatty and O'Hanlon emphasized, the feedback technique helps subjects to become aware of changes in their own arousal level and thus alerts them to take corrective steps. It is likely that this effect—if it turns out to exhibit reliability and robustness—reflects state changes comfortably subsumed under most conceptualizations of arousal; perhaps Beatty and O'Hanlon have discovered a way to teach people to stay awake without drugs or peripheral stimulation. There are, however, no consistent data indicating that background theta activity per se (i.e., theta activity generally present, and not associated with changes in arousal) is related to performance levels (Williams, Granda, Jones, Lubin, & Armington, 1962). Recent findings by the Naval Health Research Center support the conclusions of Williams *et al.* Theta feedback appears to allow the subjects to become aware of changes in state, which are reflected by changes in theta levels, rather than in theta activity per se.

Cardiovascular Activity

While only good things had been imputed to alpha enhancement at the start of the research program, there were serious concerns as to the levels beyond which cardiovascular activity should not be pushed, and as to the long-term effects of biofeedback-induced cardiovascular changes. As an initial part of the ARPA self-regulation project, Alan Harris and Joseph Brady were asked to determine safe limits and the possible chronic effects of operant control of blood pressure and heart rate (HR) in animals (Harris, Findley, & Brady, 1971; Harris, Gilliam, Findley, & Brady, 1973). A detailed presentation of this work is presented by Harris and Brady elsewhere in this volume.

Following the animal work, Harris and his colleagues concentrated on the operant control of HR and the relation of self-regulated increases and decreases in HR to performance (Harris, Stephens, & Brady, 1973–1974) and to physiological variables (Stephens, Harris, & Brady, 1972; Stephens, Harris, Brady, & Shaffer, 1975).

The results of these human studies have been evaluated with respect to the extent to which *(1)* engaging in a concurrent task modifies self-regulatory ability, and reciprocally, *(2)* autonomic self-regulation of HR affects the concurrent task performance. For 19 subjects, self-regulated HR increases averaged 15 beats per minute (bpm), decreases averaged 3 bpm, with a range from 29 bpm increase to 16 bpm decrease. Heart rate could be controlled to some extent by practically all subjects tested; HR increases were significantly easier to achieve than decreases. Significant correlations between changes in HR and blood pressure were observed, with the stronger relation appearing during the HR "increase" condition.

Subjects were tested on three kinds of tasks, ranging from a relatively simple auditory reaction-time task and a Mackworth Clock Vigilance test to mental arithmetic problems under time-limit conditions. In all cases, the task requirement had been introduced repeatedly throughout each of the self-regulation components (i.e., HR "raising," "lowering," and "rest") with problem presentations occurring on the average of approximately once per minute with a variable interval range from 15 to 95 seconds. All subjects were able to perform satisfactorily on the reaction-time task without interfering with HR self-regulation and no significant differences in the reaction-time performance could be discerned as a function of the self-regulatory HR change (i.e., "raising" or "lowering").

The Mackworth Clock Vigilance task required the subject to report the occurrence of skipped steps ("jumps") in the clockwise rotation of the sweep hand on a large clock face. The vigil was maintained continuously throughout the experimental session with "clock jumps" programmed to occur on the average of once per minute during all three phases of the self-regulatory program (i.e., HR "raising," "lowering," and "rest interval"). The interaction between the Mackworth Clock Vigilance task and HR self-regulation was studied in four subjects during a total of 20 experimental sessions under both incentive (i.e., special performance effectiveness "pay") and nonincentive conditions. The results again showed no discernible effect, either of the concurrent vigilance task upon HR self-regulation or of the self-regulation requirement upon the vigilance behavior.

In addition to the Mackworth Clock Vigilance, the Continuous Performance Task (CPT) described by Rosvold, Mirsky, Sarason, Bransome, and Beck (1956) was included as another vigilance task. The CPT requires the identification of the letter "x" from among various letters presented at a 2-per-second rate on a display in front of the subject. Correct identifications were reported by a hand switch. As earlier studies had showed no correlation between HR changes and performance in nonstressful conditions, the task situation was modified to induce a degree of stress. The assumption was that stress would be a disruptive factor which would be reflected in HR changes. If HR were under operant control, this change in HR could be prevented or counteracted and the disruptive effects of stress on performance minimized.

Superimposed upon both the self-regulation of HR and the concurrent vigilance task performance were clicker–shock pairings, which represented an additional stress factor in the environment. Each clicker presentation lasted for 1 minute and terminated with an electric shock (5–15 ma for .5 seconds) applied to the subject's lower right leg. Each subject determined his or her own "painful but tolerable" shock levels during pre-experimental instructional periods. Three such pairings were presented during a 10-minute interval of HR raising, HR lowering, or rest, with and without the added concurrent vigilance task performance.

This aversive classical cardiovascular conditioning procedure was a modification of the "conditioned emotional response" or "conditioned suppression" method extensively used in animal laboratories (Brady, 1969).

A new sample of 40 subjects was initially examined for this study, Self-regulated HR increases averaged 13 bpm while HR decreases averaged 3 bpm, with a range of from 47 bpm increases to 14 bpm decreases. Thirteen subjects were used to examine the interaction of HR control and performance in the nonstressful and stressful conditions (Brady, Harris, Anderson, & Stephens, in press). While accuracy of response was not affected by the experimental conditions or HR regulation, the reaction times under conditions of regulated HR lowering were clearly the longest. Those during HR raising were the shortest ($p < .05$), and reaction times in the absence of HR control fell at an intermediate value.

When the clicker–shock pairings were imposed on the task (i.e., there were three 1-minute clicker–shocks presented in a 10-minute segment), there was a characteristic reduction in baseline HR. The effects of stress upon the interaction between HR self-regulation and concurrent vigilance task performance resulted in the elimination of the subject's ability to produce HR decreases, and the self-regulated HR increase effects decreased to about 7 bpm. Clearly, interactions among concurrent performance, HR self-regulation, and stress occurred.

During clicker–shock pairings, concurrent performance scores (i.e., percent correct) fell to 73% during rest intervals, and to a low of 60% during periods requiring HR decreases. During periods of self-regulated HR raising, these decrements were essentially eliminated, while during self-regulated HR lowering even greater response decrements were produced. Harris, Stephens, and Brady (1973–1974) felt that the counteraction by HR raising of the performance decrement shown during clicker–shock pairings was a clear indication of the potential for autonomic self-regulation to provide an effective technique for the prevention of performance decrement due to aversive classical conditioning stress. The counteraction of stress-elicited HR changes by biofeedback control has also been demonstrated in monkeys (Ainslie & Engel, 1974), and the relationship of these interactions to human performance should be studied further.

Earlier, we noted that Morgan and Coates (1975) had required their subjects to suppress theta and raise HR concurrently. The rationale for training HR increases was the finding of Harris, Stephens, and Brady, that HR increase was associated with increased accuracy and faster reaction times on the Continuous Performance Task. As will be recalled, Morgan and Coates found no positive effects from conbined self-regulated theta suppression and HR increase during a 48-hour period of continuous performance. Moreover, in an examination of individual differences and a closer inspection of each subject's response, they found that, where relations did exist between HR increase and performance, the relations were negative. A tendency appeared toward greater HR control's occurring with larger performance decrements, and greater theta control's occurring with smaller performance decrements. Morgan and Coates felt these results suggested that "the two control functions were antagonistic in their effects on performance" (1975, p. 25).

Operant control of HR, especially HR increase, as a technique for enhancing human performance appears to be more promising than enhancement of alpha. Since there were no EEG data recorded by Harris and his co-workers, one can only speculate whether or not the poorer performance during HR lowering was a reflection of lower arousal levels, and the reverse with HR increase. If this were true, HR lowering might be expected to increase EEG theta, although the findings of Morgan and Coates suggest considerable individual difference in this relationship. Further, Hord and Barber (1971) reported that the relation between alpha enhancement and basal HR was not the same across subjects and that, when the within-correlations over subjects were averaged, the average correlation did not differ significantly from zero. Elsewhere in this volume, Gary Schwartz presents the case for the simultaneous self-regulation of more than one physiological variable.

Muscle Relaxation

If there is one technique that can claim precedence over all the current biofeedback techniques, it is muscle relaxation (Jacobson,

1938). Does operant control of muscle activity enhance performance in nonstressful situations and prevent performance decrement in stressful conditions? From the data produced under the ARPA program, the answer must be "no."

Stoyva and Budzynski (1973) examined the effects of muscle-relaxation training on tasks involving either complex decision making or simple sensory motor activity. Performance under stress, and in the recovery phase after stress, was examined. The most severe test was in a complex decision task under stress. Here subjects were presented with visual slides of intelligence test problems (Cattell Culture-Fair Test) in which the missing figure in a series of geometric figures must be inferred. While engaged in this task, loud distracting noises were presented over headphones and, at arbitrary intervals, colored slides of a gory and disturbing automobile accident were presented in place of the problems. The objective was to determine whether or not subjects trained in moderating their arousal levels by means of self-regulated muscle relaxation would perform better (make more correct decisions) than subjects who lacked such training. No significant differences were found. In related experiments, these investigators also found no enhancement of performance in *(1)* complex decision making, *(2)* a serial 7s task, *(3)* stylus steadiness, *(4)* pursuit rotor performance, or *(5)* ability to maintain a sleep state in a distracting environment.

In an operational test of the effectiveness of muscle relaxation in overcoming stress-induced physiological and performance changes, Smith (1975) examined 36 subjects in a hyperbaric chamber. Three performance environments were used: *(1)* a control condition, involving no hyperbaria (simulated or real) open hatches to the chamber, and a nonstressful briefing; *(2)* an experimental condition, with simulated hyperbaria to 100 feet and a briefing designed to induce anxiety; and *(3)* a second experimental condition involving actual hyperbaria to 30 feet for induction of modest physiological stress plus simulated hyperbaria to 100 feet.

Nine subjects were given 8 weeks of self-regulation EMG biofeedback training and were encouraged to use this training to maintain a state of physiological relaxation throughout their chamber experience. A second group of nine subjects was given 2 weeks of simulated (and largely recognized as such) self-regulation training and was also asked to use its training to maintain a state of relaxation during the study. A third group of subjects was given no preliminary training but was asked to relax physiologically as much as possible throughout the study. The fourth group had no preliminary training and was given no specialized instructions with regard to relaxation. All subjects were told casually to "sit back and relax" at several points when physiological measures were taken.

Recording of EMG, HR, and blood pressure was done periodically throughout the simulated and actual pressurization, and during an initial phase for the first and fourth groups. Immediately upon stabilization of the chamber, all subjects were given the TODAY form of the Multiple Affect Adjective Checklist (MAACL) to assess their level of anxiety, depression, and hostility. During this time, the subjects were again asked to relax, and recordings were made of all three physiological parameters. The remaining 30 minutes of each chamber run were utilized for performance measurement interrupted for ventilation and physiological recording. Performance measures included a "Mathematics Aptitude Test" and the "Ship Destination Test" designed to assess general reasoning ability, which has been shown to decline under physical stress (Smith & Armstrong, 1973). An apparently operational vigilance task was superimposed over these cognitive activities to reduce perceptual narrowing and provide a more realistic environment. This task consisted of monitoring the depth indicator in the chamber and informing the experimenter of any deviations from 100 feet, greater than ±5 feet. Such deviations were programmed to occur twice during each trial. A detailed debriefing followed the chamber experience, including "dehoaxing" the subject with regard to any deception employed.

All subjects receiving biofeedback training showed a significant decrease in EMG levels. Simulated training did not "fool" the subjects into believing they had been trained, nor did it appreciably affect their general physiological state. All subjects, however, whether under simulated or actual hyperbaria, perceived themselves to be at a pressure equivalent to a depth of at least 50 feet and some subjects assumed their depth to be 100 feet. The effectiveness of this stress was further manifested by elevated physiological parameters and depressed performance measures. There was, however, no apparent benefit of biofeedback training in the suppression of physiological response to stress (subjects who had received biofeedback training reported difficulty in concentrating on self-regulatory activity during the stressful "dive"), nor did biofeedback training enhance performance on any of the tasks. In his summary, Smith concluded, "based upon the limited data available in this study, one can conclude that the relatively mild form of perceived physical threat created in this highly controlled laboratory environment is sufficient to produce expected increments in physiological functions and a concomitant decrement in performance. However, biofeedback training as conducted for this study, while effectively reducing physiological levels in low stress situations appears ineffective for the control of physiological functions or the enhancement of performance under perceived physical threat stress" (Smith, 1975, p. 28).

In another EMG study undertaken at the U.S. Air Force Academy (Tebbs, Eggleston, Prather, Simondi, & Jarboe, 1974), cadets who had received EMG feedback training scored higher on a check flight in a T-41 trainer, as rated by instructors on a variety of specific measures in a double-blind design. No similar effects were found, however, in an earlier flight simulator test. Unfortunately, there are no data as to whether the EMG-trained cadets used their relaxation during the check ride. Training had taken place several months earlier, and there were neither instructions to use it during the check ride nor instrumentation to monitor EMG levels.

This summary of studies relating EMG and performance offers little promise for use of biofeedback-controlled muscular relaxation to achieve performance enhancement in stressful situations. Furthermore, it may be naive to search for acute situational benefits from EMG regulation; certainly muscle relaxation under stress would be maladaptive in many situations requiring sudden and vigorous physical response. The more chronic and general tension-reducing effect frequently described by those who employ a regime of relaxation training may, if real, result in increased ability to handle life stress. The aims of this program, however, did not include an evaluation of these claims.

DISCUSSION

Several conclusions offer themselves as a result of this body of work. First, it seems that biofeedback offers much less powerful and robust self-control over certain internal physiological events than many researchers anticipated on the strength of early anecdotal evidence. Clearly, from the work that has taken place in many laboratories, it is extremely difficult, if not impossible, to train subjects to regulate nervous system events to a level contrary to the best interests of their own physiology. If a subject is resting comfortably, alert but relaxed, he probably is not going to be able to lower HR from 72 to 40, or raise it to 130 simply by deciding to do so. And these data offer no apparent reason he should wish to do so, other than to please the experimenter. Effects have been, in general, obtainable only in physiologically appropriate directions; attempts to develop ability to respond autonomically contrary to spontaneous tendencies have met with very limited success. A notable exception to this, however, has been the work of Edward Taub, in which some subjects have been able to dilate peripheral vasculature in very cold environments. The work by Taub is presented in Chapter 11 of this volume.

So far, this research has failed to identify specific configurations of physiological events that have unique and reliable concomitance with specific performance or psychological states, and that can be controlled for the purpose of eliciting these behaviors. The path of psychophysiological research is strewn with the negative results of those who believed that specific physiological events are associated with specific behaviors. The general versus the specific physiological determinants of emotional states and the role of cognition in the labeling of the visceral changes are still far from settled (see Schachter & Singer, 1962; Plutchik & Ax, 1967). The difficulty of delineating unique physiological responses associated with performance over several tasks and across subjects is clearly illustrated in the many reports that have stressed not only situational specificity but also individual response specificity of physiological response patterns (Sternbach, 1966).

Quite early in the ARPA program, emphasis shifted toward the use of self-regulation to control of the physiological changes brought about by stress and to aid in the maintenance of arousal or alertness. Implicit in the first goal was the belief that, if the visceral responses to stress could be brought under control, then feelings of panic, fear, fright, anger, and so on would be reduced. This approach was motivated largely by the many observations that perceived physiological response often interacts with and intensifies the psychological state. The results of stress studies in this program, however, cast doubt on the ability of a subject to utilize previously acquired operant skills to maintain basal or near basal physiological activity during the crisis periods. Sleep loss and fatigue reduced the ability to maintain self-regulated brain activity, fear of shock changed the subject's ability to modify HR, and hyperbaric stress, plus the performance tasks, made it difficult to achieve EMG relaxation. At the moment of truth, effective self-regulation may not be possible. In any event, the usefulness of biofeedback training for handling stress has not been convincingly demonstrated.

In another area, a recent finding by McLean and Milne (1975) and McLean (personal communication, 1975) is relevant to the effect of learned control of a physiological event on emotions and behavior.

These investigators taught snake-phobic subjects to decrease GSRs elicited by the feared stimuli. This training had no apparent effect upon a subject's subsequent approach behavior to snakes. These negative results offer no support for the proposition that learned regulation of at least one physiological concomitant of subjective fear can modify the behavior associated with that fear. There were no data reported as to changes, if any, in other autonomic events.

On the basis of the brain wave, heart rate, and EMG work reviewed above, it is clear that there is no easy and powerful key available in biofeedback for significant enhancement of performance. Reliable relations between internal events and performance have not been convincingly demonstrated in this series of studies. Certainly the results of this research program offer little support for the initial goal of using voluntary regulation of physiological events to enhance performance. The few interesting laboratory results on simple tests evaporated when more complex operational tests were performed outside the laboratory. Based upon these results, further effort toward the development of biofeedback techniques for performance enhancement does not appear reasonable. While biofeedback may offer a way to learn to relax more rapidly and perhaps more deeply, and may assist in the maintenance of desired arousal levels, further search for unique cause and effect relations between specific internal events and discrete performance components seems unwarranted.

REFERENCES

Ainslie, G. W., & Engel, B. T. Alteration of classically conditioned heart rate by operant reinforcement in monkeys. *Journal of Comparative and Physiological Psychology*, 1974, *87*, 373–382.

Alluisi, E. A. Methodology in the use of synthetic tasks to assess complex performance. *Human Factors*, 1967, *9*, 375–384.

Alluisi, E. A. Influence of work–rest scheduling and sleep loss on sustained performance. In W. P. Colquhoun (Ed.), *Aspects of human efficiency*. London: English Universities Press, 1972. Pp. 199–215.

Beatty, J. *Self regulation as an aid to human effectiveness* (Annual Progress Rep. under Contract N00014-70-C-0350 submitted to San Diego State University Foundation). Los Angeles: University of California, 1973.

Beatty, J., Greenberg, A., Deibler, W. P., & O'Hanlon, J. F. Operant control of occipital theta rhythm affects performance in a radar monitoring task. *Science*, 1974, *183*, 871–873.

Beatty, J., & O'Hanlon, J. F. *EEG theta regulation and radar monitoring performance of experienced radar operators and air traffic controllers* (UCLA Tech. Rep.). Los Angeles: University of California, March 1975.

Brady, J. V. Recent developments in the measurement of stress. In B. P. Rourke (Ed.), *Explorations in the psychology of stress and anxiety*. Don Mills, Ontario: Longmans Canada, 1969. Pp. 131–164.

Brady, J. V., Harris, A. H., Anderson, D. H., & Stephens, J. Instrumental control of autonomic responses: Cardiovascular monitoring and performance interactions. *Proceedings of Fourth Symposium on Behavior Modification* (Mexico City, 1974), in press.

Gannon, L., & Sternbach, R. A. Alpha enhancement as a treatment for pain: A case study. *Journal of Behavior Therapy and Experimental Psychiatry,* 1971, *2,* 209–213.

Green, E. E., Green, A. M., & Walters, E. D. Self-regulation of internal states. In J. Rose (Ed.), *Progress of cybernetics: Proceedings of the International Congress of Cybernetics* (London, 1969). London: Gordon & Breach, 1970.

Harris, A. H., Findley, J. D., & Brady, J. V. Instrumental conditioning of blood pressure elevations in the baboon. *Conditioned Reflex,* 1971, *6,* 215–226.

Harris, A. H., Gilliam, W. J., Findley, J. D., & Brady, J. V. Instrumental conditioning of large-magnitude, daily, 12-hour blood pressure elevations in the baboon. *Science,* 1973, *182,* 175–177.

Harris, A. H., Stephens, J., & Brady, J. V. *Self-regulation of performance-related physiological processes* (Annual Progress Reps. under Contract N00014-70-C-0350 submitted to San Diego State University Foundation). Baltimore: Johns Hopkins University, 1973–1974.

Honorton, C., Davidson, R., & Bindler, P. Feedback-augmented EEG alpha, shifts in subjective state, and ESP card-guessing performance. *Journal of the American Society for Psychical Research,* 1971, *65,* 308–323.

Hord, D. J., & Barber, J. Alpha control: Effectiveness of two kinds of feedback. *Psychonomic Science,* 1971, *25,* 151–154.

Hord, D. J., Lubin, A., Tracy, M. L., Jensma, B. W., & Johnson, L. C. Feedback for high EEG alpha does not maintain performance or mood during sleep loss. *Psychophysiology,* in press.

Hord, D. J., Tracy, M. L., Lubin, A., & Johnson, L. C. Effect of self-enhanced EEG alpha on performance and mood after two nights of sleep loss. *Psychophysiology,* 1975, *12,* 585–590.

Hord, D. J., Wilson, C. E., Townsend, R., & Johnson, L. C. Theta suppression effects on complex visual sonar operation. Paper presented at the Fifth Annual ARPA Self-Regulation Symposium, Grand Teton, Wyoming, June 1975.

Jacobson, E. *Progressive relaxation.* Chicago: University of Chicago Press, 1938.

Kamiya, J. Operant control of the EEG alpha rhythm and some of its reported effects on consciousness. In C. T. Tart (Ed.), *Altered states of consciousness: A book of readings.* New York: Wiley, 1969. Pp. 507–517.

Kamiya, J. *Self-regulation as an aid to human effectiveness* (Annual Progress Rep. under Contract N00014-70-C-0350 submitted to San Diego State University Foundation). San Francisco: Langley Porter Neuropsychiatric Institute, June 1972.

McLean, P. D., & Milne, L. G. Effect of exteroceptive feedback in conditioning electrodermal activity in pre-conditional fears. *Perceptual and Motor Skills,* 1975, *40,* 487–493.

Melzack, R., & Perry, C. Self-regulation of pain: The use of alpha-feedback and hypnotic training for the control of chronic pain. *Experimental Neurology,* 1975, *46,* 452–469.

Morgan, B. B., Jr., & Alluisi, E. A. Synthetic work: Methodology for assessment of human performance. *Perceptual and Motor Skills,* 1972, *35,* 835–845.

Morgan, B. B., Jr., & Coates, G. D. *Enhancement of performance during sustained operations through the use of EEG and heart-rate autoregulation* (Annual Progress Rep. under Contract N00014-70-C-0350 submitted to San Diego State University Foundation). Norfolk, Va.: Old Dominion University, June 1975.

Nowlis, D. P., & Kamiya, J. The control of electroencephalographic alpha rhythms through auditory feedback and the associated mental activity. *Psychophysiology,* 1970, *6,* 476–484.

O'Hanlon, J. F., & Beatty, J. *EEG theta regulation and radar monitoring performance in a controlled field experiment* (Tech. Rep. under Contract N00014-70-C-0350 submitted to San Diego State University Foundation). Los Angeles: Human Factors Research and University of California at Los Angeles, 1975.

Orne, M. T., & Paskewitz, D. Adversive situational effects on ALPHA feedback training. *Science,* 1974, *186,* 458–460.

Orne, M. T., Evans, F., Wilson, S., & Paskewitz, D. *The potential effectiveness of autoregulation as a technique to increase performance under stress* (Final Summary Rep. under Contract N00014-70-C-0350 submitted to San Diego State University Foundation). Philadelphia: University of Pennsylvania, 1975.

Paskewitz, D. A., & Orne, M. T. Visual effects on alpha feedback training. *Science,* 1973, *181,* 360–363.

Plutchik, R., & Ax, A. F. A critique of determinants of emotional state by Schachter and Singer (1962). *Psychophysiology,* 1967, *4,* 79–82.

Regestein, Q. R., Buckland, G. H., & Pegram, G. V. Effect of daytime alpha rhythm maintenance on subsequent sleep. *Psychosomatic Medicine,* 1973, *35,* 415–418.

Rosvold, H. E., Mirsky, A. F., Sarason, I., Bransome, E. D., Jr., & Beck, L. H. A continuous performance test of brain damage. *Journal of Consulting and Clinical Psychology,* 1956, *20,* 343–350.

Schachter, S., & Singer, J. E. Cognitive, social, and physiological determinants of emotional state. *Psychological Review,* 1962, *69,* 379–399.

Smith, R. W. *Self-regulation as an aid to human effectiveness* (Final Rep. under Contract N00014-70-C-0350 submitted to San Diego State University Foundation). Coral Gables, Fla.: Applied Science Associates, Inc., June 1975.

Smith, R. W., & Armstrong, T. R. *Laboratory studies of the effects of physical hazard on shelter management behavior* (Final Rep.). Coral Gables. Fla.: American Institutes for Research, 1973.

Stephens, J. H., Harris, A. H., & Brady, J. V. Large magnitude heart rate changes in subjects instructed to change their heart rates and given exteroceptive feedback. *Psychophysiology,* 1972, *9,* 283–285.

Stephens, J. H., Harris, A. H., Brady, J. V., & Shaffer, J. W. Psychological and physiological variables associated with large magnitude voluntary heart rate changes. *Psychophysiology,* 1975, *12,* 381–387.

Sternbach, R. A. *Principles of psychophysiology.* New York: Academic Press, 1966.

Stoyva, J., & Budzynski, T. *Biofeedback training in the self-induction of sleep* (Annual Progress Rep. under Contract N00014-70-C-0350 submitted to San Diego State University Foundation). Denver: University of Colorado Medical Center, June 1973.

Tebbs, R., Eggleston, R., Prather, D., Simondi, T., & Jarboe, T. *Stress management through scientific muscle relaxation training and its relation to simulated and actual flying training* (Final Rep. under ARPA Order 2409 submitted to the Defense Advanced Research Projects Agency), November 21, 1974.

Williams, H. L., Granda, A. M., Jones, R. C., Lubin, A., & Armington, J. C. EEG frequency and finger pulse volume as predictors of reaction time during sleep loss. *Electroencephalography and Clinical Neurophysiology,* 1962, *14,* 64–70.

II

THE AUTONOMIC NERVOUS SYSTEM

8

Biofeedback and Patterning of Autonomic and Central Processes: CNS–Cardiovascular Interactions*

GARY E. SCHWARTZ
Yale University

INTRODUCTION AND OVERVIEW

One of the most important and intriguing discoveries involving biofeedback procedures has been the development of rapidly learned self-regulation of specific autonomic responses. The discovery of the capacity for learned specificity of visceral self-regulation has revised the classic, oversimplistic conception of the autonomic nervous system as being totally automatic, diffuse, and tightly coupled (Miller, 1969). We now know that the visceral system is, in fact, finely tuned to both anticipate and respond to specific behavioral demands in a differentiated, patterned manner (e.g., Cohen & Obrist, 1975). The patterning of visceral responses, under normal conditions, represents an adap-

* This chapter was completed while the author was on leave from Harvard University at the University of British Columbia.

tive functional CNS reaction designed to maintain the bodily structures. This capacity for patterned regulation of visceral responses by the brain in its dynamic commerce with the external environment reflects, in Cannon's words, a "wisdom of the body" that markedly extends his original statement of the phenomena (Cannon, 1939).

The concept of patterning needs to be underscored, for it has important theoretical and practical implications regarding the conception, design, and interpretation of basic and clinical research in visceral self-regulation (Schwartz, 1974, 1975, 1976). At the simplest level, it has been pointed out that the self-regulation of patterns of responses using pattern biofeedback procedures can have different consequences from those observed when controlling individual functions alone (Schwartz, 1976). This basic observation provides the foundation for the hypothesis that by training subjects to control voluntarily patterns of visceral and motor responses, it is possible to assess central and peripheral linkages between physiological responses and their relationship to human behavior and consciousness (Schwartz, 1975). However, the conceptual implications go deeper than this, because it becomes evident that even in the process of providing feedback for any "single" overt or covert physiological response, one is, in fact, providing feedback for numerous other physiological responses to varying degrees. More importantly, at a neurophysiological level, it becomes clear that in the process of providing feedback for a selected effector response, one is in fact presenting the feedback for a complex *pattern of neural system activity*. To the extent that the brain and nervous system represent the final common pathway for learned behavior and regulation (Luria, 1973), it stands to reason that visceral biofeedback (or skeletal motor biofeedback) is, ultimately, patterned neural biofeedback, and that the learned physiological regulation is ultimately patterned neural self-regulation which is expressed via the peripheral nervous system as "behavior" (Schwartz, in press-a).

The purpose of this chapter is to consider the conceptual, procedural, and practical issues regarding biofeedback and pattern self-regulation as expressed in the autonomic nervous system. Research involving cardiovascular processes as a model system will be reviewed, emphasizing a neurophysiological analysis of reflexive and learned cardiovascular self-regulation. Included are new data from our laboratory on the patterning of neural skill learning in the regulation of heart rate and the patterning of specific cortical processes in cardiac self-regulation using feedback and instructions. Clinical implications of pattern self-regulation are discussed elsewhere (Schwartz, 1973, 1974, 1976, in press-a).

THEORY AND MEASUREMENT OF ANS–CNS PATTERNING

The concept of patterning requires, first of all, the systematic assessment of multiple processes occurring simultaneously. In information processing terms, this implies the *parallel* processing of multiple sources of input, with the goal of assessing the unique gestalts or response complexes that emerge. It is beyond the scope of this chapter to consider the more advanced mathematical and computer pattern analysis procedures that have been developed for conceptually similar problems such as recognizing faces, assessing voice or finger prints, or detecting geographic landmarks. However, it is valuable to realize that advances in these fields do have important implications for the improved assessment of physiological patterning, though bridges between these fields are just beginning to be built.

The notion of parallel process analyses of multiple inputs serves the immediate function of increasing the awareness of researchers regarding the potential impact of biofeedback procedures on multiple processes. If the investigator does not consider the possibility that response systems other than those that he or she is measuring may be simultaneously receiving contingent feedback to varying degrees, the potential changes in the other systems will go unnoticed or, if measured, will not be readily understood. The simplest means of conceptualizing response patterning derives from a binary (yes–no) analysis of response presence or absence (Schwartz, 1974). Although this is often an artificial means of defining any change from a biological perspective, nonetheless it is one that has important behavioral significance because feedback and reward from the external environment often occur in binary bursts. To the extent that operant conditioning utilizes binary (yes–no) contingencies, it becomes a good starting place for integrating learning procedures with the measurement of patterning. It should be noted that it is the binary characteristic of the operant procedure that makes it so useful, conceptually and practically, in the *measurement* of patterning; the *interpretation* of the underlying systems of neurochemical processes involved in the learned self-regulation, in this writer's opinion, profits more from biobehaviorally oriented analyses of cybernetics and systems theory (e.g., Powers, 1973).

Measurement of Levels of Patterning: Blood Pressure

An example of the binary approach to patterning involves feedback and reward for human blood pressure and its underlying cardiovascular determinants. The regulation of blood pressure is a particularly good illustration of patterning; blood pressure is a response only in a sense that it is a physical quantity that can be measured. It is not a biological effector organ, or pattern of organs, and has no direct neural or humoral control. Rather, blood pressure is the integrated product of dynamically changing patterns of underlying cardiovascular changes, which are themselves neurally and humorally regulated in complex ways. Consequently, if an investigator defines some binary criterion level that represents high or low pressure, and then presents feedback contingently for this change, the subject will be receiving feedback for some *pattern* of underlying cardiovascular effectors. Since there may be numerous ways of combining the underlying patterns of cardiovascular effectors to achieve the same pressure level, it becomes clear how the binary feedback is not necessarily highly coupled with any subcomponent or pattern of subcomponents within the cardiovascular system. If the investigator desires more consistent learned regulation of specific components of underlying systems, either for theoretical or clinical reasons, it follows that it is necessary to more carefully monitor the pattern of underlying responses and provide feedback and reward accordingly (Schwartz, 1974).

Since in the normal, intact person, blood pressure is never zero, the definition of response presence or absence is described more correctly as reflecting high and low values relative to some criterion value. In our previous research on patterning of systolic blood pressure, diastolic blood pressure, and heart rate (reviewed in Schwartz, 1975, 1976; Shapiro & Surwit, 1976), we selected the approximate midpoint or median as the level for defining high and low. For ease of describing patterns, the words "up" and "down" are placed above and below the response initials, as superscripts and subscripts, respectively (Schwartz, 1974). Extending this procedure to the physiology of blood pressure regulation, the first sublevel of analysis is the recognition that blood pressure (BP—Level A) is determined by a complex interaction of the total output of the heart (Cardiac Output, or CO) and the resistance it encounters in the peripheral vasculature (Peripheral Resistance, or PR—Level B) (See Figure 8.1). Consequently, since BP at all times is the dynamic product of CO and PR, binary feedback for increases in BP can be achieved by some *pattern* of regulation of CO and PR. Feedback for BP^{up}, then, could conceivably represent, using median values of CO and PR, either a $CO^{up}PR^{up}$ pattern, a $CO^{up}PR_{down}$ pattern, or a $CO_{down}PR^{up}$ pattern. Since it is impossible at present to measure both of these hemodynamic components continually in the

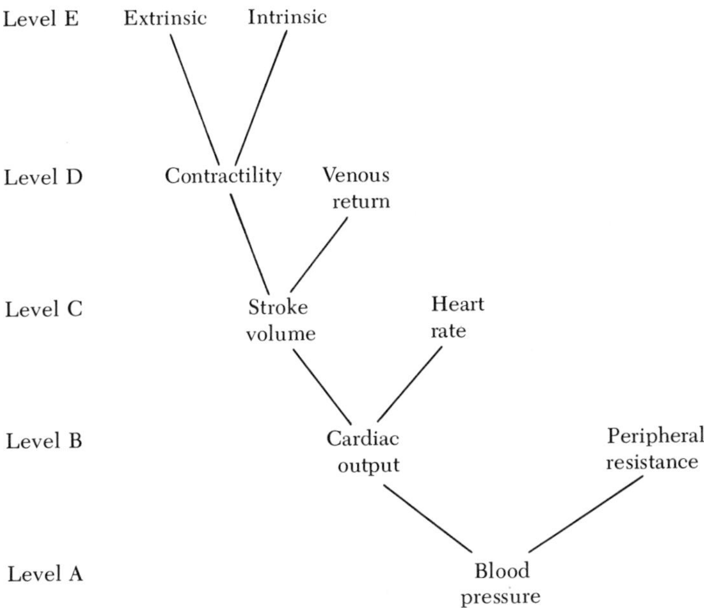

Figure 8.1 A *descriptive* analysis of patterning of processes underlying the regulation of blood pressure. The figure is not complete, but rather illustrates some of the levels of analysis as described in a standard cardiovascular textbook. A *conceptual*, more comprehensive and general description of patterns of processes underlying the expression of blood pressure is presented in Figure 8.2.

normal, intact person, it is not surprising that cardiovascular researchers have not been encouraged to develop this line of reasoning.

However, this is only the simplest level of defining the underlying patterns, and it does not address the effector organs themselves. The next lowest level (Level C) of analysis is to define the pattern of changes that determine CO and PR, respectively. For example, the total output of blood from the heart per unit time (CO) depends on the amount of blood ejected from the heart per beat (called Stroke Volume, or SV) and the rate that the heart is pumping (Heart Rate, or HR). Hence, CO^{up} actually reflects an underlying pattern that, in terms of median binary levels, can be defined as $SV^{up}HR^{up}$, $SV^{up}HR_{down}$, or $SV_{down}HR^{up}$. If we replace CO in the original equation, ($BP = CO \times PR$) with SV and HR, it becomes immediately clear that our understanding of the underlying patterns must become more complicated. A similar kind of analysis can be applied to PR.

Describing CO in terms of SV and HR brings us closer to, but not completely at, the level of the effector organs, since we have yet to define the patterns of determinants underlying stroke volume. When this is done (Level D), we find that the picture is even more complicated, because stroke volume is not determined *solely* by the cardiac organ itself, and those components that are determined by the cardiac organ are not all determined by neural influence from the brain. The volume of blood ejected by the heart per beat is determined by: *(1)* the amount of blood reaching the heart from the veins (venous return) and *(2)* the force with which the heart contracts (contractility). Venous return is substantially determined by vascular rather than cardiac factors (at least immediately preceding a given heart beat). Contractility, on the other hand, is also not a simple response and, in fact, represents a *patterned* response at the next lowest level (Level E). This is because the force with which the heart contracts is determined by *(1)* neural reflex mechanisms within the heart itself which lead the heart to automatically contract more forcefully as a function of more blood being in the heart, and *(2)* neural and humoral factors regulated by the brain, such as sympathetic tone to the ventricles.

To summarize thus far, blood pressure (Level A) represents a pattern of cardiac output and peripheral resistance (Level B) of which cardiac output is a pattern of stroke volume and heart rate (Level C). But, stroke volume is itself a pattern of venous return and contractility (Level D) and, further, contractility is a pattern including intrinsic and extrinsic influences on the heart itself (Level E). These *descriptive* levels of patterning are illustrated in Figure 8.1. A more *conceptually* accurate and general description of the five levels of patterns of processes underlying blood pressure are shown in Figure 8.2.

Referring now to Figure 8.2, once we reach the level of organ behavior (Level 3) and the pattern of mechanisms regulating this behavior (Level 4), it is finally possible to express the differential patterning of *peripheral* neural–humoral factors involved in the biofeedback regulation of blood pressure. Since, at present, most of these processes cannot be monitored continuously in the intact person, such research is being initially developed in surgically prepared lower animals. However, the *technological* difficulties of response measurement notwithstanding, a more serious problem is the *conceptual* one of keeping track of all of the various components making up these patterns and converting them into a form that can be understood by the investigator studying them.

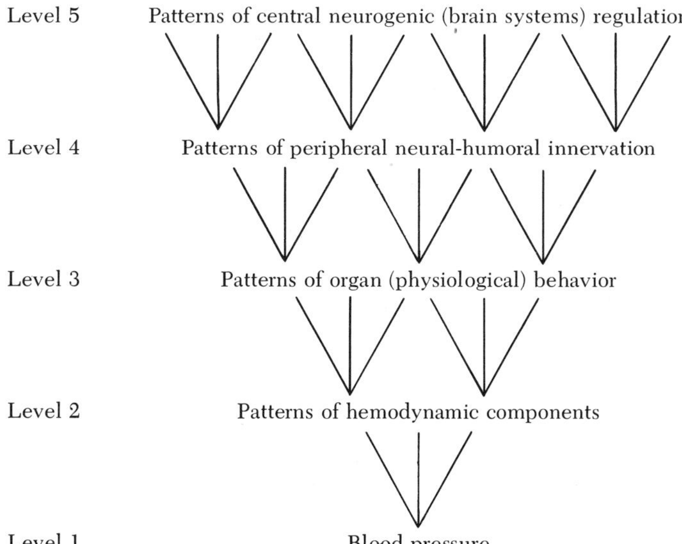

Figure 8.2 A conceptual and general description of levels of analysis underlying the behavioral regulation of blood pressure. The figure illustrates how blood pressure (Level 1) is the composite of patterns of hemodynamic factors (Level 2) which are created by patterns of effector organs (Level 3) innervated by patterns of peripheral neural and humoral mechanisms (Level 4) which are expressions of (regulated by) patterns of central neurogenic processes (Level 5). Biofeedback for "blood pressure" (Level 1) is ultimately feedback for patterns of central neurogenic processes (Level 5), the system responsible for active learning in the human organism.

Computers can be programmed, using the simple binary analysis procedure of multiple inputs, to keep track of the various combinations of processes occurring over time. For example, we have developed a computer program for a PDP-11 that *(1)* measures four different parameters simultaneously, *(2)* determines which of the 16 possible combinations of the four parameters (e.g., $A^{up}B_{down}C_{down}D^{up}$) are occurring, *(3)* generates histograms for each of the 16 possible patterns, and *(4)* makes it possible to present feedback and reward for any single parameter alone, two at a time, three at a time, or selectively for any one of the 16 possible patterns of the four parameters (described in Roemer, 1975). Although it is no easy task to develop such a program, it is solvable given current hardware, programming languages, and theoretical directions. However, the problem ultimately rests on the shoulders of the investigator who must develop the requisite perceptual and cognitive skills for keeping track of, and interpreting, the complex patterns that are uncovered.

Once the concept of patterning is recognized, even from the simple perspective of binary components, it becomes clear how the notion of "direct conditioning" or "single response" training is misleading and incorrect. Even if one thinks from a simple behavioral perspective that he or she is working with a single response such as heart rate, upon adapting a broader biobehavioral framework, one soon recognizes that the mechanisms of regulation actually involve an underlying pattern of sympathetic and parasympathetic influences on the heart, as well as additional humoral factors transmitted by the blood. This description of the *peripheral* pattern underlying the so-called "single response" is still incomplete, because various *central* patterns of cortical and subcortical processes (Level 5) are differentially involved in the ultimate generation of the pattern of peripheral factors (neural and humoral—Level 4) that is expressed via the cardiac muscle (Level 3) as a change in rate of contraction.

The concept of patterning, then, is a general one having implications regarding how we define a response and therefore how we measure and manipulate it. Although, for ease of communication, the term *specific* response training is contrasted with *pattern* feedback training, the present analysis hopefully clarifies that these terms are not dichotomous. This is because the training of any single overt behavioral response, or underlying physiological response expressed as an effector organ change, is ultimately learned as a complex pattern of neural systems (Luria, 1973). Thus, the concept of patterning has the potential to make it easier to describe more comprehensively the interaction of the underlying processes involved in learned self-regulation and the translation connecting behavioral and biological theories. In this context, *learned behavior (e.g. Level 3) is defined as the integrated expression of patterns of neural and humoral components (Level 4) generated by the central nervous system (Level 5).*

Temporal Components in Patterning

Two other aspects regarding the conceptualization and measurement of patterning need to be considered at this point. Both involve the recognition that all biobehavioral activity occurs over time, and that our description of this activity must ultimately involve defining response topography in an analogue (as opposed to binary) fashion (e.g., Powers, 1973). For example, the distinction between systolic and diastolic blood pressure is made not only in terms of magnitude, but also along a *temporal* dimension in relation to the heart (systolic pressure being the initial peak pressure *following* each contraction of

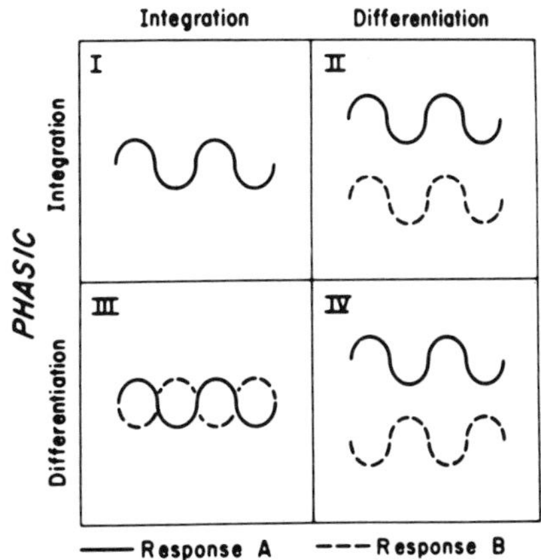

Figure 8.3 Sine waves illustrating differences between and patterning of tonic and phasic integration and differentiation for two hypothetical responses (A and B). Quadrant I represents the pattern of tonic and phasic integration; Quadrant IV represents the pattern of tonic and phasic differentiation. Quadrants II and III represent, respectively, the patterns of phasic integration and tonic differentiation and phasic differentiation and tonic integration. [From Schwartz, 1974.]

the heart, diastolic pressure being the minimum pressure reached following contraction, *after* systolic pressure and *before* the next heart beat occurs). Thus, *the definitions of systolic and diastolic pressure are themselves illustrations of the patterning concept, since they reflect specific patterns of amplitude and temporal factors.*

When the temporal dimension is recognized, it becomes evident that issues of response definition involve the temporal window through which one chooses to look. The first point is discussed in traditional psychophysiology as the distinction between tonic versus phasic changes (Sternbach, 1966). Tonic activity typically refers to underlying baseline activity which is more stable in nature, occurring and computed over tens of seconds or minutes in duration. Phasic activity, on the other hand, usually refers to responses superimposed on the tonic activity which are more labile in nature and often occur within a few seconds. It follows that when one gives binary feedback for *absolute* criterion level, one is in fact giving feedback for a specific *pattern* of the *tonic and phasic components.* To the extent that these components reflect differences in underlying neural and humoral mechanisms, then the issue of patterning becomes more acute. A schematic diagram reflecting how it is possible to obtain differential patterning of tonic and phasic factors is illustrated in Figure 8.3 (from Schwartz, 1974).

The second point is an extension of the phasic–tonic distinction and refers not only to the need to recognize patterning across responses in a parallel process sense, but also to the patterning of responses in a serial, sequential sense. Differential response topography (i.e., the shape of the waveform of a dynamically changing analogue variable) within one single variable is complex enough; differential *pattern* topography, meaning the *sequencing* of different patterns adds another dimension to the complexity. Mathematical models for time series analyses are being developed, and have the potential to be applied to the biofeedback patterning question.[1]

A simple binary model can also be extended to handle the patterned sequence of patterns question. This involves determining the differential probabilities of a given pattern's being replaced by other specific patterns. An illustration of this kind of analysis has been applied to the sequencing of patterns of systolic blood pressure and one of its components (heart rate). (See Figure 8.4; from Schwartz, 1971.) This diagram illustrates how assessing the *average* frequency of the four possible binary-derived patterns of systolic blood pressure and heart rate can result in each occurring about 25% of the time. Yet, a tightly coupled phasic interrelationship between BP and HR can coexist when viewed temporally. This temporal factor may influence the nature of learned systolic blood pressure and heart rate pattern regulation obtained with biofeedback (Schwartz, 1972).

Careful analysis reveals that phasic heart rate leads blood pressure by two to three beats. When the $BP_{down}HR_{down}$ pattern changes, the probability is over .70 that it will change to a $BP_{down}HR^{up}$ pattern. When the $BP_{down}HR^{up}$ pattern changes, the probability is again over .70 that it will change to $BP^{up}HR^{up}$. The remaining sequencing, BP^{up}-HR^{up} to $BP^{up}HR_{down}$, and $BP^{up}HR_{down}$ to $BP_{down}HR_{down}$, completes the cycle with comparable probability values. Consequently, if a subject is given feedback and reward for $BP^{up}HR_{down}$, the probability of this pattern's being immediately *preceded* by a BP^{up} HR^{up} is quite high. To the extent that immediacy of feedback influences learned visceral self-regulation (Lang, 1974), it might be predicted that subjects would learn a more complex patterned skill of regulating both $BP^{up}HR_{down}$ *and* $BP^{up}HR^{up}$ with $BP^{up}HR_{down}$ biofeedback. This prediction will be

[1] One instance is a recent time series model of mother–child interactions (Thomas & Martin, 1976). Physiological or neurophysical data can easily be substituted for overt behavioral data, and the model can be extended to handle multiple parallel processes.

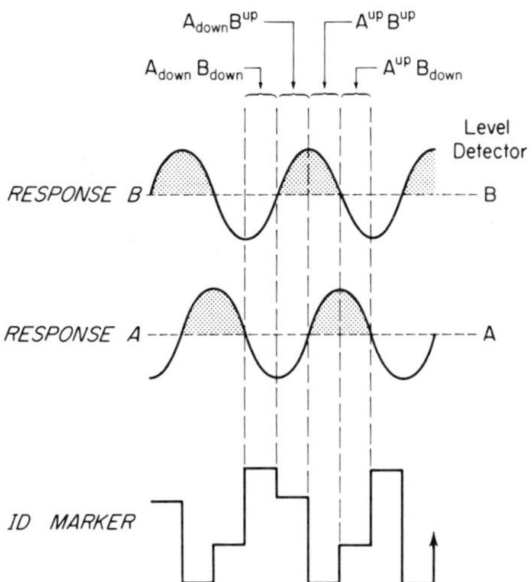

Figure 8.4 Hypothetical sine wave analysis of the observed sequencing of blood pressure (response A) –heart rate (response B) patterns. Response B leads response A by 90 degrees. The sequence of the four patterns is displayed on the ID Marker, explained in Figure 8.5. [From Schwartz, 1971.]

returned to later. The point here is to recognize that one can consider the concept of *patterned sequencing of patterns,* and that patterned sequences of patterns can be assessed within a simple binary perspective using currently available computer and mathematical procedures. However, the full implications of this issue for learned self-regulation have yet to be systematically explored.

Problems in Interpreting Patterning

The major difficulty inherent in discussing patterning is that, even using a model system as simple and artificial as the binary analysis procedure, the researcher has the tendency to become overwhelmed by the complexity of the data and issues. Clearly, the shotgun approach to pattern research, regarding the definition of variables to be measured and patterning procedures to be used, will likely lead to information overload on the part of the investigator. The research strategy preferred in this chapter is to take a more focused, systematic approach to patterning. This involves carefully selecting a few variables because of their hypothesized psychobiological relevance to the particular problem under investigation. In this way, it becomes possible to not lose sight of either the forest or the trees, and consequently develop a more pragmatic and comprehensive understanding linking the response pattern to its underlying components.

Before considering empirical data on biofeedback and patterning of cardiovascular and related processes, it is worthwhile to further consider the fundamental neurophysiological question (Level 5, Figure 8.2) underlying self-regulation. At the present time, it is indeed a mystery how it is possible for the brain (Level 5) to associate events from the outside environment with the behavior of its peripheral organs (Level 3) as expressed by the peripheral nervous system (Level 4). The brain's capability for deriving such linkages and associations, and then regulating those specific pattern processes to meet specific goals, is extraordinary. Examples of the brain's ability to finely regulate electrocortical (Mulholland, 1977) and skeletal (Basmajian, 1977) activity are discussed elsewhere in this volume. The challenge of ultimately describing learned control of visceral responses in terms of self-regulation of patterns of brain processes can be raised at this point, even though we currently lack the technology and theory to adequately address the challenge. Despite these limitations, it is possible to make a start in formulating the challenge and in obtaining rudimentary data that illustrate the patterning of electrocortical activity underlying visceral self-regulation. This challenge will be returned to later.

DETERMINANTS OF LEARNED PATTERNING: EXAMPLES OF CARDIOVASCULAR SELF-REGULATION

There is now a large body of literature on biofeedback and the regulation of various cardiovascular and related processes. Data are available regarding heart rate and other cardiac variables (Lang, 1974; Engel & Bleecker, 1974), as well as peripheral vasculature changes, including temperature (reviewed in this volume by Taub). The patterning approach can readily be applied to any of these areas, but space precludes reviewing this work here. However, it should be evident that the regulation of heart rate and contractility (Figure 8.2—Level 3) for example, involves the differential patterning of sympathetic, parasympathetic, and humoral factors (Level 4). These are ultimately regulated in the CNS by patterns of neural system activity (Level 5), some of these systems being the neural substrates for human cognitive processes. Similarly, feedback regulation of a composite response like skin temperature (Level 1) is actually feedback for various patterns of vascular and other physiological (such as sweat gland) activity (Levels 2 and 3). At the present time, there are no published studies that have systematically presented feedback and reward for specific patterns of these underlying processes with the goal of determining how the component processes contribute to the expression of the composite response. However, research on the regulation of human blood pressure provides a paradigm that illustrates one direction such research can take.[2]

Binary Assessment of Cardiovascular Patterning

In our initial studies on the regulation of human blood pressure using feedback and reward, the ultimate goal was the development of a potential behavioral approach to the treatment of hypertension. The design of a simple binary feedback system for blood pressure (Tursky, Shapiro, & Schwartz, 1972) was not only determined by the theoretical orientation prevalent at that time (operant conditioning), but also by the biomedical constraints involved in measuring relevant changes in blood pressure at each heart beat using nonsurgical procedures. The instrumentation constraint for blood pressure per se stimulated our use of simple binary feedback procedures for some of the component processes underlying blood pressure. The purpose here was to generate a comparable binary feedback display for studying the mechanisms underlying learned blood pressure regulation. since, unlike blood pressure, responses such as heart rate can be readily monitored on a continuous basis, it is possible to provide more complex analogue feedback displays reflecting their activity. However, it was a fortuitous accident of instrumentation *not* to present subjects at that time with analogue feedback for responses such as heart rate, since this stimulated the development of the binary-based patterning analysis procedure.

Figure 8.5 is a sample polygraph record illustrating the median procedure for giving binary feedback for systolic blood pressure, heart rate, and patterns of blood pressure and heart rate. For systolic blood pressure, a cuff is inflated to a pressure level approximating average systolic blood pressure and held constant, typically for a period of 50 beats (Tursky *et al.*, 1972). At each heart beat, blood pressure rises and reaches peak systolic. If the peak pressure on a given beat is greater than the constant pressure in the cuff, blood will flow under the cuff and a Korotkoff sound can be detected by a microphone placed at the

[2] The reader who has read recent reviews of this research (e.g., Schwartz, 1975, 1976) may wish to skim this section and go on to the next, which begins on page 204.

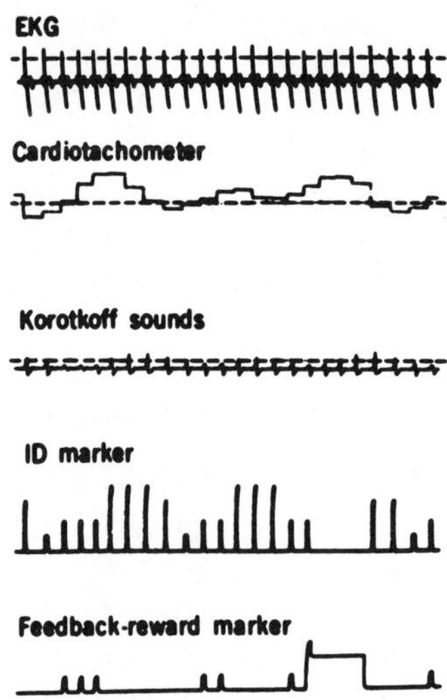

Figure. 8.5 Representative portion of a polygraph record of the binary pattern system operation. Shown are the electrocardiogram (EKG), heart rate (HR) displayed through a cardiotachometer, Korotkoff sounds measured at a constant cuff pressure, and two marker channels. Dashed lines represent the approximate levels of the three electronic level detectors. The presence or absence of a Korotkoff sound relative to the constant pressure in the cuff indicates whether blood pressure (BP) is up or down, while HR is rated up or down relative to the median HR. After each heart cycle (except during a reward), one of four possible marks appears on the ID marker channel. The longest and shortest marks indicate integration, with $BP^{up}HR^{up}$ producing the longest mark and $BP_{down}HR_{down}$ producing the shortest mark. The other two marks indicate differentiation, with $BP^{up}HR_{down}$ producing the third longest mark, and $BP_{down}HR^{up}$ producing the second shortest mark. The bottom channel indicates which one of the four possible patterns is receiving feedback (short mark) and reward (long mark). In this example, feedback is occurring for the $BP_{down}HR^{up}$ pattern. [From Schwartz, 1972.]

distal end. Conversely, if the peak pressure on a given beat is less than the constant pressure in the cuff, blood will not flow under the cuff and no sound will be detected. By autonomically assessing the percentage of Korotkoff sounds present and absent for a given 50 beat trial, it is possible to *(1)* administer binary feedback for the presence of a sound (BP^{up}) or the absence of a sound (BP_{down}), and *(2)* obtain an accurate measure of median pressure (within 2 mmHg for 50% ± 25% Korotkoff sounds) for the trial. It should be clear that binary feedback in this situation reflects a combination (pattern) of phasic and tonic changes (see Figure 8.3). If the tonic levels shift by more than 2 mmHg on a given trial, the cuff pressure is adjusted on the next trial so as to continually maintain the percentage of sounds at approximately the 50% point.

The binary model is extended to heart rate in Figure 8.5. Beat-by-beat heart rate as displayed by a cardiotachometer is bisected at the median by an electronic level detector, and the presence (HR^{up}) or absence (HR_{down}) of a criterion heart rate at each heart beat is automatically detected. In reinforcement terms, two separate contingencies have been arranged in this example, one for systolic blood pressure and the other for heart rate. To the extent that heart rate contributes both in magnitude and time to the expression of systolic blood pressure, then reinforcement for one would involve simultaneous reinforcement for the other. The procedure for detecting the patterns of systolic blood pressure and heart rate is also shown in Figure 8.5. It illustrates that when binary feedback procedures are used, the percentage of each of the four possible phasic BP–HR patterns can be about 25%, yet the relationship may not be random when *temporal* patterning of the patterns is also considered (schematically displayed in Figure 8.4).

Biofeedback for Systolic Blood Pressure or Heart Rate

In the first two studies presenting binary feedback and reward for BP^{up} (in one group of subjects) and BP_{down} (in a second group of subjects), evidence of learned regulation of median systolic blood pressure was obtained after 25 training trials (Shapiro, Tursky, Gershon, & Stern, 1969; Shapiro, Tursky, & Schwartz, 1970a). Although the magnitude of regulation ($BP^{up} - BP_{down}$) was only about 5 mmHg, the changes were important in light of *(1)* the brevity of the training, *(2)* the simplicity of the feedback, *(3)* the biobehavioral constraints placed on the subjects (e.g., they were not allowed to move), and *(4)* the minimal instructions used (Schwartz, 1974). Present research indicates that each of these factors contributes in important ways to learned cardiovascular self-regulation.

When mean heart rate was examined in the subjects given systolic BP feedback, no differences were observed between the groups. In other words, the subjects had controlled their systolic pressure without changing heart rate. This implies that feedback for systolic blood pressure must be associated more directly with other variables comprising the pressure pattern, such as stroke volume and/or peripheral resistance. To test this conclusion further, in the third experiment feedback and reward were presented for criterion level heart rate changes using the same situational conditions (and thus the same biobehavioral constraints) as the previous pressure feedback studies (Shapiro, Tursky, & Schwartz, 1970b). Here the change in feedback conditions from systolic BP to HR reversed the findings; subjects learned to regulate their heart rate (HR^{up} minus HR_{down} differences of about six bpm) without corresponding changes in systolic blood pressure.

Biofeedback for Patterns of Systolic Pressure and Heart Rate

Stimulated by these findings, the patterning procedure displayed in Figure 8.5 was developed (Schwartz, Shapiro, & Tursky, 1971; Schwartz, 1972). It was predicted that the phasic relationship between heart rate and systolic blood pressure must result in 50% integration (BP^{up} HR^{up} and $BP_{down}HR_{down}$) and 50% differentiation ($BP^{up}HR_{down}$ and $BP_{down}HR_{up}$) in order to have obtained, using binary feedback and minimal instructions, the previous specificity findings. It was further predicted that if the feedback and reward were given more explicitly for selected BP–HR patterns, then subjects would learn to regulate the relationship between systolic pressure and heart rate. However, it was anticipated that to the extent that specific constraints (both central and peripheral) underlie the relationship between heart rate and other determinants of systolic pressure, these constraints would influence the degree to which subjects could self-regulate the different BP–HR patterns. Interestingly, the pattern biofeedback procedure uncovered constraints not readily apparent using the more traditional single-system biofeedback procedure.

Figure 8.6 presents results from an experiment in which binary feedback and reward were given for each of the four BP–HR patterns in separate groups of subjects (Schwartz, 1972). Unlike the previous specificity finding, the results showed that subjects could, in a single session, learn to voluntarily make their blood pressure and heart rate change in the same direction or, to a lesser extent, change in opposite directions when feedback was given for the appropriate BP–HR pattern. Evidence for unique effects uncovered with pattern feedback emerged from three sources: *(1)* Feedback for integration patterns produced somewhat larger effects (up − down difference scores after 25 trials for both BP and HR were approximately 40% greater) than feedback for either single variable alone; *(2)* feedback for integration patterns produced more rapid learning within the first 15 trials than feedback for the individual variables; and *(3)* unlike the prior findings, subjects trained to decrease BP and HR simultaneously (BP_{down} HR_{down}) spontaneously reported feelings of relaxation and calmness, a subjective state one would expect to be associated with more general (i.e., patterned) visceral relaxation. Given that these subjects

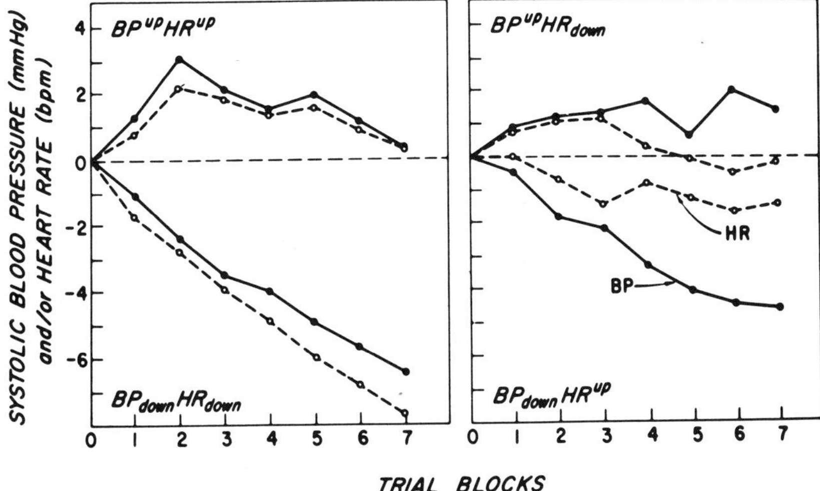

Figure 8.6 Average systolic blood pressure and heart rate for subjects (10 per group) receiving feedback and reward for patterns of BP and HR. On the left are the data from the two integration conditions; on the right are the data for the two differentiation conditions. Solid lines are BP, dashed lines are HR; millimeters of mercury and beats per minute are on the same axis. [From Schwartz, 1972.]

were *not* told what functions they were to control, nor in what direction they were to be regulated, the finding of a consistent subjective report emerging with pattern relaxation (as opposed to single-system relaxation) takes on added importance. Altogether, it appeared that in the process of trying to understand and extend biofeedback techniques to patterns of responses, the research uncovered information about the nature of the physiological systems and constraints and their relation to subjective experience.

As described in detail in Schwartz (1972), a tendency for BP–HR *tonic* (as opposed to phasic) integration can be observed when correlations are computed between *change* in tonic BP and *change* in tonic HR in response to five trials of random feedback and reward. The results show a small, but significant, correlation over 40 subjects ($r = +.36$), indicating that there is a tendency for tonic heart rate to vary with tonic systolic pressure in response to the environmental stimulation provided by the feedback situation itself. Since this tonic constraint accounts for less than 20% of the variance relating systolic blood pressure and heart rate, the degree of HR–BP dissociation that was achieved with single-system biofeedback procedures becomes understandable. On the other hand, as illustrated in Figure 8.6, this small tonic constraint apparently can be marshalled *under the appropriate pattern feedback conditions*. It may also be marshalled using other stimulus conditions, such as instructions.

Another aspect of the data deserving future consideration concerns the learning of "patterns of patterns" using pattern biofeedback procedures. As mentioned previously, the phasic relationship between heart rate and systolic blood pressure is not random; heart rate often leads systolic pressure by about two to three beats. Consequently, feedback for $BP^{up}HR_{down}$ also involves to some extent, feedback for the preceding $BP^{up}HR^{up}$ pattern; feedback for $BP_{down}HR^{up}$ also involves feedback for the preceding $BP_{down}HR_{down}$ pattern. The tendency to inadvertently couple integration feedback with differentiation training has effects on self-regulation that are evident in Figure 8.6 (right panel). It appears that the tonic integration constraint holding the systems together opposes the pattern feedback requirement that the subjects in these two groups differentiate HR and BP. The extent to which delayed feedback of this kind has predictable patterning effects on learned self-regulation, especially when the particular pattern receiving delayed feedback has a built-in positive system constraint, is not known.

Both the complexity and richness of patterning procedures and analyses are illustrated in this experiment. Yet this (Schwartz, 1972) experiment is limited for a variety of reasons, and generalizations must be made with caution. First, the experiment was limited to a single training session, using a between-subjects design and corresponding feedback training procedure. It is not known to what extent the BP–HR relationships uncovered in this experiment continue with long-term training. Nor is it known if the relationship would change depending upon the complex patterns of feedback, training, instructional, and individual difference variables that can vary from experiment to experiment. The generality of any observation ultimately depends on further research testing for its presence in a variety of different situations. The issue at the present stage of research is not whether this particular set of *observations* is generally applicable, but whether the conceptual and procedural *paradigm* is broadly applicable and comprehensive.

Interactions of Biofeedback and Instructions in Cardiovascular Patterning

Failure to recognize the complex pattern of interacting variables that contribute to learned self-regulation can lead to faulty interpretations of data. For example, in an extension of the original Shapiro *et al.* (1969) systolic blood pressure feedback study, Fey and Lindholm (1975) concluded that systolic blood pressure and heart rate were coupled, and that binary feedback for systolic blood pressure leads to corresponding changes in heart rate. This conclusion is based on two findings: *(1) mean* changes over three training sessions in heart rate comparing increase versus decrease groups in their experiment roughly paralleled the *mean* changes in systolic blood pressure observed between the two groups, and *(2)* correlations between changes in heart rate and changes in systolic blood pressure within the four different feedback groups over all sessions were positive, though none reached significance. However, careful analysis of the separate sessions reveals evidence for statistically significant heart rate–systolic blood pressure dissociation in every session. Whereas the pattern of blood pressure changes was consistent from session to session, the pattern of heart rate changes varied from session to session. For example, in Session II, the difference in systolic blood pressure between the BP^{up} and BP_{down} groups was almost 10 mmHg while the difference in heart rate was nonsignificant (only 2 bpm). Although this fully replicates the prior findings of learned specificity, it was dismissed by the authors because the identical finding was *not* observed in the first session.

Closer examination of the procedures used in the different experiments helps to clarify differences that could contribute to the corresponding, albeit idiosyncratic, changes in heart rate from session to session with systolic blood pressure binary feedback. One reason may involve the specific instructions given to the subjects. In the early Shapiro *et al.* (1969, 1970a) studies, subjects were not told that they were to regulate a cardiovascular response, nor were they told in what direction the response was to change. However, in the two studies that have reported initial coupling in Session I between heart rate and systolic blood pressure using systolic pressure feedback (Brener & Kleinman, 1970; Fey & Lindholm, 1975), subjects were instructed that the feedback reflected BP and/or the direction the response was to change. To the extent that instructions lead subjects to draw immediately on specific patterns of cognitive and somatic strategies (cortical patterns), this will result in different CNS mechanisms (Figure 8.2—Level 5) being utilized to regulate the peripheral response in question (Bell & Schwartz, 1975), which may result in corresponding differences in peripheral patterns.

An indirect strategy for assessing whether different CNS strategies are being used is to more systematically examine patterns of peripheral activity that could reflect the differentiated underlying mechanisms. A more direct strategy would be to monitor specific *patterns of electrocortical activity* occurring when different patterns of instructions and feedback for visceral self-regulation are administered. Examples of this research strategy will be described in a later section in this chapter. The point here is to highlight the fact that conclusions regarding the patterning of visceral processes must take into account factors other than just the specific stimulus parameters of the feedback itself. Instructions can be conceptualized as resulting in environmentally initiated self-regulation of differential patterns of cortical and subcortical processes, which by definition will interact with the subject's neural processing and regulation of the external biofeedback he may also be receiving.

Returning to the question of systolic BP and HR, it is possible that blood pressure and heart rate may covary, at least in initial training sessions, but the *mechanisms* underlying the regulation of BP and HR may be different and situation-specific. In the Fey and Lindholm (1975) study, the BP changes may be more specifically involved with the external biofeedback, while the HR changes may be primarily involved with the specific instructions used. Stated in this fashion, it becomes possible to generate testable hypotheses that can be evaluated in future research.

Biofeedback for Patterns of Diastolic Pressure and Heart Rate

Another example of pattern biofeedback training concerns research on the self-regulation of diastolic pressure. Shapiro, Schwartz, and Tursky (1972) observed that, when minimally instructed subjects were given direct binary feedback and reward for diastolic as opposed to systolic blood pressure, some covariation of heart rate was also observed. Interestingly, the learned changes in diastolic blood pressure emerged earlier than those for heart rate, and the magnitude of the heart rate changes were smaller than those previously observed for heart rate biofeedback alone. These data imply that some cardiovascular components of the pattern underlying the observed changes in diastolic pressure other than heart rate were initially being regulated, whereas later in training, heart rate may have been a contributing (Level 3) factor.

On the basis of these observations, it was predicted that diastolic blood pressure and heart rate must be partially, but not completely, phasically integrated. Consequently, biofeedback for diastolic

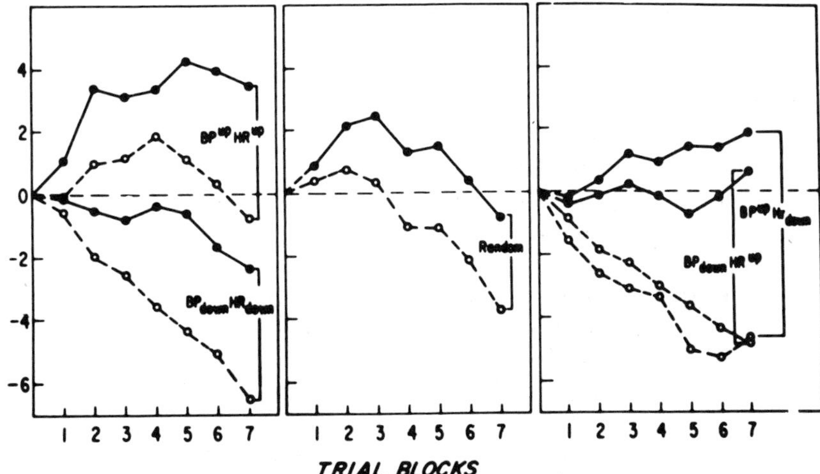

Figure 8.7 Average diastolic blood pressure and heart rate for subjects (10 per group) receiving feedback and reward for patterns of BP and HR, and randomly across the four patterns. On the left are the data from the two integration conditions; in the center are the data for the random feedback condition; on the right are the data from the two differentiation conditions. Solid lines are BP, dashed lines are HR; millimeters of mercury and beats per minuts are on the same axis. [From Schwartz, 1974.]

pressure would result in partial (but not complete) feedback for comparable heart rate changes as well. This would explain why some learning of heart rate control occurred with diastolic pressure biofeedback in minimally instructed subjects. An analysis of the resulting BP–HR patterns confirmed that the two variables changed spontaneously in the same direction about two-thirds of the time. In light of this apparent phasic constraint, it was predicted that subjects should be readily able to integrate their diastolic pressure and heart rate, but find it extremely difficult to differentiate them. Schwartz, Shapiro, and Tursky (1972) performed a pattern biofeedback experiment modeled after the previously described systolic blood pressure–heart rate pattern experiment (Schwartz, 1972), but added a fifth group as a control given random feedback and reward. The results are shown in Figure 8.7 (from Schwartz, 1974).

The curves for random feedback are interesting because they reveal that the baselines for diastolic blood pressure and heart rate not only do not remain constant over the session, but change at relatively different rates (HR decrease faster than BP). Thus, to assess learning over time accurately, self-regulation must be measured vis-à-vis the changing tonic baselines that are exposed, for example, by comparison with a random feedback control group (Crider, Schwartz, & Shnidman, 1969). It can be seen that for integration feedback, rapid learning of both diastolic pressure and heart rate occurred; again the rate of growth in learning was greater than that obtained for single-system biofeedback. This finding can be contrasted with the results for the two differentiation conditions, which show little evidence of separation beyond what occurred spontaneously with random feedback.

These data support the notion that the resting phasic relationship observed between diastolic blood pressure and heart rate reflects a biological, and probably hemodynamic, constraint. However, it should be emphasized that a simple correlation of two or more variables over time does not necessarily indicate a causal relationship between them (either at the periphery and/or in the CNS). A causal relationship can be proved only by determining the ease with which the two variables can be separated—for example, using the self-regulation pattern strategy described here. Clearly, an accurate assessment of the degree to which such relationships are fixed requires multiple sessions of pattern training. Such studies have yet to be carried out.

The data described in this section are useful to the extent that they illustrate some general conceptual and procedural issues regarding the measurement, regulation, and interpretation of patterning in biofeedback. Research that monitors multiple response contingencies simultaneously and examines the patterning of these changes, both from a parallel process and serial process perspective, is at only the most rudimentary stages. The interaction of *(1)* type of feedback (including the use of more complex analogue displays and analogue pattern analysis procedures) and *(2)* instructions used in determining *(3)* the patterns of CNS and PNS processes regulated by the subject, is just beginning to be appreciated. Further discussion of variables determining learned patterning in basic and clinical research is contained elsewhere (Schwartz, 1974, 1976).

PATTERNING OF CNS AND CARDIOVASCULAR PROCESSES

The above studies on the regulation of patterns of cardiovascular processes underlying blood pressure were not explicitly directed toward uncovering the patterning of central neural and/or humoral mechanisms that are ultimately responsible for the changes observed at the periphery. As illustrated in Figure 8.2, blood pressure (Level 1) is the composite of patterns of hemodynamic factors (Level 2) which are created by patterns of the effector organs (Level 3) innervated by patterns of peripheral neural and humoral mechanisms (Level 4) which are expressions of (regulated by) patterns of central neurogenic processes (Level 5). Biofeedback for blood pressure (Level 1), then, is ultimately feedback for patterns of central neurogenic (brain) processes (Level 5), the neural system responsible for active learning in the human. As Obrist (1976) had recently stated this principle "How else can biofeedback or any behavioral intervention technique be maximally effective other than through neurogenic mechanisms?" (p. 105).

A complete description of self-regulation of composite variables such as blood pressure will require accurate descriptions of the patterns of processes expressed at *each* of the levels. Recognizing the hierarchical pattern of structures emerging from the central nervous system to the periphery (Powers, 1973) helps to direct our attention to problems of pattern measurement and analysis in the biofeedback setting. Attempts to interconnect the five basic levels of analyses are progressing as new information in the biological sciences is obtained and integrated. Recent reviews by Smith (1974) and Cohen and Obrist (1975) provide some of the foundations for this approach. One value of conceptualizing the biological structure of the nervous system and body as composed of interacting levels of feedback systems (Powers, 1973) is that it provides a theoretical superstructure that brings physiological concepts such as homeostasis, neurological concepts such as functional systems in the brain, behavioral concepts such as biofeedback, and mathematical–mechanical concepts such as cybernetics, under one theoretical umbrella. The research to be described below incorporates this orientation at a general level, even though some of the specific experiments are derived from the behavioral literature of conditioning and motor skills learning.

Patterning of Neural Skills in Heart Rate Regulation

One example integrating motor skills theory with patterning at Level 3 (Figure 8.2) conceptualizes complex motor skills as reflecting complex peripheral nervous system skills which are composed of underlying patterns of simpler skills (Schwartz, Young, & Vogler, 1976). The analysis is an extension of Fleishman's (1966) motor skills model. He posits that motor skills are conceptually separate from motor abilities, with complex skills being comprised of a finite number of distinct, underlying abilities. The model predicts that a positive correlation (and, therefore, transfer of learning) will be found between performance on any pair of complex, integrated skills to the extent that they share a similar constellation or pattern of underlying abilities. However, the basic abilities are themselves viewed as relatively separate components involving distinct CNS learning processes.

Several of the motor abilities outlined by Fleishman (1966) can be applied to visceral learning, though the differences in effector organs in the somatic and visceral systems make direct comparisons difficult. The comparison can be illustrated by referring to peripheral neural innervation in Table 8.1 (from Schwartz, Young, & Vogler, 1976). Although the translation is shown using single neural innervation of a positive nature (increased neural firing leading to increased effector activity), this is an oversimplification when applied to complex visceral effectors such as the heart. Visceral responses are typically dually innervated by patterns of sympathetic and parasympathetic fibers, and these components may become differentially patterned in learning depending upon the nature of the skill required (e.g., HR^{up} versus HR_{down}; Engel, 1972; Lang, 1974).

The first two relevant abilities, strength and endurance, can be translated fairly directly to cardiovascular biofeedback terminology: How great was the change in heart rate (magnitude) and for how long was it sustained (duration)? Steadiness in the motor system, interpreted as the minimum of variability in the pattern of neural activity, has its counterpart in early research on reduction in cardiac rate variability (Hnatiow & Lang, 1965; Lang, Sroufe, & Hastings, 1967). The last two abilities considered here, control precision and reaction time, can also be translated into visceral skills, but they have not received empirical investigation.

The majority of cardiovascular biofeedback studies have employed a paradigm that combines the abilities of strength and endurance; that is, the experimental task is to change heart rate as much as possible and sustain it for a given interval of time. Schwartz, Young, and Vogler (1976) developed a task that measured and trained a cardiac reaction-time ability and compared performance on this task with performance on the more typical strength–endurance paradigm. According to Fleishman (1966), the degree of transfer of training between these two tasks should be a function of the component abilities they have in common. Since the particular tasks in this experiment were chosen to represent, as much as possible, separate abilities (i.e., minimal strength was required in the reaction-time task), it was expected that the performance on one task would not improve following training on the other. Therefore, despite the fact that all subjects would receive training in controlling their heart rates, it was predicted that performance improvement would be task-specific to the skill for which feedback training was given.

TABLE 8.1

Cardiac–Motor Skills Ability Factor Parallels Based on Five Ability and Performance Factors Postulated by Fleishman (1966) for the Motor System[a]

Neural activity	Motor activity	Cardiac activity
max/min firing	strength	max/min HR
maintenance of max/min firing over time	endurance	holding max/min rate
stable rate of firing	steadiness	minimum variability
regulation of firing rate in specific temporal order	control precision	cardiac control precision
quick onset of firing to a required level	reaction time	cardiac reaction time

[a] Schematicized neural activity regulating these abilities is also illustrated. To apply this analysis to parasympathetic (vagal) as opposed to sympathetic innervation of the heart rate, max neural firing should be equated with min HR and vice versa (see text for details). [From Schwartz, Young, & Vogler, 1976.]

In the experiment, subjects were pre- and posttested with instructions alone (no feedback) for degree of cardiac strength and endurance control (SE) ("maximally increase or decrease heart rate and sustain it for a minute") and degree of cardiac reaction-time control (RT) ("produce a small, 3-second burst of increased or decreased heart rate as quickly as possible at the onset of a trial"). All subjects received heart rate biofeedback during training, but half practiced SE while the others practiced RT. The data indicated that SE training led to improved SE control (30%) accompanied by a slight decrement in RT control (−5%). Conversely, RT training led to markedly improved RT control (120%) accompanied by a small decrement in SE control (−18%). Thus, specificity of skill learning within a single autonomic effector was obtained.

Regulating Patterns of Occipital EEG and Heart Rate: Coordination Training

Recognizing that patterns of neural system abilities underlie complex skills (Schwartz, Young, & Vogler, 1976) can stimulate the development of new paradigms of self-regulation and alternative procedures for studying neural system patterning underlying complex visceral behavior. Research clearly is needed to parametrically investigate how simple learning skills are combined to reflect complex temporally patterned regulations. This includes developing alternative training procedures for studying the patterning of multiphysiological systems as well.

For example, most of the previous patterning biofeedback research has used the operant procedure of computing response patterns on-line and presenting feedback and reward for specific patterns. A second procedure, based on the motor skills literature, involves the concept of learned coordination of multiple processes (Hassett & Schwartz, 1975). Stimulated in part by the concept that deep relaxation represents a pattern of reduced neural activity expressed as reduced patterns of visceral and motor activity (Davidson & Schwartz, 1976b) and, conversely, that global physiological arousal represents an increase in multiphysiological systems, we embarked on a series of experiments concerned with the self-regulation of patterns of EEG and autonomic responses. Besides bearing on the relaxation–arousal question, it was hoped that such research might aid in uncovering some of the cortical mechanisms involved in the self-regulation of autonomic responses.

In an initial single-system experiment, minimally instructed subjects were given binary feedback for increases and decreases in EEG occipital alpha from the right hemisphere, while heart rate was simultaneously monitored, or they were given binary feedback for increases and decreases in heart rate, while occipital alpha was recorded. The results show that occipital alpha feedback subjects readily learned to regulate alpha (primarily in the decrease direction) and this was associated with small corresponding changes in heart rate (e.g., alpha^{off} was accompanied by small HR increases). Heart rate feedback subjects learned to regulate their heart rates without corresponding changes in occipital alpha. In other words, relatively specific regulation of occipital alpha and heart rate learning was obtained with traditional single-system training (Hassett & Schwartz, 1975).

Upon moving to the question of learned regulation of patterns of occipital alpha and heart rate, it became clear that it would be desirable to teach an individual subject to self-regulate, on command, a host of different patterns of EEG and autonomic activity, so as to reduce problems of intersubject variability and to make it possible to assess the stability of the underlying constraints over time. Learning to perform a dual task—for example, rubbing the stomach with one hand and patting the head with the other—can be difficult. One way to achieve a patterned skill of this sort is to practice each response alone and then coordinate the two. This training strategy is valuable for a number of reasons. Unlike the direct pattern feedback approach, which requires digital logic or computer facilities to quantify complex patterns on-line, the coordination approach requires simple biofeedback equipment. Combinations of portable devices can be used to train combinations of responses outside the laboratory. In addition, this procedure stimulates the subject to develop self-control more naturally. He is allowed to experiment at his own pace in learning what strategies are effective for increasing and decreasing the feedback (Engel, 1972) and the "free play" periods interspersed with test trials make the task both more challenging and more rewarding.

Applying this concept to occipital alpha and heart rate, in the next study, subjects were given single-system training for occipital alpha control and heart rate control in one session (Hassett & Schwartz, 1975). Then, in the second session, subjects were given periods of free play with feedback presented for both responses simultaneously. Subjects were asked to practice at their own pace (during the free play period) voluntary coordination of the two responses, making them change separately or together, in the same or opposite directions. The results were quite striking, demonstrating that subjects could rapidly learn to generate during test trials all eight possible combinations of occipital alpha and heart rate ($\text{Alpha}^{\text{off}}$; Alpha_{on}; HR^{up}; HR_{down}; $\text{Alpha}^{\text{off}}\text{HR}^{\text{up}}$; $\text{Alpha}^{\text{off}}\text{HR}_{\text{down}}$; $\text{Alpha}_{\text{on}}\text{HR}^{\text{up}}$; $\text{Alpha}_{\text{on}}\text{HR}_{\text{down}}$). Interestingly, comparisons across conditions revealed that once again subjects found it relatively easier to voluntarily regulate their responses in the same direction than in opposite directions. This provides support for the notion that partial coupling exists across occipital EEG and cardiac responses.

However, the data suggest that this coupling is weak and unidirectional. As suggested by results of the initial single-system experiment, the findings for pattern training showed that occipital alpha regulation was accompanied by heart rate changes, while the opposite was not the case. This effect was especially evident in the pattern conditions, where heart rate control was actually enhanced when occipital alpha was simultaneously self-regulated in an arousal pattern ($\text{Alpha}^{\text{off}}$ HR^{up}). Conversely, differentiation of heart rate and occipital alpha led to an impairment of heart rate regulation, compared to single-system heart rate control. Such data suggest that when subjects are required via feedback to regulate neural processes in the occipital region, cardiovascular adjustments may be brought into play. However, since subjects can utilize various neural mechanisms other than their occipital cortex for regulating heart rate, the regulation of heart rate per se will not *necessarily* require the regulation of occipital processes.

Patterning of EEG Processes in Heart Rate Control

This leads us to one of the most challenging frontiers facing researchers in biofeedback and the self-regulation of visceral processes, the specification of patterns of CNS processes (Level 5, Figure 8.2) involved in the regulation of visceral responses. Phrased in this manner, the challenge becomes *(1)* to specify at a neurophysiological level what patterns of functional systems in the brain (both cortical and subcortical) are involved in the regulation of visceral responses, and *(2)* to develop electrophysiological procedures to reflect the underlying spatial and temporal patterning of neural activity. Although neurophysiological theory, psychophysiological techniques, and behavioral paradigms each have their own limitations at this time, it is possible to make initial inroads by integrating current neuropsychology, recent cerebral psychophysiology of localization of function, and advances in specifying behavioral tasks that reflect more focused and definable patterns of underlying biocognitive processes.

Consider some of the possible cortical mechanisms involved in the regulation of heart rate. It has long been noted that cardiac and skeletal motor processes are often, but not always, coupled (Obrist, 1976), since one of the functions of the cardiovascular systems is to meet the needs of the skeletal tissues. As reviewed in Cohen and Obrist (1975), skeletal activity does not simply initiate brain regulation of cardiovascular processes via peripheral feedback from the musculature itself. There are also cortical–subcortical feedback loops between the motor cortex and the brain stem that can integrate these processes as well. It would be predicted from current neuropsychology (reviewed in Davidson & Schwartz, 1976a), that if a subject regulated his or her heart rate by means of skeletal motor strategies, the subject would be typically regulating left hemisphere activity of the sensorimotor cortex. On the other hand, if the subject were regulating his or her heart rate by using a more cognitive strategy, such as thinking arousal thoughts, he or she would likely be regulating right hemisphere activity in the mode specific sensory regions.

We have conducted a series of experiments to provide initial data on EEG patterning during heart rate regulation. In one experiment, Neyer and Schwartz (in preparation) recorded monopolar EEG activity using surface electrodes over the left sensorimotor cortex and left occipital region. Subjects were instructed either to control their heart rate by increasing and decreasing their muscle activity, or to regulate their heart rate by sitting still and thinking arousing and relaxing thoughts. It was predicted that subjects instructed to regulate their heart rate by controlling their skeletal muscle activity would show corresponding changes in EEG activation over the left sensorimotor region and not over the left occipital region. It was further predicted that, to the extent that affective imagery involves right hemisphere processes (Schwartz, Davidson, & Maer, 1975), subjects instructed to regulate heart rate by thinking arousing thoughts would show little differential EEG activity over either site recorded in this experiment. The results supported these basic predictions. EEG alpha over the left sensorimotor region (in right-handed subjects) changed differentially when subjects regulated their heart rate via somatic instructions, but showed little change with affective imagery instructions. Importantly, occipital alpha showed little change in either instructional condition.

These data have been recently replicated and extended in an experiment by Schwartz and Bergman (in preparation). Again, heart rate, EEG alpha from the sensorimotor and occipital region were recorded, only now a 2 × 2 between-groups design was employed. Half the subjects were given binary feedback for criterion HR changes, the other half were given binary feedback for criterion *occipital* alpha changes (using integrated alpha measures; Hardt & Kamiya, 1976). Within each of these groups, half the subjects were instructed to regulate the feedback by tensing and relaxing their muscles (somatic instructions), the other half by generating arousing and relaxing imagery (cognitive instructions). Each subject was given training in both increasing and decreasing the feedback. Up minus down change scores, separately for the three physiological measures and the four groups, are shown in Figure 8.8. The EEG data are arranged in the "arousal" direction, with higher bar graphs reflecting less alpha.

It can be seen that all four patterns of the two EEG variables are obtained. When subjects are given heart rate biofeedback and somatic instructions (HRS), they show corresponding changes in heart rate and sensorimotor EEG, but not in occipital EEG. When subjects are given heart rate biofeedback and cognitive instructions instead (HRC), they show changes predominantly in heart rate. However, when subjects are given *occipital* alpha feedback and cognitive instructions (OC), they now show regulation of occipital EEG as well as heart rate, but little change in sensorimotor EEG. Finally, changes in *both* EEG sites *and* heart rate are obtained when subjects are given biofeedback for occipital alpha and instructed to regulate it with somatic instructions (OS).

This EEG demonstration is of particular importance because it illustrates how patterning of brain processes is influenced by biofeedback *and* instructions, and that the neural components underlying this patterning can be assessed and differentiated in a meaningful manner. In one sense, biofeedback can itself be viewed as an "instruction" in that it is information from the *external* environment that instructs the subject regarding the state of his biological processes. It follows that dif-

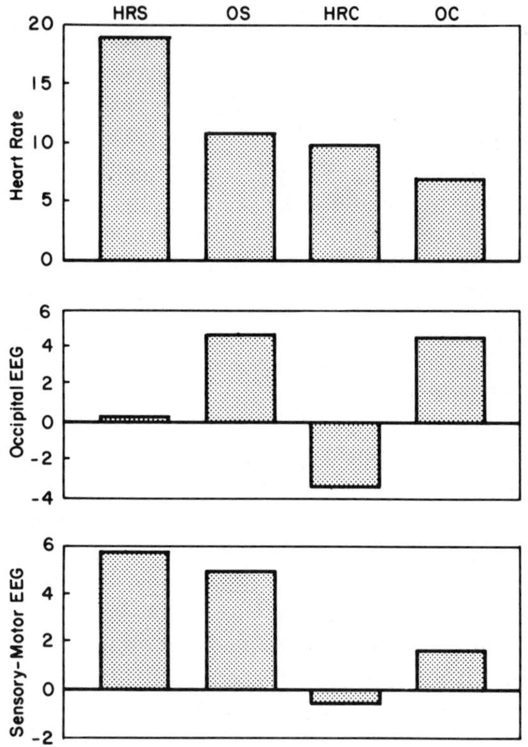

Figure 8.8 Average change (up minus down scores) for subjects (10 per group) given feedback for heart rate (HR) or occipital (O) EEG and instructions for using somatic (S) or cognitive (C) strategies. Heart rate values represent change in beats per minute; EEG values represent change in integrated 8–13 Hz activity, inverted so that positive values reflect greater EEG activation. The data show that all groups regulated heart rate, especially subjects given the pattern of heart rate biofeedback and somatic instructions (HRS). Occipital EEG shows little effect of cognitive versus somatic instructions; changes are primarily due to the presence of occipital biofeedback (OS and OC groups). Sensory–motor EEG, on the other hand, shows little effect of occipital biofeedback; changes are primarily due to the utilization of somatic instructions (HRS and OS groups). [From Schwartz & Bergman, in preparation.]

ferent patterns of neural system activity can be expressed as different patterns of peripheral organ activity as a function of the different instructions used.

The separation of sensorimotor and occipital EEG activity is one of the simplest of EEG differentiations, yet the questions stimulated by this observation are numerous and deserving of further consideration. For example, it might be useful to train subjects to regulate patterns of these EEG processes using pattern biofeedback procedures and look for corresponding patterns in cardiovascular activity. Or, it might be interesting to extend the Hassett and Schwartz (1975) study to train patterns of sensorimotor EEG and heart rate versus patterns of occipital EEG and heart rate. To the extent that sensorimotor EEG reflects neural processes that are more tightly linked to the regulation of heart rate, voluntary differentiation of sensorimotor EEG and heart rate should be more difficult to achieve than voluntary differentiation of occipital EEG and heart rate.

It also might be of interest to examine the self-regulation of more psychologically defined processes as related to the patterning of occipital and sensory motor alpha. Recent research from our laboratory has demonstrated differential patterning of these two EEG variables in the voluntary control of mode-specific attention to visual versus kinesthetic stimulation (Schwartz, Davidson, & Margolin, in preparation) and the self-regulation of mode-specific visual versus kinesthetic imagery (Davidson & Schwartz, in preparation). The corresponding patterning of autonomic effectors during these tasks is a question awaiting future research.

More sophisticated EEG procedures, including evoked potential and contingent negative variation measures, can be incorporated within a biofeedback patterning framework to investigate CNS processes in visceral regulation. The important considerations are to: *(1)* select recording sites on the basis of current neurophysiological theory; *(2)* select the behavioral tasks to match the theory; and *(3)* analyze the EEG patterning both across sites (parallel process) and over time (serial process). This writer believes that programmatic research in this direction will, in the long run, increase our understanding of general CNS mechanisms underlying self-regulation in the intact person, and more specific CNS mechanisms involved differentially in the regulation of specific visceral responses and patterns of responses. Such research would include analyses within the hemispheres (as described above) as well as between the hemispheres (e.g., see Davidson & Schwartz, 1976a, regarding hemispheric patterning in male and female subjects comparing heart rate biofeedback with instructions to generate affective imagery).

SUMMARY AND CONCLUSIONS: PATTERN BIOFEEDBACK AND EMERGENT PROPERTIES

This chapter has illustrated that patterning has important theoretical and practical implications regarding the conception, design, and interpretation of research in visceral self-regulation. Although the concept of patterning increases the complexity of research methodology and analysis, it also increases correspondingly the kinds of questions that can be raised and the potential comprehensiveness that can be developed concerning our understanding of learned self-regulation. As illustrated in Figure 8.2, variables like blood pressure (Level 1) can be meaningfully broken down into their underlying components: initially as the patterning of processes at hemodynamic (Level 2) and peripheral effector (Level 3) levels, and ultimately as the patterning of peripheral (Level 4) and central neurohumoral (Level 5) levels. The importance of viewing the self-regulation of visceral responses in psychobiological perspective, including both peripheral and central mechanisms, has been emphasized. This is not to deny the importance of instructional, cognitive, or personality variables in biofeedback-aided visceral self-regulation. Rather, the goal is to translate these more psychological terms into their neurobiological substrates so as to increase our potential for uncovering the patterns of underlying processes involved, (e.g., Davidson & Schwartz, in preparation).

To the extent that the brain and nervous system represent the final common pathway for learned behavior and regulation (Luria, 1973), it follows that visceral (or skeletal motor) biofeedback is actually patterned neural biofeedback, and that learned peripheral organ regulation is ultimately patterned neural self-regulation in the central nervous system which is expressed via the peripheral nervous system as behavior (Figure 8.2). This is not meant to imply that proprioceptive and interoceptive feedback from the periphery is not important to learned self-regulation. Rather, this information is used to varying degrees *by the brain* in a similar, but not identical, manner to the way the brain uses exteroceptive information provided by the addition of biofeedback. As stated in the section beginning on page 185, one of the major challenges for future research is to begin to describe the learned self-regulation of visceral responses as the patterning of brain processes. Pattern biofeedback procedures and patterning approaches to data analysis, emphasizing parallel and serial (temporal) aspects, can play a useful role in this research.

The concept of patterning should be a general one having implications regarding how one defines a response and, therefore, how one measures and manipulates it. It has been suggested that the training of any overt behavioral response, or the measured physiological response expressed as an effector organ change, is ultimately learned as a complex pattern of neural systems (Luria, 1973). Even at the periphery, the regulation of a visceral response such as heart rate can involve the differential patterning of sympathetic and parasympathetic influences as well as humoral factors. Since a variety of combinations of these processes may be expressed as similar changes in heart rate, it becomes important to specify more precisely what these potential patterns are, and provide feedback and reward more explicitly for selected patterns if more consistent self-regulation of particular patterns is desired. It follows that the use of the word *specificity* at one level can simultaneously involve the concept of *patterning* when *(1)* other concurrently changing responses at the same level are also considered, or when *(2)* the pattern of underlying processes at the next level is recognized.

The general thesis slowly emerging from biofeedback research is that patterns of physiological processes can be both generated and processed by the brain, producing unique cross-system interactions and perceptual gestalts that make up a significant component of human behavior and subjective experience (Schwartz, 1975). The concept of pattern here refers not simply to viewing in isolation, combinations of processes, but rather goes beyond the individual components making up the pattern to recognize the novel, interactive, or emergent property that patterns acquire. Simply stated, *the whole can have properties that are qualitatively and/or quantitatively different from the sum of its parts, and yet be dependent upon the organization of its parts for its unique properties.* This phenomenon is seen at all levels of physics and chemistry and extends through biology and neuropsychology (Weiss, 1969). The term "synergism" is also used to describe emergent property, as recently elucidated in a comprehensive volume by Fuller (1975).

The concept of emergent property or synergism needs to be considered in patterning. Although it is not a new concept, with few exceptions, it is still ignored. Neuropsychologists concerned with the biology of consciousness employ a similar idea when they speak of cell assemblies (Hebb, 1974), hyperneurons (John, 1976), holograms (Pribram, 1971), dynamic neural patterns (Sperry, 1969), or functional systems in the brain (Luria, 1973). Emotion was described by William James (1890) as the brain's perception of patterns of visceral consequences of its action. More recent psychologists, such as Schachter and Singer (1962), have added biocognitive processes to the visceral activity as an integral part of the pattern. Modern comprehensive theorists like Tomkins (1962–1963) and Izard (1971) stress the interaction of combinations of neurophysiological systems, including discrete patterns of postural and facial muscle activity, as mechanisms underlying the emergent experience of emotion. Recent data from our laboratory has documented that complex cognitive–affective tasks can be dissected into their underlying subcomponents having predictable effects on patterning of hemispheric activity (Schwartz, Davidson, & Maer, 1975), and that the self-generation of different classes of affective imagery involves the generation of different patterns of facial muscle activity (Schwartz, Fair, Salt, Mandel, & Klerman, 1976).

Research on biofeedback and the regulation of combinations of responses extends the emergent nature of patterning by providing a new paradigm for investigating physiological relationships in the intact human. Self-regulation as a general research strategy can be useful to the extent that it enables researchers to isolate component parts of systems and then examine how they combine to provide unique physiological and associated subjective states.

Previous research from our laboratory has indicated that the regulation of patterns of responses can produce effects that are different from those observed when single components are regulated (Schwartz, 1975, 1976). The same phenomena can likely be extended to the patterning of patterns as well. For example, in a recent experiment applying a binary feedback and analysis procedure for regulating patterns of EEG activity across the two hemispheres, it was found that the training of left $\text{Alpha}^{\text{off}}$ right Alpha_{on} was accompanied by verbal cognitions, the training of left Alpha_{on} right $\text{Alpha}^{\text{off}}$ was accompanied by spatial cognitions, while left $\text{Alpha}^{\text{off}}$ right $\text{Alpha}^{\text{off}}$ training resulted in a third pattern of subjective experience not readily predicted from the regulation of the separate hemispheric asymmetry patterns themselves (Schwartz, Davidson, & Pugash, in press).

Although the simple principle of pattern regulation and emergent property can have important basic research as well as clinical implications, there are limitations to the use of pattern regulation procedures. It is not inconceivable, for example, that the act of regulating a particular pattern of responses will have emergent consequences that are somewhat different from those found when a similar pattern is generated by other means. If future research proves this to be true, it will restrict the general applicability of the approach accordingly. On the other hand, such a finding might provide a further key regarding the unique characteristic of self-regulation processes themselves.

REFERENCES

Basmajian, J. V. Learned control of single motor units. In G. E. Schwartz & J. Beatty (Eds.), *Biofeedback: Theory and research.* New York: Academic Press, 1977.

Bell, I. R., & Schwartz, G. E. Voluntary control and reactivity of human heart rate. *Psychophysiology*, 1975, *12*, 339–348.

Brener, J., & Kleinman, R. A. Learned control of decreases in systolic blood pressure. *Nature*, 1970, *226*, 1063–1064.

Cannon, W. B. *The wisdom of the body*. New York: Norton, 1939.

Cohen, D. H., & Obrist, P. A. Interactions between behavior and the cardiovascular system. *Circulation Research*, 1975, *37*, 693–706.

Crider, A., Schwartz, G. E., & Shnidman, S. R. On the criteria for instrumental autonomic conditioning: A reply to Katkin and Murray. *Psychological Bulletin*, 1969, *71*, 455–461.

Davidson, R. J., & Schwartz, G. E. Patterns of cerebral lateralization during cardiac biofeedback versus the self-regulation of emotion: Sex differences. *Psychophysiology*, 1976, *13*, 62–68. (a)

Davidson, R. J., & Schwartz, G. E. The psychobiology of relaxation and related states: A multi-process theory. In D. I. Mostofsky (Ed.), *Behavior control and modification of physiological activity*. Englewood Cliffs, N.J.: Prentice-Hall, 1976. (b)

Davidson, R. J., & Schwartz, G. E. Patterns of occipital and sensorimotor EEG during self-generated visual and kinesthetic imagery. In preparation.

Engel, B. T. Operant conditioning of cardiac function: A status report. *Psychophysiology*, 1972, *9*, 161–177.

Engel, B. T., & Bleecker, E. R. Application of operant conditioning techniques to the control of the cardiac arrhythmias. In P. A. Obrist, A. H. Black, J. Brener, & L. V. DiCara (Eds.), *Cardiovascular psychophysiology*. Chicago: Aldine, 1974.

Fey, S. G., & Lindholm, E. Systolic blood pressure and heart rate changes during three sessions involving biofeedback or no feedback. *Psychophysiology*, 1975, *12*, 513–519.

Fleishman, E. A. Human abilities and the acquisition of skill. In E. A. Bilodeau (Ed.), *Acquisition of skill*. New York: Academic Press, 1966.

Fuller, R. B. *Synergetics*. New York: Macmillan, 1975.

Hardt, J. V., & Kamiya, J. Conflicting results in EEG alpha studies: Why amplitude integration should replace percent time. *Biofeedback and Self-Regulation*, 1976, *1*, 63–76.

Hassett, J., & Schwartz, G. E. Relationships between heart rate and occipital alpha: A biofeedback approach. *Psychophysiology*, 1975, *12*, 228. (Abstract)

Hebb, D. O. What psychology is about. *American Psychologist*, 1974, *29*, 71–79.

Hnatiow, M., & Lang, P. J. Learned stabilization of cardiac rate. *Psychophysiology*, 1965, *1*, 330–336.

Izard, C. E. *The face of emotion*. New York: Appleton, 1971.

James, W. *Principles of psychology*. New York: Holt, 1890.

John, E. R. A model of consciousness. In G. E. Schwartz & D. Shapiro (Eds.), *Consciousness and self-regulation: Advances in research*. Vol. 1. New York: Plenum, 1976.

Lang, P. J. Learned control of human heart rate in a computer directed environment. In P. A. Obrist, A. H. Black, J. Brener, & L. V. DiCara (Eds.), *Cardiovascular psychophysiology*. Chicago: Aldine, 1974.

Lang, P. J., Sroufe, L. A., & Hastings, J. E. Effects of feedback and instructional set on the control of cardiac rate variability. *Journal of Experimental Psychology*, 1967, *75*, 425–431.

Luria, A. R. *The working brain*. New York: Basic Books, 1973.

Miller, N. E. Learning of visceral and glandular responses. *Science*, 1969, *163*, 434–445.

Mulholland, T. B. Biofeedback as scientific method. In G. E. Schwartz & J. Beatty (Eds.), *Biofeedback: Theory and research.* New York: Academic Press, 1977.

Neyer, M. A., & Schwartz, G. E. Heart rate regulation with somatic versus cognitive instructions: Effects on sensorimotor and occipital alpha. In preparation.

Obrist, P. A. The cardiovascular–behavioral interaction: As it appears today. *Psychophysiology,* 1976, *13,* 95–107.

Powers, W. T. *Behavior: The control of perception.* Chicago: Aldine, 1973.

Pribram, K. H. *Languages of the brain.* Englewood Cliffs, N.J.: Prentice-Hall, 1971.

Roemer, R. A. Computer applications in a physiological psychology laboratory. *American Psychologist,* 1975, *30,* 295–298.

Schachter, S., & Singer, J. E. Cognitive, social and physiological determinants of emotional state. *Psychological Review,* 1962, *69,* 379–399.

Schwartz, G. E. Operant conditioning of human cardiovascular integration and differentiation. Unpublished doctoral dissertation, Harvard University, 1971.

Schwartz, G. E. Voluntary control of human cardiovascular integration and differentiation through feedback and reward. *Science,* 1972, *175,* 90–93.

Schwartz, G. E. Biofeedback as therapy: Some theoretical and practical issues. *American Psychologist,* 1973, *28,* 666–673.

Schwartz, G. E. Toward a theory of voluntary control of response patterns in the cardiovascular system. In P. A. Obrist, A. H. Black, J. Brener, & L. V. DiCara (Eds.), *Cardiovascular psychophysiology.* Chicago: Aldine, 1974.

Schwartz, G. E. Biofeedback, self-regulation, and the patterning of physiological processes. *American Scientist,* 1975, *63,* 314–324.

Schwartz, G. E. Self-regulation of response patterning: Implications for psychophysiological research and therapy. *Biofeedback and Self-Regulation,* 1976, *1,* 7–30.

Schwartz, G. E. Psychosomatic disorders and biofeedback: A psychobiological model of disregulation. In J. D. Maser & M. E. P. Seligman (Eds.), *Psychopathology: Experimental models.* San Francisco: Freeman, in press. (a)

Schwartz, G. E., & Bergman, T. Heart rate, sensorimotor alpha and occipital alpha patterning with biofeedback and instructions. In preparation.

Schwartz, G. E., Davidson, R. J., & Maer, F. Right hemisphere lateralization for emotion in the human brain: Interactions with cognition. *Science,* 1975, *190,* 286–288.

Schwartz, G. E., Davidson, R. J., & Margolin, R. Meditation and the self-regulation of attention: Intrahemispheric EEG patterning. In preparation.

Schwartz, G. E., Davidson, R. J., & Pugash, E. Voluntary control of patterns of EEG parietal asymmetry: Cognitive concomitants. *Psychophysiology,* in press.

Schwartz, G. E., Fair, P. L., Salt, P., Mandel, M., & Klerman, G. L. Facial muscle patterning to affective imagery in depressed and non-depressed subjects. *Science,* 1976, *192,* 489–491.

Schwartz, G. E., Shapiro, D., & Tursky, B. Learned control of cardiovascular integration in man through operant conditioning. *Psychosomatic Medicine,* 1971, *33,* 57–62.

Schwartz, G. E., Shapiro, D., & Tursky, B. Self-control of patterns of human diastolic blood pressure and heart rate through feedback and reward. *Psychophysiology,* 1972, *9,* 270. (Abstract)

Schwartz, G. E., Young, L. D., & Vogler, J. Heart rate regulation as skill learning: Strength-endurance versus cardiac reaction time. *Psychophysiology,* 1976, *13,* 472–478.

Shapiro, D., Schwartz, G. E., & Tursky, B. Control of diastolic blood pressure in man by feedback and reinforcement. *Psychophysiology,* 1972, *9,* 296–304.

Shapiro, D., & Surwit, R. S. Learned control of physiological function and disease. In H. Leitenberg (Ed.), *Handbook of behavior modification and behavior change.* Englewood Cliffs, N.J.: Prentice-Hall, 1976.

Shapiro, D., Tursky, B., Gershon, E., & Stern, M. Effects of feedback and reinforcement on the control of human systolic blood pressure. *Science,* 1969, *163,* 588–589.

Shapiro, D., Tursky, B., & Schwartz, G. E. Control of blood pressure in man by operant conditioning. *Circulation Research,* 1970, *26*(Suppl. 1), *27,* I-27–I-32. (a)

Shapiro, D., Tursky, B., & Schwartz, G. E. Differentiation of heart rate and blood pressure in man by operant conditioning. *Psychosomatic Medicine,* 1970, *32,* 417–423. (b)

Smith, O. A. Reflex and central mechanisms involved in the control of the heart and circulation. *Annual Review of Physiology,* 1974, *36,* 93–123.

Sperry, R. W. A modified concept of consciousness. *Psychological Review,* 1969, *76,* 532–536.

Sternbach, R. A. *Principles of psychophysiology.* New York: Academic Press, 1966.

Thomas, E. A. C., & Martin, J. A. Analysis of parent–infant interaction. *Psychological Review,* 1976, *83,* 141–156.

Tomkins, S. S. *Affect, imagery, consciousness* (2 vols.). New York: Springer, 1962–1963.

Tursky, B., Shapiro, D., & Schwartz, G. E. Automated constant cuff pressure system to measure average systolic and diastolic pressure in man. *IEEE Transactions on Biomedical Engineering,* 1972, *19,* 271–275.

Weiss, P. A. The living system: Determinism stratified. In A. Koestler & J. R. Smythies (Eds.), *Beyond reductionism: New perspectives in the life sciences.* Boston: Beacon Press, 1969.

9

Visceral Learning in the Curarized Rat*

BARRY R. DWORKIN
NEAL E. MILLER
The Rockefeller University

GENERAL CONSIDERATIONS

The relatively meager changes in visceral function demonstrated by most human subjects in instrumental learning experiments can be interpreted to suggest limits on the ultimate exploitation of this area of research Roberts, Kewman, & MacDonald, 1973; Miller, DiCara, Solomon, Weiss, & Dworkin, 1970; Miller & Dworkin, 1974; Miller, 1975; Shapiro, Tursky, Gershon, & Stern, 1969). Because a variety of subtle maneuvers can affect heart rate, blood pressure, or hand temperature, some strategy—"legitimate" or not—is almost certain to emerge when shaping procedures are employed and reinforcement is contingent upon the production of a small response.[1] At present, learned visceral

* Work described from this laboratory was supported by U.S. Public Health Services research grant MH 13189 awarded to NEM.

[1] Hefferline and Perera (1963) demonstrated that very subtle skeletal responses could be shaped without subject awareness. In visceral learning experiments, we found that shaping frequently results in the inadvertent reinforcement of skeletal behaviors. A postdoctoral fellow in our laboratory, David VanDercar (VanDercar, Feldstein, & Solomon, 1972), did a very careful analysis of respiratory records using two simultaneous pneumograph recordings and some other novel instrumentation. He consistently found altered breathing in people being trained to change heart rate. These changes were not evident with either casual examination of the respiration records or direct visual obser-

responses of generally accepted therapeutic value have not been demonstrated (Blanchard & Young, 1974; Hubel, 1974). Based on new insights or discoveries, effective training techniques may be developed in the future.

To evaluate and provide basic support for programs of applied research we need knowledge of the properties of the relationship among external stimuli, the brain, and the internal organs. The viscera are innervated exclusively by the autonomic nervous system. A learned visceral response may be direct, originating in the brain and being transmitted through the autonomic nervous system to the ground plexus of the organ (Figure 9.1c). It may also be mediated by both the somatic and autonomic nerves, originating in the brain and being transmitted over somatic efferents to skeletal muscles and through a mechanical or chemical linkage to the afferent limb of a peripheral autonomic reflex (Figure 9.1b). It may also be mediated by a mechanical or chemical action of the skeletal muscles on the visceral structure (Figure 9.1a). Characteristically, a direct response is more specific and reliable because articulation of a mediated response is limited by the properties of the linkage.

While the general therapeutic utility of visceral learning remains unproven, a peculiar assortment of human subjects have demonstrated impressively effective control over several autonomically innervated systems (Anand, Chhina, & Singh, 1961; Engel & Bleecker, 1974; Hadfield, 1920; Maslach, Marshall, & Zimbardo, 1972; Miller *et al.*, 1970; Miller, 1975; A. H. Roberts, personal communication, 1971; Veterans Administration videotape, 1974; Weiss & Engel, 1971). The behavior of these people is perplexing and raises some important questions. Are they visceral geniuses having central or peripheral anatomical anomalies that others lack? Have they learned to produce unusual artifacts which we have not been clever enough to detect? Or have they acquired behavior that anyone could acquire if given

---

vation of the subjects. Wesley Lynch in this laboratory has observed a variety of subtle changes in finger positions in subjects being trained in differential hand temperature control (Lynch & Schuri, 1976). With Henry Erle, we attempted to train human colon motility. Although we may have obtained some evidence for genuine learned changes in smooth muscle activity, much of what we observed was mechanically related to skeletal movement. Subjects frequently learned to mimic intestinal contractions by manipulating their abdominal muscles and diaphragm. We were able to partially exclude reinforcement of this type of behavior by monitoring skeletal electromyograms and inhibiting the reinforcing stimulus when too much EMG activity appeared. However, the subtlety of some of these maneuvers makes this "behavioral strait jacket" approach very difficult and less than totally effective.

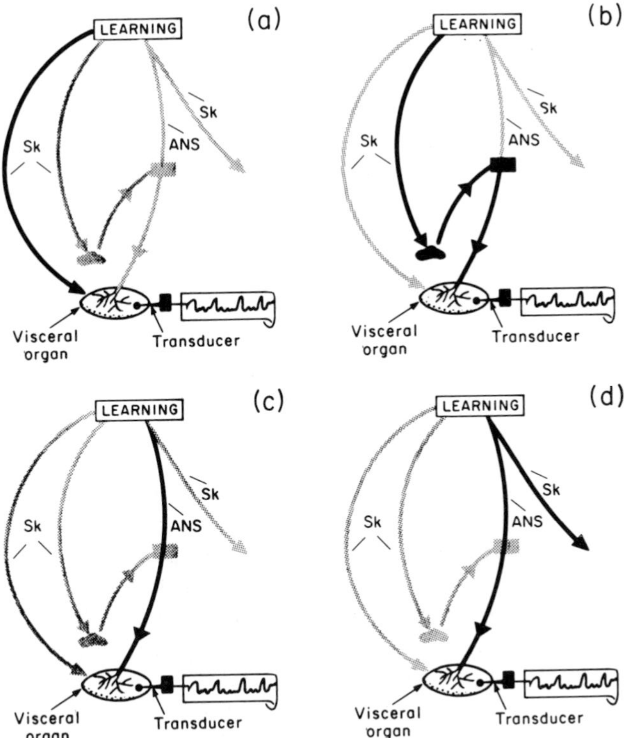

Figure 9.1 Learning can influence the observed behavior of a visceral organ in several different ways: (a) through a learned skeletal response (sk) which is mechanically (or chemically linked to the visceral organ or inadvertently directly to the transducer (see Footnote 1); (b) through the mechanical or metabolic action of a learned skeletal response on the receptive field of an unconditioned autonomic reflex; or (c) directly through the autonomic nervous system (ANS) to the organ via its motor ground plexus. Frame (d) shows a direct autonomically transmitted visceral response which is also concomitant with a particular skeletal response. Such an association between somatic and visceral behavior may be innate or itself a consequence of learning, i.e., the central and/or the peripheral manifestations of one response may be the discriminative stimulus for the other response. Curare will block the visceral response in Frames (a) and (b) but not in Frame (c). In Frame (d), if the skeletal response is primary and the discriminative stimulus or innate connection is central, curare will not block the response.

adequate instruction? Thorough study of these extraordinary people would probably provide the most direct answers, but detailed mechanisms cannot be conveniently analyzed within the ethical constraints on human research.

Nevertheless, these individuals intensify our curiosity and raise our hopes. If they are exceptionally endowed, then their performances are interesting curiosities—probably nothing more. If they are conscious or unconscious magicians, to the extent that their tricks are therapeutically valuable to themselves or others, they are worthy of study. But if common mechanisms exist through which central control of autonomic function can be modified by appropriately chosen reinforcement contingencies, then the potential for understanding pathology and developing therapy is very great.

The work in the mid-1960s by Neal Miller's group at Yale provided a great impetus to research on learned autonomic control. The series of experiments which Miller conceived and which were performed by Alfredo Carmona, Jay Trowill, Leo DiCara, and others were thought to provide incontrovertible evidence for a general instrumental visceral learning capability. To what extent they actually did so has been a subject of lively and continuing debate for the past several years. There has been difficulty replicating the experiments (Miller & Dworkin, 1974), and much discussion has concerned technical issues. The problem of reproducibility remains at least partially unresolved. However, the more important question being asked is: If replicable, what of importance do the experiments demonstrate?

It may be helpful to begin with what they cannot demonstrate. The experiments were performed on rats paralyzed with the heterocyclic neuromuscular blocking agent, *d*-tubocurarine.[2] With the doses employed, *d*-tubocurarine has little effect on the autonomic nervous system[3] and is not known to cross the blood–brain barrier in significant quantities. Its primary action is on the junctions between the efferent somatic nerves and the skeletal muscles. At relatively low doses, it blocks almost all neuromuscular transmission. Even direct maximal electrical stimulation of the nerve axon will not produce a muscle action potential (Chagas, 1959). Consequently, curare eliminates skeletal movement.

The other functions of the organism continue relatively intact. Cu-

[2] Unless a particular compound is specified, the terms "curare" and "curarization" are used generically for a neuromuscular blocking agent and its primary pharmacological effect.

[3] There have been reports of the effects of *d*-tubocurarine on the autonomic nervous system in a variety of experiments (Black, 1967; Howard, Galosy, Gaebelien, & Obrist, 1974). Some vagal blocking effects have been reported in rats. However, Robert Vertes in our laboratory has prepared rats with stimulating electrodes in the dorsal motor nucleus of the vagus and shown only minimal effects of curare on cardiac decelerations produced by this type of stimulation (Miller & Dworkin, 1974). The experiments on classical conditioning of heart rate to be reported later in this chapter show that, when the rat is respirated properly, its autonomic nervous system remains functional even after several days of paralysis by curare.

rare does not isolate central autonomic and skeletal pathways, and there is no evidence that it affects sensation in visceral or somatic structures. If a skeletal pattern ordinarily has associated autonomically mediated responses, the initiation of the pattern will manifest the visceral but not the somatic aspects. Thus, curare is not a tool for the neurochemical dissection of visceral and somatic components in the central nervous system. In fact, in the brain, the distinction may be meaningless in the usual sense.

Curare can, however, eliminate the autonomic consequences of skeletal muscle activity which is mediated by the mechanical, chemical, or reflex pathways (see Figure 9.1a,b). Systems affected in this manner are common: Intralumenal intestinal pressure reflects changes in abdominal muscle tension; increases intrathoracic pressure reduces return blood flow to the heart, increasing heart rate. Changes of tidal volume or of respiratory rate affect blood CO_2 with important consequences for a number of visceral functions, including heart rate and cerebral circulation. Increased lactic acid production by active muscles has major vasomotor effects on adjacent tissue; stretch receptors which respond to lung volume have reflex effects on heart rate; similarly, bladder mechanoreceptors are included in the afferent pool of general vasomotor reflexes. Most visceral structures or receptive fields for visceral reflexes can be affected by the mechanical or metabolic activity of adjacent skeletal muscle. Consequently, in a noncurarized preparation, no less than painstaking detective work is necessary to establish the origin of a visceral response. And, in practice, no matter how thorough and conscientious, any survey of peripheral mediators is probably incomplete.

It should be clear that a *general* instrumental visceral learning capability—the ability to improve the adjustment of function of the internal organs with successive perturbations from homeostatic balance—cannot be demonstrated unless peripheral skeletal mediation is excluded. Since physiology is ultimately inductive, the ubiquity and versatility of a property that an observed phenomenon is understood to represent determines the importance of its being attributed to a particular system. The viscera receive direct innervation from the autonomic nervous system, and for many visceral structures the autonomic nervous system provides a high degree of organized functional control. Thus, to show that a particular learned change in visceral function is directly mediated by the autonomic nervous system (Figure 9.1c) is to imply generality to other visceral functions and suggest potential flexibility.

These general considerations are important in evaluating visceral learning as a potential therapeutic technique, a pathophysiological mechanism, or a component of normal physiological regulation. They are equally relevant to the analysis of plasticity in all visceral systems.

Nonetheless, the cardiovascular system is frequently given special consideration because of its extensive interpenetration with skeletal structure and function. Undoubtedly, much of the complex apparatus of cardiovascular regulation eventually serves the highly variable metabolic requirements of specific skeletal muscles; this, along with the role of the skeletal muscles in the general behavior of the organism, sometimes leads to the conclusion that central skeletal and vasomotor patterns are functionally inseparable and that only the skeletal component is independent. However, little experimental evidence exists supporting this contention; the visceral component has not been shown to be centrally mediated by the skeletal component or vice versa. Individual responses have been observed to be concomitant or to "go together" (Figure 9.1d), but the hypothesis that particular autonomic and skeletal responses are inexorably interconnected—"wired together"—is only one of many that may account for these observations.

To lift a 10-pound weight, an athlete may activate a certain skeletal pattern. He may activate a similar pattern to lift one of 50 pounds, but with different cardiovascular consequences. As his training progresses, the concomitant patterns may also change. An innate central effect related to effort, and unrelated to specific tissue requirements, may be involved (Dworkin, Pickering, Miller, Eisenberg, & Brucker, 1975); but instrumental learning may also participate in the association between particular visceral and skeletal patterns. The 10-pound weight may become the discriminative stimulus for one set of cardiovascular responses and the heavier weight for another. If restoration of homeostatic balance is intrinsically rewarding (Miller, DiCara, & Wolf, 1968), then the requirements for instrumental learning of the appropriate cardiovascular response are satisfied by a simple repetition of the skeletal pattern under the appropriate load.

Animal experiments using curare can test hypotheses of this kind. For example, activity in a somatic efferent nerve may be innately associated with increased blood flow to the corresponding muscle group. However, if the strength of the association is subject to modification by learning, the probability and/or magnitude of the local vascular response may also depend upon the history of contingent reinforcement. With inadequate cardiovascular adjustment, vigorous muscle contraction can cause a homeostatic imbalance, such as tissue anoxia or lowered pH, producing an autoregulatory drive. Rectification of the deficiency by increased blood flow would reduce this autoregulatory drive and presumably reinforce the vasomotor response. Using curarized animals, nerve activity can be dissociated from muscle contraction. With reduced metabolic requirements, a tissue deficit would not develop and the vasomotor response would cease to have rewarding consequences. Thus, the hypothesis predicts that under curare, repeated activation of a somatic nerve will cause the learned component of the concomitant vascular response eventually to extinguish.[4]

EARLY EXPERIMENTS

Following Miller and Carmona's (1967) report of modification of salivation by instrumental learning in noncurarized dogs, Trowill (1967) published the first visceral learning study with rats "maintained at a constant level of artificial respiration," while the skeletal muscles were paralyzed by curare. Trowill reinforced spontaneous changes in heart rate with "positively rewarding electrical stimulation of the brain." Continuing the strategy established by Miller and Carmona, he demonstrated that increase or decrease of heart rate was dependent only upon reinforcement contingency. This bidirectional training control was intended to reduce the possibility that the observed changes in baseline were attributable to a cumulative unconditioned effect of brain stimulation reward. The effect reported by Trowill was modest: only a few percentage points of change, with reliabilities between the 2% and 5% levels.

Trowill accomplished respiration with a rubber mask snugly fitted

[4] Inessa Koslovskaya and Robert Vertes in our laboratory trained curarized rats to sustain precise levels of sciatic nerve activity (Koslovskaya, Vertes, & Miller, 1973). By similarly training noncurarized animals, this technique could be used to study the extinction and reacquisition of a concomitant cardiovascular response.

Normally, sciatic activity produces muscle contraction and with it increased metabolism, thereby creating a local homeostatic imbalance, i.e., elevated lactic acid levels, anoxia, hypercapnea, etc. Presumably, this imbalance is corrected by increased blood flow into the muscle. Under the usual conception of the instrumental learning paradigm, the vascular response causing enhanced perfusion is reinforced by the after-coincident restoration of homeostatic balance.

With curare, muscle contraction is eliminated, and along with it local metabolic effects; thus, a learned compensatory vascular flow, being without reinforcement value, should eventually extinguish. A demonstration of gradual reacquisition of the vasomotor response with recovery of neuromuscular integrity would add credence to the hypothesis of learned adjustment by controlling for a morphological deterioration of the response system.

over the snout and a standard constant pressure rodent respirator. He did not attempt to control core temperature. In subsequent discussions (personal communication, 1971), he has indicated that rectal temperature was monitored and that it remained relatively constant. Following publication of Trowill's work, many papers on visceral learning emerged from the Yale laboratory. With the exception of two studies performed by Banuazizi, one under the direction of Wagner (Banuazizi, 1968, 1972) and one in collaboration with Miller (Miller & Banuazizi, 1968), the experiments were planned by Miller and DiCara (DiCara & Miller, 1968a,b,c,d, 1969a,b; Miller & DiCara, 1968) and performed by DiCara. Most of the experiments were of similar design. Either avoidance—escape from electric shock—or positively rewarding electrical brain stimulation was used for reinforcement. These studies differed fundamentally from Trowill's original design only in that the learning criterion was adjusted according to a shaping procedure. Two groups of curarized male rats were employed; one group was rewarded for increasing the magnitude of a visceral parameter, the other for decreasing it. An attempt was made to maintain a similar reinforcement density for both groups. At the end of a baseline period, the direction of training was assigned randomly to each animal. It was implicit in the protocol that both groups be treated identically aside from the specific reinforcement contingency.[5]

There was an explicit effort in the design of the experiments to minimize experimenter bias. However, as with any new area of investigation, many of the relevant variables are not immediately identified. The original visceral learning experiments were complicated; the methods employed were relatively sophisticated for psychological research; however, by our current standards, the maintenance procedures and reinforcement systems were primitive.

[5] In principle, a coin flip was part of the bidirectional control procedure used in all of the original experiments. Some subjects were trained to increase and others to decrease their response levels from an initial baseline. A particular subject was assigned to either increase or decrease only after all of the experimental parameters were satisfactorily adjusted. The experimenter then flipped a coin and set a single switch. Aside from criterion adjustments, he made no changes in the apparatus after that switch was set. This procedure was assumed to have two major features: *(1)* The training of subjects in both directions assured that a cumulative unconditioned effect of the reinforcer would both add and subtract from the training effect, i.e., a comparison between increase and decrease groups would cancel the unconditioned effect, since it would presumably always be in the same direction (for a more detailed discussion of this control procedure and its possible shortcomings, see Banuazizi, 1972); and *(2)* the experimenter could not inadvertently influence the outcome of the experiment while making initial adjustments because he did not know the direction of training until after the adjustments were completed.

Figure 9.2 The larynx is engaged above the soft palate and the nostrils communicate directly with the trachea. This is the normal position for negative pressure ventilation. The reduced pressure in the air passages tends to hold the larynx in place.

The rubber mask respiration technique is intrinsically unreliable. In principle, air is periodically supplied at a relatively constant pressure to the mask, from which it passes through the nostrils and other respiratory passages into the lungs. However, because the conjunction of the rat's trachea, soft palate, and nasal passages is relatively loose and precarious, any small, even temporary proximal obstruction can generate a pressure peak sufficient to displace the trachea (Figure 9.2).[6] In that event, the arrangement breaks down; the nasal passages and the entire oral cavity communicate, with air diverted out from the mouth or down into the gut (Figure 9.3). Either path reduces the tidal volume, and air diverted into the intestine also causes painful distention.

Even barring a catastrophic event of this type, more subtle, less detectable changes are possible. Quantitative analysis of gas exchange in an ideal system, using a leak-free constant pressure mask, is a complicated problem involving the interaction between discrete and continuous processes. In general, with room air as the respiratory medium, inspiratory CO_2 concentration is a function of cycle rate, I–E ratio, tidal volume, mask volume, and CO_2 production by the preparation.

Aside from rate and I–E ratio, none of these variables was carefully determined or controlled in the early experiments.[7] Using tra-

[6] This problem does not arise in normal respiration, when the negative pressure in the lungs tends to seat the junction of the soft palate and trachea.

[7] Tidal volume is roughly a monotonic function of peak inspiratory pressure, but many other variables are involved in the relationship. The basic parameter in respiration is tidal volume, which determines the aveolar surface area as well as the available size of

cheotomized rats and respiratory gas mixtures containing different concentrations of CO_2, we have shown a high proportion of the heart rate variance in curarized rats to be accounted for by the inspiratory CO_2 concentration and the resultant arterial pCO_2 (Dworkin, 1973; Miller & Dworkin, 1974) (see Figure 9.4). Consequently, exactly controlled respiration is a precondition for using heart rate as a dependent variable. Possibly because these relationships were not known for the rat until recently, the respiration technique in the early visceral learning experiments was inappropriately casual.

Heart rate in the curarized rat is also highly temperature-dependent, and the core temperature was not systematically recorded nor the environmental temperature automatically controlled in the early visceral learning experiments.

With a gradually increasing sense of the problems involved, we have attempted to duplicate the original experimental conditions. As

---

the O_2 and CO_2 diluent pool. Consequently, most respirators are designed to produce a constant tidal volume. Although these devices are of relatively simple design, for fixed inspiration–expiration (I–E) ratios they are expensive to produce, requiring precision machine work in the linkages and the volume-controlling cylinder. They are more mechanically complicated if the required I–E ratio is different from 1:1. The E & M Physiograph Company (now known as Narco Biosystems) developed a respirator using an electronically timed solenoid valve to control the respiratory cycle and a 60-Hz vibrating diaphragm fish-tank-type pump to supply the inspiratory flow. The result is inexpensive, flexible, and allows infinitely variable control over rate and I–E ratio. However, a major drawback to the design is that the use of a free-running diaphragm instead of a cycle-coordinated cylinder eliminates direct control of tidal volume. Instead, in place of volume control, a gauge and a parallel connected bleed valve are provided for measuring and controlling the peak inspiratory pressure—analogous in electronics to the use of a large-series resistance to regulate a constant current circuit. Because of this design, and variation in bronchopulmonary resistance is reflected in a change in the tidal volume (to a linear approximation of the fourth power of the radius) and that in the blood gas composition. Nevertheless, when Eric Stone developed the mask respiration technique, later used by Jay Trowill and his successors in the visceral conditioning studies, the E & M respirator represented a good compromise. With the mask technique, the rat breathes through its nostrils, while its snout is held in the stretched mouthpiece of a toy balloon. Unfortunately, the rat's snout is irregularly shaped and covered with fur. Constant volume respiration is impossible because the furry interface leaks. Since the unknown leak volume and inspiratory volume are additive, a small change in the leak volume can have a rather large proportional effect on the 2–3 cc tidal volume of the rat. The E & M respirator was useful because—in principle—it provided a constant leak, which was large when compared to the sum of interface leak and the tidal volume. Consequently, a change in the interface leak would have a small effect upon the peak inspiratory pressure. As with a constant current circuit, a small change in load resistance is of little consequence. Unfortunately, in our experience, the pump in the E & M is underrated, and it is necessary to restrict the size of the constant leak to the point where it begins to lose its constant pressure characteristics.

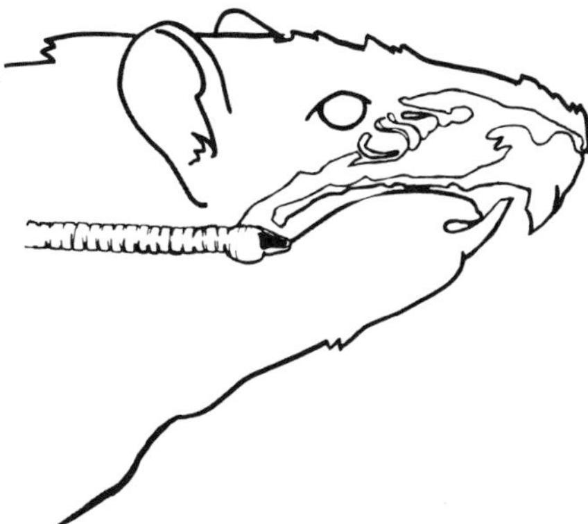

Figure 9.3 During positive pressure ventilation through the nostrils, a pressure peak can blow the larynx out of position. When this happens, air passes into the gut and out of the mouth as well as into the trachea. Intermediate positions are also possible.

of a year ago, using what we believe to be almost identical procedures and equipment, we were unable to replicate the results.

What can be concluded about the early visceral learning experiments? Because of the careful design and large reported effects, it is improbable that they were a statistical artifact. Either the original results were influenced by experimenter expectations, or very stringent conditions are necessary for obtaining the phenomena. For many reasons, neither explanation is entirely satisfactory. If exact procedures were critical, then it is difficult to understand how consistent results could have been obtained in many different studies without the several investigators[8] ever having identified the major sources of heart rate variance.

RECENT DEVELOPMENTS

We now understand that the maintenance requirements for curarized rats in visceral learning experiments are more stringent than for other types of physiological studies. Neuromuscular blockade has been most commonly used as an adjunct to general anesthesia. It has been applied only recently to conditioning and learning experiments requiring reliable responsiveness to subtle exteroceptive stimuli and drive states.

[8] In addition to the early Yale group consisting of Miller, Carmona, Trowill, DiCara, and Banuazizi, studies using the same procedures and confirming the phenomena were eventually reported by Hothersall and Brener (1969), Slaughter, Hahn, and Rinaldi (1970), Fields (1970), and Yagi (1973).

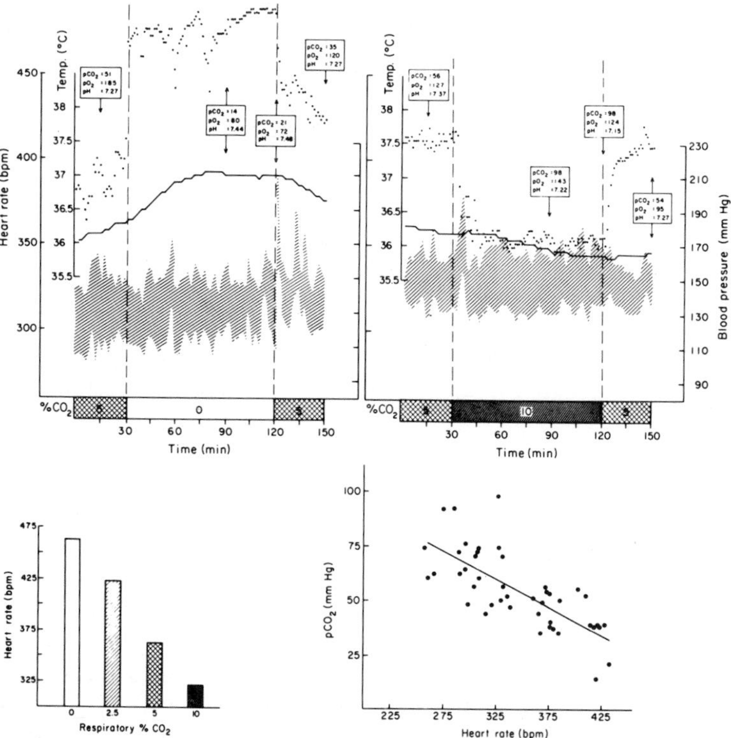

Figure 9.4 Key: dotted line is heart rate; solid line is core temperature; stippled area is blood pressure range (systolic–diastolic). Top of figure shows the effect of changing the concentration of CO_2 in the respiratory gas mixture. A decrease from 5% to 0% (left) causes an immediate rise in heart rate and a gradual increase in core temperature. An increase from 5% to 10% (right) causes an immediate fall in heart rate. The O_2 concentration in all of the mixtures was 40%. The boxed numbers are the blood gas values. Note the absence of a tonic effect on blood pressure. At the bottom left, the mean effect of different respiratory CO_2 concentrations is summarized. A one-way analysis of variance for linear regression was reliable ($p < .001$). The regression in bottom right, based on arterial pCO_2 shows the importance of blood gas composition as a determinant of heart rate in the curarized rat ($r = -.70$; $p < .001$; $N = 48$). For a more detailed discussion of these data, see Dworkin (1973).

Most reversible blocking agents do not cross the blood–brain barrier, and do not, per se, affect central processes. However, by their paralytic action, they do severely impair or eliminate normal regulation of blood gas composition, temperature, caloric intake, and fluid consumption; thus, they can indirectly alter central nervous system function. The consequences of inadequate regulation are disruptive in relatively short-term experiments and become intolerable in studies lasting for several days. Even minor distortions in blood carbon dioxide content or electrolyte balance can profoundly affect brain metabolism (Purves, 1972). Moderate distortion, 10%–25%, causes radical changes in function; and larger distortions lead to rapid loss of detectable sensory function, progressing sometimes to an irreversible deterioration of the entire preparation. Consequently, with total neuromuscular blockade, the physiological state of the preparation must be monitored and perturbations continuously corrected.

In addition to readily measurable shifts in blood chemistry and temperature, improperly managed curarized preparations can suffer chronic discomfort from general distress or specific sources of pain, and these may not be immediately evident. Localized pressure on the skin surface, accumulation of fluid and mucus in the lungs, gaseous distention of the gut, drying of the mucosal surfaces of the mouth and cornea, excessive distention of the bladder, etc., cause immediately noticeable compensatory behavior in freely moving animals. The same discomforts are even more likely to afflict the relatively "behaviorally mute" curarized subjects.

In learning experiments, a mild electric shock is often used as punishment. Presented against an elevated background of aversive stimulation, it may be less effective. Chronic discomforts create competing drives which are not under experimental control.

Weber's Law being what it is, learning experiments require better controlled curarized preparations than are standard in other types of physiology experiments. We now realize that the curarized rat preparation used in the early visceral learning experiments left much to be disired even with respect to the maintenance of vital functions. Respiration is the one most important factor. Tracheal cannulas are superior to the face mask for administering constant and accurate positive pressure ventilation; they are standard technique for animals or medium and large size. However, until recently, they were not routinely used for the rat because the small diameter catheter became blocked within several hours by accumulations of mucus, and it was difficult to see the larynx clearly enough to pass the catheter between its bands.

Tracheal cannulas traditionally consist of a Y-tube with the common channel (Palacěk, 1969), like the trachea itself, carrying fresh air in during inspiration and CO_2-laden air out during expiration but the trachea, unlike the cannula, has a special surface that helps transport mucus out of the air passages. Since the cannula does not have cilia, with unbiased two-way flow, mucus continuously accumulates in the common segment of the "Y." Eventually, if the mucus is not removed, the cannula clogs. In physiology experiments on large animals obstruction is alleviated when necessary, by momentarily opening the cannula and aspirating the mucus. This technique is unsuitable for learning experiments with rats because of the size of the cannula and the possibility that ad libitum interruption of the respiration by the experimenter could bias the results.

We have found that a cannula of the type shown in Figure 9.5 eliminates the problem of mucus accumulation. It consists of two entirely separate channels: the smaller, 19 gauge, inside the larger, 12 gauge. The inspiratory aliquot is forced through the small tube at approximately 1–3 psi during the first third of the respiratory cycle, then passive expiration is allowed for the remainder of the cycle through the large tube. Overhumidification of the inspiratory gas mixture keeps the mucus at the cannula tip in a liquid state and it is continuously discharged through the larger tube with the unidirec-

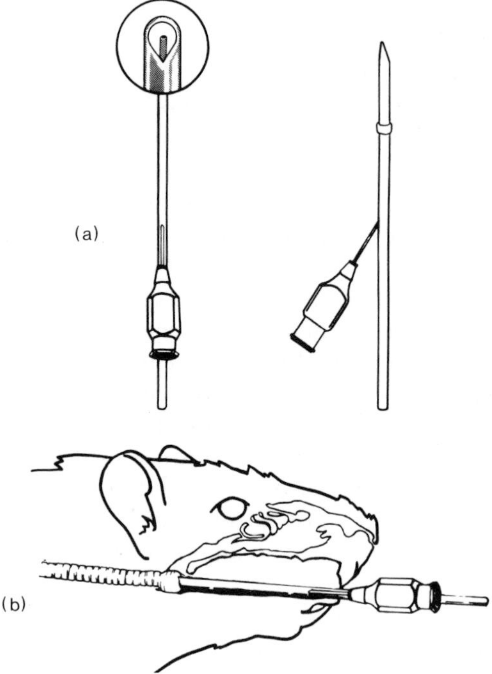

Figure 9.5 (a) This cannula consists of two entirely separate channels: the smaller, 19 gauge, inside the larger, 12 gauge. The inspiratory aliquot is forced through the small tube at approximately 1–3 psi during the first third of the respiratory cycle, then passive expiration is allowed for the remainder of the cycle through the large tube. (b) The cannula in place. It forms an airtight junction with the trachea.

tional flow of expired air. The secretions are separated from the expiratory gas in an automatically emptied trap before reaching the respirator. A transducer in the trap measures the peak inspiratory pressure, which rarely exceeds 10 cm H_2O.

The tip of the cannula is shaped much like the prow of a ship, with a large opening on either side. The shape facilitates passage between the bands of the larynx and the two openings prevent formation of a one-way "flutter valve" between a single level opening and the tracheal wall. This latter phenomenon, while it sounds unlikely, killed several of our early animals.

To facilitate cannula placement, retraction and illumination is aided with a spatula-like tongue depressor made of fused-glass, light-conducting fibers. Using this device makes the larynx clearly visible. Figure 9.6 shows a cannula (a) being placed. The rat's incisors are hooked over a narrow bar suspended above an inclined block (b).

With this cannula, constant volume respiration of the chronically curarized rat became a possibility. However, to realize this end, we were obliged to design an entirely new respirator. The rodent instruments available on the market were so imperfect in volume reproducibility and rate stability as to be virtually useless for careful work. In this new respirator, a fixed minute volume is delivered through a precision, constant-speed rotary valve (Figure 9.6c) which has only one moving part. The entire system maintians a set minute volume for many days within ±.1% for any reasonable variation in peak inspiratory pressure. A constant infusion, low dead volume humidifier (Figure 9.6f) was also developed to complement the rodent respiration system. As an additional feature, the rotary valve shunts the last 5% of each expiration to a separate port where it can be collected for end tidal CO_2 determination (Figure 9.6g). The dual channel of the tracheal cannula helps to make the end tidal sample a particularly reliable reflection of arterial pCO_2. When this respiratory technique is used with a gas mixture containing 40% O_2 and 4%–6% CO_2, and the rat is supported by procedures to be described below, heart rate and blood gas can be continuously maintained at stable preselected values for at least 6 days.

Depth of neuromuscular blockade is automatically regulated by monitoring the size of evoked potentials in the extraocular muscles to stimulation in the nucleus of the III nerve.

After a long evaluation, we have found ordinary electromyographic recording unreliable because it is inherently dependent on centrally produced nerve activity. A single pulse of 50 μa and 30 μsec delivered via a chronic monopolar electrode evokes a muscle response of 5–9 mv

Figure 9.6 The setup for passing the tracheal cannula and respirating a curarized rat. The cannula (a) is being placed with the aid of the support block (b) and fiber optic illuminator (H). The gas supply enters a precision regulator (J) and passes through a flow-regulating needle valve (K) and a flow meter (L) which directly reads the respiratory minute volume, and into the reservoir tank (M). When the respirator valve (c) begins inspiration, gas flows from the reservoir through the valve into the chamber of the transducer, and through the humidifier (F), the inspiratory channel of the tracheal cannula (a) and into the lungs of the rat. The infusion pump (o) supplies water to the stream through the humidifier at a rate of 1.0 ml/hour. When expiration begins, gas flows out of the lungs through the cannula (a) into the dome of the transducer and out through the respirator valve (c). Mucus is separated from the expiratory stream in the dome of (P) and continuously removed from the bottom port by the peristaltic pump (Q). The E & M respirator (R) is used with a mask for the first 5 minutes of paralysis while the neuromuscular blocking agent takes complete effect. Total muscular relaxation greatly facilitates passing the cannula.

across bipolar recording electrodes chronically implanted in the orbit. The latency is consistent at approximately 1 msec. Using signal averaging, with fewer than five individual stimulations, we can reliably detect evoked responses of less than 5 μv, and we can quantitatively control neuromuscular blockade to any specified level from .1 to 100% junctional transmission. Stimulation sampling cycles are programmed at 1 per minute; and infusion of blocking agent is automatically begun when the criterion response is exceeded, and terminated when the predetermined response size has been achieved.

Temperature control is also entirely automatic. A dual loop, direct current, proportional heater control varies the surface temperature of the rat to maintain constant rectal temperature. With an initial stabilization period of 1 hour, core temperature varies less than ±.2°C from the set point throughout an experiment.

Using these respiration, temperature, and infusion control techniques, survival limits for a curarized rat preparation were extended from several hours to several days. This, a particularly desirable development for learning experiments, has itself presented some additional problems. Fluid balance and nutritional intake have to be continuously maintained by infusion of electrolytes, glucose, and amino acids, and the exposed surfaces of the mouth and eyes must be carefully protected from dessication.

However, even using this improved preparation, consistently reliable discriminative classical conditioning of heart rate—an intermediate goal in our effort to demonstrate instrumental learning—was not readily obtained; yet another detail needed attention. We had noticed that blood appeared in the urine of most animals after 1 or 2 days of curarization, and autopsy usually revealed abnormally distended and frankly ulcerated bladders. Systematic observation showed that excessive bladder distention, known to be painful for humans, was present within the first hours of curarization and persisted throughout most experiments. The distention results from a valve formed by a slight twisting of the bladder neck. In rat, unlike man, the bladder is on a delicate stalk, adjacent to the junction of the ureters and the urethra. This anatomy also made for a solution of welcome simplicity; the bladder is easily removed, and in the laboratory environment the rat is not handicapped without its bladder.

DISCRIMINATIVE CLASSICAL CONDITIONING OF HEART RATE[9]

Figure 9.7 shows the timing diagram for the classical conditioning procedure. A 25-second CS+ is terminated with a single 300-msec, 1-ma, 60-Hz shock. The neutral stimuli are a 72-db (uncompensated RMS power), 1000-pps square wave and a light produced by a 24-volt panel lamp placed 4 cm from the left eye. The right eye is relatively unilluminated. Bilateral light is comparatively ineffective as a con-

[9] These studies were done in collaboration with Ethel Eissenberg, who was a USPHS postdoctoral fellow in this laboratory. Michelle Flaum prepared a number of the graphic illustrations.

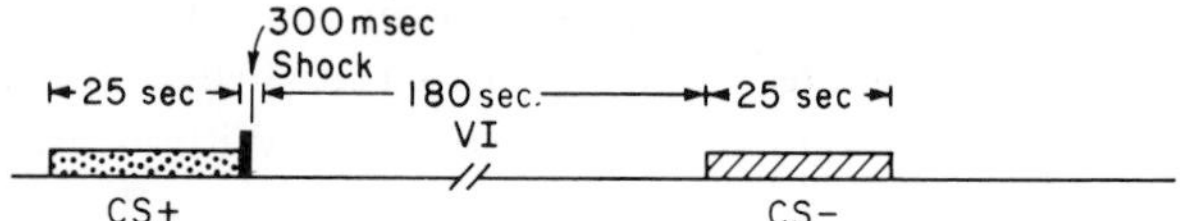

Figure 9.7 The timing diagram for the classical conditioning procedure. A 25-second CS+ is terminated with a single 300-msec, 1-ma, 60-Hz shock. The neutral stimuli are a 72-db (uncompensated RMS power), 1000-pps square wave and a light produced by a 24-volt panel lamp placed 4 cm from the left eye.

ditioned stimulus. Figures 9.8–9.11 are representative of our classical conditioning results. The particular experiments have been chosen to give an impression of the various patterns of learning rather than to provide "median" data. We do, in fact, obtain classical conditioning of heart rate with all subjects we attempt to train. Figure 9.8 shows a modal result. At the end of training, the response to the CS+ for a mean block of 20 trials is typically 5%–6% reduction from the baseline heart rate which persists for the duration of the 25-second positive stimulus. The response is usually terminated by the unconditioned stimulus, which causes a rapid acceleration of heart rate. The response is rarely less than a 3% change, and some subjects have produced consistent responses of 25%, which is a change of nearly 100 beats per minute. Often there is an unconditioned change in heart rate to one of the conditioned stimuli, which usually habituates within the first 10 presentations, but occasionally, as in Figure 9.9, persists to bias the

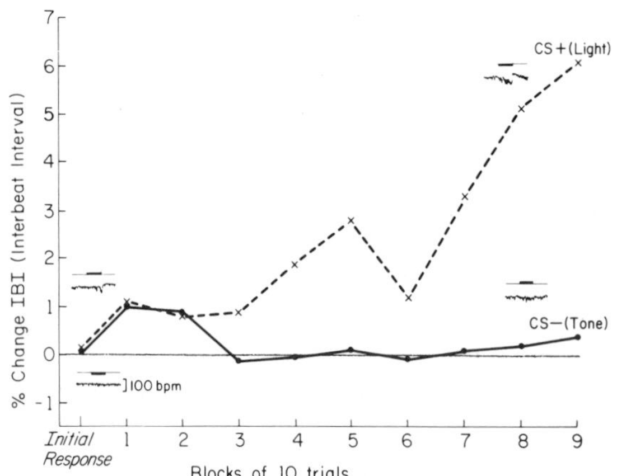

Figure 9.8 Modal learning result. The inserted tachograph trace shows the responses to the conditioned stimuli and shock at the beginning and end of training. Note the progressive nature of the conditioned decrease. The plotted result is based on the mean interbeat interval during the entire positive stimulus.

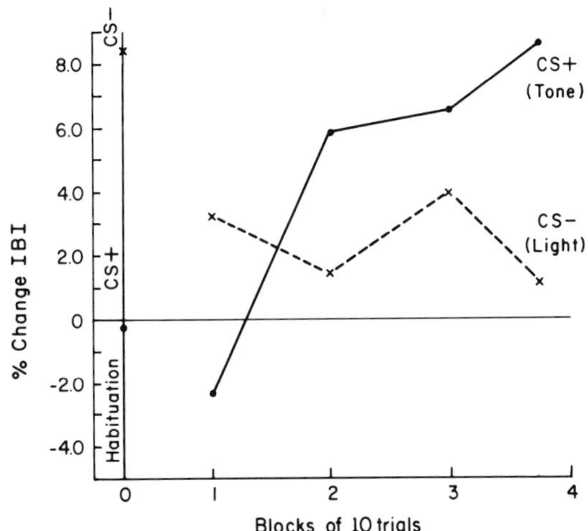

Figure 9.9 An unconditioned change in heart rate to a neutral stimulus usually habituates in the first few trials but in this subject the response to the light (CS−) persisted throughout the entire experiment.

result throughout the experiment. The subject in Figure 9.8 showed no unconditioned response to either stimulus, which is somewhat unusual.

Figure 9.10 shows one of a series of experiments with which we have been attempting to determine the role of respiratory parameters

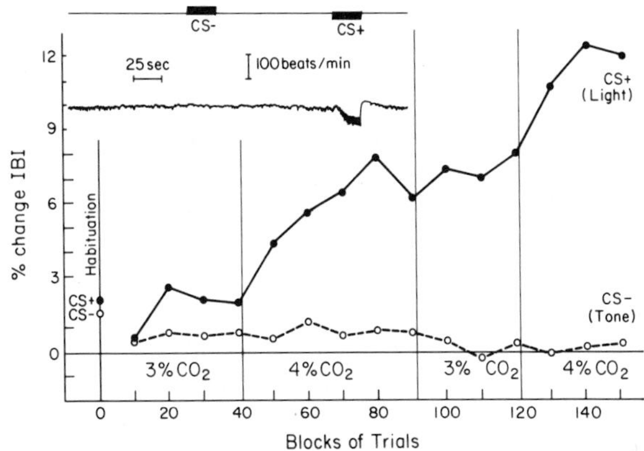

Figure 9.10 In this subject, learning was more rapid with a respiratory mixture containing 4% than with one containing 3% CO_2. Performance, as distinguished from learning, is relatively unaffected by the respiratory gas mixture. The insert shows a typical response to the CS+ and CS− at the end of the last 4% CO_2 period.

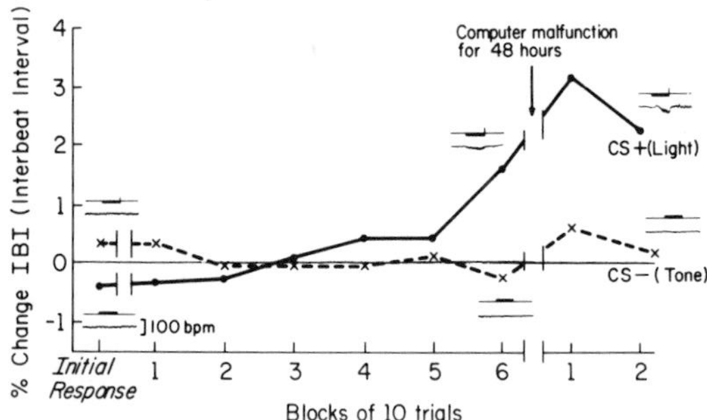

Figure 9.11 This figure shows the retention of the discriminated behavior during a 2-day apparatus failure. The degree of retention and the increment to the CS+ is not unusual after a long rest period.

in acquisition of classical conditioning. In this subject, learning was more rapid with a respiratory mixture containing 4% than with one containing 3% CO_2. Performance, as distinguished from learning, is relatively unaffected by the respiratory gas mixture. However, most animals in this series show a loss of performance as well with 3% CO_2. The insert shows a typical response to the CS+ and CS− at the end of the last 4% CO_2 period.

Figure 9.11 shows the retention of the discriminated behavior during a 2-day apparatus failure. The degree of retention and the increment to the CS+ is not unusual after a long rest period.

In conclusion, we would contend that these classical conditioning studies substantiate the long-term physiological and psychological integrity of the properly maintained curarized rat.

While developed primarily for our ongoing studies of instrumental modification of visceral systems, the curarized rat may be useful for a variety of neuropsychological investigations requiring both immobility and intact central function, and for the analysis of the peripheral components of cardiovascular–skeletal interdependence.

REFERENCES

Anand, B. K., Chhina, G. S., & Singh, B. Studies on Shri Ramanand Yogi during his stay in an airtight box. *Indian Journal of Medical Research,* 1961, *49,* 82–89.

Banuazizi, A. Modification of an autonomic response by instrumental learning. Unpublished doctoral dissertation, Yale University, 1968.

Banuazizi, A. Discriminative shock-avoidance learning of an autonomic response under curare. *Journal of Comparative and Physiological Psychology,* 1972, *81,* 336–346.

Black, A. H. Operant conditioning of heart rate under curare (Technical Report No. 12).

Hamilton, Ontario: Department of Psychology, McMaster University, October 1967.

Blanchard, E. B., & Young, L. D. Clinical application of biofeedback training. *Archives of General Psychiatry*, 1974, *30*, 573–589.

Chagas, C. Studies on the mechanism of curarization. *Annals of New York Academy of Sciences*, 1959, *81*, 345–357.

DiCara, L. V., & Miller, N. E. Instrumental learning of systolic blood pressure responses by curarized rats: Dissociation of cardiac and vascular changes. *Psychosomatic Medicine*, 1968, *30*, 489–494. (a)

DiCara, L. V., & Miller, M. E. Instrumental learning of vasomotor responses by rats: Learning to respond differentially in the two ears. *Science*, 1968, *159*, 1485–1486. (b)

DiCara, L. V., & Miller, N. E. Changes in heart rate instrumentally learned by curarized rats as avoidance responses. *Journal of Comparative and Physiological Psychology*, 1968, *65*, 8–12. (c)

DiCara, L. V., & Miller, N. E. Long-term retention of instrumentally learned heart rate changes in the curarized rat. *Communications in Behavioral Biology*, 1968, Part A, *2*, 19–23. (d)

DiCara, L. V., & Miller, N. E. Heart rate learning in the noncurarized state, transfer to the curarized state, and subsequent retraining in the noncurarized state. *Physiology and Behavior*, 1969, *4*, 621–624. (a)

DiCara, L. V., & Miller, N. E. Transfer of instrumentally learned heart-rate changes from curarized to noncurarized state: Implications for a mediational hypothesis. *Journal of Comparative and Physiological Psychology*, 1969, *68*, 159–162. (b)

Dworkin, B. R. An effort to replicate visceral learning in rats. Unpublished doctoral dissertation, The Rockefeller University, 1973.

Dworkin, B. R., Pickering, T. G., Miller, N. E., Eisenberg, L., & Brucker, B. Continuous noninvasive recording of blood pressure changes during attempted muscular contraction in patients with severe muscular paralysis. Manuscript submitted for publication, 1975.

Engel, B. T., & Bleecker, E. R. Application of operant conditioning techniques to the control of the cardiac arrhythmias. In P. A. Obrist, A. H. Black, J. Brener, & L. V. DiCara (Eds.), *Cardiovascular psychophysiology*. Chicago: Aldine, 1974. Pp. 456–476.

Fields, C. Instrumental conditioning of the rat cardiac control systems. *Proceedings of the National Academy of Sciences* (USA), 1970, *65*, 293–299.

Hadfield, J. A. The influence of suggestion on body temperature. *Lancet*, 1920, *2*, 68–69.

Hefferline, R. F., & Perera, T. B. Proprioceptive discrimination of a covert operant without its observation by the subject. *Science*, 1963, *139*, 834–835.

Hothersall, D., & Brener, J. Operant conditioning of changes in heart rates in curarized rats. *Journal of Comparative and Physiological Psychology*, 1969, *68*, 338–342.

Howard, J. L., Galosy, R. A., Gaebelien, C. J., & Obrist, P. A. Some problems in the use of neuromuscular blockade. In P. A. Obrist, A. H. Black, J. Brener, & L. V. DiCara (Eds.), *Cardiovascular psychophysiology*. Chicago: Aldine, 1974. Pp. 353–361.

Hubel, K. A. Voluntary control of gastrointestinal function: Operant conditioning and biofeedback. *Gastroenterology*, 1974, *66*, 1085–1090.

Koslovskaya, I. B., Vertes, R. P., & Miller, N. E. Instrumental learning without proprioceptive feedback. *Physiology and Behavior*, 1973, *10*, 101–107.

Lynch, W. C., & Schuri, U. H. Some methodological issues in the study of vasomotor self-regulation. In preparation, 1976.

Maslach, C., Marshall, G., & Zimbardo, P. G. Hyponotic control of peripheral skin temperature: A case report. *Psychophysiology,* 1972, *9,* 600–605.

Miller, N. E. Applications of learning and biofeedback to psychiatry and medicine. In A. M. Freedman, H. I. Kaplan, & B. J. Sadock (Eds.), *Comprehensive textbook of psychiatry—II.* Baltimore: Williams & Wilkins, 1975. Pp. 349–365.

Miller, N. E., & Banuazizi, A. Instrumental learning by curarized rats of a specific visceral response, intestinal or cardiac. *Journal of Comparative and Physiological Psychology,* 1968, *65,* 1–7.

Miller, N. E., & Carmona, A. Modification of a visceral response, salivation in thirsty dogs, by instrumental training with water reward. *Journal of Comparative and Physiological Psychology,* 1967, *63,* 1–6.

Miller, N. E., & DiCara, L. V. Instrumental learning of urine formation by rats; changes in renal blood flow. *American Journal of Physiology,* 1968, *215,* 677–683.

Miller, N. E., DiCara, L. V., Solomon, H., Weiss, J. M., & Dworkin, B. Learned modifications of autonomic functions: A review and some new data. *Circulation Research,* 1970, *26, 27* (Suppl. 1), 3–11.

Miller, N. E., DiCara, L. V., & Wolf, G. Homeostasis and reward: T-Maze learning induced by manipulating antidiuretic hormone. *American Journal of Physiology,* 1968, *215,* 684–686.

Miller, N. E., & Dworkin, B. Visceral learning: Recent difficulties with curarized rats and significant problems for human research. In P. A. Obrist, A. H. Black, J. Brener, & L. V. DiCara (Eds.), *Cardiovascular psychophysiology.* Chicago: Aldine, 1974. Pp. 312–331.

Palaček, F. Measurement of ventilatory mechanics in the rat. *Journal of Applied Physiology,* 1969, *27,* 149–156.

Purves, M. J. *The physiology of the cerebral circulation.* Cambridge: Cambridge University Press, 1972, Pp. 179–191.

Roberts, A. H., Kewman, D. G., & MacDonald, H. Voluntary control of skin temperature: Unilateral changes using hypnosis and feedback. *Journal of Abnormal Psychology,* 1973, *82,* 224–235.

Shapiro, D., Tursky, B., Gershon, E., & Stern, M. Effects of feedback and reinforcement on the control of human systolic blood pressure. *Science,* 1969, *163,* 588–590.

Slaughter, J., Hahn, W., & Rinaldi, R. Instrumental conditioning of heart rate in the curarized rat with varied amounts of pretraining. *Journal of Comparative and Physiological Psychology,* 1970, *72,* 356–359.

Trowill, J. A. Instrumental conditioning of heart rate in the curarized rat. *Journal of Comparative and Physiological Psychology,* 1967, *63,* 7–11.

VanDercar, D. H., Feldstein, M. A., & Solomon, H. Instrumental conditioning of human heart rate during free and controlled respiration. Unpublished manuscript, 1972.

Veterans Administration. *A dialogue on biofeedback.* Videotape, 1974.

Weiss, T., & Engel, B. T. Operant conditioning of heart rate in patients with premature ventricular contractions. *Psychosomatic Medicine,* 1971, *33,* 301–321.

Yagi, F. The physiological mechanisms of operant conditioning of cardiac function: The effects of the autonomic nervous system blocking agents. Unpublished manuscript, 1973.

10

Long-Term Studies of Cardiovascular Control in Primates

ALAN H. HARRIS
JOSEPH V. BRADY
The Johns Hopkins University
School of Medicine

INTRODUCTION

The observation that cardiovascular functions are altered, sometimes in profound ways, by environmental circumstances and behavioral activities has been repeatedly confirmed in both the laboratory and clinic (Guttman & Benson, 1971; Henry & Cassel, 1969; Zanchetti, 1972). Systematic experimental inquiry into the nature of such relationships began almost a century ago with studies of I. P. Pavlov (1879). Research and experimentation within the broad conceptual framework defined by behavioral conditioning effects upon the cardiovascular system, however, have not as yet provided a convincing analysis of the way in which such psychological influences bear upon the etiology, treatment, and prevention of even the most common circulatory disorders (e.g., essential hypertension).

For the most part, accounts of the relationship between such psychogenic factors and cardiovascular functions have been framed in the context of traditional psychophysiological models emphasizing *antecedent* or *concurrent* environmental–behavioral stress effects upon the elicitation of cardiovascular responses. More recently, attention has been focused upon the cardiovascular effects of environmental–behavioral events that *follow* circulatory changes and that bear a close temporal relationship to their occurrence. Several experimental reports, recently reviewed (Harris & Brady, 1974), have established that a broad range of visceral and glandular responses (with particular emphasis upon the cardiovascular system) can be modified by operant learning procedures that make environmental stimulus events (e.g., food reward, shock avoidance) contingent upon prespecified physiological changes. Significant increases and decreases in both heart rate (DiCara, 1971; Engel & Hansen, 1966; Engel & Chism, 1967) and blood pressure (Benson, Herd, Morse, & Kelleher, 1969; Shapiro, Tursky, & Gerson, 1969; Shapiro, Tursky, & Schwartz, 1970) have been shown to result from the application of such operant conditioning procedures to the control of cardiovascular responses, and additional studies have established that a remarkable degree of specificity can be observed with respect particularly to the operant learning of vasomotor responses (DiCara & Miller, 1968b). It has also been demonstrated that such operantly conditioned visceral and glandular responses can be brought under the control of explicit discriminative stimulus events in the environment (Miller & DiCara, 1967), can be maintained by several modes of reinforcement (DiCara & Miller, 1968a), and can be extinguished by discontinuing reinforcement (Fields, 1970; Miller & Banuazizi, 1968). Although numerous methodological and theoretical issues continue to be raised with regard to this relatively new operant conditioning approach to experimental psychophysiology (Blanchard & Young, 1973; Katkin & Murray, 1968), several reports have described a range of promising clinical applications involving such operant learning procedures with particular attention to the development of novel treatment modalities for cardiovascular disorders (Engel, 1973; Schwartz & Shapiro, 1973).

Of particular relevance to the work described in the present summary review are several reports in the recent literature of changes in blood pressure produced by such instrumental conditioning procedures in a variety of different primate species and man. Squirrel monkeys (Benson *et al.*, 1969), Rhesus monkeys (Plumlee, 1968, 1969), baboons (Harris, Findley, & Brady, 1971; Harris, Gilliam, Findley, & Brady, 1973) and human subjects (Shapiro *et al.*, 1969; Benson, Shapiro, Tursky, & Schwartz, 1971; Shapiro, Tursky, & Schwartz, 1970), all have shown alterations in both systolic and diastolic blood pressure levels in response to the programming of environmental consequences (i.e., "reward" and "punishment") made contingent upon specific increases or decreases in systemic vascular pressure. A prominent focus of the work in our own laboratories over the past several years has been upon this more contemporary "contingent" psychophysiological model in relationship to the interaction between cardiovascular changes and environmental consequences.

EXPERIMENTAL SUBJECTS AND SURGICAL PROCEDURES

Baboons (*Papio* sp.) of 12 to 15 kg (minimum weight) have been used in this research because of the animal's size, hardiness, adaptability to surgery and long-term experimental conditions, and the similarity of their circulatory parameters (i.e., blood pressure, heart rate, clinical biochemistry) to man (McGraw & Sim, 1972; Weber, Brede, Retief, & Melby, 1971). The animals are restrained in specially designed primate chairs (Findley, Robinson, & Gilliam, 1971) and housed in sound-resistant experimental chambers that provide access to a work panel containing multiple stimulus lights, operant manipulanda, a food tray, and a water spout. Electric shocks (5–10 ma, for .25 sec) are administered through plate electrodes attached with conducting paste to a shaved portion of the animal's tail.

Each baboon is surgically prepared, using a modification of previously described techniques (Perez-Cruet, Plumlee, & Newton, 1966; Werdegar, Johnson, & Mason, 1964) with two silicone-coated polyvinyl catheters, one implanted in the femoral artery to a point just above the level of the iliac bifurcation, and the other inserted in the vein and advanced to the inferior vena cava. The distal end of each catheter is tunneled under the skin, exited in the interscapular region, fitted with an 18-gauge Luer stud adapter, and connected to a Statham strain gage (P23De) transducer shock-mounted on the outside top of the experimental chamber. Patency of the catheter is maintained by continuous infusion of lightly heparinized saline (5000 USP units per liter) at a constant rate of approximately 4 ml/hour, and by a more rapid "flush" once each day. Daily calibration of the system is accomplished without dismantling the components by integration of a mercury manometer through a series of three-way valves (Findley, Brady, Robinson, & Gilliam, 1971). The special conditions of long-term operant cardiovascular control and observation essential to these studies require attention to the maintenance of catheter patency with such procedures as periodic (approximately 3–4 months) "blowing out" of the catheters with a 1-hour "flush" of fibrinolysin (Lyovac Thrombolysin) 1000 MSD units/cc at an infusion rate of 1 cc per minute. Despite this precaution, catheters can be expected to occlude within a year or two, well before the useful lifespan of the laboratory baboon. In our experience, however, such animals are readily recatheterized using the other femoral vessels, carotid artery, and jugular vein during the course of these long-term studies with no untoward effects.

APPARATUS AND LABORATORY SETTING

Pressure signals from the strain gauge transducer are amplified and displayed on an Offner Polygraph (Type R) which provides continuous heart rate and beat-by-beat blood pressure recordings. In addition, the pressure and rate signals are analyzed by an electronic averager (Swinnen, 1968) which provides on-line printout of heart rate (in beats per minute) and both systolic and diastolic blood pressure (in millimeters of mercury) over consecutive prespecified intervals. Throughout the extended course of the experiments, blood pressure and heart rate are monitored continuously each day, and adjustable meter relays integrated with the physiological recording system provide for selection of criterion diastolic blood pressure and/or heart rate levels and automatic programming of contingent food and shock events. All programming of the experimental procedures and recordings of both physiological and behavioral responses is accomplished automatically and remotely using a system of relays, timers, switches, cumulative event markers, polygraphs, electronic averagers, and printout counters.

CONDITIONING PROCEDURES

The instrumental conditioning procedure requires the animals to produce prespecified changes in blood pressure and/or heart rate and to maintain these altered levels for progressively increasing intervals in order to obtain food and avoid shock. Five 1-gm food pellets are delivered to the animal for every 10 minutes of accumulated time that the specified circulatory function (e.g., diastolic blood pressure) remains above criterion, and a single shock is programmed for every 60 seconds below criterion level. Additionally, each food reward delivery resets the shock timer (thus providing an additional 60 seconds of accumulated shock-free time), and each occurrence of an electric shock resets the food timer (thus postponing the delivery of food for at least an additional 10 minutes of accumulated time). Beginning with

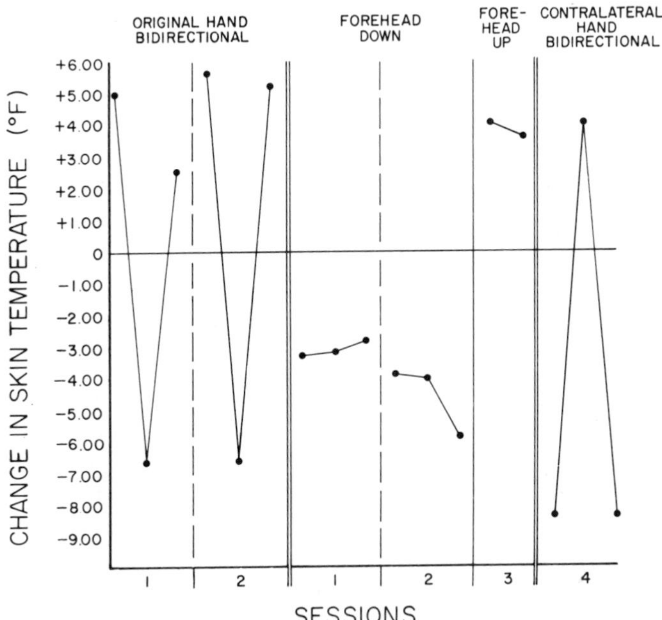

Figure 11.8 Range of self-regulatory temperature change during transfer of training sessions for one subject. One day of training with the original hand was interpolated between the last day of forehead-up testing, shown to the left of the second double line, and the day of transfer testing to the contralateral hand, shown to the right of the second double line.

The subject was then asked to bring the temperature of her forehead down. She succeeded in achieving a 3°F change in the appropriate direction in each of three 10-minute periods on the first transfer testing day, and was then able to improve her performance on the next day to a level close to the mean for the originally trained hand. On the third day of transfer testing, the subject was asked to reverse the direction of control and bring the temperature of her forehead up. She was able to do this, going up 4°F in the first 5 minutes; but during the second control period, she stopped performing the task after producing a change of 3.5°F and urgently requested release from the experimental situation. She reported a severe headache that seemed to center on the thermistor taped to her forehead. The headache disappeared shortly afterward. A second subject tested in similar fashion gave virtually identical results. Neither of these two subjects had ever reported a headache or any other disc[illegible]nd each had been involved in over 40 [illegible]

Friar and Beatty (in pr[illegible]eported that

self-regulated reduction of blood flow in a forehead vessel during a migraine aura decreases the incidence of migraine headache attacks. Our results may represent the opposite phenomenon.

The Question of Somatic Mediation

EMG recordings from the lateral aspect of the trained forearm were not well correlated with the observed self-regulatory changes in skin temperature. Other aspects of our data provide additional evidence that the temperature regulation was produced as a direct effect on local tissue-temperature control mechanisms (presumably volume blood flow) and was not mediated by somatic muscular activity (Taub & Emurian, 1976). *(1)* Direct observation of subjects indicated little or no movement or isometric muscular contraction during performance. *(2)* Subjects performing maneuvers involving powerful muscular contraction for periods of 20 seconds produced skin temperature changes that were a small fraction of those observed during temperature self-regulation periods. *(3)* Those subjects performing best, in either an upward or downward direction, usually reported being physically relaxed. *(4)* Anatomical precision of the response was considerable and developed gradually. If muscular contraction and relaxation were responsible for the temperature change, one would expect a more diffuse response, especially since there was not particular advantage to be gained from developing a precise, as opposed to a generalized, response.

Temperature Control of the Whole Hand

The specificity of the response that developed when feedback was given from one locus is of interest as a preliminary step in defining the precision of neural control possible over learned vasomotor responses. From the standpoint of practical applications, however, it would be desirable to have the subjects retain the original diffuse response permanently. To facilitate whole-hand training in naive subjects, a harness was constructed containing five thermistors, with a control device that enabled averaged feedback to be provided from one to five locations over a given portion of the body in any combination. For this work, the method of providing visual feedback was changed from the original single analog light to a digital information display, schematized in Figure 11.9, in order to correct certain apparent defects of the analog system (discussed in the next section). The digital system contained arrays of unit and cumulator lights; each unit light represented .02°F and each cumulator light represented 1.0°F.

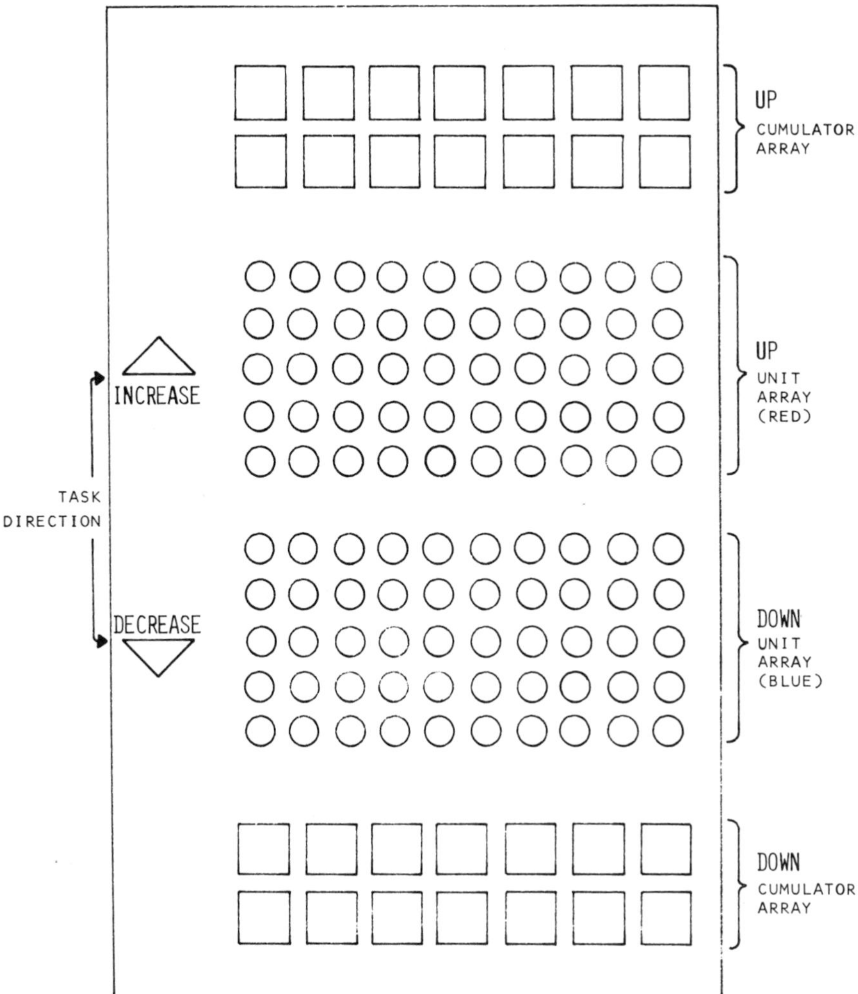

Figure 11.9 Digital feedback display panel.

The first 10 subjects trained with this device displayed a mean temperature change over the whole hand of 1.95°F on Training Days 4, 5, and 6 ($p < .001$, t-test) (Taub, Emurian, & Howell, 1974). Of the 10 subjects, 8 displayed significant temperature self-regulation ($p < .05$, t-test). Two of the subjects who originally learned to reduce whole-hand temperature were also able subsequently to learn to increase whole-hand temperature. Since this work, 18 additional subjects have learned to produce self-regulated whole-hand temperature changes of a magnitude similar to that of the first 10. Thus, self-regulation of whole-hand temperature would appear to be no more difficult than self-regulation of temperature around a single point.

Effects of Improving Discriminability of Feedback

While the original analog feedback system employed in these experiments proved satisfactory for virtually all subjects, two major deficiencies were noted. First, since the rate of temperature change controlled the rate of light-intensity change, very slow temperature changes resulted in such slow brightness changes that subjects had difficulty in discriminating them, especially when the feedback light was in the higher intensity range. Second, the light could not register large changes in temperature. Although it was reset to a standard intensity at the end of every 1-minute trial, it could not indicate changes larger than .25°–.3°F within a given trial. Subjects at the beginning of training, when still heavily dependent on feedback, would often self-regulate skin temperature considerably more than this feedback-limited value, and would then not uncommonly fall back. It appeared that these temperature reversals following large spurts in the correct direction resulted from the lack of temperature feedback information to support the new, high level.

The digital feedback system employed in the whole-hand conditioning work was designed to correct these deficiencies. The smallest unit that could be resolved by the system was always represented by a light with a spatial location easily discriminable from all others, and the subject therefore never had a discrimination problem with respect to the visual feedback system. In addition, the temperature range over which feedback could be presented to a subject on any given trial was ±12°F.

The digital feedback system also embodied other important principles of information presentation (Notterman, Filion, & Mandriota, 1971): *(1)* In general, differences in rate of change of spatial location or extent are more readily perceived than differences in rate of change in energy content (i.e., intensity); and *(2)* discontinuous change in spatial location is more easily discriminated than continuous change. According to this second principle, on–off changes along a row of individual lights of given length would be discriminated more easily than identical changes in extent along a continuous bar of light of the same length.

It will be remembered that one of the considerations that originally prompted this line of research was the desire to develop a test system for the hypothesis that improving the discriminability of augmented feedback would increase an organism's ability to self-regulate autonomic response systems. The digital information display corrected what appeared to be clear deficiencies in the earlier analog feedback system, but this did not improve the ability to self-regulate skin temperature. Two groups of four subjects participated in an experiment of crossover design in which they used one feedback system for eight training sessions and then switched to the other for an additional eight sessions. The digital feedback system did not provide any advantage. The hypothesis cannot be considered to have been disconfirmed on the basis of this single case; however, the results were certainly contrary to expectation.

Temperature Self-Regulation in Patients with Raynaud's Disease

An initial attempt at clinical application was directed toward Raynaud's disease, a condition in which paroxysms of cutaneous vasospasm occur, usually in the fingers. The vasospastic attacks can be precipitated by emotional upsets, but are usually due to exposure to cold. Each of three Raynaud's disease patients was trained to self-regulate increases in whole-hand temperature. Their performance was as good as that of normal subjects. The data for these three patients are shown in Figure 11.10. (Results of preliminary training of two other patients are consistent with those for the first three.) At times, these patients began a session with their hand temperature either at, or only 1°–2°F above, ambient room temperature, indicating that there was little or no blood flow in the skin. With training, they were frequently able to increase hand temperature into the normal range. On one day, one patient increased her hand temperature by 17.75°F—which is the largest change in one direction that has been observed to date in this laboratory.

Two of the Raynaud's disease patients, who began training in the winter, were frequently exposed to cold environments and other situations conducive to vasospastic attacks. These patients kept daily records of their condition. After approximately 20 sessions, each reported a greatly decreased incidence of such attacks and an ability to reduce the severity of incipient attacks or even to prevent them, by employing, without feedback, the technique learned in the laboratory. The third patient, who was also trained in winter, took elaborate measures to avoid exposure to cold, which could precipitate an attack.

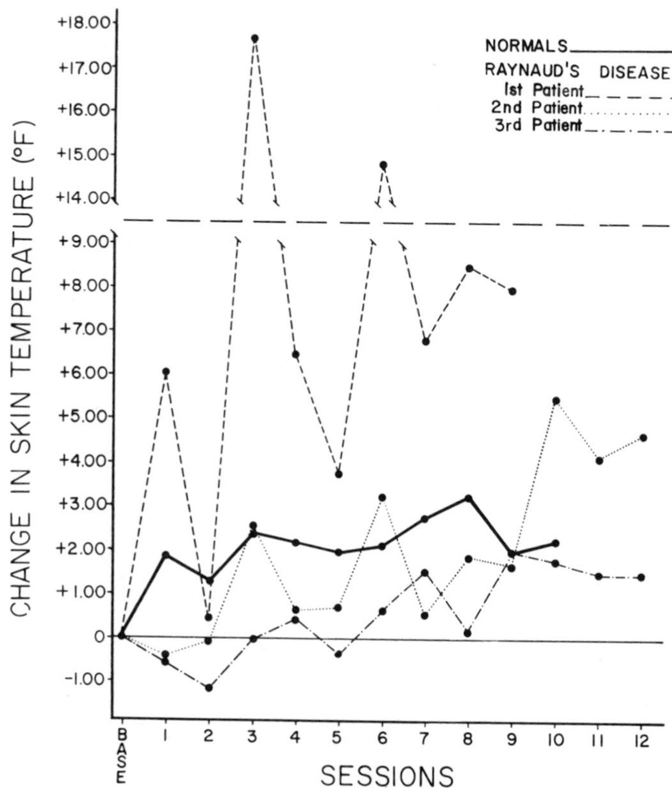

Figure 11.10 Course of learning self-regulatory control of whole-hand skin temperature by three patients with Raynaud's disease, compared to a group of four normal subjects who were trained just prior to the Raynaud's patients and under similar conditions.

While these results are of interest, clinical or diary-based data from just a few subjects are insufficient to demonstrate the therapeutic effectiveness of a training technique for Raynaud's disease. Since this condition is known to be greatly influenced by emotional state, it is probably quite sensitive to suggestion and placebo effects. Consequently, an effort is currently being made to determine, in direct experimental fashion, the value of the technique in preventing vasospastic attacks. Patients are required to don a "cold suit" which leaves only the hands and head bare and whose inner surface is lined with 300 feet of 1/16 inch tygon tubing. Cold water of specified temperature can be circulated rapidly through this suit, thereby posing a sudden whole-body cold challenge.

In control sessions, normal subjects typically exhibited a drop of

5°–8°F in hand temperature during a 10-minute cold challenge (suit inlet temperature at 60°F) when asked to simply sit quietly and not temperature self-regulate. Figure 11.11 provides an example of performance during a cold-suit session for one Raynaud's disease patient who prevented such a drop through self-regulation. After the stability criterion was reached at the beginning of the session, the information display was activated and the patient began to perform the task. Average hand temperature was increased by approximately 1°F in 5 minutes, at the end of which time water at 60°F was circulated into the suit. This was sufficiently cold so that the patient reported distress and could be observed to shiver frequently. She was nevertheless able to continue increasing hand temperature by another .9°F during the next 5 minutes. For the remaining 5 minutes of the cold challenge, she maintained her hand temperature at an essentially stable level. Circulation of the cold water was then discontinued, the information display was deactivated, and the patient stopped performing the task. Note the drop in hand temperature that occurred, even though suit temperature

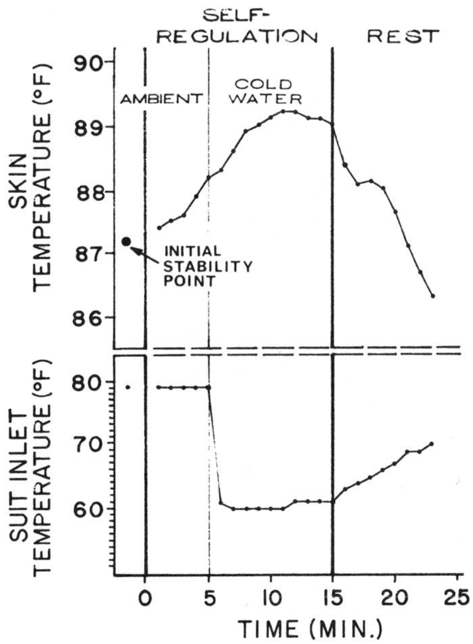

Figure 11.11 Self-regulated temperature increases by a Raynaud's disease patient during whole-body cold challenge. The upper curve represents skin temperature averaged over three locations on the fingers of the controlling hand; the lower curve represents temperature of the water in the inlet tube, 30 cm from the cold suit. (Note the difference of scales for skin and suit inlet temperatures on the ordinate.)

began to increase as soon as water circulation ceased. In contrast, the hands of normal subjects began to rewarm immediately after the period of cold challenge.

Prior to the work in this laboratory, temperature or photoplethysmographic feedback had been employed in an attempt to treat five individual cases of Raynaud's disease or allied conditions in four laboratories—two in one laboratory (Shapiro & Schwartz, 1972), and one in each of three others (Peper, 1972; Jacobson, Hackett, Surman, & Silverberg, 1973; Surwit, 1973). Each of these studies was undertaken on a preliminary pilot basis, and the reports rely heavily on the patients' general opinion; therefore, the results cannot be taken as providing anything more than suggestive evidence. However, the reports in four of the five cases were positive. More recently, several other investigators have reported success in treating Raynaud's disease with augmented feedback techniques—Adler and Adler, Peper, Russell, and Stroebel and Glueck (personal communications).

TEMPERATURE SELF-REGULATION, HYPNOSIS, AND HYPNOTIC SUSCEPTIBILITY

It has been known for some time that some individuals can produce hand-temperature changes on the basis either of suggestions made in the waking state (Hadfield, 1920; Schultz & Luthe, 1969) or of instructions to recall previous experiences involving thermal sensations (Menzies, 1941). In our own work, however, we have found that thermal imagery alone is insufficient to enable most people to self-regulate skin temperature (e.g., see Figure 11.5). However, the slide presentation of thermally relevant scenes with simultaneous verbal suggestion by the experimenter does appear to enhance temperature self-regulation reliably when feedback is available (Herzfeld & Taub, 1976).

It is also known that some individuals can change peripheral vasomotor tone on the basis of suggestions made after hypnotic induction (McDowell, 1959). A recent study by Maslach, Marshall, and Zimbardo (1972) demonstrating large temperature changes between the two hands following suggestions to hypnotized subjects was prompted by biofeedback research and has therefore gained particular attention, though augmented feedback was not employed. Roberts, Kewman, and Macdonald (1973) employed hypnotic suggestion to produce hand-temperature changes, but, in addition, they also used auditory feedback. The experimental design prevented determination of the relative contributions of the two factors. However, the authors did recognize that it might be possible to obtain the experimental effect they reported without hypnosis; and, indeed, in an excellent later study (Roberts, Schuler, Bacon, Zimmermann, & Patterson, 1974) where hypnosis was not used but the method was otherwise virtually identical, they did obtain similar results. Moreover, the magnitude of the learned temperature changes was also similar to that observed in the initial training series in this laboratory.

In the first study by Roberts and co-workers (1973), there was a suggestion that there might be a correlation between depth of hypnotic trance and magnitude of the self-regulated effect. In the second study (Roberts *et al.*, 1974), however, the relationship was reported to be disconfirmed, since no correlation was found between hypnotic susceptibility and the ability to self-regulate temperature. It should be pointed out, however, that the subjects in the first study were hypnotized while attempting to self-regulate, but those in the second study were not. Thus, results of the second study do not necessarily invalidate the relationship that may have begun to emerge in the first one.

In our own work, we have confirmed the lack of correlation between hypnotic susceptibility and temperature self-regulation ability. Ten subjects who were still available from our original series of 21 were recalled to the laboratory and tested for hypnotic susceptibility. The scores on the second repetition of the Stanford Hypnotic Susceptibility Scale correlated +.51 with the subjects' mean performance on the fourth and fifth training days, but this correlation was not significant. When these same subjects were later tested on Form C of the Stanford Hypnotic Susceptibility Scale by Charles Graham, the correlation was somewhat smaller and, again, not significant. However, as mentioned above, the lack of a significant, positive correlation between hypnotic susceptibility and the ability to self-regulate temperature in no way implies that temperature self-regulation might not be enhanced by hypnosis during task performance. For example, in our own work, one subject who showed high hypnotic susceptibility evidenced little self-regulatory ability during 10 training sessions; indeed, in later sessions, he exhibited an anomalous tendency to change hand temperature in a direction opposite to that desired, going as much as 4.3°F in the wrong direction on Day 9. He was then hypnotized on 3 consecutive days during which he was not asked to self-regulate, and baseline recordings were made of his skin temperature. Next, he was hypnotized during each of eight sessions and asked to perform the task. In the first five sessions, he was given direct suggestions, and during Sessions 3, 4, and 5 was able to self-regulate temperature by a mean of 1.25°F in the correct direction. During the last three hypnosis sessions, he was given indirect suggestions involving thermal imagery, and his control increased by .5°F. Finally, he was given six sessions without hypnosis, during which he not only retained his ability to control temperature, but actually improved it, achieving a temperature change of almost 3°F. These results are from only one subject, and must therefore be considered tentative. However, they are certainly suggestive and do seem to indicate the value of pursuing this approach further.

SELF-REGULATION TRAINING IN THE TREATMENT OF MIGRAINE

Training the Hand

In the mid-1960s, a group at the Menninger Clinic began using temperature feedback in conjunction with EMG and alpha feedback in an effort to improve autogenic training (Green, Green, & Walters, 1970). Autogenic training is a technique for promoting relaxation developed by Schultz and Luthe (1969) and used in the treatment of various psychosomatic disorders. The method involves autosuggestion, and one of the basic formulae is the suggestion that warmth is flowing into the hands. To enhance this aspect of the technique, the Menninger group used temperature feedback provided by a meter device. The measure represented either the temperature of a finger or the temperature difference between a finger and a midforehead location. In the latter case, the subject's instruction was to raise the temperature of his hand while lowering that of his forehead. Most subjects were reported to be successful in learning the task. However, the work was pilot in nature, and no data were given.

Since then, the Menninger group has employed temperature self-regulation as a therapeutic approach to the treatment of migraine headache (Sargent, Green, & Walters, 1972, 1973).[2] Feedback was originally given in terms of the temperature difference between a finger and the forehead, but it was later found that the major—and frequently, the only—temperature change was taking place in the finger[3]; consequently, this is now being used as the sole feedback site.

[2] Schultz and Luthe (1969) had previously reported that autogenic training relieved the symptoms of some migraine sufferers.

[3] Similar results were obtained by Keefe (1975).

Patients received several training sessions in the clinic, where they were asked to use autogenic phrases while receiving feedback, and were then given a portable device to use for home practice. They were expected to discontinue use of this device as soon as they felt they could dispense with it, and then to use the technique during the prodromal period that signals the beginning of a headache. Records were kept of the incidence of attacks, the intensity of the headache pain, and the amount and type of medication used. On the basis of these data and information obtained during clinical interviews, the senior author made a judgment concerning whether the patient had benefitted. Of the 42 migraine patients whose data were available, 81% were judged to have improved over 150 days of follow-up.

The Menninger group reported that this work was undertaken as a pilot study and was, therefore, preliminary in nature. A number of factors prevent unambiguous interpretation of the results. No data were given on temperature self-regulation performance, with respect to either the number of subjects who succeeded unequivocally in learning the task, or the extent of control that was achieved. The conditions of training and testing were not held constant; and while this would be difficult to achieve for home practice, and perhaps even counterproductive, it is clearly necessary for laboratory measurement of performance. The assessment of headache symptoms was also unstandardized, and the criteria for determining the effectiveness of the technique could be specified only in approximate terms. Finally, no attempt was made to employ a control procedure for placebo effects, and migraine headache is known to be particularly susceptible to this type of influence. However, the findings from this study are certainly suggestive; they have aroused a great deal of interest and stimulated additional work.

The later investigators have uniformly reported confirmatory results. Among them are Adler (1974), Diamond and Franklin (1974, 1975), Drury, DeRisi, and Liberman (1975), Gladman and Estrada (1974), Mitch, McGrady, and Iannone (1975), Pearse, Sargent, Walters, and Meers (1975), Peper and Grossman (1974), Turin (1975), and Wickramasekera (1973). Though the sheer number of these reports is impressive, all of this research is based heavily on the earlier work at the Menninger Clinic and preserves its primarily clinical character. Consequently, none of it can be considered to add to the conclusiveness of the original demonstration.

In comparing the temperature-control aspect of the work from the Menninger Clinic with the work from the author's laboratory, one is led to question whether the two involve the same type of mechanism.

We have been interested in training specific control of blood flow in a localized region of the body. When feedback was given from a single location, control was greatest around that point and decreased inversely with distance. In order to generalize control of temperature to even so small an area as the whole hand, feedback had to be given from multiple loci. Subjects were asked to relax, but they did so both when bringing hand temperature up and when bringing it down.

In contrast, the Menninger group used temperature feedback in conjunction with autogenic phrases as a means of establishing a generalized relaxation effect. An increase in hand temperature is a typical accompaniment of relaxation; consequently, it is a useful indicator of this process. However, many other major physiological changes, including large-scale alterations in blood distribution in other parts of the body, occur simultaneously, and these could, of course, be easily observed if an attempt were made to record them. It would probably not be possible to obtain a localized blood-flow change when autogenic phrases are used to induce a generalized state of relaxation, no matter what type of feedback were employed.

Thus, it is possible that the two laboratories are dealing with two different techniques based on two separate mechanisms: One involves establishing control of blood flow confined to a single region of the body, while the other involves training subjects to relax, one indication of which is an increase in hand temperature.

Training the Forehead

A second approach to the relief of migraine symptoms has been carried out by Friar and Beatty (in press), who asked subjects to reduce forehead blood flow, using feedback based on pressure plethysmographic recording from the temporal artery or some other vessel in the extracranial circulation coursing through the forehead. This technique resulted in a significant reduction in headaches, at least over the follow-up period, which was confined to 1 month. Zamani (1975), employing a similar technique, has obtained similar results.

Training in the Friar and Beatty experiment was carried out in rigorous fashion, and the demonstration of subject control of the designated parameter—first with, and later without, feedback—was unambiguous. In addition, unlike other work in this area, including the study by Zamani, the experiment benefitted from the use of a placebo control group, in which subjects were asked to decrease blood flow to the hand. A question arises, however, as to whether learning to self-regulate physiological events in a region where pain occurs would not have more intuitive value for placebo effects than learning to self-regulate that type of event in some location remote from the pain. The possibility that some placebo effects may have been operating in this experiment is suggested by the fact that there was a decrease in the incidence of headaches in the control group, although this decrement was not significant. There was also a decrease in the amount of medication taken by control group subjects.

It is of interest that large decreases in blood flow took place in the hands of the experimental subjects in this study at the same time as the decreases in blood flow in the extracranial vessel from which they were receiving feedback—the manipulation that presumably resulted in the alleviation of headache symptoms. In the work of the Menninger group and the studies based upon it, headaches were averted or terminated by warming a hand—a hand-temperature change in the opposite direction. Thus, if both techniques were effective in reducing migraine headache incidence, they would appear to involve different mechanisms. The hand-warming technique would presumably work because it involves induction of a state of relaxation, thereby reducing the level of the postulated migraine-triggering factor, while the effective mechanism in the Friar and Beatty technique would be vasoconstriction of vessels that would otherwise produce pain because of excessive vasodilatation.

OTHER FINDINGS

Most attempts at training temperature self-regulation have met with success. Much of this work is recent and has not yet been published. The findings are frequently available only in the form of preliminary reports or abstracts, and are therefore difficult to evaluate. In a majority of the studies, investigators have attempted to produce temperature changes in a finger. In addition to the workers cited in the preceding sections, these include Bertelson and Klein (1974); Keefe (1975); Leeb, Fahrion, French, and DeJoseph (1974); Russell (1972); and Thompson (1974). A number of investigators in addition to those mentioned in the preceding section have reported positive results in obtaining blood-flow changes in the forehead, either on the basis of temperature feedback (Engel & Schaeffer, 1974; Keefe, 1974) or plethysmographic feedback (Koppman, McDonald, & Kunzel, 1974; Savill & Koppman, 1975). Success in training has also been reported for such other regions of the body as the earlobes (Steptoe, Mathews, & Johnston, 1974), the mouth (Morgan & Coates, 1975), and the scrotum

(French, Leeb, & Fahrion, 1974). In the sole reported study to date involving temperature self-regulation in animals, Walsh, Wilcox, and Hartz (1975) were able to train squirrel monkeys to decrease skin temperature on a thigh.

In two important, well-controlled investigations, however, the results have not been uniformly positive. Surwit and Shapiro (1974) at first reported an inability to obtain operant control of finger temperature. More recently, they have reported success in training subjects to produce substantial decreases in temperature, but subjects asked to increase temperature were unable to do so reliably (Surwit, Shapiro, & Feld, 1975). Lynch, Hama, Kohn, and Miller (1974) found that, while a few of their adult subjects could self-regulate finger temperature, the majority could not. In contrast, these investigators have been able to train a number of children to self-regulate increases in finger temperature, and some of these young subjects were also able to learn to decrease finger temperature. The reason for the negative aspects of the work in these two laboratories are at present unknown.

Children have been the subjects in two other self-regulation studies. Peper and Grossman (1974), on the basis of two cases, arrived at the opinion that it is easier to train children than adults. Russell, Hunter, and Russell (1974) were able to train children to produce reliable increases in finger temperature, using movements of a toy train as reward and one source of feedback. Some of these subjects were "learning disabled" children. Adult retardates have also demonstrated the ability to self-regulate finger temperature (French, Leeb, & Fahrion, 1975).

Several studies indicate that both instructions and feedback are important factors in learning temperature self-regulation. Instructions by themselves, if they involve suggestions concerning thermal sensations, can be enough to produce temperature changes in the extremities in many subjects, even when there is no feedback—as, for example, in autogenic training (Schultz & Luthe, 1969). However, if subjects are simply instructed to increase or decrease the temperature of an area of the body, and there are neither thermal suggestions nor feedback, then learning does not appear to take place (Engel & Schaefer, 1974; Keefe, personal communication).[4]

[4] Thompson (1974), working in collaboration with Russell, has found that subjects with instructions to increase finger temperature performed even better in a no-feedback condition than in a feedback condition. In their laboratory, however, an attempt was made to promote relaxation and a warm experimenter–subject relationship, and this may have functioned in a manner similar to autogenic training in producing finger-temperature increases. They might not have obtained similar results if the task had been to decrease finger temperature.

Feedback alone is apparently sufficient to produce learning; it can overcome not only a lack of instructions but even misleading instructions. In one set of studies involving feedback, instructions to subjects to increase or decrease temperature were found to be important for learning early in training (Keefe, 1975), but, in a longer training series, the performance of subjects uninstructed in the nature of the parameter producing the feedback changes attained the same level as that of fully instructed subjects (Keefe, personal communication). Engel and Schaefer (1974) found that subjects given temperature-related feedback, but told incorrectly that the feedback was contingent on skin-resistance changes, showed no retardation in learning as compared with correctly instructed subjects.

PRACTICAL APPLICATIONS

Attempts have been made to employ temperature self-regulation for the prevention of vasospastic attacks in patients with Raynaud's disease and for the relief of migraine headache (see preceding sections). The symptoms in both of these clinical entities are episodic. Thus, in order for self-regulation to be effective in these cases, it need be carried out only for short periods of time—just long enough to terminate or prevent an attack. This is a simpler requirement to place on a self-regulation task than the control of some chronic condition, which would involve continuous self-regulation over long periods of time—for example, the control of hypertension through self-regulated decreases in blood pressure. Thus, if temperature self-regulation is found to be effective in the laboratory in controlling the symptoms of either migraine or Raynaud's disease, then the technique would stand an excellent chance of being useful in the control of the condition in the life situation. At this point, however, the evidence is not yet conclusive for either disease.

With respect to migraine, the results are suggestive and even exciting, but there is still a need for rigorous experiments in which *(1)* the temperature training is well controlled, *(2)* the data taking is unambiguous with respect to both self-regulatory ability and headache symptomology, *(3)* there are adequate controls for placebo effects, and *(4)* there is a long-term follow-up. The data for Raynaud's disease are also promising, but here, again, there is need for more data from a larger sample of subjects than is presently available, especially under laboratory conditions where patients are asked to avert vasospastic attacks that would otherwise occur as a result of cold stress.

The fact that subjects can produce self-regulated increases in hand temperature in a cool environment suggests that the technique may have cold-weather applications. For example, when a hand is suddenly exposed to very cold temperatures, as when a glove is removed in arctic environments, there is a rapid vasoconstriction of the vessels in the hand, resulting in marked reduction in tactile sensitivity and severe impairment in manual dexterity. If a person could generate an overriding self-produced vasodilatation of the vessels of the hand for a short period of time, the cold-induced clumsiness might be overcome to a degree that tasks requiring fine manipulation, as of instruments, could be carried out. Self-regulation of temperature increases in the extremities might also conceivably confer some protection against cold injury. Another use of the technique, suggested by French, Leeb, and Fahrion (1974), involves the use of self-induced increases in scrotal temperature to produce temporary sterility.

It is not difficult to conceive of still other potential applications for temperature self-regulation in cases where truly powerful control of the parameter has been achieved. These might include:

Self-regulation of vasoconstriction

- Alleviation of pain in various chronic ailments, such as arthritis
- Reduction of the edema and pain that follow tissue damage
- Control of diffuse bleeding that cannot readily be stanched
- Induction of sleep by lowering core temperature
- Reduction in the size of tumorous growths by reducing the nutrition to these hypermetabolic regions

Self-regulation of vasodilatation

- Promotion of wound healing
- Combating local infection by increasing phagocyte concentration, nutrition, and oxygenation in the affected tissues.

However, any list of this nature can represent only an interesting exercise in imagination until data are supplied indicating feasibility.

CONCLUSIONS

The demonstration that human beings can control blood flow in peripheral vascular beds is not new. It has long been known that some people can alter skin temperature of the hand on the basis of vivid thermal imagery, hypnotic suggestion, or suggestion given in the waking state. The classical conditioning of peripheral blood flow also has a long history. What is new is the development of techniques that permit training the ability to consistently self-regulate sustained alterations in parameters associated with peripheral blood flow. All of these techniques are based upon the use of some form of augmented feedback. The first investigators to employ such techniques were Lisina, using an operant–respondent overlap method; Snyder and Noble, working with transient vasoconstrictive events; and Green and co-workers, who employed temperature feedback as a means of enhancing autogenic training.

Work in the author's laboratory was designed to enable subjects to produce both increases and decreases in hand skin temperature that could be learned rapidly and sustained over a reasonably long period of time. The method involved operant shaping of small variations in skin temperature by means of changes in a visual information display. Following a period of development, it was found that a large majority of the population could perform the task. After learning bidirectional control, some subjects routinely displayed changes of 8°–15°F in 15 minutes. Subjects were also found capable of retaining the response over a period of months, of maintaining a considerable increase in skin temperature over approximately three-quarters of an hour while performing a concurrent task, and of self-regulating temperature increases when subjected to different types of cold stress. All of these phenomena have clear practical implications.

The data indicated that there is a surprisingly large difference between experimenters in the ability to train subjects to self-regulate skin temperature. It was also found that, when feedback was given from a single, punctate locus, subjects developed considerable anatomical precision of response as training progressed. In contrast, when temperature feedback is used in conjunction with autogenic phrases to promote relaxation, as in the experiments of Green and co-workers, a temperature increase measured at one point on the hand probably represents not only a change in blood distribution over that particular area, but a response involving changes in many physiological parameters over the entire body. The two techniques may therefore involve entirely different mechanisms.

In recent years, a substantial number of investigators have been successful in training subjects to establish self-regulatory control over peripheral blood flow, using either temperature or plethysmographic feedback. The work of Roberts and co-workers, Surwit and Shapiro, and Friar and Beatty is of particular interest because of methodological rigor. Several investigators, starting with Sargent, Green, and co-workers, have employed either self-induced increases in hand temperature or decreases in blood flow to some regions of the head as a means of reducing the incidence of migraine headache. Other workers have attempted to employ handwarming as a therapeutic approach to Raynaud's disease. At this time, the results are promising, but in neither case can the demonstration of efficacy be considered conclusive. Many other potential applications appear feasible, including the self-regulation of temperature increase in the extremities in cold environments. Consequently, there will probably be a great deal of research activity in this area in the future. Previous attempts to employ biofeedback techniques in the treatment of clinical entities lead one to be cautious about predicting the outcome. However, many possible applications of temperature self-regulation appear to involve situations where performance of the task need be carried out over relatively short periods of time, as in the prevention of episodes in either migraine or Raynaud's disease, rather than the continuous maintenance of a self-regulated change, as would be required in the treatment of hypertension or cardiac arrhythmia. This fact, and the rapid advances in the field over a period of only a few years, probably justify a guarded optimism concerning the future.

REFERENCES

Adler, S. M. The headache swamp: Pragmatic problems of biofeedback treatment. Paper presented at Biofeedback Research Society meeting, Colorado Springs, 1974.

Baer, P. E., & Fuhrer, M. J. Cognitive processes in the differential trace conditioning of electrodermal and vasomotor activity. *Journal of Experimental Psychology*, 1970, *84*, 176–178.

Bertelson, A., & Klein, M. The effects of autogenic and anti-autogenic phrases on ability to increase and decrease hand temperature. Paper presented at Biofeedback Research Society meeting, Colorado Springs, 1974.

Burch, G. E., & Thorpe, R. Cardiovascular system as the effector organ in psychosomatic phenomena. *Journal of the American Medical Association*, 1948, *136*, 1011–1017.

Diamond, S., & Franklin, M. Indications and counterindications for the use of biofeedback therapy in headache patients. Paper presented at Biofeedback Research Society meeting, Colorado Springs, 1974.

Diamond, S., & Franklin, M. Intensive biofeedback therapy in the treatment of headache. Paper presented at Biofeedback Research Society meeting, Monterey, California, 1975.

DiCara, L. V., & Miller, N. E. Instrumental learning of peripheral vasomotor responses by the curarized rat. *Communications in Behavioral Biology*, 1968, *1*, 209–212. (a)

DiCara, L. V., & Miller, N. E. Instrumental learning of vasomotor responses by rats: Learning to respond differentially in the two ears. *Science*, 1968, *159*, 1485–1486. (b)

Drury, R. L., DeRisi, W., & Liberman, R. Temperature feedback treatment for migraine headache: A controlled study. Paper presented at Biofeedback Research Society meeting, Monterey, California, 1975.

Emurian, C. S., & Taub, E. Self-regulation of skin temperature using a variable intensity light. Paper presented at Eastern Psychological Association meeting, New York, 1972.

Engel, R. R., & Schaefer, S. Operant control of forehead skin temperature. Paper presented at Biofeedback Research Society meeting, Colorado Springs, 1974.

French, D., Leeb, C., & Fahrion, S. Self-induced scrotal hypothermia: An extension. Paper presented at Biofeedback Research Society meeting, Colorado Springs, 1974.

French, D. J., Leeb, C. S., & Fahrion, S. Biofeedback hand temperature training in the mentally retarded. Paper presented at Biofeedback Research Society meeting, Monterey, California, 1975.

Friar, L. R., & Beatty, J. T. Migraine: Management by operant control of vasoconstriction. *Journal of Consulting and Clinical Psychology,* in press.

Gladman, A. E., & Estrada, N. Biofeedback, some clinical applications. Paper presented at Biofeedback Research Society meeting, Colorado Springs, 1974.

Green, E. E., Green, A. M., & Walters, E. D. Voluntary control of internal states: Psychological and physiological. *Journal of Transpersonal Psychology,* 1970, *II,* 1–26.

Hadfield, J. A. The influence of suggestions on body temperature. *Lancet,* 1920, *2,* 68–69.

Herzfeld, G. M., & Taub, E. Effect of suggestion on feedback-aided self-regulation of hand temperature. Paper presented at Biofeedback Research Society meeting, Colorado Springs, 1976.

Jacobson, A. J., Hackett, T. P., Surman, O. S., & Silverberg, E. L. Raynaud phenomenon: Treatment with hypnotic and operant technique. *Journal of the American Medical Association,* 1973, *225,* 739–741.

Keefe, F. J. The effect of instructions upon the conditioning of changes in absolute skin temperature. Paper presented at Biofeedback Research Society meeting, Colorado Springs, 1974.

Keefe, F. J. Conditioning of changes in differential skin temperature. *Perceptual and Motor Skills,* 1975, *40,* 282–288.

Keller, F. S., & Schoenfeld, W. N. *Principles of psychology.* New York: Appleton, 1950.

Kiritz, S., & Moos, R. H. Physiological effects of social environments. *Psychosomatic Medicine,* 1974, *36,* 96–114.

Koppman, J. W., McDonald, R. D., & Kunzel, M. G. Voluntary regulation of temporal artery diameter by migraine patients. *Headache,* 1974, *14,* 133–138.

Leeb, C., Fahrion, S., & French, D. The effect of instructional set on autogenic biofeedback hand temperature training. Paper presented at Biofeedback Research Society meeting, Colorado Springs, 1974.

Leeb, C., Fahrion, S., French, D., & DeJoseph, F. Voluntary control of hand temperature: Increase and decrease. Paper presented at Biofeedback Research Society meeting, Colorado Springs, 1974.

Lisina, M. I. The role of orientation in the transformation of involuntary reactions into voluntary ones. In L. G. Veronin, A. H. Leontiev, A. R. Luria, E. N. Sokolov, & O. S. Vinogradova (Eds.), *Orienting reflex and exploratory behavior.* Washington, D.C.: American Institute of Biological Sciences, 1965.

Lynch, W. C., Hama, H. Kohn, S., & Miller, N. E. Instrumental learning of vasomotor responses: A progress report. Paper presented at Biofeedback Research Society meeting, Colorado Springs, 1974.

Maslach, C., Marshall, G., & Zimbardo, P. G. Hypnotic control of peripheral skin temperature: A case report. *Psychophysiology,* 1972, *9,* 600–605.

McDowell, J. Hypnosis in dermatology. In J. M. Schneck (Ed.), *Hypnosis in modern medicine* (2nd ed.). Springfield, Ill.: Charles C Thomas, 1959.

Menzies, R. Further studies of conditioned vasomotor responses in human subjects. *Journal of Experimental Psychology,* 1941, *29,* 457–482.

Miller, N. E., & DiCara, L. V., Instrumental learning of urine formation by rats: Changes in renal blood flow. *American Journal of Physiology,* 1968, *215,* 677–683.

Mitch, P. A., McGrady, A., & Iannone, A. Autogenic feedback training in treatment of migraine: A clinical report. Paper presented at Biofeedback Research Society meeting, Monterey, California, 1975.

Mittelmann, B., & Wolff, H. G. Affective states and skin temperature: Experimental study of subjects with "cold hands" and Raynaud's syndrome. *Psychosomatic Medicine,* 1939, *1,* 271–292.

Morgan, B. B., Jr., & Coates, G. D. Enhancement of performance during sustained operations through the use of EEG and heart-rate autoregulation (Advanced Research Projects Agency Technical Report). Louisville, Ky., 1975.

Notterman, J. M., Filion, R. D. L., & Mandriota, F. J. Perception of changes in certain exteroceptive stimuli. *Science,* 1971, *173,* 1206–1211.

Pearse, B. A., Sargent, J. D., Walters, E. D., & Meers, M. Exploratory observations of the use of an intensive autogenic biofeedback training (LAFT) procedure in a follow-up study of out-of-town patients having migraine and/or tension headaches. Paper presented at Biofeedback Research Society meeting, Monterey, California, 1975.

Peper, E. Case report presented at Biofeedback Research Society meeting, Boston, 1972.

Peper, E., & Grossman, E. R. Thermal biofeedback training in children with headache. Paper presented at the Biofeedback Research Society meeting, Colorado Springs, 1974.

Razran, G. The observable unconscious and the inferrable conscious in current Soviet psychophysiology: Interoceptive conditioning, semantic conditioning and the orienting reflex. *Psychological Review,* 1961, *68,* 81–147.

Roberts, A. H., Kewman, D. G., & Macdonald, H. Voluntary control of skin temperature: Unilateral changes using hypnosis and feedback. *Journal of Abnormal Psychology,* 1973, *82,* 163–168.

Roberts, A. H., Schuler, J., Bacon, J. G., Zimmerman, R. L., & Patterson, R. Individual differences and autonomic control: Absorption, hypnotic susceptibility, and the unilateral control of skin temperature. Paper presented at Biofeedback Research Society meeting, Colorado Springs, 1974.

Russell, H. L. Fingertip temperature changes during relaxation and psychotherapy. *Psychophysiology,* 1972, *9,* 279. (Abstract)

Russell, H. L., Hunter, S. H., & Russell, E. D. The ability of elementary school children to learn autoregulation of fingertip skin temperature: Preliminary results. Paper presented at Biofeedback Research Society meeting, Colorado Springs, 1974.

Sargent, J. D., Green, E. E., & Walters, E. D. The use of autogenic feedback training in a pilot study of migraine and tension headaches. *Headache,* 1972, *12,* 120–124.

Sargent, J. D., Green, E. E., & Walters, E. D. Preliminary report on the use of autogenic feedback techniques in the treatment of migraine and tension headaches. *Psychosomatic Medicine,* 1973, *35,* 129–135.

Savill, G. E., & Koppman, J. W. Voluntary temporal artery regulation compared with finger blood volume and temperature. Paper presented at Biofeedback Research Society meeting, Monterey, California, 1975.

Schultz, J. H., & Luthe, W. *Autogenic therapy*. Vol. 1. New York: Grune and Stratton, 1969.

Shapiro, D., & Schwartz, G. E. Biofeedback and visceral learning: Clinical applications. *Seminars in Psychiatry*, 1972, *4*, 171–184.

Shmavonian, B. M. Methodological study of vasomotor conditioning in human subjects. *Journal of Comparative and Physiological Psychology*, 1959, *52*, 315–321.

Singer, M. T. Engagement-involvement: A central phenomenon in psychophysiological research. *Psychosomatic Medicine*, 1974, *36*, 1–17.

Slattery, P., & Taub, E. Specificity of temperature self-regulation to feedback loci. Paper presented at Biofeedback Research Society meeting, Colorado Springs, 1976.

Snyder, C., & Noble, M. E. Operant conditioning of vasoconstriction. *Journal of Experimental Psychology*, 1968, *77*, 263–268.

Steptoe, A., Mathews, A., & Johnston, D. The learned control of differential temperature in the human earlobes: Preliminary study. *Biological Psychology*, 1974, *1*, 237–242.

Surwit, R. S. Biofeedback: A possible treatment for Raynaud's disease. In Lee Birk (Ed.), *Biofeedback: Behavioral medicine*. New York: Grune and Stratton, 1973.

Surwit, R. S., & Shapiro, D. Skin temperature feedback and concomitant cardiovascular changes. Paper presented at Biofeedback Research Society meeting, Colorado Springs, 1974.

Surwit, R. S., Shapiro, D., & Feld, J. L. Digital temperature autoregulation and associated cardiovascular changes. Paper presented at Biofeedback Research Society meeting, Monterey, California, 1975.

Taub, E., Bacon, R., & Berman, A. J. The acquisition of a trace-conditioned avoidance response after deafferentation of the responding limb. *Journal of Comparative and Physiological Psychology*, 1965, *58*, 275–279.

Taub, E., & Berman, A. J. Movement and learning in the absence of sensory feedback. In S. J. Freedman (Ed.), *The neuropsychology of spatially oriented behavior*. Homewood, Ill.: Dorsey Press, 1968.

Taub, E., Ellman, S. J., & Berman, A. J. Deafferentation in monkeys: Effect on conditioned grasp response. *Science*, 1966, *151*, 593–594.

Taub, E., & Emurian, C. S. Operant control of skin temperature. Paper presented at Biofeedback Research Society meeting, St. Louis, 1971.

Taub, E., & Emurian, C. S. Self-regulation of skin temperature using a variable intensity light. In J. Stoyva, T. Barber, L. V. DiCara, J. Kamiya, N. E. Miller, & B. Shapiro (Eds.), *Biofeedback and self-control: 1972*. Chicago: Aldine, 1973. P. 504. (Abstract)

Taub, E., & Emurian, C. S. Feedback-aided self-regulation of skin temperature with a single feedback locus: I. Acquisition and reversal training. *Biofeedback and Self-Regulation*, 1976, *1*, 147–168.

Taub, E., Emurian, C. S., & Howell, P. Further progress in training self-regulation of skin temperature. Paper presented at Biofeedback Research Society meeting, Colorado Springs, 1974.

Taub, E., Perrella, P. N., & Barro, G. Behavioral development following forelimb deafferentation on day of birth in monkeys with and without blinding. *Science*, 1973, *181*, 959–960.

Teichner, W. H., & Levine, I. M. Digital vasomotor conditioning and body heat regulation. *Psychophysiology*, 1968, *5*, 67–76.

Thompson, D. J. An investigation of some parameters of acquisition of voluntary peripheral vasomotor control. Unpublished doctoral dissertation, University of Houston, May 1974.

Turin, A. Biofeedback for migraines. Paper presented at Biofeedback Research Society meeting, Monterey, California, 1975.

Walsh, J. M., Wilcox, R. H., & Hartz, N. Voluntary regulation of skin temperature in the squirrel monkey. Paper presented at Biofeedback Research Society meeting, Monterey, California, 1975.

Wickramasekera, I. E. Temperature feedback for the control of migraine. *Journal of Behavior Therapy and Experimental Psychiatry*, 1973, *4*, 343–345.

Zamani, R. Treatment of migraine headache: Bio-feedback versus deep muscle relaxation. Paper presented at Biofeedback Research Society meeting, Monterey, California, 1975.

ACKNOWLEDGMENTS

This research was carried out in collaboration with a number of co-workers, chief among whom were Susan N. Rice, in pilot work; Cleeve Emurian, in the experiments involving feedback from a single locus; and Priscilla Howell, in the experiments involving temperature self-regulation of the whole hand in normal subjects and Raynaud's disease patients. The patients were referred by Andrew G. Prandoni, who collaborated in this aspect of the work. Thanks are due Joseph Rothberg for the design and construction of the analog feedback system, Maurice Swinnen for the design and construction of the thermistor probes and thermistor bridges, Alfred Jakniunas for the design and construction of the digital feedback system, and Jean Swauger for technical assistance. The cold suit was supplied courtesy of ILC Industries, Dover, Delaware, and modified by Robert Heitmann. Portions of the data described in this paper were presented at meetings of the Biofeedback Research Society, St. Louis, October 1971; Boston, November 1972; Colorado Springs, 1974; and the Eastern Psychological Association, New York, April 1972.

12

Operant Control of Sexual Responses in Man

RAYMOND C. ROSEN
CMDNJ–Rutgers Medical School

Current accounts of human sexual behavior range along a broad spectrum of explanatory levels: from an entirely social approach (Gagnon & Simon, 1973) to a biological or clinical perspective (Masters & Johnson, 1966, 1970; Kaplan, 1974). In order to deal with the issues of operant control of sexual response, it will be necessary to restrict the empirical focus of the current chapter to studies dealing with penile-tumescence changes in the human male. There is certainly much more to sex than erections (in more senses than one). However, the psychophysiological processes involved in the engorgement of the penis do reflect a very fundamental aspect of human sexual response.

Masters and Johnson (1966) have demonstrated the major significance of vasomotor engorgement of the genitals during the early phase of the sexual arousal cycle of both genders. Moreover, in two previous studies (Bancroft & Mathews, 1971; Wenger, Averill, & Smith, 1968) penile erection was found to be the only consistent index of male sexual arousal elicited in the laboratory situation. Fewer studies have been conducted on female vaginal blood-flow changes, due to the obvious problems of measurement. Recent technological developments (Shapiro, Cohen, DiBianco, & Rosen, 1967; Sintchak & Geer, in press) have made measurement of female vaginal blood flow possible, and this measure will no doubt be incorporated in future research in this area.

At the present time, penile tumescence measurement appears to be the most reliable and valid method for the laboratory study of sexual arousal (Zuckerman, 1971). The mercury-in-rubber strain gauge provides an excellent, easy-to-use measure of momentary changes in penile blood flow, and is thus highly suitable as a dependent measure in operant studies of human sexual response. Moreover, the strain gauge has become standard apparatus for the assessment of certain behavior therapy techniques (Barlow, 1973; Marks & Gelder, 1967).

PSYCHOPHYSIOLOGY OF MALE SEXUAL AROUSAL

The prevailing account of the process of erection in the human male has tended to view that response as an involuntary, reflexive, stimulus-bound flow of blood to the spongy corpora of the penis. This tumescence response was once thought to be related to the flexion of two groups of striate muscle: *ischiocavernosus* and *bulbospongiosus*. However, Masters and Johnson (1966) have demonstrated that these skeletal muscles have little effect on the normal process of erection. In fact, there is no doubt at this time that erection is mediated entirely by the autonomic nervous system.

Penile tumescence is achieved through the engorgement of three cylindrical, sponge-like bodies of erectile tissue in the penis. The *corpora cavernosa* are two parallel dorsal cylinders, with a third ventral cylinder, the *corpus spongiosum*. These cylinders are composed of many small compartments separated by bands of smooth-muscle tissue, the *trabeculae*. The arterioles supplying blood to these bodies are derived from the internal pudendal artery.

Erection results from direct vasodilation of the arterioles, instigated by the action of *parasympathetic* vasodilator fibers from the sacral cord *(nervi erigentes)*. Certain authors (e.g., Bard, 1961) also consider the possibility of sympathetic vasodilator innervation of the penis. He refers to Muller's work in 1901, which demonstrated that erections could be produced in dogs that had had the entire sacral cord removed. However, the human research showing that abdominal sympathectomy does not interfere with erection, only ejaculation (Learmonth, 1931), suggests that the sympathetic innervation is relatively unimportant for tumescence. Furthermore, Nocenti (1961) notes that abatement of erection is caused by the vasoconstrictive action of sympathetic stimulation.

Weiss (1972) draws an important distinction between "psychogenic" and "reflexogenic" erections, with the former mediated primarily by thoraco-lumbar pathways and the latter by an entirely sacral, parasympathetic reflex arc. Moreover, Weiss cites evidence that after spinal injury severing all suprasegmental connections, reflexogenic erections can occur on the basis of this sacral reflex alone. In the intact adult male, erection probably represents the synergistic action of dual innervation. The neurophysiology of detumescence remains obscure at this time.

Voluntary Control of Erection?

The distinction between voluntary and operant control of behavior is rather complex and is discussed in detail in another chapter. Mediation of voluntary erection is easily accomplished through sexual fantasy. For many men, however, direct tactile stimulation of the glans and shaft of the penis is a necessary adjunct to mental imagery.

Advocates of the techniques of *yoga* have made some remarkable claims for the ability of experienced yogas to control a variety of physiological processes, including sexual arousal. One of the more incredible such claims if for the technique of "vajroli mudra" which is described by Arthur Koestler:

> The highest technique of vajroli consists in successfully withholding the ejaculation of sex secretions prior to or during orgasm under sexual excitement and thus cause their resorption through the lymphatics. In case the secretions happen to be ejected, the Yogi is advised to withdraw the secretion from the vagina where it may have become deposited, with the aid of Madhavadasa vacuum (part of the vajroli technique) [Koestler, 1965, p. 95].

While such extravagant claims await the scrutiny of sceptical scientific investigation, the possibilities of such control are certainly most provocative.

Though not so dramatic as the claims made for the vajroli technique, Laws and Rubin (1969) showed that employees of Anna State Hospital are capable of some degree of "voluntary control" of penile tumescence. Having found four subjects who showed full erections (measured by mercury strain gauge) to erotic films, they instructed the subjects to attempt to inhibit their erections during the showing of the film. With these instructions, the subjects appeared capable of suppressing erections to some extent, as compared to subsequent control presentations of the films in which the subjects were instructed to no longer inhibit their responses. Laws and Rubin also demonstrated that the subjects were capable of producing moderate tumescence in the absence of any external stimuli.

In a follow-up study (Henson & Rubin, 1971), these researchers developed a more stringent control for attention to the erotic material in the suppression condition. The subjects were required to provide a verbal description of the material they were viewing, which supposedly prevented the subject from generating competing fantasy material. Notwithstanding this additional control, normal male volunteers were still capable of some voluntary suppression of erection.

Even if it is assumed that normal male volunteers are capable of controlling erections on a purely "voluntary" basis, there appear to be certain individuals who are incapable of such voluntary control in the presence of certain stimuli. Fetishism, voyeurism, exhibitionism, transvestism, pedophilia, and homosexuality often involve elements of *involuntary* sexual arousal. While aversive methods are still resorted to in the treatment of some cases, positive reorientation techniques are becoming increasingly popular (Lazarus & Rosen, 1976). New methods for developing voluntary control of tumescence should greatly enhance this latter approach.

LABORATORY RESEARCH

Experiment 1: Contingent Suppression of Tumescence

The purpose of the first study was to investigate the learned control of elicited tumescence in the laboratory. Specifically, an attempt was made to demonstrate that, under controlled laboratory conditions, an instrumental conditioning procedure could produce substantial suppression of tumescence in normal male volunteers. Details of the procedure can be found in Rosen (1973). Susceptibility of tumescence to instrumental contingencies would have important implications for both etiology and treatment of psychogenic erectile disorders.

Penile tumescence in this experiment was elicited by erotic tape-recorded passages of approximately 10 minutes' duration. A standard mercury-in-rubber strain gauge, placed directly behind the coronal ridge, was used to measure changes in penile tumescence. Forty normal male volunteers were randomly divided into four experimental conditions: *(1)* a contingent feedback procedure illustrated in Figure 12.1; *(2)* a yoked control; *(3)* a group that received instructions to inhibit their erection with no external feedback; and *(4)* a no-treatment group. All subjects received one pretreatment and three treatment sessions.

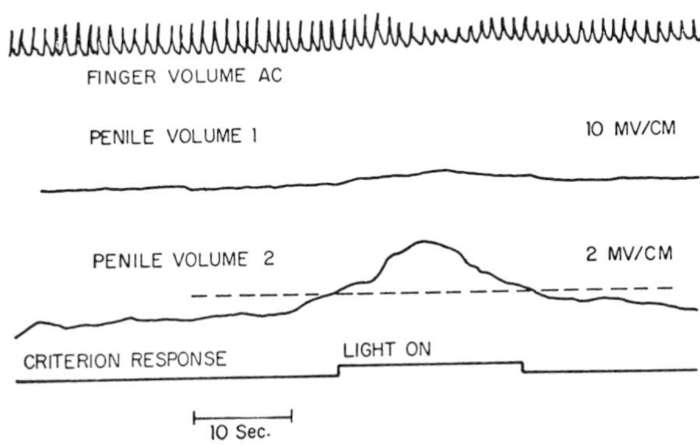

Figure 12.1 Representative portion of the polygraph record from a contingent feedback subject.

Due to the use of a binary feedback procedure (light-on or light-off), the tumescence records could be scored in terms of percentage time above criterion for each experimental session. Data from all four groups over all four experimental sessions is illustrated in Figure 12.2.

Significant ($p < .01$) suppression of tumescence was obtained as a result of the contingent feedback procedure. None of the control groups showed such suppression, indicating that the feedback procedure is particularly effective in producing suppression of erection.

Postexperimental questionnaires were administered after each experimental session. Although subjects in the control conditions tended

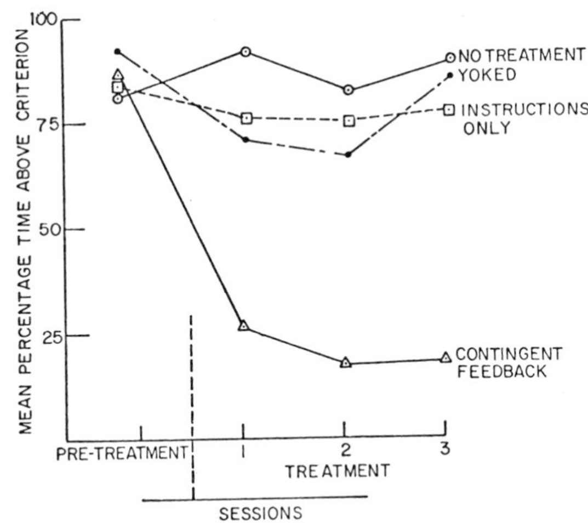

Figure 12.2 Average time above criterion (.5 mm penile diameter increase from flaccid level) of four groups over four experimental sessions. [Reprinted by permission of American Elsevier Publishing Co. for *Psychosomatic Medicine*.]

to rate themselves as having been less successful during the suppression phase, there was no evidence that the yoked subjects doubted the veridicality of the feedback. Another questionnaire finding of note was that subjects appeared to be able to rate with reasonable accuracy the extent to which they had been successful in inhibiting their tumescence during the session. That is, subjective ratings of suppression correlated significantly ($p < .01$) with actual strain gauge scores.

Experiment 2: Control of Erection without External Stimulation

A second study (Rosen, Shapiro, & Schwartz, 1975) investigated the *facilitation* of tumescence. The purpose of this experiment was to establish optimal conditions for the observation of penile tumescence in the absence of direct sexual stimulation. Both analogue feedback and reward were introduced to maximize voluntary control.

Twenty-four adult male volunteers without any history of sexual dysfunction were screened for the study. All subjects were instructed to increase tumescence (get hard) without direct stimulation of the penis during S+ (orange signal light) periods. During S− (blue light), subjects allowed tumescence to return to basal level. During the S+ period, the subject could earn monetary bonuses by increasing penile diameter to a predetermined criterion level. Following the usual operant shaping procedure, the criterion was raised each time the subject earned a bonus. This experimental procedure is illustrated in Figure 12.3.

A control group was employed to determine the extent to which analogue feedback and reward contributed to the tumescence control.

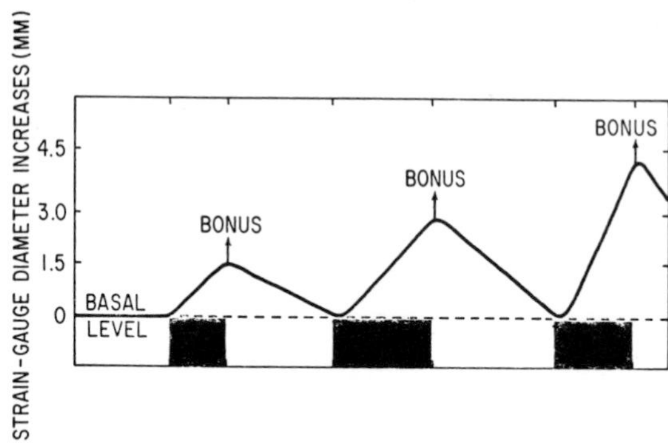

Figure 12.3 Shaping procedure for facilitation of penile tumescence. Feedback light is presented during solid blocks in figure.

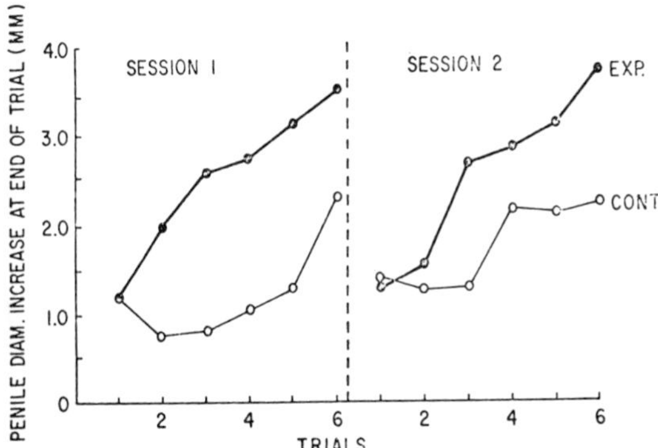

Figure 12.4 Mean penile diameter increase over six trials in the two experimental sessions. The 12 subjects receiving feedback and reward are indicated by the solid dots, and the controls by the open dots. [Reprinted by permission of American Elsevier Publishing Co. for *Psychosomatic Medicine*.]

Experimental subjects received varying intensities of the orange light, proportional to the strain gauge resistance, and a 2-second white light signaled the bonus $.25 whenever the tumescence attained the criterion on a trial. Twelve control subjects received similar instructions and experimental conditions except that a constant orange light and a yoked white light were used. All subjects were given two 20-minute training sessions.

The data can be analyzed with regard to a variety of measures. One basic conclusion that can be drawn is that subjects rapidly learned to increase tumescence in the presence of the orange light, and decrease tumescence in the presence of the blue light. Moreover, the shaping procedure appeared relatively effective in that progressively larger penile diameters were obtained in the presence of the orange light. These results for both experimental and control groups are shown in Figure 12.4.

Conclusions that can be drawn from these data are:

1. Both groups showed significant voluntary control of penile tumescence in the absence of any external erotic stimulus.
2. This control seemed to improve from the first to the second training session, suggesting that the skill could be improved with practice. Strictly speaking, however, another control group should be added in which subjects simply receive repeated exposures to the situation. It is conceivable that increasing comfort in the situation, rather than any direct learning effect, was responsible for improved performance from Session 1 to Session 2.
3. While both groups showed evidence of voluntary control, the

> feedback and reward group obtained greater and more consistent changes, suggesting that these variables could assist subjects in developing voluntary control over the response.

In addition to penile tumescence, we had also recorded cardiotachometer heart rate data, as well as respiration by means of a strain gauge belt. In reviewing these results, as well as the questionnaire and subjective reports, it became apparent that two different response patterns were identifiable. Some subjects could be characterized as showing a *tension* pattern, involving marked heart rate acceleration, irregular respiration and more variable strain gauge changes. The relaxation pattern, on the other hand, was accompanied by relatively constant heart rates and respiration records, and smooth, regular penile tumescence curves. On the basis of ratings by four independent raters, we selected penile tumescence records on which there was 100% agreement on whether they were relaxation or tension patterns. Figure 12.5 shows four samples of the averaged heart rates associated with these tumescence records. Both Subjects 9 and 5 were judged to have "relaxed" penile records, while Subjects 4 and 7 were judged as "tension" patterns. The heart-rate differences between these two types of response patterns is evident in Figure 12.5.

It should be noted that the tension-like patterns observed were very likely increased by the demands of our experimental situation. Subjects were trying to obtain erections in order to obtain bonuses. The situation might be somewhat analogous to the "performance demand" sexual condition, in which anxiety is often a concommitant of increased sexual arousal. This anxiety could possibly interfere with performance in more demanding interpersonal situations where sustained, prolonged erections are called for. In fact, a noteworthy difference between the relaxed and tense subjects was that detumescence in the relaxed subjects was a slower and more gradual process.

CLINICAL IMPLICATIONS OF OPERANT CONTROL

Although both the above studies were conducted on normal male volunteers, certain tentative clinical inferences can be drawn from the results. Masters and Johnson (1970) have stated that: "Erections develop just as involuntarily, and with just as little effort as breathing" (p.196). On the other hand, the results of the above studies suggest that instrumental contingencies could control tumescence in a manner analogous to the control of somatic behavior. Naturally, this raises the possibility of feedback-assisted laboratory training methods in the

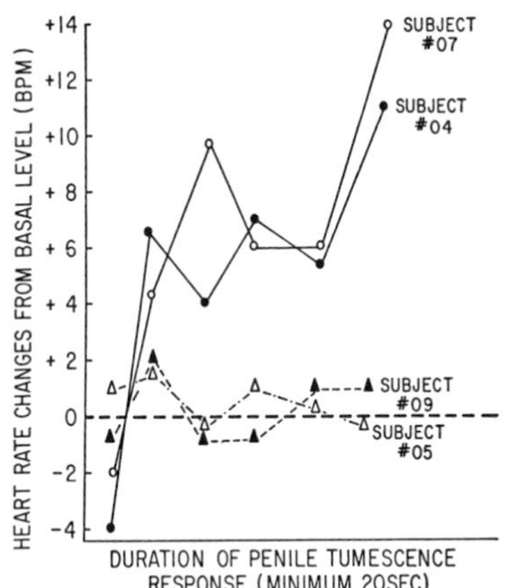

Figure 12.5 Heart rate averaged over tumescence responses for four subjects. Subjects 7 and 4 had irregular tumescence records, while Subjects 9 and 5 were judged to have "relaxed" tumescence responses.

treatment of erectile dysfunctions. At this time, several researchers, including this author, are attempting to develop such clinical applications. However, certain potential limitations must be considered:

1. The majority of erectile dysfunction cases are associated with strong *interpersonal conflicts* (Kaplan, 1974; Masters & Johnson, 1970). The impotent man usually needs to learn to cope with the demands of his relationship (with wife or other sexual partner) before any meaningful progress can be made with the erectile dysfunction. A laboratory feedback program is unlikely to provide any remedy for such problems.
2. The question of *transfer* of treatment gains from the laboratory to the real-life situation must be raised with respect to all feedback-assisted therapy programs. The issue appears particularly crucial in the case of sexual dysfunction, where unique stimulus conditions may play a major role in causing the problem.
3. The second study described above suggests another potential difficulty. To the extent that an operant training program places performance demands on the subject, this may tend to increase, rather than alleviate, anxiety. Performance anxieties are associated as either the cause or the consequence of erectile dysfunction, and must be dealt with before erection can be restored. Perhaps the answer lies in a feedback program for an integrated *pattern* of autonomic response: relaxation plus penile tumescence.

The first study reported above (Rosen, 1973) has led to the development of a clinical procedure for the treatment of inappropriate sexual behavior. Instrumental contingencies and laboratory feedback can be used as the basis for a self-control training program with certain clients. The following case study illustrates the considerable clinical potential of such procedures.

Mr. W is a 45-year-old married teacher with two teenage girls. He has worked for the past 17 years in the same professional position in a small, suburban town. Following a history of transvestite masturbation scripts, he was arrested in a supermarket parking lot for exposing himself in female clothing. A referral was made to the Rutgers Sexual Counseling Service for behavioral treatment.

In conference with my cotherapist, Steve Kopel, a three-track therapy program was elaborated. The immediate crisis demanded a procedure for gaining control over the problem behavior. For the longer haul, however, we decided to implement sexual counselling for the client and his wife (she was anorgasmic). We also stressed that gaining a broader perspective on his life would help to prevent the recurrence of such problems in the future. Mr. W agreed to enter our inpatient service for the initial conditioning phase of the therapy program.

Having identified the target behavior as *transvestite* exhibitionism, we videotaped a 30-minute sequence in which the client masturbated to orgasm in his customary female outfit. On viewing this videotape, the client showed consistent, protracted erections as measured in the usual way with a strain gauge. This response defined our therapy baseline, and we proceeded to shape a progressively diminished tumescence response in the presence of the videotape. This was accomplished with the use of a novel feedback stimulus—an amplified recording of the client's alarm clock. Whenever tumescence exceeded the preestablished criterion for the session (following the procedure in the first study, above), the alarm went off. In order to provide Mr. W with additional analogue feedback, the volume of the alarm was regulated according to the degree of erection. This relatively sophisticated feedback program seemed to facilitate rapid acquisition of self-control, and total suppression of response was possible by the twelfth session. This is shown in Figure 12.6.

One important concern in the use of such a procedure is the possibility of generalization of such tumescence suppression. We therefore showed a portion of a

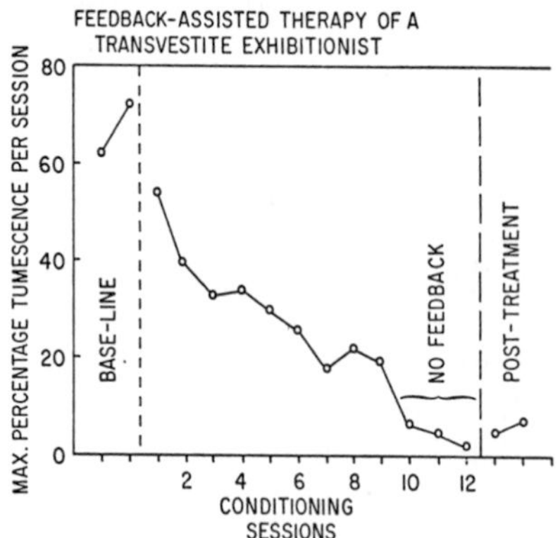

Figure 12.6 Feedback-assisted therapy of a transvestite exhibitionist.

typical heterosexually oriented stag film at the beginning and end of each conditioning session. His large tumescence amplitude and short latency on this film remained virtually unchanged throughout the 12 sessions. In fact, the specificity of the effect was quite remarkable.

At this time, successful suppression has been maintained. The emphasis has shifted to enhancement of sexual functioning with Mrs. W. In this respect, Mr. W is a relatively inhibited, naive lover, whose sexual repertoire is currently being expanded. Response acquisition, rather than suppression, is now the current focus for therapy.

It is noteworthy that the instrumental training paradigm in the above case utilized a combination of a punishment procedure (turning the alarm on whenever the response exceeded criterion) and an analogue feedback training program (diminution of volume with decreased response). This particular combination seemed to be successful for bringing the impulse to expose under control, and enhancing "voluntary" control of erection in such situations.

To date, there have been few reported attempts to utilize feedback techniques to enhance erectile responses in the clinical situation. A pioneering, if somewhat crude, attempt has been reported by Quinn, Harbisan, and McAllister (1970). They attempted to develop heterosexual penile responding in a homosexually oriented patient (Kinsey rating 5), who had previously received a series of aversive conditioning trials. Aversive conditioning treatment is focused on suppression of "deviant" responding, and in this case had resulted in a loss of all sexual interest. In order to develop heterosexual interest, the authors began reinforcing penile responses in the presence of appropriate stimuli. The reinforcement of cold lime juice seemed very effective while the patient was in a water deprivation state. After 20 sessions, during which time successively larger erectile responses had been shaped, the goal of full erection had not quite been attained. Follow-up is completely lacking.

Notwithstanding the limitations discussed above, feedback techniques may offer an interesting new approach to the treatment of specific cases of erectile dysfunction in a heterosexual context. With the development of sophisticated penile feedback systems (Laws & Pawlowski, 1973), it is only a matter of time before the appropriate applications are made. Several projects in this regard are currently in progress in our laboratory.

REFERENCES

Bancroft, J. H. J., & Mathews, A. Autonomic correlates of penile erection. *Journal of Psychosomatic Research*, 1971, *15*, 159–167.

Bard, P. Control of the systemic blood vessels. In P. Bard (Ed.), *Medical physiology* (11th ed.). St. Louis: C. V. Mosby, 1961. Chap. 11.

Barlow, D. H. Increasing heterosocial responsiveness in the treatment of sexual deviation: A review of the clinical and experimental evidence. *Behavior Therapy*, 1973, *4*, 655–671.

Gagnon, J. H., & Simon, W. *Sexual conduct: The social sources of human sexuality.* Chicago: Aldine, 1973.

Henson, D. E., & Rubin, H. B. Voluntary control of eroticism. *Journal of Applied Behavior Analysis*, 1971, *4*, 37–47.

Kaplan, H. S. *The new sex therapy.* New York: Brunner/Mazel, 1974.

Koestler, A. *The lotus and the robot.* New York: Harper and Row, 1965.

Laws, D. R., & Pawlowski, A. V. A multipurpose biofeedback device for penile plethysmography. *Behavior Therapy and Experimental Psychiatry*, 1973, *4*, 339–341.

Laws, D. R., & Rubin, H. B. Instructional control of an autonomic sexual response. *Journal of Applied Behavior Analysis*, 1969, *2*, 93–99.

Lazarus, A. A., & Rosen, R. C. Behavior therapy techniques in the treatment of sexual disabilities. In J. K. Meyer (Ed.), *Clinical management of sexual disorders.* Baltimore: Williams & Wilkins, 1976.

Learmonth, J. R. A contribution of the neurophysiology of the urinary bladder in man. *Brain*, 1931, *54*, 147–176.

Marks, I. M., & Gelder, M. G. Transvestism and fetishism: Clinical and psychological changes during faradic aversion. *British Journal of Psychiatry*, 1967, *113*, 711–729.

Masters, W. H., & Johnson, V. E. *Human sexual response.* Boston: Little, Brown, 1966.

Masters, W. H., & Johnson, V. E. *Human sexual inadequacy.* Boston: Little, Brown, 1970.

Nocenti, M. R. Reproduction. In P. Bard (Ed.), *Medical physiology* (11th ed.). St. Louis: C. V. Mosby, 1961. Chap. 48.

Quinn, J. T., Harbisan, J. J., & McAllister, H. An attempt to shape human penile responses. *Behavior Research and Therapy*, 1970, *8*, 213–216.

Rosen, R. C. Suppression of penile tumescence by instrumental conditioning. *Psychosomatic Medicine*, 1973, *35*, 509–514.

Rosen, R. C., Shapiro, D., & Schwartz, G. E. Voluntary candral of penile tumescence. *Psychosomatic Medicine*, 1975, *37*, 479–483.

Shapiro, A., Cohen, H., DiBianco, P., & Rosen, G. Vaginal blood flow changes during sleep and sexual arousal. *APSS proceedings*, 1967, *4*, 394.

Sintchak, G., & Geer, J. A vaginal plethysmograph system. *Psychophysiology*, in press.

Weiss, H. D. The physiology of human penile erection. *Annals of Internal Medicine*, 1972, *76*, 793–799.

Wenger, M. A., Averill, J. A., & Smith, D. B. Autonomic activity during sexual arousal. *Psychophysiology*, 1968, *4*, 468–478.

Zuckerman, M. Physiological measures of sexual arousal in the human. *Psychological Bulletin*, 1971, *75*, 297–329.

13

Biofeedback and Self-Regulation in Essential Hypertension*

DAVID SHAPIRO
J. ALBERTO MAINARDI
University of California, Los Angeles
RICHARD S. SURWIT
Harvard Medical School, Massachusetts Mental Health Center, Boston

Hypertension is a major public health problem in the United States, estimated to occur in 5% to 10% of the general population. High levels of arterial blood pressure increase the risk of life-threatening disorders such as coronary artery disease, atherosclerosis, and nephrosclerosis (Kannel, Gordon, & Schwartz, 1971). Even occasional large increases in resting levels of pulse rate and blood pressure are thought to be associated with a shortening of the life span (Merrill, 1966). A vast proportion of all cases of hypertension are diagnosed as "essential hypertension," defined by idiopathic elevations in blood pressure. While investigators do not entirely agree about the significance of psychological factors in hypertension, incidence of the disorder ap-

* Supported by National Institute of Mental Health Research Grants MH-26923 and MH-25104, Training Grant MH-06415, and Office of Naval Research Contract N00014-75-C-0150. Portions of this chapter were adapted from D. Shapiro and R. S. Surwit, "Learned control of physiological function and disease," in H. Leitenberg (Ed.), *Handbook of behavior modification and behavior therapy* (Englewood Cliffs, N.J.: Prentice-Hall, 1976).

pears related to various behavioral, social, and environmental conditions (Gutmann & Benson, 1971). A good body of literature indicates that such environmental factors play a critical "triggering" role in the development of the disorder. Excessive reactivity of the sympathetic nervous system may be associated with elevations of blood pressure in the early stages of hypertension as evidenced by increases in heart rate, cardiac output, and cardiac contractility (Frohlich, Tarazi, & Dustan, 1969; Frohlich, Ulrych, Tarazi, Dustan, & Page, 1967; Julius & Conway, 1968). This reactivity probably occurs in individuals who are particularly susceptible by reason of genetic, constitutional, or other factors. In addition, recent evidence indicates that there are interactions between autonomic and renin-angiotensin systems which play a significant role in hypertension (Buñag, Page, & McCubbin, 1966; Davis, 1971; Ganong, 1973; Stokes, Goldsmith, Starr, Gentle, Mani, & Stewart, 1970; Ueda, Kaneko, Takeda, Ikeda, & Yagi, 1970; Ueda, Yasuda, Takabatake, Iizuka, Iizuka, Ihori, & Sakamoto, 1970).

Current medical practice advocates active treatment when there is reason to suspect that the hypertension is becoming severe and fixed (Freis, 1974; Merrill, 1966; Veterans Administration Cooperative Study Group on Antihypertensive Agents, 1967, 1970, 1972). In view of assumed environmental, personality, and autonomic nervous system components of essential hypertension, biofeedback or other behavioral approaches offer nonpharmacologic means of lowering pressure that can augment or facilitate methods in medical practice. Two important problems in the management of hypertension, besides detection and diagnosis, are effectiveness of drug therapy and treatment compliance. Behavioral treatments such as biofeedback may be important in cases where drug control is not adequate or results in disturbing side effects. They can be used as adjuncts to drug therapy in order to provide more adequate control of blood pressure levels or to reduce required dosage. Behavioral treatments offer alternatives for patients who do not want to comply with drug treatment, for whatever reasons, in the same way that drug treatment offered an alternative for patients who did not want to undergo sympathectomy in the early 1950s. Behavioral treatments may expand the number of treated patients, aid in prevention, and help make patients more aware of responsibility for their health.

BIOFEEDBACK AND BLOOD PRESSURE REGULATION: BASIC RESEARCH

Basic research on biofeedback in the regulation of blood pressure provides evidence for the extension of such techniques into a therapeutic setting. In the curarized rat, instrumental conditioning of systolic blood pressure was demonstrated using shock escape and avoidance (DiCara & Miller, 1968). Learned changes in pressure were about 20% of baseline in both increase and decrease directions, and they were not associated with changes in heart rate or rectal temperature. In a subsequent study in noncurarized rats, changes obtained were about 5% of baseline (Pappas, DiCara, & Miller, 1970). Diastolic pressure elevations of large magnitude (50–60 mmHg) were obtained in the rhesus monkey using a shock avoidance procedure in which the elevations functioned as an avoidance response (Plumlee, 1969). More modest elevations of mean arterial pressure (25 mmHg) were observed in the squirrel monkey using similar procedures (Benson, Herd, Morse, & Kelleher, 1969). In the dogfaced baboon, substantial elevations in blood pressure were established by an operant procedure in which food delivery and shock avoidance were made contingent upon increases in diastolic pressure (Harris, Findley, & Brady, 1971; Harris, Gilliam, Findley, & Brady, 1973). In their recent work, these investigators reported sustained increases of about 30–40 mmHg in both systolic and diastolic blood pressure. The changes in blood pressure were associated with elevated, but progressively decreasing, heart rates (Harris & Brady, 1974).

Having an experimental animal with behaviorally induced hypertension is of significance for the study of associated physiological and biochemical processes, and it suggests that the illness may develop in this fashion. Arterial blood pressure in squirrel monkeys can be modulated in characteristic ways by different operant conditioning schedules, and sustained hypertension can be associated with schedule-controlled performances (Morse, Herd, Kelleher, & Grose, 1971). In exploring the value of an operant conditioning therapy in squirrel monkeys, Benson *et al.* (1969) put them on a work schedule in which they were required to press a key in order to avoid electric shock. Prolonged and persistent elevations in pressure resulted. Then, the schedule was reversed, and a decrease in pressure became the criterion for shock avoidance. Pressures were shown to decline 10 to 20 mmHg. However, the capacity to reduce blood pressure using an operant procedure may be related to the length of time that the high level is present (Teplitz, 1971). It is not known whether or not similar reversals can occur in animals with chronic high levels of pressure.

Most of the human studies on blood pressure control with biofeedback methods follow the procedures first described in Shapiro, Tursky, Gershon, and Stern (1969). The "constant cuff" technique was devised to obtain a relative measure of blood pressure on each beat of the heart so as to be able to provide continuous feedback to subjects.

Intermittent measurements (once or twice a minute) using an ordinary pressure cuff (Riva–Rocci method) can provide information on only 2% to 3% of the changes. They are inadequate because of the inherent variability of blood pressure. A single determination of systolic or diastolic pressure every half-minute can vary by chance as much as 20–30 mmHg from typical values. For example, in a minute's direct recording of pressure obtained via an arterial catheter, two successive casual clinical measurements using a standard cuff procedure would have yielded 124/90 and 144/60 mmHg, while the median reading based on the 50 pressure waves was actually 128/68 mmHg (Tursky, Shapiro, & Schwartz, 1972). Direct arterial catheterization is not a feasible alternative for routine repetitive training, although it may be possible in some hospitalized patients.

In the constant cuff method, a blood pressure cuff is wrapped around the upper arm, and a crystal microphone is placed over the brachial artery under the distal end of the cuff. The cuff is inflated to about average systolic pressure and held constant at that level. Whenever the systolic pressure rises and exceeds the occluding cuff pressure, a Korotkoff sound is detected from the microphone. When the systolic level is less than the occluding pressure, no Korotkoff sound is detected. Using a regulated low-pressure source and programming apparatus, it is possible to find a constant cuff pressure at which 50% of the heart beats yield Korotkoff sounds. This pressure is, by definition, median systolic pressure. Inasmuch as the time between the R-wave in the electrocardiogram and the occurrence of the Korotkoff sound is approximately 300 milliseconds, it is possible to detect either the presence of the Korotkoff sound (high systolic pressure relative to the median) or its absence (low systolic pressure relative to the median) on each heart beat. In this way, the system provides information about directional changes in pressure relative to the median on each successive heart beat, and this information can be used in a biofeedback procedure. Subjects are provided with binary (yes–no) feedback of either relatively high, or low, pressure on each heart beat. After a prescribed number of feedback stimuli or a change in median pressure, rewarding slides or other incentives are presented.

The cuff is inflated for a trial period of 50 heart beats and then deflated for about 30 seconds to allow recirculation of the blood. Whenever the percentage of Korotkoff sounds in a single 50-beat trial is greater than 75% or less than 25%, the constant pressure is increased or decreased in the next trial by a small amount (±2 mmHg) to return the cuff pressure to the subject's median. In addition to providing blood pressure feedback on each heart beat, the system can also track median pressure from trial to trial. The system has been evaluated against simultaneous data obtained using a direct arterial recording, and a close correspondence has been obtained for all of its essential features (Tursky *et al.*, 1972). Comparable procedures are used to determine diastolic values. In this case, the cuff is set at a constant pressure close to the median diastolic level, and the presence or absence of the Korotkoff sound at this level is used to track median diastolic pressure.

Some investigators have used the same constant cuff procedure but with a smaller number of heart beats per trial (Goldman, Kleinman, Snow, Bidus, & Korol, 1975; Kristt & Engel, 1975;. For further information on the constant cuff method and other methods of indirect recording of human blood pressure, see Tursky (1974). Efforts are currently under way to develop a simple portable blood pressure biofeedback device that can be used in the doctor's office or in the home.

Initial studies with the constant cuff method attempted to determine whether normal volunteer subjects could learn to modify their systolic or diastolic blood pressure. Complete details of the experiments may be found in Shapiro *et al.* (1969), Shapiro, Tursky, and Schwartz (1970a,b), Schwartz, Shapiro, and Tursky (1971), Schwartz (1972), and Shapiro, Schwartz, and Tursky (1972). In these studies, subjects were told that the feedback represented information about "a physiological response usually considered involuntary." Subjects were simply told to make the feedback stimulus occur as much as possible and thereby to earn as many rewards as possible. They were not told that the feedback was being given for changes in blood pressure; nor were they told whether to increase it or decrease it. This procedure controlled for any results that are due to the natural ability of subjects to control their pressure "voluntarily," and tested the specific effects of feedback and reward contingency. Voluntary control of blood pressure and other circulatory changes has been reported in individual cases (Ogden & Shock, 1939) and may be more widespread than previously believed. However, voluntary control of blood pressure unassisted by external feedback was not obtained, on the average, in a sample of normal subjects (Shapiro, 1973). Brener (1974) has also reported failure to obtain blood pressure control with instructions only.

To summarize these studies, normal subjects were able to modify their blood pressure with feedback and reward. Average differences in systolic pressure between increase and decrease conditions for groups of subjects at the end of a single session of training varied from 3% to 10% of baseline. The best results were obtained for diastolic pressure

(Shapiro *et al.*, 1972) with individuals showing increases up to 25% and decreases up to 15% of baseline values. Heart rate was not associated with learned changes in systolic pressure, and systolic pressure was not associated with learned changes in heart rate (Shapiro *et al.*, 1970b). However, Fey and Lindholm (1975), using the constant cuff method, reported that heart rate increased or decreased in groups receiving contingent feedback for increasing and for decreasing systolic blood pressure, respectively. Brener (1974) cited data from a dissertation by Emily M. Shanks in which continuous recordings of heart rate, chin electromyogram, and respiratory activity were obtained while subjects were given both increase and decrease feedback training for diastolic blood pressure. The results indicated that diastolic blood pressure biofeedback tended to have an effect specific to blood pressure (see also Brener & Kleinman, 1970). However, Shapiro *et al.* (1972) reported that heart rate was not independent of learned changes in diastolic pressure. Clearly, the evidence on specificity of learned blood pressure control is not entirely consistent.

To explain the conditions under which specificity of conditioning occurs, Schwartz (1972) hypothesized that when feedback is given for one response, simultaneous learning of other responses will depend on the degree to which these other responses are directly associated with the response for which feedback is given, as well as on other homeostatic mechanisms. He developed an on-line procedure for tracking both phasic and tonic patterns of blood pressure and heart rate in real time and showed that subjects could learn to control patterns of simultaneous changes in both functions. Subjects learned to integrate systolic blood pressure and heart rate (i.e., make both increase or both decrease simultaneously) and to some extent to differentiate both functions (i.e., make one increase and the other decrease simultaneously). Further analysis of the patterning of both functions over time and of natural tonic reactivity in this situation made it possible to predict the extent and time course of pattern learning in the different conditions. Subjective reports of a "relaxed" state were associated with learned reduction in both systolic pressure and heart rate (see also Schwartz, 1975).

Although the average curves suggest that it is easier to obtain reductions than increases in pressure in a single session (Shapiro *et al.*, 1969), further data under conditions of random reinforcement indicated a tendency for baseline pressure values to habituate over time (Shapiro *et al.*, 1970a). Therefore, increases in pressure over baseline values may be more likely in normal subjects. Unpublished data (Shapiro) indicated that the same pattern of pressure reduction occurs whether subjects try to reduce their pressure with or without feedback or simply rest in the laboratory and do nothing. On the other hand, Fey and Lindholm (1975), using the constant cuff method, reported reliable decreases in systolic blood pressure over three 1-hour sessions of feedback training for reduced pressure as compared with no changes in no-feedback, random, or increase-training groups. As in the case of heart rate, the processes involved in increasing blood pressure may be different from those involved in decreasing pressure (see Engel, 1972; Lang & Twentyman, 1974). In normal subjects, typical resting pressures are close to minimal waking values, but there is a potential for large increases above baseline. For individuals having significantly elevated pressure levels, significant decreases may be more likely.

By and large, uninstructed normal subjects, though they were able to produce changes in blood pressure, could not consistently report whether they were, in fact, learning to raise or lower their pressure; nor did they report the consistent use of specific thoughts, images, or physical strategies, such as respiratory maneuvers or muscle tension, as a means of achieving control. The determination of effective related strategies of control would be useful in practical applications of biofeedback methods, and additional research is needed to examine associated physiological and cognitive processes in detail.

Finally, Brener and Kleinman (1970) used a finger-cuff method of following systolic pressure. In an experimental group, normotensive subjects were instructed to decrease their blood pressure with the aid of pressure feedback. In a control group, subjects were instructed to observe the feedback, but they were not informed of its meaning. Differences of about 20–30 mmHg were obtained between the two groups after about 30 minutes of training, and the differences were not associated with heart rate. Inasmuch as blood pressure values obtained with a finger cuff are larger than those obtained with an arm cuff, it is difficult to compare these results with the smaller changes reported previously (Shapiro *et al.*, 1969).

All told, this research suggests that blood pressure can be self-regulated by normal subjects with a fair degree of consistency and specificity. The degree of change achieved, especially in a decrease direction, is relatively small. However, most of the research consists of one-session experiments in subjects already low in pressure to begin with. More work is needed to determine whether larger and persistent changes can be brought about with long-term training. In addition, further research is needed on the biofeedback regulation of other cardiac and vasomotor functions (e.g., cardiac output, heart contractile force, blood flow in muscles and other organs) as well as a more comprehensive physiological and hemodynamic assessment of changes taking place in blood pressure feedback studies. We should also investigate the effects on blood pressure and other cardiovascular indices when subjects are given biofeedback training for reductions in activity at various muscle sites, for reductions in electrodermal activity and other autonomic functions, for changes in various respiratory indices, and for alterations in various brain wave rhythms. Aside from these physiologically oriented questions, investigation has to proceed further into the effects of different behavioral and psychological factors in association with and comparison to biofeedback training. These include the use of particular instructions or training sets, suggestion, imagery, cognitive processes, incentives, reinforcers, and individual or personality differences. Clearly, there are great holes in our basic knowledge of self-regulatory psychophysiological processes, not only with respect to blood pressure control but also to other, related processes. To a large extent, clues concerning the direction of such basic research will derive from a variety of perspectives and from the clinical research, described below, which is rapidly accumulating observations and critical questions. Answers to these questions will permit a more rational and comprehensive approach to clinical application.

CLINICAL APPLICATIONS OF BLOOD PRESSURE BIOFEEDBACK IN HYPERTENSION

The basic laboratory data provided a foundation for the clinical application of biofeedback to hypertension. Benson, Shapiro, Tursky, and Schwartz (1971) used feedback techniques in the lowering of systolic blood pressure in seven patients, five of whom had been diagnosed as having essential hypertension. Medication dosage, diet, and other factors were kept constant during the course of the study. Of the two other patients, one did not have elevated systolic pressure and the other had renal artery stenosis. No reductions were observed in as many as 15 pretreatment control sessions. The five patients responding positively showed decreases of 34, 29, 16, 16, and 17 mmHg with 33, 22, 34, 31, and 12 sessions of training, respectively. The two patients diagnosed as not having essential hypertension showed little or no decrease in systolic pressure as a result of the conditioning procedure. Inasmuch as no reliable pressure readings were taken outside of the laboratory, the general effectiveness of the training could not be determined.

In the Benson *et al.* study (1971), the average amount of within-session decrease in systolic pressure for the patients was about 5 mmHg, about the same as in studies of normal subjects. Although the lowered pressure tended to carry over from one session to the next, the trends were not always consistent. Curves of individual patients suggested a pattern of successive cycles of decreasing pressure interspersed with increases and subsequent decreasing trends. Apparently, certain events in the life of the patient, or other factors not presently understood, interfered with the process of self-regulation. The pressure would bounce back, although not to original levels, and then the pattern of pressure reduction would resume. The feedback–reward techniques may facilitate a process of habituation. It is not entirely clear whether random feedback, attempts at voluntary control without feedback, muscular relaxation, or simply sitting in the laboratory would not achieve comparable results in patients with high blood pressure (see below).

It is important to have well-established, stable baseline values in clinical studies such as these. For example, patients may overrespond to initial sessions with higher than typical pressures for themselves. Subsequently, reductions in pressure would be observed as patients got used to the laboratory situation. Such reductions may be misinterpreted as a therapeutic effect. In the Benson *et al.* (1971) study, little or no reduction in pressure was observed in these patients after as many as 15 control sessions under resting conditions with no feedback or rewards. However, nonspecific placebo effects cannot be ruled out as an explanation of the observed reductions in pressure. The patients studied had been in treatment for hypertension for long periods of time, and no changes in their drug treatment were made. The innovation of "biofeedback" as a new technique involving unusual instrumentation, feedback displays, and the idea of self-control may be a very good placebo (Stroebel & Glueck, 1973).

Parenthetically, there is nothing wrong with placebo effects. Indeed, Miller (1974) cites a number of studies in which powerful effects on physiological responses, including blood pressure, could be obtained by pill placebos and simple suggestions. Such phenomena are well known, although insufficiently studied or understood in terms of mechanism (see A. K. Shapiro, 1960). Moreover, they underscore the potential for human beings to bring their blood pressure under control without active medication and simply through psychological mechanisms. In the final analysis, the value of any procedure in medicine depends upon how effective and for how long it can bring the symptom and the illness under control. Clearly, the better we understand mechanisms of therapeutic effects, including placebo effects, the more probable it is that the benefits will be long-lasting and significant.

Using the constant cuff procedure, Goldman *et al.* (1975) reported average decreases of 4% and 13% in systolic and diastolic pressure, respectively, in seven patients with average baseline values of 167/109 mmHg who were diagnosed as having essential hypertension and who were willing to participate in the study prior to having medication. Although feedback was given for systolic pressure, the significant reductions occurred only in diastolic pressure over the course of the nine training sessions. Those patients who showed the greatest decreases in both systolic and diastolic pressure during biofeedback training also showed the greatest improvement on the Category Test of the Halstead–Reitan Neuropsychological Test Battery for Adults (Reitan, 1966). As this test is related to cognitive dysfunctioning, Goldman *et al.* speculate that biofeedback may be useful in lowering pressure *and* in overcoming a cognitive impairment associated with hypertension. This kind of impairment has been suggested in previous research (Reitan, 1954; Richter-Heinrich & Läuter, 1969). Moreover, the improvement in cognitive functioning suggests that the effects of biofeedback training may not be entirely laboratory-specific. The need for further evaluation of independent criteria of the results of treatment, including cognitive, social, and psychological factors as well as the critical medical and physiological changes, is obvious.

Miller (1975) attempted to train 28 patients with essential hypertension to reduce their diastolic blood pressure. A few patients appeared to reduce their blood pressure, but, after reaching a plateau, the pressure drifted up again. One patient showing good results was trained to alternate in increasing and decreasing her pressure. Over a period of 3 months, this patient acquired the ability to change pressure over a range of 30 mmHg. Her baseline pressure decreased from 97 to 76 mmHg, and similar decreases were observed on the ward; medication was discontinued. Later on, she lost voluntary control and was put back on drugs as a result of life stresses. When the patient came back to training 2½ years later, she rapidly regained a large measure of control. Such multiple courses of treatment need to be done more often and evaluated thoroughly.

Kristt and Engel (1975) reported evidence that patients with essential hypertension having a variety of cardiovascular and other complications can learn to control and reduce their pressure over and above the effects produced by drugs. In Phase 1, the patients took their pressure at home daily over a 7-week period and mailed in their reports to the laboratory. In Phase 2, patients were trained to raise, to lower, and to alternately raise and lower systolic blood pressure. The constant cuff method (Shapiro *et al.*, 1969) was used to record pressure and provide feedback. In Phase 3, the patients again took their pressure at home and mailed in daily reports. Learned control of pressure was observed in all patients during the training sessions, and reductions in pressure of about 10%–15% were observed from pretraining baselines to values recorded at a 3-month follow-up. Although feedback training was provided for systolic pressure, diastolic pressure was also reduced. Medication was reduced in three patients, including one patient whose blood pressure had been progressively rising which would have otherwise required a change in the medication schedule. This study is particularly relevant because it shows that biofeedback can be used to provide direct control of blood pressure in the laboratory and at home, even in patients with cardiovascular complications such as cardiac arrhythmias, left ventricular hypertrophy, malignant hypertension, aortic atherosclerosis, cardiomegaly, and diabetes. It also shows that biofeedback can at least aid in the management of hypertension by reducing the dosages required to control blood pressure. At least in some patients, biofeedback may be used as a successful substitute for and/or an adjunct to antihypertensive medication.

Since systolic blood pressure has been found to be more closely associated with morbidity and mortality than diastolic pressure in males over 45 years of age, reductions in systolic pressure could be a treatment of choice for this particular age–sex population. Also, morbidity and mortality in females seem to be more dependent upon systolic than diastolic pressure at almost all ages (Kannel *et al.*, 1971). In younger men, diastolic pressure is more closely associated with morbidity and mortality (Kannel *et al.*, 1971), in agreement with traditional concepts of hypertension (Merrill, 1966). Diastolic pressure is thought to be more critical in later or final stages of hypertension because of its closer relation to peripheral resistance (Merrill, 1966). Preliminary research (Benson, Shapiro, & Schwartz, unpublished) suggests that it is difficult to reduce abnormally high diastolic levels in patients with hypertension (see Schwartz & Shapiro, 1973). Part of the problem may be related to unreliability in obtaining consistent diastolic values over repeated sessions. Learned control of diastolic pressure was observed in a single-session study of normal subjects, with consistent changes occurring in almost all subjects (Shapiro *et al.*, 1972). However, positive results of biofeedback training for decreases in diastolic pressure in patients have been reported in other laboratories. Using feedback and verbal praise, 20%–30% reductions in diastolic pressure were obtained in patients diagnosed as essential hypertensives (Elder, Ruiz, Deabler, & Dillenkoffer, 1973). None of the 18 patients studied was under antihypertensive medication, although many were on central nervous system depressants. As discussed previously, other clinical studies have reported significant reductions in diastolic pressure, even though the feedback training was related to control of systolic pressure.

Surwit and Shapiro (in press) report preliminary findings of a clinical study in which two types of biofeedback training were compared to a form of meditation in the treatment of borderline hypertension. The subjects were 24 borderline hypertensives, who were evenly divided into three treatment conditions. All subjects received two 1-hour baseline sessions and eight hour-long biweekly treatment sessions. The first treatment group received binary feedback for simultaneous reductions of blood pressure and heart rate (Schwartz, Shapiro, & Tursky, 1972). The second group received analogue feedback for combined forearm and frontalis electromyographic activity. The third group received a meditation–relaxation procedure (Benson, 1975). Six weeks following the last treatment session, all subjects received a 1-hour treatment follow-up session. Preliminary analysis indicates that all three treatment groups showed significant reductions in pressure over trials during each session, implying that each of the behavioral methods tested was equally effective as a clinical intervention. Carryover effects from session to session or in follow-up evaluations were not significant. Borderline or labile patients may reveal normal pressure levels in a quiet laboratory, suggesting that the conditions of training may not be appropriate for retraining purposes. Related to this issue, high levels of pressure may be under the control of particular situational events, and patients would therefore need to learn to reduce their reactivity in relation to such triggering stimuli.

The above clinical studies provide supportive evidence concerning the potential of biofeedback techniques in the direct reduction of blood pressure in patients with essential hypertension. Similar biofeedback procedures have been used in independent laboratories with relatively consistent positive results. However, wide differences exist in characteristics of patients studied, duration of treatments, availability of follow-up data, and amount of systematic documentation of physiological effects and changes in drug regimes. The total number of patients studied is still few, and only large-scale clinical trials accompanied by comprehensive medical, physiological, and psychological evaluations can provide the information required before biofeedback can be routinely applied in essential hypertension.

OTHER BIOFEEDBACK AND SELF-REGULATION METHODS

The clinical studies discussed above attempted direct control of blood pressure by means of blood pressure feedback. Other approaches have been investigated that involve biofeedback of physiological responses assumed to be associated with blood pressure. These approaches are based on the belief that reductions in response levels of associated functions will bring about concomitant reductions in blood pressure. Other behavioral methods not involving the use of complex feedback techniques include progressive relaxation, meditation, yogic practices, autogenic training, and suggestion.

Patel (1973) used a combination of yogic relaxation and electrodermal (GSR) feedback in a group of 20 patients (11 women and 9 men) of mixed diagnostic categories (essential, renal, and intracranial hypertension, and essential hypertension following toxemia of pregnancy). All patients were under antihypertensive medication at the beginning of the trial. Their ages varied from 39 to 78 years with an average of 57. When they were first found to be hypertensive, systolic pressure varied from 160 to 230 mmHg (average 190), and diastolic pressure varied from 100 to 150 mmHg (average 122). When the patients entered the trial, systolic pressure varied from 130 to 190 mmHg (average 160), and diastolic pressure varied from 88 to 113 mmHg (average 102). The duration of hypertension varied from 1 to 20 years (average 6.8 years). Before entering the trial, any attempt to reduce drug dosage increased blood pressure. The study consisted of half-hour sessions, three times a week, for a period of 3 months. At the conclusion of the study, antihypertensive medication was discontinued in 25% of the patients, and reduced by 33% to 60% in seven other patients. Blood pressure control was better in four other patients, while four patients did not respond to therapy. Patel (1975), reporting on a 12-month follow-up in the patients previously studied, concluded that both blood pressure and drug reductions were maintained. Moreover, in a control procedure involving simple blood pressure measurement and regular medical care, no significant reductions in blood pressure were observed. The rationale for using electrodermal feedback is not entirely clear, but its effectiveness may depend upon its role in facilitating relaxation by lowering sympathetic nervous system function. Altogether, from a practical standpoint, the positive results reported by Patel are encouraging and supportive of a combined biofeedback–relaxation approach.

Weston (1974), using the constant cuff method (Shapiro *et al.*, 1969) and providing feedback for diastolic blood pressure or forehead electromyographic activity, with or without additional relaxation practice, and combinations of these modalities, obtained reductions in systolic and diastolic blood pressures in four groups of hypertensive subjects, 42 in all. Although no controlled diagnosis was made prior to acceptance in the study, these subjects were required to keep their medication and diet constant for the 8 weeks of the study. Subjects were males and females younger than 55 years of age. Mean group reductions varied between 13 and 36 mmHg for systolic and between 6 and 20 mmHg for diastolic pressures. Initial group mean systolic pressures varied between 143 and 167 mmHg, final pressures between 129 and 139 mmHg; initial mean diastolic levels were between 90 and 105 mmHg, final levels between 84 and 89 mmHg. The various treatment procedures produced roughly comparable effects, suggesting again that a generalized relaxation process may be involved. Moreover, the absence of a control group does not rule out the possibility that observed changes were due to habituation or other nonspecific effects.

Shoemaker and Tasto (1975) failed to reveal any significant reductions in blood pressure when a noncontinuous feedback procedure was used. However, there were important methodological differences in this study: The subjects had not been previously diagnosed as essential hypertensives; there was no control for medication and diet; systolic and diastolic blood pressures were recorded using a procedure similar to the Riva–Rocci method; and the feedback procedure did not provide continuous information to the subject. These authors also used tape-recorded muscular relaxation instructions as a method of treatment. Relaxation was found to be the more effective method of reducing blood pressure, resulting in mean group reductions across sessions of 4 and 5 mmHg for systolic and diastolic blood pressure, respectively, and 10 and 7 mmHg within sessions, respectively. Although the subjects' ages were not reported, initial blood pressure levels seemed to have been within normotensive range, around 137/92 mmHg. These latter factors might also account for the relatively small decreases observed.

Moeller (1973) and Moeller and Love (personal communication) hypothesized that by teaching subjects to relax their muscles, it may be possible to reduce blood pressure, which they assume is associated with increased muscle tension. Their procedure has a possible added advantage in that patients may be more likely to be able to "sense" and control their muscles (proprioceptive feedback) and thereby possibly develop a means of self-control of blood pressure outside of the laboratory. In a preliminary study by Moeller and Love, a sample of six patients with average baseline pressures of 153/110 mmHg was given exercises that included muscle feedback and autogenic training as a means of facilitating general bodily relaxation. The training covered a period of 17 weeks. Both systolic and diastolic pressure were reduced by 13% in this program. In a larger study, Moeller (1973) replicated these findings in a sample of 36 patients. Group mean pretreatment pressures ranged between 157/102 mmHg and 169/115 mmHg; posttreatment pressures ranged from 144/91 to 154/95 mmHg, respectively, These studies did not include controls for nonspecific effects.

Benson, Rosner, Marzetta, and Klemchuk (1974a,b), using procedures based on meditation techniques in which the physiological effects seem to mimic Hess's (1957) "trophotropic" response, have shown that elicitation of what they call the "relaxation" response (Benson, Beary, & Carol, 1974; Benson, 1975) effectively reduced blood pressure levels in 14 pharmacologically treated hypertensive subjects and in 22 untreated borderline hypertensives. Although etiology of hypertension was not investigated, the group of pharmacologically treated hypertensives reduced systolic pressure from 146 to 135 mmHg and diastolic pressure from 92 to 87 mmHg (Benson *et al.*, 1974a). The pretreatment control period lasted 5.6 weeks and the experimental period 20 weeks. In the prospective study with borderline hypertensives (Benson *et al.*, 1974b), during the 6-week pretreatment control period, blood pressures averaged 147 mmHg systolic and 95 mmHg diastolic. During the subsequent 25-week experimental period, when the patients regularly elicited the relaxation response, blood pressures fell to 139 mmHg systolic and 91 mmHg diastolic. This relaxation procedure is very simple to explain and easy for patients to practice by themselves.

Datey, Deshmukh, Dalvi, and Vinekar (1969) used a yogic relaxation exercise to treat 32 essential, 12 renal, and 3 arteriosclerotic hypertensive patients (37 men, 10 women, mean age 46 years, range 22 to 64 years of age). Most of the patients on drug therapy had been under treatment for an average of about 2 years at a hypertensive clinic. During this period, their drug treatment had been stabilized, and any attempt to reduce the drug dosage caused a rise in blood pressure. The patients who had not received any antihypertensive drugs were first given placebo tablets for at least a month before learning the relaxation technique. Ten patients were not taking any drugs, 22 had their blood pressure well controlled with drugs, and in 15 blood pressure was inadequately controlled in spite of drugs. In the group of patients not taking any drugs, the average mean blood pressure was reduced from 134 mmHg to 107 mmHg. In the group of 22 patients whose blood pressure was well controlled with drugs, the mean blood pressure was 102 mmHg. Since the blood pressure was well controlled, no attempt was made to reduce it further. The drug treatment was gradually reduced, keeping the mean blood pressure constant, and it was possible to reduce the average drug requirement to 32% of the original in 13 patients. In the remaining 9 patients in whom the drug requirement could not be reduced, 6 were irregular in performing the exercise, but 3 were regular. The average mean blood pressure after the yogic exercise in this group of 22 patients was about the same (102–100 mmHg). Out of 15 patients whose blood pressure was inadequately controlled in spite of drugs, the drug required was reduced to 29% of the original in 6 patients. The dose was unchanged in 7 (of these, 2 were irregular and 2 could not perform the exercise correctly). The dose had to be slightly increased in two other patients who were regular in their exercise. In those cases with essential hypertension, 62.5% responded favorably to this treatment as did 42% of renal hypertensives. However, of the three patients with arteriosclerotic hypertension, none responded. The study lasted about 40 weeks.

An innovative approach to relaxation was utilized with some success in lowering pressure in patients with essential hypertension (Brady, Luborsky, & Kron, 1974). It is called "metronome-conditioned relaxation" and requires that the patient lie down for half an hour with eyes closed and listen to a tape recording (Brady, 1973). The recording consits of suggestions to "re–lax" and "let–go" of the muscles paced with rhythmic beats of an auditory metronome set at 60 beats per minute. With repeated training, several patients showed significant reductions in pressure, but the reductions were observed only during the practice periods. Two patients who used the tape recording at home for a protracted period showed further reductions in pressure.

Luthe (1963) has also described good reductions in blood pressure with the use of autogenic training, a procedure basically aimed at producing physical and psychological relaxation. It involves self-suggestions of warmth, passivity, and total bodily relaxation.

While the various behavioral procedures have all been shown to be effective in reducing high blood pressure to some degree, comparative studies are needed to determine their relative effectiveness. It is reasonable to expect that different training procedures will show up in differences in the degree and persistence of achieved self-control and in the physiological patterns associated with this control. However, the fact that the various procedures, including biofeedback, have more or less similar results suggests that a relaxation or low arousal state may be a common underlying factor (see Benson, 1975; Stoyva & Budzynski, 1974). This state may well be facilitated if the patient is confident that he is able, in fact, to exert control over his own blood pressure. In a disorder as complex as hypertension, it will take a larger body of empirical studies than is currently available to be able to conclude that any particular combination of biofeedback with other methods of self-regulation is ready for routine medical practice in specific varieties of hypertension or in particular subgroups of patients. Experimental treatment programs with systematic efforts at evaluation are proceeding in a number of hospitals, clinics, and research institutes. Systematic, well-controlled studies are needed, and time will tell.

MEDICAL AND PHYSIOLOGICAL COMPLICATIONS IN ESSENTIAL HYPERTENSION

Application of biofeedback procedures in the treatment of essential hypertension is a fertile ground for clinical and basic research through the combined efforts of physiologists, physicians, psychologists, and biomedical engineers. Ideally, such work should be performed in a setting that provides adequate medical backup. The need for team work is dictated by the complexity of the cardiovascular system; subtleties in differential diagnosis of essential hypertension; required clinical knowledge of, and experience with, the disorder; medical, ethical, and legal responsibility towards the patient; and mastery of the behavioral and recording procedures to be employed in the treatment. Seldom can one single investigator deal with all of these problems by himself. For example, patients should have a thorough medical workup to rule out secondary hypertension, for which adequate treatment procedures are available. Administration of behavioral treatments carries with it the same responsibility as the prescription of medication in the case of drug treatment. Because biofeedback for blood pressure involves the treatment of disease, it is one area where traditional medical models of illness cannot be dismissed. While hypertension can be exacerbated by emotional and environmental variables, it has a distinct physical etiology and represents profound physiological dysfunction. Also, at certain stages it may be associated with permanent destruction and/or alteration of tissue, which may or may not be amenable to a behavioral amelioration. In most cases, medication will have to be used in association with biofeedback training. As Pinkerton (1973) aptly remarked, "no single factor is of overriding importance in symptom production [in psychosomatic illness]. The

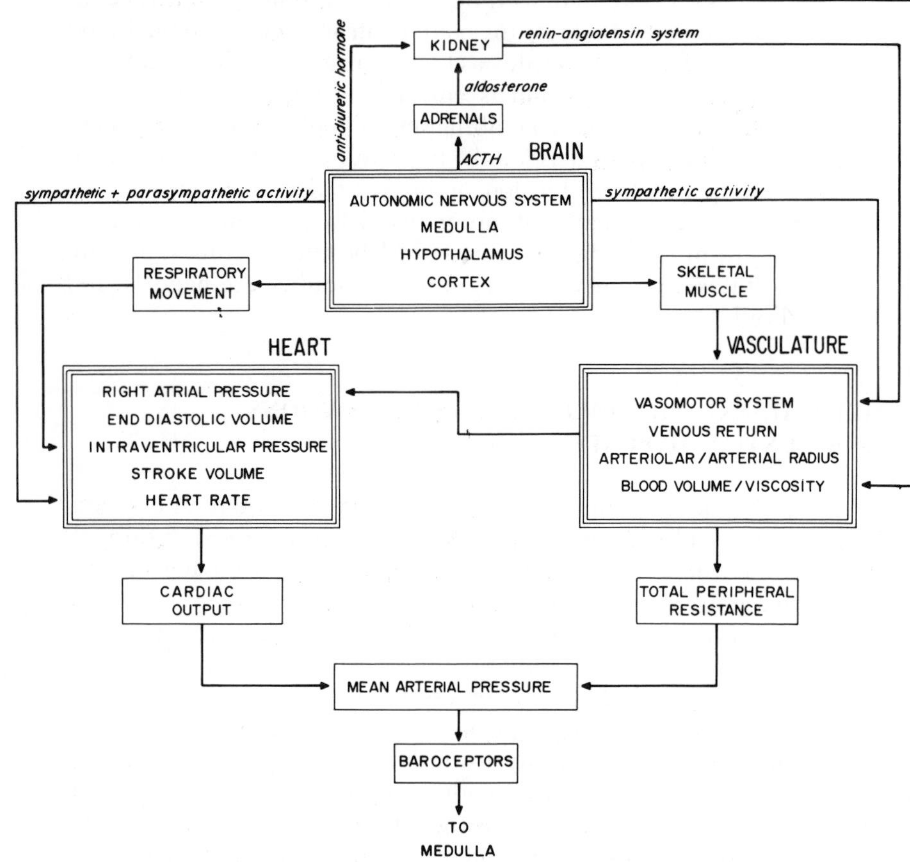

Figure 13.1 Schematic diagram summarizing the physiological mechanisms involved in the regulation of arterial blood pressure. The diagram oversimplifies the processes involved in order to provide a general overview of mechanisms most relevant to behavioral manipulation. Boxes labeled Heart, Brain, and Vasculature each contain a subset of relevant systems and functions. While these are not necessarily temporally or functionally related in the order presented, the outside arrows indicate the site at which other systems exert their influence on the system described in the box. The reader should note the numerous and diverse pathways through which behavioral control over blood pressure could be exerted. For example, relaxation techniques acting on the muscles could have their main effect on the vasculature, producing a decrease in peripheral resistance. Yogic exercises emphasizing breath control might have their main effect on cardiac output by changing intraventricular pressure. While the diagram suggests that a feedback approach including both cardiac and vascular parameters would be most efficacious, it illustrates how verbal instruction acting on the cortex might also be seen to affect blood pressure. [From "Learned control of physiological function and disease" by

clinical outcome is always determined by a composite etiological sequence, so that the key to successful management lies in correctly evaluating each factor's importance in any given case" (p. 462).

In any event, it is clearly not up to the psychologist alone to decide how biofeedback will contribute to the treatment of hypertension. Consequently, biofeedback should be applied clinically only after a competent medical diagnosis has been made, and the examining physician and biofeedback specialist have decided that biofeedback may be of value. The need for medical participation in any biofeedback case is both an ethical and legal responsibility of the psychological practitioner. Conversely, it is also the ethical responsibility of a physician who wishes to employ biofeedback in treatment to collaborate with a psychologist in designing the behavioral procedures of the proposed therapy. Medical training does not usually provide the in-depth knowledge of behavioral variables of which the practitioner must be cognizant in order for training to be successful. Therefore, the use of biofeedback in therapy for hypertension should be an endeavor involving both medical and behavioral specialists.

Figure 13.1 gives a general picture of the network of interacting systems and processes involved in the regulation of systemic arterial pressure in healthy human beings. In normal states, the cardiovascular system operates to maintain homeostasis, its principal physiological function being to provide adequate cell nutrients to the body tissues in response to actual metabolic demands. The cardiovascular system is exquisitely regulated to maintain cell nutrients proportional to tissue metabolic requirements by means of control of cardiac output, systemic arterial pressure usually remaining within narrow limits. Arterial blood pressure changes when metabolic demands are excessive, such as during exercise. Moreover, the metabolic-dependent regulation of the cardiovascular system is easily overridden by cortical or subcortical stimulation under "stress" conditions or in preparation for exercise or "action" (Brod, 1964; Folkow & Rubinstein, 1966). It is well known that systemic arterial blood pressure is significantly influenced by psychogenic factors, emotional stress, and behavioral and physiological environmental demands. Such neurogenic influences, perfectly adaptive where action follows the preparatory rise in cardiovascular activity, are not adaptive in typical life situations where

---

"fight" or "flight" responses are not compatible with accepted social behavior. Furthermore, neurogenic factors have often been postulated as being implicated in the hypertensive process (DeQuattro & Miura, 1973; Dustan, Tarazi, & Bravo, 1972; Pfeffer & Frohlich, 1973).

The disorder called essential hypertension (or of unknown cause) means only that blood pressure is elevated above certain arbitrary age–sex norms. The disorder tends to progress ("hypertension begets hypertension"), and the whole system stabilizes again and again around higher and higher levels of blood pressure (Rushmer, 1970). In contrast, in a normal organism, the system would compensate to reduce acute increases in blood pressure or cardiac output to normal levels. Thus, changes in one part of the cardiovascular system by means of biofeedback or other methods may produce changes in other parts of the system, whether to compensate for the imposed deviation from homeostasis, or just as associated changes. Furthermore, the nature of the readjustment depends on the particular functioning of the system in the given individual or variety of disorder.

The complexity of physiological factors thought to be involved in the development or maintenance of essential hypertension is shown in Figure 13.2. This diagram illustrates the need to be aware of the complexity of the disorder, rather than taking the oversimplified view of modifying blood pressure directly, which may or may not turn out to be the most successful approach to treatment.

In its "fixed" state, hypertension involves changes in anatomical structures; that is, the medial walls of the arteries are swollen, while neurogenic vasoconstrictor discharges are minimal or normal (Folkow, 1971; Rushmer, 1970). However, after 10 or 20 years of drug treatment, blood pressure sometimes returns to normal even after drug treatment is discontinued. This seems to support the hypothesis that hypertrophy of the medial arterial walls is reversible under conditions of reduced arterial pressure (Folkow, 1971; Folkow, Hallbäck, Lundgren, Sivertsson, & Weiss, 1973). However, the time required for such reversions to take place in humans is not known, though it may be short. The structural changes suggest that blood pressure feedback in the treatment of fixed essential hypertension might not meet much success, unless it can result in keeping blood pressure at low levels in the same way that drugs are presumed to do.

Since diastolic pressure is known to be closely associated with peripheral resistance, a possible approach to fixed hypertension would be to use biofeedback for reducing diastolic pressure while at the same time preventing compensatory increases in heart rate. This could be

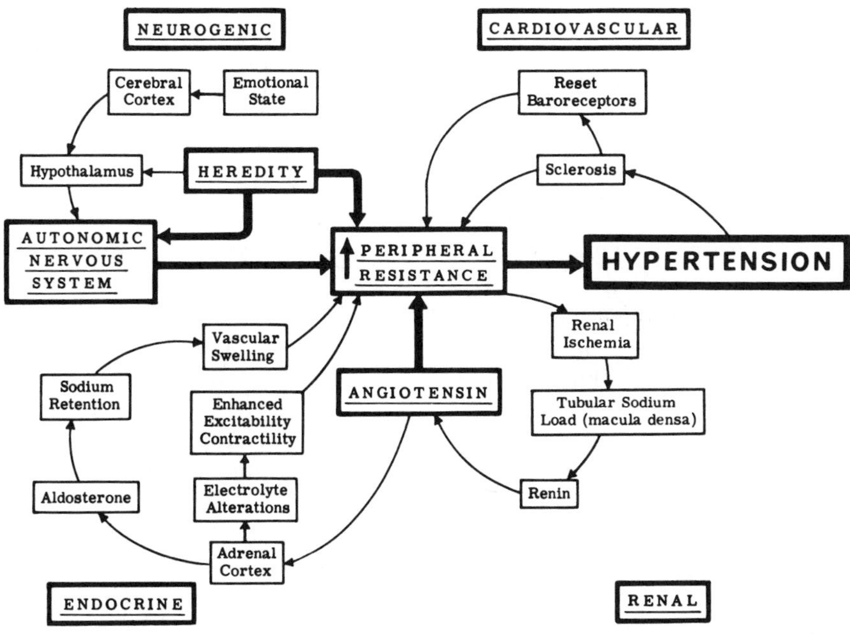

Figure 13.2 Possible participation of various factors in the development of hypertension. [From "Pathological physiology of the cardiovascular system. A. Hypertension" by J. J. Friedman, in E. E. Selkurt (Ed.), *Physiology* (3rd ed.) (Boston: Little, Brown, & Co.). © 1971 by Ewald E. Selkurt. Reprinted by permission.]

accomplished with a pattern approach in which feedback is given for a decrease in diastolic pressure except when it is associated with an increase in heart rate. The main objective in the therapy of fixed essential hypertension is to reduce blood pressure in a permanent fashion, and this implies a re-resetting of the mechanoreceptor reflex working range to normal pressure levels, as well as providing the conditions for the arterial walls to return to their normal structural characteristics. Again, much research is needed in this area, since the research of Shapiro *et al.* (1972) showed that acute reductions in diastolic pressure by means of biofeedback and operant conditioning were not accompanied by compensatory increases in heart rate. Indeed, the results of this experiment raise an important empirical question regarding behavioral–physiological interactions in intact organisms which is not clearly explained by traditional physiology, namely, how does behavioral modification of individual cardiovascular parameters affect the total function of the cardiovascular system in an intact organism? For a discussion of compensatory changes in cardiovascular responses resulting from controlled physiological manipulation of selected parameters, see Rushmer (1970, Chap. 3) and Rothe and Friedman (1971).

There are also reports in the literature (DeQuattro & Miura, 1973; Schmid & Abboud, 1974) indicating that some cases of fixed essential hypertension are characterized by elevated sympathetic activity. Direct recording of sympathetic activity in specific neural pathways is a field now in its infancy (Wallin, Delius, & Hagbarth, 1973), and we are not yet technologically and theoretically sophisticated enough to undertake modifications of sympathetic activity in specific pathways, such as selectively modifying parameters of cardiac function and/or of peripheral circulation. A combination of relaxation techniques and blood pressure feedback might turn out to be effective for such patients. Indeed, even if sympathetic smooth muscle arteriolar tone is normal or subnormal in fixed essential hypertension, a procedure (such as general relaxation, meditation, or biofeedback) that can produce an *active* inhibition of "normal" sympathetic tone may facilitate reduction in peripheral resistance and, consequently, blood pressure. Continuous practice of such a procedure might accomplish the desired result, especially if the patient also changes his whole mode of responsiveness to environmental events.

Many investigators believe that fixed essential hypertension develops as a compensatory process in response to idiopathic, high cardiac output states (Guyton, Coleman, Bower, & Granger, 1970). The process apparently develops in genetically predisposed young adults who are cardiovascular hyperreactors under emotional or environmental stress (Eich, Cuddy, Smulyan, & Lyons, 1966; Forsyth, 1974; Frohlich, Kozul, Tarazi, & Dustan, 1970; Frohlich *et al.*, 1969; Gorlin, Brachfeld, Turner, Messer, & Salazar, 1959; Tobian, 1972). Consequently preventive treatment of this prehypertensive high cardiac output state may turn out to be the treatment of choice. This stage of hypertension is also known as "labile" essential hypertension because it is often accompanied by large variability in blood pressure and/or hyperresponsiveness to stimuli of various sorts. The main physiological derangement in "labile" hypertension is an increased cardiac output, with or without correspondent abnormal increases in blood pressure. Total peripheral resistance often remains "abnormally normal"; that is, it fails to decrease in order to compensate for the high cardiac output. Treatment of the disorder at this stage thus requires monitoring of cardiac output or associated cardiovascular indices. Biofeedback training for such indices of relevant cardiac functioning would likely be advantageous in this disorder. However, the development of adequate noninvasive methods of recording cardiac output and other critical cardiovascular indices presents a major challenge for investigators in the field (see Obrist, Black, Brener, & DiCara, 1974). A now-feasible alternative possibility in labile patients who have significantly elevated heart rates is biofeedback training for simultaneous decreases in heart rate and systolic pressure.

Though it has not been proved that labile hypertension is a necessary and sufficient condition for the transition to fixed essential hypertension to occur, this prehypertensive state represents an area of research where biofeedback procedures might be most useful. Indeed, labile hypertension and the hyperkinetic syndromes in general may be especially amenable to behavioral treatment because important neurogenic factors seem to be involved in their etiology (Frohlich *et al*., 1970; Schmid & Abboud, 1974). At the present time, this large at-risk population (Freis, 1972, 1974) remains basically untreated, since the risk of later development of fixed hypertension is not clearly known.

An alternative approach of significance for the control of blood pressure in labile hypertension might be a decrease of total sympathetic activity. General physiological functions, such as sympathetic activity, may be more readily subject to "voluntary" control because they involve a number of common nervous pathways that are integrated at higher levels of the nervous system. That biofeedback training may be used to modify patterns of simultaneous change in two (and possibly more) physiological functions is illustrated in the research of Schwartz (1972). He found that patterns of heart rate and blood pressure could be modified. Moreover, larger decreases (or increases) in both heart rate and systolic blood pressure were found when feedback and rewards were given for the simultaneous occurrence of decreases (or increases) in both, as compared to earlier results when only one or the other function was reinforced (Shapiro *et al*., 1970b). The strategy of training may be to go from the general to the specific, at first utilizing as many common sympathetic functions as possible and then selectively controlling those responses most related to pressure reduction. Irrelevant responses in the global pattern would then drop out as training progresses (Kimble & Perlmuter, 1970).

An effective way to modify blood pressure in either labile or fixed essential hypertension might be through the control of higher cortical activity, such as in meditation (Benson, 1975). The process may have its effect by direct downstream control of subcortical centers and, hence, autonomic activity. Since this process requires that the patient focus his attention and maintain a specific cognitive set, it is not certain how its therapeutic effects might generalize during the day when normal cortical pressures are occurring. In contrast to the feedback approach, the effectiveness of meditation would seem to be predicated upon producing an all-encompassing change in the hypertensive patient's behavior. This suggests that it is not reasonable to reduce blood pressure alone while leaving the remainder of a high stress behavioral repertoire intact.

The above-mentioned variations in approaches, findings, and theories concerning the physiological derangement underlying idiopathic high blood pressure, together with several abnormalities in plasma renin activity and levels of circulating catecholamines, illustrate the point that several subcategories of hypertension are masked under the heading of "essential." We have speculated on a number of different biofeedback strategies that may be useful in addition to those already applied in clinical studies. Clearly, clinical practice and research in this area will benefit greatly from long-term intensive case studies, where careful observations and thorough evaluations are the rule.

Finally, we should point out that there are many factors affecting blood pressure levels which need to be adequately controlled, if not accounted for, during clinical trials and research (Pickering, 1968):

1. posture
2. muscle activity and strenuous exercise
3. emotional states and current life stress
4. place of recording (home, clinic, emergency room)
5. professional status of person recording blood pressure (self, relative, nurse, student, physician)
6. spontaneous variability—familiarity with or habituation to the treatment environment
7. accumulation of urine in the bladder ("bladder reflex")
8. respiratory maneuvers and patterns
9. time of day
10. basal metabolic versus nonbasal conditions
11. time and amount of last food or liquid taken
12. diet

A brief look at the above partial list again underscores the complexity of the problem. It suggests at the least that blood pressure recordings and feedback training should occur at the same time of the day and in the same social setting. Several baseline sessions are needed in order to allow for habituation effects to wear out and to determine the patient's characteristic blood pressure and other important physiological functions (e.g., heart rate, respiration) before starting treatment. Also to be considered are weight, age, sex, and ethnic and socioeconomic background of the patient. Of great importance are prescription, change, or discontinuance of medication concurrent with behavioral treatments and the use of appropriate criteria, beyond mere blood pressure readings, in diagnosis, treatment, and evaluation. It is obvious that all of these factors cannot be experimentally or statistically controlled for. They should all be considered in addition to a thorough hypertensive workup. They add to the complicated picture of hypertension in its various phases, and emphasize the need for a comprehensive approach to treatment and research.

Furthermore, not only is control of the above variables desirable, but their therapeutic potential might well be tapped independently of or in conjunction with other means of behavioral intervention. For example, current life stress or other social factors influencing blood pressure might be attended to by means of counseling, psychotherapy, behavior therapy, or direct alterations in life style or occupation. As discussed previously, changes in muscle tension and respiratory patterns can be approached by means of biofeedback, meditation, or other behavioral methods. Similarly, biofeedback procedures might be used to decrease spontaneous variability of blood pressure or of other variables related to blood pressure, for example, heart rate and respiration. Regarding diet, it is well known that dietary prescriptions concerning caloric, salt, and cholesterol intake are often part of conventional hypertensive treatment.

SOME PRACTICAL CLINICAL ISSUES

The first, and perhaps most obvious, question of practical concern in the evaluation of biofeedback as a clinical tool in the treatment of hypertension is economy. How much time and effort on the part of both the patient and the practitioner is needed to obtain a clinically useful result? Even if biofeedback techniques can be shown to be therapeutically effective, what patient would opt for a costly time-consuming training course if equal reduction of blood pressure could be obtained from pills? Unless the side effects of the medication are serious or biofeedback is shown to be superior to medication, it is unlikely that biofeedback will be considered as a treatment of choice.

A related issue has to do with patient motivation. Several articles (e.g., Schwartz, 1973; Schwartz & Shapiro, 1973; Shapiro & Schwartz, 1972; Surwit, 1973) have commented on the importance of patient motivation in biofeedback programs. It is not sufficient to assume that feedback indicating therapeutic improvement will, in and of itself, act as a reinforcer and maintain the persistent practice required to gain therapeutic benefit. Hypertension has no short-term aversive consequences. It usually works its insidious destruction within the cardiovascular system without causing any serious discomfort to the patient. By the time a painful heart attack occurs, it may be too late to correct the damage. It is only the knowledge that the patient has hypertension and that the disorder is not good for him that provides motivation to undergo treatment. In light of the fact that many hypertensive patients will not even take their medication regularly, it is uncertain whether biofeedback training, requiring long periods of practice, will prove generally useful. It depends, of course, on how really successful biofeedback methods turn out to be.

A second possible area of motivational difficulty arises from other behaviors strongly entrenched in the patient's repertoire that may be in conflict with the aims of therapy. This is best illustrated in a case discussed by Schwartz (1973). A patient was treated for essential hypertension and, over a week of treatment, lowered his blood pressure by as much as 20 mmHg. Over the weekend, his pressure would become elevated again. The difficulty turned out to be that the patient liked to gamble on weekends and persisted in doing so despite the fact that such activities were countertherapeutic. This last point is extremely important. There is good evidence that certain schedules of reinforcement for somatomotor behaviors can induce high blood pressure in normal animals (Benson *et al*., 1969; Benson, Herd, Morse, & Kelleher, 1970; Brady, 1958; Harris *et al*., 1973; Morse *et al*., 1971). It would seem futile to attempt to treat a disorder with biofeedback training unless work were also done on analyzing and correcting behavioral processes that may be associated with the problem.

An issue closely related to motivation and equally important in the successful application of biofeedback techniques to hypertension is transfer of training. It is often all too easy to forget, even for psychologists, that learning techniques cannot be administered as are most medical treatments. There is no reason to believe that biofeedback, in and of itself, like radiation therapy and diathermy, can be expected to produce sustained effects outside of the treatment session. It is completely logical that a patient may show perfect control over his problem during a feedback session and no control at home. In basic research in normal subjects, some investigators have explored the use of intermittent reinforcement schedules as an aid to generalization

(Greene, 1966; Shapiro & Crider, 1967; Shapiro & Watanabe, 1971), but the evidence is insufficient to conclude that partial reinforcement increases resistance to extinction in the case of visceral responses, such as learned reductions of blood pressure in the laboratory. In their study of the control of premature ventricular contractions, Weiss and Engel (1971) phased the feedback out gradually, making it available all the time at first, then 1 minute on and 1 minute off, then 1 on and 3 off, and finally 1 on and 7 off. The purpose of the procedure was to wean the patient from the feedback and enable him to become more aware of the arrhythmia through his own sensations and to become less dependent upon the feedback. Hefferline and Bruno (1971) described a similar technique of slowly fading out the feedback as a means of transferring external to internal control. There is also evidence for the short-term maintenance of learned control of diastolic pressure (Shapiro *et al.*, 1972), but the need is great for comprehensive research on extinction and reconditioning processes in autonomic learning and on self-regulation without feedback.

A related, but more complex, issue concerns the need of patients to control their reactivity to stressful stimuli or situations. In most cases, biofeedback procedures are applied in resting, nonstimulating laboratory settings. Will the patient be able to transfer this training to the relevant situations in everyday life? Patel (1975) has reported that, with a combination of yoga exercises and biofeedback, patients were able to lower their systolic and diastolic pressures during both rest and in response to everyday emotional stresses. Working with heart rate, Sirota, Schwartz, and Shapiro (1974) showed that, in anticipation of receiving noxious electrical stimulation, subjects learned to control their heart rate when provided with external heart rate feedback and reward for appropriate changes. Voluntary slowing of heart rate led to a relative reduction in the perceived aversiveness of the noxious stimuli, particularly for those subjects who reported experiencing cardiac reactions to fear situations in their daily lives. Sirota *et al.* concluded:

> Taken together, the results support the general conclusion that direct feedback control of autonomic functions which are appropriate for given subjects in terms of their normal fear responding and/or whose relevance for fear has been instructionally induced may possibly be used in systematic desensitization to inhibit anxiety from occurring in response to phobic stimuli and as an adjunct to other therapeutic techniques for the prevention and reduction of anxiety and fear reactions. [1974, p. 266]

Procedures such as these should be studied as a means of increasing the potential for greater transfer of learned control of blood pressure to relevant situations for the individual.

In addition to motivation, Shapiro and Schwartz (1972) have pointed out that patient characteristics must also be considered in determining the feasibility of biofeedback as a treatment. Because most clinical and experimental work on biofeedback has been done with highly educated, motivated individuals, it is at present unclear how the variables of intelligence, socioeconomic status, and overall life adjustment are related to treatment outcome. Until more data shed light on these questions, therapists should be cognizant of the particular characteristics of the population from which successful behavior therapy patients have been drawn.

Finally, in a previous review (Shapiro & Surwit, 1976), it was concluded, "There is *not one* well-controlled scientific study of the effectiveness of biofeedback and operant conditioning in treating a particular physiological disorder." We are not so sure now about the prerequisites of such a study in biofeedback research, especially given the complexities and varieties of a disorder such as hypertension. Moreover, the evaluation of placebo and nonspecific effects is particularly troublesome in behavioral treatment situations, which involve repeated contacts of a positive and cooperative nature between doctor and patient. Unlike drug studies in which a pill can be handled with either single- or double-blind methods, a behavioral treatment is not so easily manageable. Various beliefs, biases, and attitudes in either patient or doctor, either initially or in the course of intercommunication during treatment, can easily complicate administration or evaluation of particular experimental or control procedures. With these considerations in mind, single group and crossover designs are still possible in which various biofeedback and behavioral procedures can be applied singly or in various combinations and compared with commonly accepted medical treatments (drugs). At a later stage of research, it should also be possible to devise placebo treatments involving levels of attention, contact, and personal relationship that are comparable to those employed in biofeedback and related methods. This research will require a great deal of ingenuity, care, and effort. It will also require adequate financial support. As emphasized previously, clinical research in this area will also gain from intensive case studies involving careful observations, thorough evaluations, and good documentation.

CONCLUSION

In one of the first reports of the use of biofeedback in the regulation of blood pressure in humans, it was concluded, "The apparatus and results suggest a possible approach to the treatment of essential hypertension" (Shapiro *et al.*, 1969, p. 588). In the interim, both basic and clinical research have moved us closer to the realization of this goal. Unlike other, more specific or unitary physiological responses that have been studied in biofeedback experiments, blood pressure is a complex biological function involving biochemical, humoral, central, and autonomic nervous system processes. Yet, despite its complexity, blood pressure appears to function like some of the other, simpler physiological responses in regard to behavioral interventions. Thus, changes in blood pressure, either separately or in combination with heart rate, can be modified by means of biofeedback and reinforcement. This apparent selectivity in the control of cardiovascular patterns is of particular significance, given the complexity of the entire cardiovascular system and the various homeostatic systems of regulation. To facilitate clinical application of biofeedback in the control of blood pressure, we obviously need to know a great deal more about the cardiovascular system in response to various biofeedback techniques and other means of behavioral regulation of different cardiovascular and associated physiological indices. Biofeedback offers a valuable research tool in investigating such processes in the intact organism.

Not only is blood pressure a complex biological function, but so is essential hypertension a disorder that involves many different physiological, behavioral, and environmental processes. Knowledge of the disorder in its various stages and varieties is essential to an eventual practical behavioral therapy. We have tried to outline some of the salient facts about the disorder, and have speculated about particular physiological and behavioral approaches to clinical application. A slowly growing body of research indicates that biofeedback techniques can produce significant reductions in blood pressure in patients with essential hypertension or result in reductions of antihypertensive medications. The techniques also have been effectively applied in conjunction with other behavioral, cognitive, and physiological methods. Systematic comparative studies are needed to determine which behavioral interventions are most critical in achieving therapeutic benefits.

We believe that the attractiveness of biofeedback and other behavioral procedures lies in that they might provide alternative or adjunctive modalities in the treatment of high blood pressure, thereby perhaps increasing patient compliance and satisfaction and maximizing the effectiveness of, or providing alternatives to, drug therapy. Again, a word of caution. The research to date suggests, though as yet does not conclusively demonstrate, the effectiveness of biofeedback and other behavioral techniques in the treatment of high blood pressure. The behavioral studies reported so far are simply basic demonstrations. Long-term effects and the feasibility of implementation of behavioral procedures need to be thoroughly investigated. We are hopeful that continued systematic research and sound clinical practice will bring us still closer to converting biofeedback and other behavioral approaches into accepted medical practices. Through interdisciplinary efforts, this area of research will contribute significantly to our basic understanding of psychosomatic interactions and, hopefully, lead to practical applications in clinical medicine.

REFERENCES

Benson, H. *The relaxation response.* New York: William Morrow, 1975.

Benson, H., Beary, J. F., & Carol, M. P. The relaxation response. *Psychiatry,* 1974, *37,* 37–46.

Benson, H., Herd, J. A., Morse, W. H., & Kelleher, R. T. Behavioral induction of arterial hypertension and its reversal. *American Journal of Physiology,* 1969, *217,* 30–34.

Benson, H., Herd, J. A., Morse, W. H., & Kelleher, R. T. Behaviorally induced hypertension in the squirrel monkey. *Circulation Research,* 1970, *26–27* (Suppl. I), 21–26.

Benson, H., Rosner, B. A., Marzetta, B. R., & Klemchuk, H. M. Decreased blood pressure in pharmacologically treated hypertensive patients who regularly elicited the relaxation response. *Lancet,* 1974, *7852,* 289–291. (a)

Benson, H., Rosner, B. A., Marzetta, B. R., & Klemchuk, H. P. Decreased blood pressure in borderline hypertensive subjects who practiced meditation. *Journal of Chronic Diseases,* 1974, *27,* 163–169. (b)

Benson, H., Shapiro, D., Tursky, B., & Schwartz, G. E. Decreased systolic blood pressure through operant conditioning techniques in patients with essential hypertension. *Science,* 1971, *173,* 740–742.

Brady, J. P. Metronome-conditioned relaxation: A new behavioral procedure. *British Journal of Psychiatry,* 1973, *122,* 729–730.

Brady, J. P., Luborsky, L., & Kron, R. E. Blood pressure reduction in patients with essential hypertension through metronome-conditioned relaxation: A preliminary report. *Behavior Therapy,* 1974, *5,* 203–209.

Brady, J. V. Ulcers in "executive" monkeys. *Scientific American,* 1958, *199,* 95–103.

Brener, J. A general model of voluntary control applied to the phenomena of learned cardiovascular change. In P. A. Obrist, A. H. Black, J. Brener, & L. V. DiCara (Eds.), *Cardiovascular psychophysiology.* Chicago: Aldine, 1974.

Brener, J., & Kleinman, R. A. Learned control of decreases in systolic blood pressure. *Nature,* 1970, *226,* 1063–1064.

Brod, J. Circulation in muscle during acute pressor responses to emotional stress and during chronic sustained elevation of blood pressure. *American Heart Journal,* 1964, *68,* 424–426.

Buñag, R. D., Page, I. H., & McCubbin, J. W. Neural stimulation of release of renin. *Circulation Research,* 1966, *19,* 851–858.

Datey, K. K., Deshmukh, S. N., Dalvi, C. P., & Vinekar, S. L. "Shavasan": A yogic exercise in the management of hypertension. *Angiology,* 1969, *20,* 325–333.

Davis, J. O. What signals the kidney to release renin? *Circulation Research*, 1971, *28*, 301–306.

DeQuattro, V., Miura, V. Neurogenic factors in human hypertension: Mechanism or myth? *American Journal of Medicine*, 1973, *55*, 362–378.

DiCara, L. V., & Miller, N. E. Instrumental learning of systolic blood pressure responses by curarized rats: Dissociation of cardiac and vascular changes. *Psychosomatic Medicine*, 1968, *30*, 489–494.

Dustan, H. P., Tarazi, R. C., & Bravo, E. L. Physiologic characteristics of hypertension. *American Journal of Medicine*, 1972, *52*, 610–622.

Eich, R. H., Cuddy, R. P., Smulyan, H., & Lyons, R. H. Haemodynamics in labile hypertension. *Circulation*, 1966, *34*, 299–307.

Elder, S. T., Ruiz, Z. R., Deabler, H. L., & Dillenkoffer, R. L. Instrumental conditioning of diastolic blood pressure in essential hypertensive patients. *Journal of Applied Behavior Analysis*, 1973, *6*, 377–382.

Engel, B. T. Operant conditioning of cardiac function: A status report. *Psychophysiology*, 1972, *9*, 161–177.

Fey, S. G., & Lindholm, E. Systolic blood pressure and heart rate changes during three sessions involving biofeedback or no feedback. *Psychophysiology*, 1975, *12*, 513–519.

Folkow, B. Regulation of the peripheral circulation. *American Heart Journal*, 1971, *33* (Suppl.), 27–31.

Folkow, B., Hallbäck, M., Lundgren, Y., Sivertsson, R., & Weiss, L. Importance of adaptive changes in vascular design for establishment of primary hypertension, studied in man and in spontaneously hypertensive rats. *Circulation Research*, 1973, *32* (Suppl. I), 12–116.

Folkow, B., & Rubinstein, E. H. Cardiovascular effects of acute and chronic stimulations of the hypothalamic defense area in the rat. *Acta Physiologica Scandinavica*, 1966, *68*, 48–57.

Forsyth, R. P. Mechanisms of the cardiovascular responses to environmental stressors. In P. A. Obrist, A. H. Black, J. Brener, & L. V. DiCara (Eds.), *Cardiovascular psychophysiology*. Chicago: Aldine, 1974.

Freis, E. D. The treatment of hypertension: Why, when and how. *American Journal of Medicine*, 1972, *52*, 664–671.

Freis, E. D. The clinical spectrum of essential hypertension. *Archives of Internal Medicine*, 1974, *133*, 982–987.

Friedman, J. J. Pathological physiology of the cardiovascular system. A. Hypertension. In E. E. Selkurt (Ed.), *Physiology* (3rd ed.). Boston: Little, Brown, 1971.

Frohlich, E. D., Kozul, V. J., Tarazi, R. C., & Dustan, H. P. Physiological comparison of labile and essential hypertension. *Circulation Research*, 1970, *27* (Suppl. I), 155–163.

Frohlich, E. D., Tarazi, R. C., & Dustan, M. P. Reexamination of the hemodynamics of hypertension. *American Journal of Medical Sciences*, 1969, *257*, 9–23.

Frohlich, E. D., Ulrych, M., Tarazi, R. C., Dustan, H. P., & Page, I. H. A hemodynamic comparison of essential and renovascular hypertension. *Circulation*, 1967, *35*, 289–297.

Ganong, W. F. Biogenic amines, sympathetic nerves, and renin secretion. *Federation Proceedings*, 1973, *32*, 1782–1784.

Goldman, H., Kleinman, K. M., Snow, M. Y., Bidus, D. R., & Korol, B. Relationship between essential hypertension and cognitive functioning: Effects of biofeedback. *Psychophysiology*, 1975, *12*, 569–573.

Gorlin, R., Brachfeld, N., Turner, J. D., Messer, J. V., & Salazar, E. The idiopathic high cardiac output state. *Journal of Clinical Investigation*, 1959, *38*, 2144–2153.

Greene, W. A. Operant conditioning of the GSR using partial reinforcement. *Psychological Reports*, 1966, *19*, 571–578.

Gutmann, M. C., & Benson, H. Interaction of environmental factors and systemic arterial blood pressure: A review. *Medicine*, 1971, *50*, 543–553.

Guyton, A. C., Coleman, T. G., Bower, J. D., & Granger, H. J. Circulatory control in hypertension. *Circulation Research*, 1970, *26* (Suppl. II), 135–147.

Harris, A. H., & Brady, J. V. Animal learning—Visceral and autonomic conditioning. In M. R. Rosenzweig & L. W. Porter (Eds.), *Annual review of psychology*. Vol. 25. Palo Alto: Annual Reviews, Inc., 1974.

Harris, A. H., Findley, J. D., & Brady, J. V. Instrumental conditioning of blood pressure elevations in the baboon. *Conditional Reflex*, 1971, *6*, 215–226.

Harris, A. H., Gilliam, W. J., Findley, J. D., & Brady, J. V. Instrumental conditioning of large magnitude, daily, 12-hour blood pressure elevations in the baboon. *Science*, 1973, *182*, 175–177.

Hefferline, R. F., & Bruno, L. J. J. The psychophysiology of private events. In A. Jacobs & L. B. Sachs (Eds.), *The psychology of private events*. New York: Academic Press, 1971.

Hess, W. R. *The functional organization of the diencephalon*. New York: Grune & Stratton, 1957.

Julius, S., & Conway, J. Hemodynamic studies in patients with borderline blood pressure elevation. *Circulation*, 1968, *38*, 282–288.

Kannel, W. B., Gordon, T., & Schwartz, M. J. Systolic versus diastolic blood pressure and risk of coronary heart disease. *American Journal of Cardiology*, 1971, *27*, 335–343.

Kimble, G. A., & Perlmuter, L. C. The problem of volition. *Psychological Review*, 1970, *77*, 361–384.

Kristt, D. A., & Engel, B. T. Learned control of blood pressure in patients with high blood pressure. *Circulation*, 1975, *51*, 370–378.

Lang, P. J., & Twentyman, C. T. Learning to control heart rate: Binary versus analogue feedback. *Psychophysiology*, 1974, *11*, 616–629.

Luthe, W. Autogenic training: Method, research and application in medicine. *American Journal of Psychotherapy*, 1963, *17*, 174–195.

Merrill, J. P. Hypertensive vascular disease. In J. V. Harrison, R. D. Adams, I. L. Bennett, W. H. Resnik, G. W. Thorn, & M. M. Wintrobe (Eds.), *Principles of internal medicine*. New York: McGraw-Hill, 1966.

Miller, N. E. Preface. In N. E. Miller, T. X. Barber, L. V. DiCara, J. Kamiya, D. Shapiro, & J. Stoyva (Eds.), *Biofeedback and self-control 1973: An Aldine Annual on the regulation of bodily processes and consciousness*. Chicago: Aldine, 1974.

Miller, N. E. Applications of learning and biofeedback to psychiatry and medicine. In A. M. Freedman, H. I. Kaplan, & B. J. Sadock (Eds.), *Comprehensive textbook of psychiatry–II*. Baltimore: Williams & Wilkins, 1975.

Moeller, T. A. Reduction of arterial blood pressure through relaxation training and correlates of personality in hypertensives. Unpublished doctoral dissertation, Nova University, Fort Lauderdale, Fla., 1973.

Morse, W. H., Herd, J. A., Kelleher, R. T., & Grose, S. A. Schedule-controlled modulation of arterial blood pressure in the squirrel monkey. In H. Kimmel (Ed.), *Experimental psychopathology: Recent research and theory*. New York: Academic Press, 1971.

Obrist, P. A., Black, A. H., Brener, J., & DiCara, L. V. (Eds.) *Cardiovascular psychophysiology*. Chicago: Aldine, 1974.

Ogden, E., & Shock, N. W. Voluntary hypercirculation. *American Journal of Medical Sciences,* 1939, *198,* 329–342.

Pappas, B. A., DiCara, L. V., & Miller, N. E. Learning of blood pressure responses in the noncurarized rat: Transfer to the curarized state. *Physiological Behavior,* 1970, *5,* 1029–1032.

Patel, C. H. Yoga and biofeedback in the management of hypertension. *Lancet,* 1973, *7837,* 1053–1055.

Patel, C. 12-Month follow-up of yoga and biofeedback in the management of hypertension. *Lancet,* 1975, *7898,* 62–64.

Pfeffer, M. A., & Frohlich, E. D. Hemodynamic and myocardial function in young and old normotensive and spontaneously hypertensive rats. *Circulation Research,* 1973, *32–33* (Suppl. I), 128–135.

Pickering, G. *High blood pressure.* London: Churchill, 1968.

Pinkerton, P. The enigma of asthma. *Psychosomatic Medicine,* 1973, *35,* 461–462.

Plumlee, L. A. Operant conditioning of increases in blood pressure. *Psychophysiology,* 1969, *6,* 283–290.

Reitan, R. Intellectual and affective changes in essential hypertension. *American Journal of Psychiatry,* 1954, *110,* 817–828.

Reitan, R. A. A research program on the psychological effects of brain lesions in human beings. In N. R. Ellis (Ed.), *International review of research in mental retardation.* Vol. 1. New York: Academic Press, 1966.

Richter-Heinrich, E., & Läuter, J. A psychophysiological test as diagnostic tool with essential hypertensives. *Psychotherapy and Psychosomatics,* 1969, *17,* 153–168.

Rothe, C. F., & Friedman, J. J. Control of the cardiovascular system. In E. E. Selkurt (Ed.), *Physiology* (3rd ed.). Boston: Little, Brown, 1971.

Rushmer, R. F. *Cardiovascular dynamics.* Philadelphia: Saunders, 1970.

Schmid, P. G., & Abboud, F. M. Neurohumoral control of vascular resistance. *Archives of Internal Medicine,* 1974, *133,* 935–946.

Schwartz, G. E. Voluntary control of human cardiovascular integration and differentiation through feedback and reward. *Science,* 1972, *175,* 90–93.

Schwartz, G. E. Biofeedback as therapy: Some theoretical and practical issues. *American Psychologist,* 1973, *28,* 666–673.

Schwartz, G. E. Biofeedback, self-regulation, and the patterning of physiological processes. *American Scientist,* 1975, *63,* 314–324.

Schwartz, G. E., & Shapiro, D. Biofeedback and essential hypertension: Current findings and theoretical concerns. *Seminars in Psychiatry,* 1973, *5,* 493–503.

Schwartz, G. E., Shapiro, D., & Tursky, B. Learned control of cardiovascular integration in man through operant conditioning. *Psychosomatic Medicine,* 1971, *33,* 57–62.

Schwartz, G. E., Shapiro, D., & Tursky, B. Self control of patterns of human diastolic blood pressure and heart rate through feedback and reward. *Psychophysiology,* 1972, *9,* 270. (Abstract)

Shapiro, A. K. Contribution to a history of the placebo effect. *Behavior Science,* 1960, *5,* 109–135.

Shapiro, D. Role of feedback and instructions in the voluntary control of human blood pressure. *Japanese Journal of Biofeedback Research,* 1973, *1,* 2–9. (in Japanese)

Shapiro, D., & Crider, A. Operant electrodermal conditioning under multiple schedules of reinforcement. *Psychophysiology,* 1967, *4,* 168–175.

Shapiro, D., & Schwartz, G. E. Biofeedback and visceral learning: Clinical applications. *Seminars in Psychiatry,* 1972, *4,* 171–184.

Shapiro, D., Schwartz, G. E., & Tursky, B. Control of diastolic blood pressure in man by feedback and reinforcement. *Psychophysiology,* 1972, *9,* 296–304.

Shapiro, D., & Surwit, R. S. Learned control of physiological function and disease. In H. Leitenberg (Ed.), *Handbook of behavior modification and behavior therapy.* Englewood Cliffs, N.J.: Prentice-Hall, 1976.

Shapiro, D., Tursky, B., Gershon, E., & Stern, M. Effects of feedback and reinforcement on the control of human systolic blood pressure. *Science,* 1969, *163,* 588–590.

Shapiro, D., Tursky, B., & Schwartz, G. E. Control of blood pressure in man by operant conditioning. *Circulation Research,* 1970, *26–27* (Suppl. I), 27–32. (a)

Shapiro, D., Tursky, B., & Schwartz, G. E. Differentiation of heart rate and systolic blood pressure in man by operant conditioning. *Psychosomatic Medicine,* 1970, *32,* 417–423. (b)

Shapiro, D., & Watanabe, T. Timing characteristics of operant electrodermal modification: Fixed interval effects. *Japanese Psychological Research,* 1971, *13,* 123–130.

Shoemaker, J. E., & Tasto, D. L. The effects of muscle relaxation on blood pressure of essential hypertensives. *Behavior Research and Therapy,* 1975, *13,* 29–43.

Sirota, A. D., Schwartz, G. E., & Shapiro, D. Voluntary control of human heart rate: Effect on reaction to aversive stimulation. *Journal of Abnormal Psychology,* 1974, *83,* 261–267.

Stokes, G. S., Goldsmith, R. F., Starr, L. M., Gentle, J. L., Mani, M. K., & Stewart, J. H. Plasma renin activity in human hypertension. *Circulation Research,* 1970, *26–27* (Suppl. II), 207–214.

Stoyva, J., & Budzynski, T. Cultivated low-arousal—an anti-stress response? In L. V. DiCara (Ed.), *Recent advances in limbic and autonomic nervous system research.* New York: Plenum, 1974.

Stroebel, C. F., & Glueck, B. C. Biofeedback treatment in medicine and psychiatry: An ultimate placebo? *Seminars in Psychiatry,* 1973, *5,* 379–393.

Surwit, R. S. Biofeedback: A possible treatment for Raynaud's disease. *Seminars in Psychiatry,* 1973, *5,* 483–490.

Surwit, R. S., & Shapiro, D. Biofeedback and meditation in the treatment of borderline hypertension. In J. Beatty (Ed.), *Biofeedback and behavior: A NATO symposium.* New York: Plenum, in press.

Teplitz, T. A. Operant conditioning of blood pressure: A critical review and some psychosomatic considerations. *Communications in Behavioral Biology,* 1971, *6,* 197–202.

Tobian, L., Jr. A viewpoint concerning the enigma of hypertension. *American Journal of Medicine,* 1972, *52,* 595–609.

Tursky, B. The indirect recording of human blood pressure. In P. A. Obrist, A. H. Black, J. Brener, & L. V. DiCara (Eds.), *Cardiovascular psychophysiology.* Chicago: Aldine, 1974.

Tursky, B., Shapiro, D., & Schwartz, G. E. Automated constant cuff-pressure system to measure average systolic and diastolic blood pressure in man. *IEEE Transactions on Biomedical Engineering,* 1972, *19,* 271–276.

Ueda, H., Kaneko, Y., Takeda, T., Ikeda, K., & Yagi, S. Observations on the mechanism of renin release by hydralazine in hypertensive patients. *Circulation Research,* 1970, *27* (Suppl. II), 201–206.

Ueda, H., Yasuda, H., Takabatake, Y., Iizuka, M., Iizuka, T., Ihori, M., & Sakamoto, Y. Observations on the mechanism of renin release by catecholamines. *Circulation Research,* 1970, *27* (Suppl. II), 195–200.

VA Cooperative Study Group on Antihypertensive Agents. Effects of treatment on morbidity in hypertension. Results in patients with diastolic blood pressures averaging 115 through 129 mmHg. *Journal of the American Medical Association,* 1967, *202,* 116–122.

VA Cooperative Study Group on Antihypertensive Agents. Effects of treatment on morbidity in hypertension. II. Results in patients with diastolic blood pressure averaging 90 through 114 mmHg. *Journal of the American Medical Association,* 1970, *213,* 1143–1152.

VA Cooperative Study Group on Antihypertensive Agents. Effects of treatment on morbidity in hypertension. III. Influence of age, diastolic pressure, and prior cardiovascular disease; further analysis of side effects. *Circulation,* 1972, *45,* 991–1004.

Wallin, B. G., Delius, W., & Hagbarth, K. Comparison of sympathetic nerve activity in normotensive and hypertensive subjects. *Circulation Research,* 1973, *33,* 9–21.

Weiss, T., & Engel, B. T. Operant conditioning of heart rate in patients with premature ventricular contractions. *Psychosomatic Medicine,* 1971, *33,* 301–321.

Weston, A. Perception of autonomic processes, social acquiescence, and cognitive development of a sense of self-control in essential hypertensives trained to lower blood pressure using biofeedback procedures. Unpublished doctoral dissertation, Nova University, Fort Lauderdale, Fla., 1974.

III

THE CENTRAL NERVOUS SYSTEM

14

Learned Regulation of Alpha and Theta Frequency Activity in the Human Electroencephalogram*

JACKSON BEATTY
University of California,
Los Angeles

Much of the popular interest in biofeedback procedures stems from Kamiya's early work (Kamiya, 1969) demonstrating that human subjects could learn to regulate the abundance of alpha frequency activity in the electroencephalogram (EEG). Kamiya conjectured that the presence of large amounts of alpha activity signaled a special state that is similar to that obtained by meditational and other related techniques. A variety of more recent reports suggests that this, however, is not the case; large amounts of alpha frequency activity do not correspond to a special state of subjective experience (see Johnson, 1970; Walsh, 1974). Current research on the learned regulation of brain function addresses quite different issues. In the present paper, I shall selectively review the literature of the past few years in an attempt to clarify just what biofeedback experiments have revealed about brain

* This research was supported by the Advanced Research Projects Agency of the Department of Defense and monitored by the Office of Naval Research under contract N00014-70-C-0350.

events and behavior. I will do so from the perspective of previous work in my own laboratory and in that of James O'Hanlon of Human Factors Research, Inc., Santa Barbara. Two topics will be considered with respect to brain function and behavior: the regulation of occipital alpha rhythms and the control of posterior theta frequency activity. The question of the regulation of the sensorimotor rhythm and its behavioral effects is treated by Sterman elsewhere in this volume (see Chapter 16).

SOME GENERAL ISSUES

EEG as a Data Source for the Study of Brain and Behavior

Since Berger's (1929) original discovery that time-varying voltages of cerebral origin may be recorded from the scalp of man, the electroencephalogram (EEG) has appeared to be a promising tool for basic research on human brain function and behavior. The reasons for this are several. First, the EEG is formed by the integration of electrical events in vast numbers of brain cells. Although the rules by which such integration is achieved are quite unclear (Elul, 1972) and the resulting waveform of the EEG is complex (Walter, Rhodes, Brown, & Adey, 1966), the EEG is nonetheless much simpler than the brain events that generate it; simplicity is an attractive feature of any method of studying exceedingly complex systems. Second, the argument has been made that the EEG, in integrating the output of large numbers of individual neurons, extracts information about the activation of whole populations of cortical units and, therefore, may characterize the activity of the whole brain at a level appropriate to the study of behavior (John, 1966). Third, the EEG is a tool of importance by default; there are very few alternative methods of gaining information about ongoing events in the normal human brain.

Despite such arguments, and over five decades of serious experimental work, the demonstration of a detailed, systematic relationship between spontaneous electroencephalographic phenomena and other brain or behavioral events is still lacking (Johnson, 1970). When reliable findings have been reported, they tend to link the pattern of EEG activity and behavior at either the general level of state, as in the electroencephalographic categorization of the levels of arousal and sleep (Rechtschaffer & Kales, 1968), or at the level of regional activation of brain tissue, as in the sensorimotor or posterior alpha rhythms. There is little reliable evidence linking shifts in the patterns of the

EEG with more subtle behavioral events; similar EEG patterns may be generated under quite different behavioral circumstances.

Paradigms and Terminology

Even a cursory review of the recent literature on learned control of the spontaneous EEG reveals a certain uneasiness and indecision on the part of the various contributers as to the appropriate terms to use in describing the experiments, data, and findings. One reads of self-regulation, autoregulation, learned control, operantly conditioned EEG, feedback control, feedback regulation, and various other combinations of these elements as descriptors of process. The issue is, of course, not simply terminological; rather, it reflects the absence of a wholly appropriate model or framework with which to conceptualize the processes that underlie the observed alterations of EEG spectra as a function of experimental conditions. We have used the term "operant control" or "learned control" in the descriptive sense as it adequately characterizes the experiments that we have performed at procedural level (Beatty, 1971, 1972; Beatty, Greenberg, Deibler, & O'Hanlon, 1974, for example). But at a more theoretical level, I would not claim that these experiments or any others reported in the present literature demonstrate that spectral shifts of the EEG are the result of operant conditioning in the stricter sense of the term (Paskewitz & Orne, 1973). Thus, the metaphor of operant control is useful, but not wholly appropriate to the phenomena under consideration.

Similarly, the use of terms drawn from system and control theory are sometimes useful but, in many experimental situations, not completely appropriate. While it is true that the signal that the operant conditioning paradigm regards as a reinforcer also serves as a feedback loop in the experimental situation, in most instances, the total system is too poorly specified to allow the relatively precise formulations of system theory (Riggs, 1970) to be employed. Thus, by drawing a system of boxes and arrows with recurrent paths, we may give the impression of a deeper understanding than we have in point of fact.

LEARNED CONTROL OF THE POSTERIOR ALPHA RHYTHMS

It is not surprising that the first attempts to condition EEG rhythms were concerned with the alpha rhythms; alpha frequency activity is certainly the most obvious feature of the human electroencephalogram (Berger, 1929). These 8–13 Hz, high-amplitude waveforms are easily observed in the waking EEG, clustering together to form bursts of alpha activity that contrast sharply with surrounding periods of faster, low-voltage activity. Thus, alpha activity has somewhat the character of an electroencephalographic event or state, and it is natural to inquire whether or not a person can be trained to regulate these relatively well-defined waveforms. Several early attempts were made to demonstrate that the blocking of posterior alpha frequency activity could be classically conditioned (Jasper & Shagass, 1941; Shagass, 1942; Shagass & Johnson, 1943), but these experiments bear only tangentially upon the issues at hand.

The use of operant procedures to gain control of EEG activity is a considerably more recent undertaking. In an attempt to demonstrate that operant control procedures may be applied to responses other than those of the skeletal musculature, one of Miller's students, Carmona (1967), trained cats to increase or decrease EEG amplitude when electrical stimulation of the medial forebrain bundle was used as reinforcement (Miller, 1969). Kamiya (1969) at the same time was publishing data indicating that humans trained to discriminate periods of high-amplitude alpha activity from cortical desynchrony were able to exert some voluntary control over the EEG spectrum as a result of discrimination training. Similar results were obtained with naive subjects provided with a tone indicating the state of the EEG (alpha or nonalpha activity).

In the flurry of publications that followed these initial reports, little attention has been paid to the question of mechanism: What are the brain processes that give rise to alpha activity and how are they related to behavior or to brain function? Instead, most of the current literature addresses itself to questions that are primarily demonstrational (Can the alpha rhythm be operantly regulated?), technological (Which procedure yields the most effective control?), or correlational (If the alpha rhythms are operantly modified, does something else also change?). Such experimental questions can, of course, help disclose the characteristics of underlying brain mechanisms, but do not constitute a direct frontal attack on the question of mechanism. For example, the correlational question is quite capable of addressing the issue of mechanism if the "something else" that is measured is a variable that is implicated by a process model of either brain function or behavior. Often, however, the correlative measure is a behavioral variable selected in an attempt to demonstrate that regulation of alpha activity is of some practical utility.

Much of the literature on the learned control of the cortical alpha rhythms may be understood if synchronous brain activity is interpreted as an indicator of reduced activity in the cortical area from which the rhythm is recorded. Thus, the momentary level of synchronous activity should vary as an inverse function of the momentary level of specific activation in the recording area, and the general level of activation of the cortex as a whole, either as a function of brainstem alerting mechanisms (Lindsley, 1960) or as the result of local activation of restricted cortical regions (Kahneman, 1973). Further, individuals differ markedly in the degree to which they exhibit synchronous, alpha frequency activity, so that the absolute level of alpha abundance must also depend upon an individual difference factor or set of factors describing the tendency to cortical synchrony. Each of these putative factors in the learned regulation of alpha activity will be considered in turn.

Individual Differences in Alpha Abundance as a Factor in the Learned Regulation of Alpha Activity

The degree to which the synchronous alpha rhythms are apparent in the EEG record differs widely among individuals, but within any single person, the profile of the spectrum is quite constant over repeated tests (Matousek & Petersen, 1973). This suggests that constitutional factors contribute to the relative abundance of alpha activity observable in an individual. Such individual differences in tendency toward synchronous activity probably play only a minor role in the acquisition of control of posterior alpha activity, except in extreme cases. Suppression of alpha activity is extremely difficult to achieve in subjects in which alpha activity is virtually absent under unregulated conditions. Conversely, alpha augmentation may be difficult to demonstrate in subjects with highly synchronous alpha activity in the unregulated EEG. Nonetheless, the characteristic level of alpha activity for an individual determines only the range of values within which he will be able to regulate under conditions of bidirectional reinforcement; it does not predict the degree of control or differentiation of augment and suppress conditions. Baseline alpha activity is nonsignificantly correlated (*rho* = − .20) with the difference in alpha abundance at the end of training trials in which significant discriminant control was observed (Beatty, 1971).

Visual System Activation as a Factor in the Learned Regulation of Posterior Alpha Frequency Activity

The importance of visual system activity as a determinant of alpha frequency activity in the posterior EEG has long been known. Berger (1930) supplied the first evidence of this relation in his second published paper on the human electroencephalogram. More recent work confirms the extent to which the activation of the cortical visual system controls alpha activity in occipital cortex. The power of this relationship is evident in Mulholland's work (see Chapter 2, this volume) in which the techniques of systems analysis are used to describe the effects of EEG-contingent visual stimulation upon alpha frequency activity over occipital cortex.

Similar specific relations between degree of visual system activation and local EEG synchrony in the alpha frequency band have been demonstrated to hold within individual regions of the visual cortex as well. Morrell (1967) has reported that specific blocking of alpha activity in restricted areas of occipital cortex may be produced by selective stimulation of the corresponding portions of the visual field. Morrell recorded multiple electrocorticograms from the exposed surface of the brain in an awake patient undergoing surgery for the removal of epileptogenic tissue anterior to the left occipital pole. Fixation upon the visual display initially resulted in a reduction of alpha frequency activity from all occipital sites, but this suppression was short-lived as alpha activity quickly returned. Illumination of small sectors of the contralateral visual field resulted in regional suppression of alpha activity in specific segments of occipital cortex. Morrell reports that this local suppression of alpha activity was orderly and reliable, occurring consistently in 10 or 12 replications.

More directly relevant to the concerns of this chapter is that similar local effects of regulation of alpha activity by processing activity in restricted regions of brain tissue may also be observed from scalp electrodes in normal subjects. For example, Cavonius and Estevez-Uscanga (1974) report that stimulation of the contralateral visual field with complex pictorial stimuli results in a specific, unilateral suppression of alpha frequency activity recorded between occipital and temporal cortex (O_1–T_5 versus O_2–T_6).

From such evidence, it is reasonable to argue that control of alpha frequency activity recorded at the scalp over posterior cortex could be regulated by brain mechanisms intrinsic to the cortical visual systems.

Paskewitz and Orne (1973) provide data that indicate visual system activation is an important factor in the regulation of occipital alpha frequency activity even when the feedback signal is not presented in the visual modality. Using a binary auditory indicator of alpha frequency activity in the occipital EEG, Paskewitz and Orne attempted to train two groups of paid volunteers to increase the abundance of alpha activity over no-task resting control levels interspersed among the training trials. In the presence of room illumination, a group of seven subjects showed no difficulty in acquiring control; the percent time in which alpha activity was present increased steadily over experimental trials, whereas percent alpha activity in the rest periods remained approximately constant. However, when compared with alpha activity levels in preceding eyes-closed and eyes-open control periods, it appears that opening the eyes in an illuminated environment results in a marked suppression of alpha activity. The percent time alpha activity, even in the later training trials, never exceeds the eyes-closed baseline measure.

A somewhat different pattern is present in the data of nine subjects in which a comparable experiment was conducted without illumination. As before, a significant difference in the abundance of alpha activity occurred between the eyes-closed and eyes-open baseline measures. However, during the testing periods, no differences in percent alpha activity appeared between the alpha-augment feedback conditions and the interspersed rest periods. A similar failure of feedback to yield alpha augmentation appeared on 5 subsequent days of testing for this group.

Eight of these nine subjects were subsequently retested in a seventh training day, but with low-level illumination of the experimental chamber. Under these conditions, they performed as did the previous subjects tested with illumination; a significant difference between test and rest conditions appeared for the first time. These data strongly suggest that visual system activation serves as a controlling variable for occipital alpha activity even when the reinforcing or feedback stimulus is not presented in the visual modality.

That successful regulation under alpha augmentation reinforcement contingencies is accomplished by reducing visual system activity is also supported by data from a detailed spectral intensity and coherence analysis performed on two subjects by Hord, Naitoh, and Johnson (1972). Spectral intensity and coherence functions were obtained from frontal, temporal, and occipital monopolar leads before, during, and after a 60-minute period of attempted enhancement of occipital alpha activity. High-amplitude, low-frequency activity in the frontal (F_2) and temporal (T_4) leads indicative of eye movements was characteristically observed during the baseline periods. During successful regulated enhancement of occipital alpha, the electrical signs of eye movements were suppressed. Suppression of involuntary eye movements may be taken as a peripheral sign of reduced activity in the thalamocortical visual system (Kahneman, 1973). During regulation, the intensity of alpha activity at the occipital (O_2) lead was selectively and specifically increased.

General Activation as a Factor in Learned Regulation of Alpha Activity

The role that slow shifts in cortical activation might play in the learned regulation of occipital alpha activity is less clear. It is known that the spectral power in the alpha frequencies is sensitive to changes in general alertness (Anliker, 1963; Lindsley, 1960; Lynn, 1966). Under certain experimental conditions, such generalized shifts in arousal might be employed in the regulation of cortical alpha rhythms. For example, with prolonged trials in which alpha augmentation was reinforced, one might expect to observe changes in other physiological systems that indicate a general alteration of tonic activation.

Such changes, however, are not necessary for discriminant control of alpha frequency activity. When trials are short and interspersed among them are frequent breaks in the experimental procedure that permit movement of the subject, bidirectional discriminant control of alpha activity may be easily observed (Beatty & Kornfeld, 1972). Under such conditions, however, no differences in either heart period or respiratory rate are observed between the alpha-augment and the alpha-suppress trials. Shifts in the general level of physiological activation are not a necessary accompaniment of regulated posterior alpha activity.

REGULATION OF THE THETA RHYTHMS

Unlike the prominant alpha rhythms, cortical theta frequency (3.5 to 7.5 Hz) activity in man is a low-amplitude, poorly organized component of the electroencephalogram. Barely visible in the record of the alerted subject, periods of visually identifiable theta activity appear under conditions of prolonged monotonous monitoring or after periods of sleep loss. Clinical electroencephalographers often regard posterior theta as an indicator of increasing drowsiness (Kooi, 1971). However, even under such conditions, theta activity rarely dominates the EEG record. For this reason, sensitive spectral or period-analytic analysis procedures are needed to reliably discriminate theta frequency activity from higher amplitude activity in other frequency ranges.

Several pieces of evidence suggest that under well-defined circumstances, the level of theta frequency activity in the EEG is closely related to general alertness level and sometimes to behavioral performance efficiency. For example, Williams, Granda, Jones, Lubin, and Armington (1962) examined performance in a short, auditory vigilance task as a function of sleep loss. Using visual methods of EEG scoring, increases in theta frequency activity during deprivation were apparent in five of seven subjects. If such theta periods immediately preceded the delivery of a critical target, the subject was highly likely to fail to detect that target. The probability of detection was high, however, if the dominant frequency of the EEG was within the alpha range in the 1-second period before target presentation.

A similar relation between theta activity and vigilance was observed by O'Hanlon (O'Hanlon & Beatty, in preparation) under monotonous monitoring conditions without sleep deprivation using a sensitive period-analytic indicator of theta frequency activity in the EEG. Twenty paid undergraduate volunteers were required to monitor a simulated radar display for infrequent targets over a 2-hour period. EEG was recorded and analyzed on-line by a period-analytic algorithm in a digital computer (Beatty & Figueroa, 1974; Legewie & Probst, 1969). A theta ratio was formed for each second by counting the number of waves with periods (between positive-going zero crossings) in the theta frequency band (periods between 133 and 286 milliseconds) divided by the total number of waves in the theta, alpha, and beta frequencies (periods between 33 and 286 milliseconds). The average theta ratio over the entire 2-hour period of the watch was related significantly to the average level of performance over subjects; the correlation between the number of sweeps in which a target was present before detection and the theta ratio was .67 ($p < .01$). Thus, theta activity appears to be related to behavior under monotonous conditions in which subject drowsiness is likely to affect performance efficiency.

Reinforcement of appropriate values of the theta ratio determined by the period-analytic method (Beatty & Figueroa, 1974) results in statistically reliable discriminant control of the posterior theta rhythm in experimentally naive subjects (Beatty, Palmer, & Edelston, in preparation). Five university students served as volunteer subjects to fulfill the requirements of an introductory psychology course. They were told nothing concerning the nature of the task other than instructions to minimize electromyographic and electrocular artifacts in the EEG recording. Specifically, they were not told that the EEG criterion and the direction of reinforced change would vary over trials, but were instructed to attempt to maintain a binary auditory reinforcement signal at its louder state.

The experimental session was divided into five trial blocks of four trials each, two of which employed a theta augmentation reinforcement contingency, and the other two, a theta suppression contingency. Each trial was 90 seconds in duration.

Under these conditions of reinforcement and without knowledge that the experimental procedure required bidirectional control of the theta rhythms, each of the five subjects was able to achieve stable discriminant control of the theta ratio. As illustrated in Figure 14.1, average value of the theta ratio under the theta-augment contingency is nearly twice that obtained under the theta-suppress contingency over the five trial blocks ($t(4) = 2.89$; $p < .05$).

Further, the theta ratio computed on-line using a period-analytic algorithm is closely related to power-spectral estimates of the same ratio. To test for this correspondence, EEG from the experiment was recorded on FM magnetic tape for off-line power-spectral analysis. Averaged over 90-second trials, period-analytic and power-spectral estimates are quite similar. The correlation between the two estimators was .86 ($p < .01$). It appears that the period-analytic procedure, which is computationally more rapid and less difficult, may serve as a reasonable approximation of the more complex power-spectral method.

Operantly induced changes in theta activity of the posterior EEG systematically affect behavior in a monotonous monitoring task. Beatty *et al.* (1974) trained two groups of university student volunteers to regulate posterior theta activity using procedures similar to those described above. Twelve subjects were trained to suppress, and seven to augment, posterior theta frequency activity. Following EEG training and a 2-hour familiarization session with the Human Factors Research General Purpose Radar Simulator, all subjects were tested on two separate days on a 2-hour radar vigilance test. On one day, EEG-contingent reinforcement was provided to the subject for the entire

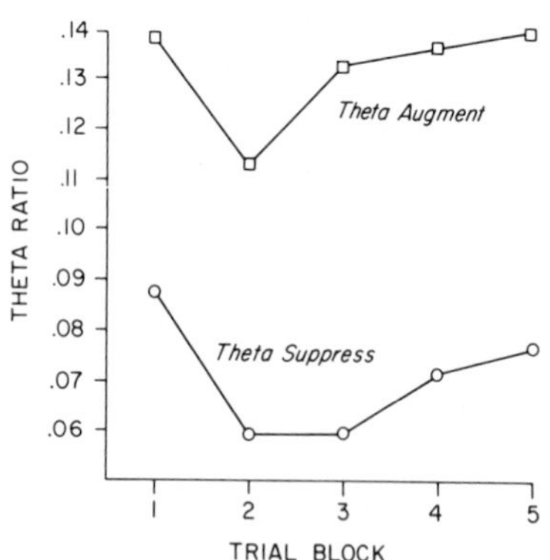

Figure 14.1 The effect of response-contingent reinforcement upon the posterior EEG in five university student subjects as a function of trial block and reinforcement contingency. The theta ratio was computed on-line using the period-analytic algorithm.

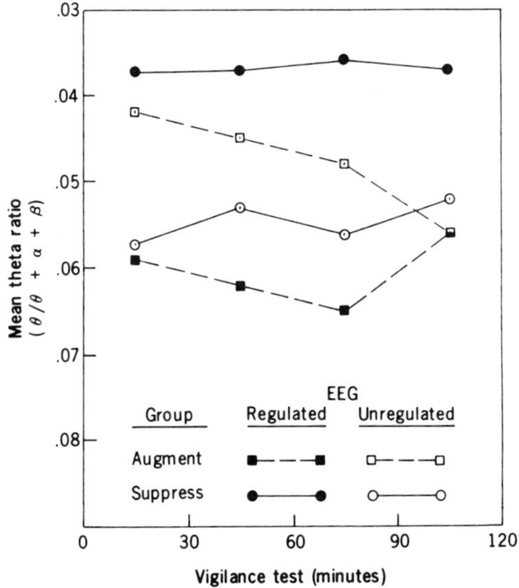

Figure 14.2 Mean theta ratio as a function of time in vigilance test, for the theta-augment group and the theta-suppress group with regulated and unregulated EEG. Subjects were volunteer university students. The ordinate is inverted. [From Beatty *et al.*, 1974, in *Science*, Vol. 183, pp. 871–873. Copyright 1974 by the American Association for the Advancement of Science.]

period of the vigilance test. On the other day, EEG was monitored but no reinforcement was provided.

The EEG reinforcement procedures led to a selective alteration of the theta ratio (Figure 14.2). As predicted, the theta-suppress group showed significantly less occipital theta activity while simultaneously performing the monitoring task and regulating EEG than while performing the monitoring task alone ($t = 1.97$; $df = 11$; $p < .05$). The theta-augment group produced more theta activity in the monitoring task while regulating ($t = 1.81$; $df = 6$; $p < .10$). Thus, EEG-contingent reinforcement appears effective in inducing discriminate control of theta frequency activity in the occipital EEG of subjects simultaneously performing a prolonged radar monitoring task.

Changes in monitoring performance accompanied regulation of theta activity (Figure 14.3). The incidence of theta frequency activity in the occipital EEG is inversely related to monitoring efficiency. The poorest performance in any condition was exhibited by the theta-augment group while regulating EEG. Conversely, the best monitoring performance was shown by the theta-suppress group while reg-

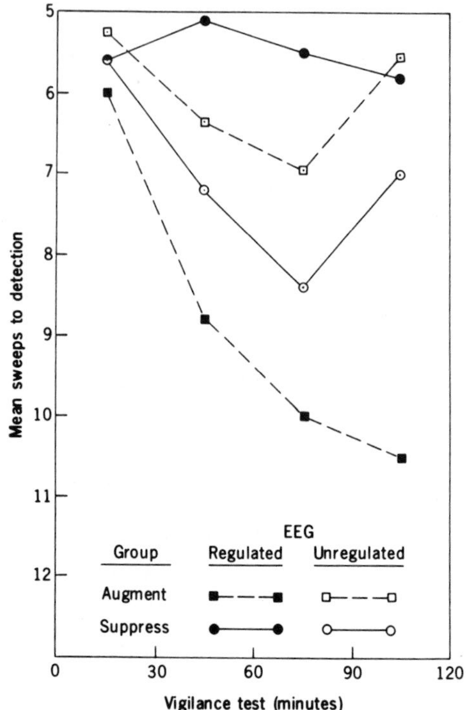

Figure 14.3 Mean number of sweeps to detect targets as a function of time in the vigilance test for the theta-augment group and the theta-suppress group with regulated and unregulated EEG. The ordinate is inverted. [From Beatty *et al.*, 1974, in *Science*, Vol. 183, pp. 871–873. Copyright 1974 by the American Association for the Advancement of Science.]

ulating. These groups performed at intermediate levels in the absence of EEG-contingent reinforcement (unregulated conditions). Statistical analyses confirmed these observations. The mean vigilance test performance of the theta-augment group was significantly worse while regulating EEG ($t = 2.84$; $df = 6$; $p < .025$), whereas performance was improved during regulation for the theta-suppress group ($t = 2.50$; $df = 11$; $p < .025$). During the EEG-unregulated monitoring session, the mean vigilance test performances of these two groups were not significantly different ($t = 1.31$; $df = 17$; $p > .20$).

If learned suppression of the posterior theta rhythms improves performance under monotonous conditions by helping the subject maintain an alerted level of cortical arousal, then such performance-enhancing effects should be most obvious in those who have difficulty maintaining alertness without the aid of EEG-contingent reinforcement. This appears to be the case; the three subjects in the theta suppression group that showed no improvement during EEG regulation were the first, third, and fourth most efficient performers in the unregulated condition. Conversely, the number of sweeps required before detection in the single worst subject under unregulated conditions was shortened by 15 sweeps (90 seconds) in the presence of reinforcement.

Such effects cannot be attributed to any nonspecific aspects of the experiment, such as the mere presence of the EEG-regulation task; under the regulation conditions, the subjects in the theta-augment group performed more poorly, whereas the performance of the theta-suppress group improved. The single factor differentiating these two groups was the contingency of EEG reinforcement.

These data indicate that learned regulation of specific, arousal-sensitive brain rhythms affects arousal-sensitive behavior, but leave open the question of the uniqueness of the effect. For example, one might argue that EEG-contingent reinforcement in the theta-suppress group simply aided a group of task-naive subjects—who were unaccustomed to performing under prolonged, monotonous conditions—by teaching them a method of maintaining wakefulness that a more experienced operator would have acquired by other means. For this reason, and to investigate the practical utility of these methods, the experiment was repeated using a group of highly experienced military radar operators and air traffic controllers (Beatty, Royal, & O'Hanlon, in preparation).

Subjects were 11 volunteers from the Point Mugu Naval Air Station, located 40 miles north of the UCLA campus. All had had extensive radar monitoring experience and were currently rated as Radar Operators or Air Traffic Controllers. While most of their regular duties required radar monitoring for periods of 1 hour or less, all subjects reported occasionally serving as the sole radar operator, unrelieved for periods of 8 to 12 hours.

The main experiment involved 2 consecutive days of training and testing for each subject. The first day was devoted to training the operators to suppress theta activity using EEG-contingent reinforcement and to familiarize them with a 3-hour radar-monitoring vigilance test.

In the second day, the effects of learned theta suppression upon the monitoring performance of experienced radar operators were tested. Each subject was tested in two 3-hour vigilance tests, one with and the other without concurrent theta-suppression reinforcement. The order of testing was determined randomly for every pair of subjects, a procedure that assured that one-half the subjects would first be tested with, and the other half without, theta suppression feedback. The two testing sequences were separated by a luncheon rest period. A 10-minute dual task practice period preceded the theta suppression sequence, in which the subject practiced EEG regulation and simultaneous radar monitoring.

These experienced radar operators, like the university students previously tested, were able to suppress parietal–occipital theta frequency EEG activity while simultaneously monitoring the radar for infrequent signals. The probability of theta activity during target periods was reduced from .039 in the EEG-unregulated vigilance test to .029 with EEG regulation ($t = 1.68$; $df = 8$; $p < .10$). Thus, theta suppression feedback reduces the incidence of theta band activity by 25% in these experienced radar operators.

Further, like the university subjects, the experienced radar operators were able to detect weak targets in fewer sweeps when their performance was aided with theta suppression feedback. Over the entire 3-hour period of the vigilance test, experienced subjects averaged 5.52 sweeps to detection without feedback and 4.80 sweeps with feedback ($t = 2.84$; $df = 9$; $p < .01$).

The demonstration of a facilitory effect of EEG theta suppression feedback upon performance in experienced radar operators and air traffic controllers indicates that such feedback does not act to simply aid the naive subject in learning to monitor a complex target for prolonged periods under monotonous conditions. The subjects in the second experiment have had a wide variety of opportunities in their years of navy experience to learn many techniques of maintaining alertness under monotonous conditions, yet their performance was aided by theta suppression feedback. This suggests that such feedback provides the experienced operator with new information concerning his state of central nervous system arousal, permitting him to maintain alertness in a manner not otherwise possible.

However, the disturbing possibility remained that the performance-enhancing effects of theta suppression feedback observed in the present experiment might be attributed to nonspecific effects of the experimental treatment, and not to the specific effects of the EEG-contingent reinforcement that we employed. Such an explanation is not likely to be correct, but it is logically possible. In the experiment with naive observers (Beatty *et al.*, 1974), any nonspecific interpretation of the experimental results could be rejected through the use of a bidirectional control design. The experiment with trained operators did not embody the full bidirectional procedure, in which

one group is trained to increase, and the other to decrease, EEG theta activity, but replicates only the theta suppression and EEG-unregulated conditions. Since the procedures employed in the two experiments are identical, it is reasonable to assume that the facilitory effects of learned theta suppression observed in the present experiment are due to the specific effects of the training procedure, as they were in the complete experiment. Nonetheless, to provide further evidence of the specific nature of the observed facilatory effects in the experienced observers, an additional control experiment was undertaken.

The six of the experienced subjects who had participated in the main experiment and were still available for further testing were brought to UCLA for an additional 1-day experiment. These subjects performed on the same experimental schedule as they had on the critical testing day of the main experiment, one with and one without EEG-contingent feedback, in the same order in which they were originally tested. They were instructed that another feedback procedure was being evaluated and, prior to testing with the EEG feedback sequence, each was given a 1-hour period of training with reinforcement for increased theta activity. Each subject in this second, control experiment tested in a theta augmentation and EEG-unregulated condition. If nonspecific effects of the experimental procedure mediated the facilitory effects of EEG feedback that were observed with theta suppression reinforcement, then these six subjects should continue to show improved performance in the feedback condition. If, however, the performance-enhancing effects of EEG feedback were a specific result of the suppression of EEG theta, then feedback acting to augment theta activity should increase the magnitude of the vigilance decrement.

The results of this control experiment support the specificity hypothesis. Theta augmentation feedback acts to increase the abundance of theta frequency activity in the parietal–occipital EEG compared to unregulated conditions and also to increase the magnitude of the vigilance decrement observed over the 3-hour period of the watch. A t-test of the difference between regulated and unregulated EEG on each of the 2 days of testing shows specific control of theta activity in these six subjects [$t(5) = 2.21$; $p < .05$]. The mean theta ratio during target presentation over the entire period of the vigilance test is larger for the theta augmentation condition (.064) than for the unregulated EEG condition on the same day (.026).

Figure 14.4 presents the corresponding behavioral data for these six

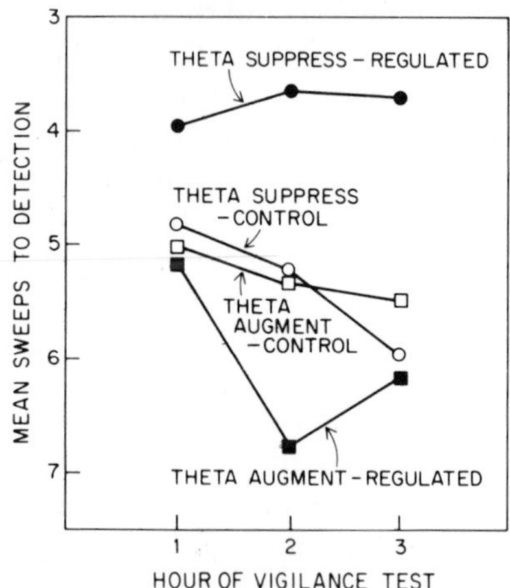

Figure 14.4 Mean number of sweeps to detect targets for six experienced radar operators who participated in both the theta-suppress and theta-augment conditions with same-day control vigilance tests. The ordinate is inverted.

operators in the control experiment. In addition, the behavioral data for these same subjects in the main experiment are also displayed. It can be seen that performance in the vigilance test without EEG regulation is quite equivalent in the two separate experiments, but that the introduction of feedback acts to improve performance in the theta suppression condition and degrade performance in the theta augmentation condition. These effects are of the same magnitude as those previously reported, and are statistically significant by t-test on the difference between regulated and unregulated performance on each of the 2 days of testing ($t = 2.66$; $df = 5$; $p < .05$).

Thus, it appears that the relation between operantly regulated theta frequency activity and performance previously observed in university students also holds for experienced radar operators. This finding suggests that the performance-enhancing effects of the theta-suppression procedure are at least partially independent of practice on radar monitoring tasks.

One test of the efficacy of operant theta suppression as a performance aid has been conducted by O'Hanlon, Royal, and Beatty (1975) using volunteers from the population of radar operators and air traffic controllers at the Point Mugu Naval Air Station. Fourteen volunteers participated in two 3-hour vigilance tasks, one with and one without theta-suppression feedback, using real radar equipment and imagery. Actual air traffic in the Point Mugu–Los Angeles area served as a background against which simulated high-speed targets occasionally

appeared. Mean time to target detection was computed for each 20-minute period of the vigilance test under both control and regulation conditions.

The detection performance of these operators was stable over the entire 3-hour period of the vigilance test under both control and experimental conditions; a vigilance decrement did not occur in this simulation. Nonetheless, a marginal ($p < .10$) tendency for detection to be more rapid in the final hour of the watch under theta suppression was present. However, the magnitude of the effect was small (detection time without regulation was 16.1 seconds; with regulation, it was 11.9 seconds). As in previous experiments, operant suppression of theta frequency activity in the posterior EEG does not improve performance over alerted levels. The performance-enhancing effects of theta suppression appear only in situations that yield a vigilance decrement under control conditions.

In summary, this series of studies provides evidence for a reliable and systematic relationship between theta activity in the posterior EEG and behavioral efficiency in prolonged, monotonous watchkeeping tasks as well as indicating the limiting conditions under which the relationship may be observed. However, the absolute magnitude of the performance-enhancing effects of operant theta suppression is such that any direct application of these procedures at present does not seem warranted under most operational conditions.

SOME CONCLUSIONS

Thus, it appears that operant procedures, when properly employed, may serve to regulate various components of the human electroencephalogram. There is little doubt that operant procedures may effect specific changes in alpha activity, posterior theta activity, or the sensorimotor rhythm. The mechanisms by which such regulation occurs, however, are far less clear. In some instances, however, operant reinforcement procedures may serve as an additional scientific tool for the study of brain–behavior relations. They provide the investigator with a technique for securing systematic control of particular patterns of electroencephalographic activity which may be useful in testing the relations between brain and behavioral events.

In contrast, the role of these procedures in applied settings appears quite limited at present. Despite the current proliferation of alpha feedback devices, there is little reason to believe that the learned regulation of alpha frequency activity is of practical consequence. The series of investigations on learned theta suppression and vigilance decrement reported above suggest that application may be warranted only under most unusual conditions. Work on the clinical application of learned control of the sensorimotor rhythm in the treatment of epilepsy is still inconclusive; biofeedback as therapy cannot be justified by the evidence available at present. Thus, it appears that the hope of applying biofeedback procedures to the behavioral or clinical purposes that stimulated much of the early research was not justified.

Operant EEG regulation is no longer new. It is no longer a technique of unknown potential and promise. Experimental research has provided the information necessary to evaluate these procedures more exactly. The essential phenomenon—that EEG rhythms may be operantly regulated—appears sound. Numerous experiments in a variety of laboratories have established that fact beyond question. However, the early hopes that operant regulation of the EEG may be of major behavioral or clinical value have been dampened. We are left then with a more modest view of the phenomenon, one stressing the continuity between operant and other experimental procedures, the usefulness of these methods for selected research problems, and a realization that any justifiable application of such procedures as treatment or performance aid is much farther away than was originally supposed.

REFERENCES

Anliker, J. Variations in alpha voltage of the electroencephalogram and time perception. *Science*, 1963, *140*, 1307–1309.

Beatty, J. Effects of initial alpha wave abundance and operant training procedures on occipital alpha and beta wave activity. *Psychonomic Science*, 1971, *23*, 197–199.

Beatty, J. Similar effects of feedback signals and instructional information on EEG activity. *Physiology and Behavior*, 1972, *9*, 151–154.

Beatty, J., & Figueroa, C. Period analytic algorithms for the estimation of selected spectral properties of short segments of EEG data. *Behavior Research Methods & Instrumentation*, 1974, *6*, 293–295.

Beatty, J., Greenberg, A., Deibler, W., & O'Hanlon, J. Operant control of occipital theta rhythm affects performance in a radar monitoring task. *Science*, 1974, *183*, 871–873.

Beatty, J., & Kornfeld, C. Relative independence of conditioned EEG changes from cardiac and respiratory activity. *Physiology and Behavior*, 1972, *9*, 733–736.

Beatty, J., Palmer, L., & Edelston, J. M. Power spectrum shifts induced by reinforcement of theta frequency EEG activity using a period-analytic algorithm. In preparation.

Beatty, J., Royal, J., & O'Hanlon, J. Operant regulation of theta frequency activity in the posterior EEG affects detection efficiency in experienced radar operators. In preparation.

Berger, H. Uber des Elektrenkephalogramm des Menschen. *Archiv für Psychiatrie und Nervenkrankheiten*, 1929, *87*, 527–570. (P. Gloor, trans. and Ed. Hans Berger on the electroencephalogram of man. *Electroencephalography and Clinical Neurophysiology*, 1969, Suppl. 28).

Berger, H. Uber des Elektrenkephalogramm des Menschen. *Journal für Psychologie und Neurologie,* 1930, *40,* 160–179. (P. Gloor, trans. and Ed. Hans Berger on the electroencephalogram of man. *Electroencephalography and Clinical Neurophysiology,* 1969, Suppl. 28).

Carmona, A. Unpublished doctoral dissertation, Yale University, 1967.

Cavonius, C. R., & Estevez-Uscanga, O. Local suppression of alpha activity by pattern in half the visual field. *Nature,* 1974, *251,* 412–414.

Elul, R. The genesis of the EEG. *International Review of Neurobiology,* 1972, *15,* 227–272.

Hord, D., Naitoh, P., & Johnson, L. Intensity and coherence contours during self-regulated high alpha activity. *Electroencephalography and Clinical Neurophysiology,* 1972, *32,* 429–433.

Jasper, H., & Shagass, C. Conditioning the occipital alpha rhythm in man. *Journal of Experimental Psychology,* 1941, *28,* 373–388.

John, E. R. Neural processes during learning. In R. W. Russell (Ed.), *Frontiers in physiological psychology.* New York: Academic Press, 1966.

Johnson, L. C. A psychophysiology for all states. *Psychophysiology,* 1970, *6,* 501–516.

Kahneman, D. *Attention and effort.* Englewood Cliffs, N.J.: Prentice-Hall, 1973.

Kamiya, J. Operant control of the EEG alpha rhythm and some of its reported effects on consciousness. In C. Tart (Ed.), *Altered states of consciousness.* New York: Wiley, 1969.

Kooi, K. A. *Fundamentals of electroencephalography.* New York: Harper & Row, 1971.

Legewie, H., & Probst, W. On-line analysis of EEG with a small computer (period-amplitude analysis). *Electroencephalography and Clinical Neurophysiology,* 1969, *27,* 533–536.

Lindsley, D. B. Attention, consciousness, sleep and wakefulness. In J. Field (Ed.), *Handbook of physiology.* Section I, Vol. 3. Washington, D.C.: American Physiological Society, 1960.

Lynn, R. *Attention, arousal and the orientation reaction.* Oxford: Pergamon Press, 1966.

Matousek, M., & Petersen, I. Frequency analysis of the EEG in normal children and adolescents. In P. Kellaway & I. Petersen (Eds.), *Automation of clinical electroencephalography.* New York: Raven, 1973.

Miller, N. Learning of visceral and glandular responses. *Science,* 1969, *163,* 434–445.

Morrell, F. Electrical signs of sensory coding. In G. C. Quarton, T. Melnechuk, & F. O. Schmitt (Eds.), *The neurosciences: A study program.* New York: Rockefeller, 1967.

O'Hanlon, J. F., & Beatty, J. EEG and neuropharmacological predictors of detection efficiency in a monotonous monitoring task. In preparation.

O'Hanlon, J. F., Royal, J. W., & Beatty, J. EEG theta regulation and radar monitoring performance in a controlled field experiment (Technical Report 1738-F, Santa Barbara, Ca.: Human Factors Research, Inc., September 1975.

Paskewitz, D. A., & Orne, M. T. Visual effects on alpha feedback training. *Science,* 1973, *181,* 360–363.

Rechtschaffer, A., & Kales, A. *Manual of standardized terminology, techniques and scoring system for sleep stages of human subjects.* USPHS. Washington, D.C.: U.S. Government Printing Office, 1968.

Riggs, D. S. *Control theory and physiological feedback mechanisms.* Baltimore: Williams and Wilkins, 1970.

Shagass, C. Conditioning the human occipital alpha rhythm to a voluntary stimulus: A quantitative study. *Journal of Experimental Psychology,* 1942, *31,* 367–379.

Shagass, C., & Johnson, E. P. The course of acquisition of a conditioned response of the occipital alpha rhythm. *Journal of Experimental Psychology,* 1943, *33,* 201–209.

Walsh, D. H. Interactive effects of alpha feedback and instructional set on subjective state. *Psychophysiology*, 1974, *11*, 428–435.

Walter, D. O., Rhodes, J. M., Brown, D., & Adey, W. R. Comprehensive spectral analysis of human EEG generators in posterior cerebral regions. *Electroencephalography and Clinical Neurophysiology*, 1966, *20*, 224–237.

Williams, H. L., Granda, A. M., Jones, R. C., Lubin, A., & Armington, J. C. EEG frequency and finger pulse volume as predictors of reaction time during sleep loss. *Electroencephalography and Clinical Neurophysiology*, 1962, *14*, 64–70.

15

The Meaning of Operantly Conditioned Changes in Evoked Responses*

J. PETER ROSENFELD
Northwestern University
Evanston, Ill.

INTRODUCTION AND METHODOLOGY

This chapter deals with the operant conditioning of sensory-evoked potentials.

Procedure

The general procedure used for evoked potential conditioning was introduced by Fox and Rudell (1968), and involves the following phases.

1. The investigator chooses the particular aspect of the evoked response specified as the neural event designated for reinforcement-controlled change. In much previous work, a 10–30-millisecond segment of an evoked component has been selected as the candidate

* Supported in part by NIH grants 5-50-RR07028 and FR7028-05 and NSF grant 75-17770 to Northwestern University (J.P.R.) and NIMH training grants 5TO1MH11284-06PO and 5TO1MH11284-05 to the Psychology Department, Northwestern University.

neural operant and referred to as the criterion segment (SC). The aspect of the SC that has been most typically used for conditioning is amplitude; for example, subjects are contingently rewarded for generating only a certain range of SC amplitude samples. It is noted that amplitude may not be the only conditionable aspect of the wave; slope, topography, frequency, latency, and any other aspects of the macropotential believed to possess adequate plasticity for conditioning might be utilized in accordance with investigators' interests. Walker (1974), for example, has utilized topographical features of photic-evoked responses with considerable success. Neither does the to-be-conditioned event need to be confined to one component, even if amplitude is utilized. Often it is desirable to utilize peak-to-peak or prestimulus baseline-to-peak measures of evoked amplitudes so as to control steady potential effects (Rudell & Fox, 1972). Whatever aspect of the wave is chosen, trials are the elements of the sample space, and designation of the criterion aspect is statistical: On a given trial, one might obtain any one of the following measures—the mean value of amplitude of an evoked component during a particular time segment, the difference between mean values of amplitudes during two time segments, the mean slope of a wave during some interval, and so on. Let us assume for purposes of the following discussion that mean component amplitude, *A*, during a single, predefined time interval is utilized.

2. In a *prebaseline* observation period, the mean value, $\bar{A}$, of A is obtained over repeated trials.[1] It is typically useful to collect and store the distribution of A if the necessary data storage facility is available. The subject can be run for about 2–5 days to allow observation of the stability of $\bar{A}$. When the investigator is satisfied that $\bar{A}$ is not fluctuating intolerably, a choice is made of a defined criterion. Often the criterion used has been an A value 1 standard deviation (SD) from $\bar{A}$ in a single, prespecified direction. For purposes of ruling out that any ultimately obtained outcomes are due to nonassociative or noncontingent and unconditional reinforcement effects, it has been convenient to use a bidirectional control design (Black, 1972) in which some subjects are rewarded for increasing A and others for decreasing A, or in which within-subject task reversals are called for in consecutive time periods.[2] Criteria defined as functions of SD (such as +1SD, +.5SD,

[1] $\bar{A}$ is often actually a mean of means since *A* may be a mean over milliseconds on one trial. $\bar{A}$, however, is the mean over trials.

[2] There is of course no a priori reason to restrict the direction of the conditioned change; e.g., it may be desireable for some purposes to reward both $A = \bar{A} + 1SD$ and $A = \bar{A} - 1SD$ in single sessions so as to develop a bimodal distribution of A. Appropriate controls would have to be designed.

−.8SD) are convenient because the theoretically expected (or a priori) proportion of criterion responses due to chance factors is readily available from tables of the normal distribution. If the assumption of a normal distribution is not warranted, percentiles can be determined.

3. Usually, a *baseline* period of about 5–10 days is run in which the chosen reinforcement contingency (such as $A = \overline{A} + 1SD$) is applied to trialwise *A* values. The subject is not contingently rewarded for criterion responses in *baseline*, but a record of them is kept so that the investigator can validate the theoretical expectation of prebaseline distribution data. It may be desirable to give random (noncontingent) reinforcements during *baseline* at a rate related to the proportion of operant successes expected later in training so that *(a)* a further control for noncontingent reinforcement effects is available, and *(b)* the transition from baseline to training periods will involve only changes restricted to the reinforcement *contingency*, rather than to state changes and contrast effects which otherwise might occur (as discussed by Rosenfeld and Hetzler, 1973a, b) if the subject were abruptly shifted from nonreward to contingent-reward conditions.

The subject is now put into *training;* the reinforcement contingency is put into effect. This may last 2–30 days, depending upon task difficulty (see Figures 15.1, 15.2). The subject can now be given *reversal training* (if he has been rewarded for $A = \overline{A} + 1SD$, now he is rewarded

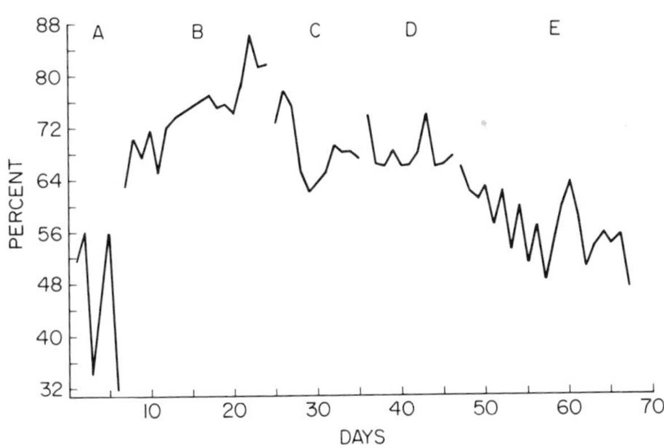

Figure 15.1 Percent successful responses as a function of training days in various conditions for one rat in the Rosenfeld *et al.* (1974) study. Rat was rewarded for increasing amplitude of evoked component in B–D, and extinguished in E. A is baseline data; the a priori reinforcement probability was 50%. The intensity of the evoking flash was manipulated by training the rat to press one of two bars following the neural operant. The two bars were at different distances from the flasher. In B, the rat was trained on the first bar. In C, it was switched to the second bar and, in D, it was returned to the first bar. Performance seemed unrelated to these manipulations.

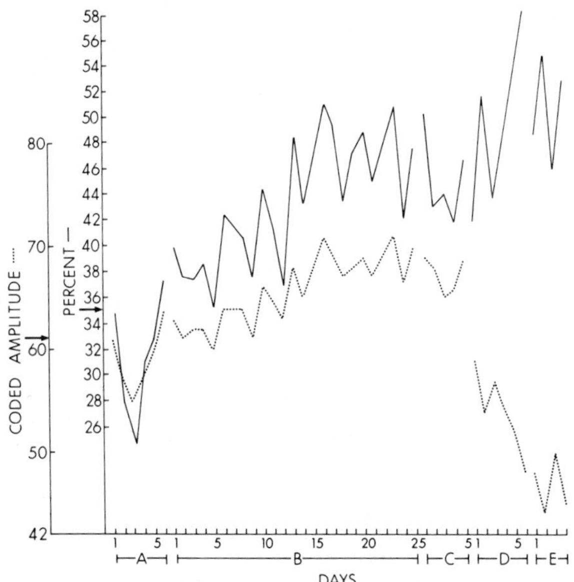

Figure 15.2 Conditioning of visual cortical potentials evoked by optic chiasm shocks in total darkness. Percent successful responses (continuous curve) and computer-coded values of evoked amplitude differences, prestimulus-to-peak (dotted line), as a function of training days for one rat in Hetzler (1977). The arrows denote the a priori reinforcement probability (35%) and mean coded amplitude value from *prebaseline* (61) on the Percent and Coded Amplitude ordinates, respectively. A is data from *baseline* period during which 35% of trials were reinforced randomly and noncontingently. In B, animal was contingently reinforced for evoked components of increased size. In C and thereafter, the intertrial interval was made to randomly vary; it was regular in A and B. In D, the animal was given the first shaping phase of *reversal training*; it was reinforced for producing smaller amplitudes of 35% a priori probability based on the distribution of amplitudes collected in C. In E, the final *reversal training* was imposed; the rat was rewarded for producing small amplitudes of 35% a priori probability, based on the *baseline* distribution. [From J. Rosenfeld, B. Hetzler, P. Birkel, R. Kowatch, & D. Antoinetti, "Operant conditioned potentials, centrally evoked at random intervals," in *Behavioral Biology*, 1976, *16*(3), 312.]

for $A = \bar{A} - 1SD$), or *extinction* which involves the reimposition of *baseline* or similar conditions.

4. The evaluation of performance could involve any subset of the following comparisons: $\bar{A}_b$ in *baseline* versus $\bar{A}_t$ in *training;* the proportion of $A = \bar{A}_b = 1SD$ responses in *baseline* versus the proportion in training; similar measures for *training* versus *extinction;* or similar measures for subjects in an $A\text{-}\bar{A} + 1SD$ contingency versus scores of subjects in an $A = \bar{A} - 1SD$ contingency. Training proportions could alternatively be compared with the theoretically expected a priori values assuming a normal distribution and no learning.

Concluding Remarks

Using variants of the above procedures, successful operant-controlled evoked potential features have been reported by the following workers: Fox and Rudell (1968, 1970); Hetzler (1977); Rosenfeld and Fox (1971, 1972b); Rosenfeld and Hetzler (1973a, b); Rosenfeld, Hetzler, and Kosnik (1974); Rosenfeld and Owen (1972); Rosenfeld, Rudell, and Fox (1969); Rudell (1970); Rudell and Fox (1972). Reviews have been provided by Fox (1970); Rosenfeld (1974); Rosenfeld and Rudell (in press); Walker, (1974).

AIMS OF OPERANTLY CONTROLLING EVOKED POTENTIALS

Historical Perspective

The initial idea for operantly conditioning evoked potentials is attributed to S. S. Fox. His reasons for initiating the program are best understood in terms of certain directions in which physiological psychology seemed to be going during the period 1960–1968. At that time, often for reasons pertaining to "the state of the art," evoked macropotentials were popular neural events to use as dependent variables or correlates in behavioral experiments. Fox and Rudell (1968) reviewed this neural correlates literature critically, noting that an investigator's desire to see reliable changes in evoked responses might be better served by explicitly reinforcing such changes rather than by directly manipulating behavior and hoping for robust evoked-potential correlates. Although this suggestion has had considerable empirical support[3] in the last several years, the interpretation of the new data generated new problems of a logical nature: Fox (1970) suggested that the application of the reinforcement contingency to the neural event was tantamount to manipulating the neural event as an independent variable. It followed that other (behavioral or physiological) events observed in consequence could be interpreted as causally dependent effects. Thus, one might hope to obtain a neural *code* for behavior by listing relations of other events with operantly reinforced evoked-potential changes.

[3] The present writer agrees with Fox's often-expressed personal communication that, apart from gross manipulations involving surgical, pharmacological, and electrical intervention, the only behavioral method of producing highly *specific* evoked potential effects of *appreciable magnitude* is the operant conditioning method, and the only other behavioral correlate of *large* evoked potential effects is sleep state.

The difficulty in the above argument is that in operant-evoked-potential conditioning, the evoked potential is *not*, in fact, the variable independently manipulated by the experimenter. The *reinforcement contingency* is directly manipulated.[4] Thus, whether one explicitly reinforces behavior and also observes simultaneous electrophysiology, or whether one explicitly reinforces electrophysiology and also observes behavioral concommitants, the behavioral and the electrophysiological events remain correlates of each other. It is, then, illogical to infer causalities or representations or codes from the correlations.

The reservations about coding interpretations just given naturally lead to a rejection of the notion that a translational view of neural coding is the goal of the operant neural conditioning methodology. Fox (1970) suggests instead that there are two other aspects of coding that should be emphasized: *(a)* One may not learn the behavioral translation of a conditionable neural event, but one does quickly *identify* an event that, because of its response to psychological manipulations (i.e., the reinforcement contingency), must be a "candidate code" for a psychological event; and *(b)* one can learn the internal rules of the candidate code without a translation. One can learn, for example, whether or not neighboring components of evoked potentials can vary independently by directly rewarding independent alterations of neighboring waves.

These aims of the technique may be easily justified as a function of investigators' creativities. Rose, Norman, Naifeh, and Collins (1974), for example, in one of the most original and important applications of evoked potential conditioning that come to mind, used the methodology to determine the learning capacities of neonatal kittens. This important developmental question previously had not been adequately answered because the motor repertoire normally employed in previously available performance assessment procedures undergoes rapid (daily) changes in such subjects. To show learning capacity, the specific act performed is irrelevant; Rose *et al.* (1974) were most content to operantly condition evoked potentials even in the absence of knowledge about what the conditioned changes represented.

Recent Directions: The Mediation Issue and Functional Significance

The writer's aims in conditioning evoked potentials have had a different emphasis from that just described. Our laboratory has been con-

[4] This point was originally provided the author by John Platt of McMaster University, Hamilton, Ontario, Canada.

cerned mainly with two aspects of operantly conditioned evoked potentials: First, we have been concerned with establishing that evoked potential conditioning is not a trivial phenomenon; second, we have been concerned with identifying uses to which the phenomenon can be put.

It should be immediately obvious that these two issues are closely related, as we have discussed elsewhere (Rosenfeld, 1974; Rosenfeld & Rudell, in press). The issue of triviality arises from the question of how evoked potential conditioning is mediated, and it is obvious that what one can do with evoked potential conditioning depends on the nature of the phenomenon's mediation. A brief analysis of the notions of mediation and triviality is in order at this point.[5]

To say that an event is mediated is to say that the subject controls it secondarily. It changes not because the subject controls it directly but because it varies in consequence of the subject's controlling some other (primary) phenomenon. What the experimenter explicitly reinforces may not even be directly perceivable to the subject. A convenient illustration is drawn from the field of cardiovascular biofeedback discussed elsewhere in this volume: A subject rewarded for increasing heart rate might, if not properly constrained, learn to do so by running. The heart rate would change in consequence of running, but one could clearly infer that it was the control of the skeletal leg musculature the subject was directly or primarily learning, and the heart rate changed secondarily. The question of primary mediation soon leads to a difficult philosophical obstacle, and we do not yet possess the means of dealing with it. One might discover that X is mediated by Y, and Y by Z, and so on—but ultimately one wants to identify, and is eluded by, the primary phenomenon. Thus we pose the question: What mediates spurious heart rate control? Muscular control. How does the subject learn to control his muscles? By learning to control impulse patterns in the lower motor neurons innervating the muscles. How does he learn to control these? By controlling his upper motor neurons. And so on, until one encounters elusive notions such as willpower, mind, intention, or internal command. These are infered constructs, still in search of good hypothetical physiological substrates.

Obviously, much useful research has proceeded in broad areas of learning and physiology, even though there has been no identification of the primary mediators of behavior. This is because there are other

[5] It is applied here to evoked potential conditioning but it is relevant in any operant situation, particularly those involving behaviors not usually regarded as voluntary, such as autonomic phenomena and spontaneous electroencephalographic events.

things worth knowing about. We may not know the identity of the primary mediator of operant running behavior, but we may simply need to know the laws that relate firing patterns of upper and lower motor neurons during running. This question could be straightforwardly answered in the absence of knowledge about primary mediation.

The above insights lead to a notion of trivial mediation, as well as a revaluation of the relevance of trivial mediation when it does occur: If the control of operant *X* is mediated by *Y*, the mediation of *X* by *Y* is trivial only if the needs of the investigation are ill served by the knowledge and fact of *XY* mediation. Several situations (some real, some hypothetical) may be adduced to illustrate this notion, which actually has several levels of interpretation. To approach these situations, we may consider an unrestrained subject who is being rewarded for generating, let us say, increased values of a certain component amplitude of a photic cortical-evoked potential. The underlying mediation of this often utilized potential could involve any one or more of the following.

Orientation

Clearly, a subject could arrange for larger photic cortical responses by controlling orientation to the light source, eye closures, pupil size, and so on.

Cross-Modality Influences

In view of the demonstrations by Rosenfeld and Fox (1972a) and Megirian, Buresova, Bures, and Dimond (1974) that somatosensory feedback from discrete voluntary (skeletal muscular) movements is directly represented in phasic cortical macropotential activity, the possibility arises that subjects change flash-evoked cortical potentials by learning to make discrete movements whose evoked responses add to the evaluated record in such a way as to satisfy the reinforcement contingency. By *phasic* activity, we imply activity of short duration. In this case, there must be some kind of signal in the situation that cues the subject to generate the discrete movement so that its feedback will be appropriately timelocked to the criterion segment. We note in passing that, in the operant-evoked potential conditioning situation most extensively employed to date, the cue can be a regular intertrial interval or the evoking stimulus itself.

It has also been shown that tonic or long-enduring macropotential phenomena may be associated with voluntary movement (Vaughn, Costa, & Ritter, 1968). As noted in the first section of this chapter, it is possible to rule out direct, steady potential mediation by programming a peak-to-peak or "difference" contingency. However, it is not only intuitively reasonable that even peak-to-peak measures of evoked potentials may depend on the cortical steady potential level but, in fact, correlations of such steady potentials and evoked potentials are not uncommon (Donald & Goff, 1973; McAdam, 1969). This is especially important in view of the fact that steady potentials have been operantly conditioned (Rosen, Loiselle, & Stamm, 1973). Of course, it may be that peak-to-peak evoked components and steady potentials may covary to the extent that both have been related to motivational, emotional, and arousal processes. These are tonic states, possibly triggerable by one or a series of discrete voluntary movements, or by a voluntarily maintained state of muscular contraction. It is also a logical possibility that tonic muscular contraction could be *directly* represented in evoked components. Such mediation could be quite subtle, though not necessarily trivial as will be argued in the next section.

Internal States Independent of the Skeletal Musculature

Elsewhere in this volume, operant control of autonomic nervous system processes is discussed at length. There is considerable evidence of such control, despite recent difficulties (Shapiro, 1973), and it must be considered at least a logical possibility that operant control of evoked potentials is mediated by operant control of the central representation of autonomic processes.

Finally, it is intuitively reasonable, though perhaps impossible to document, that controlled neural events represent purely mentalistic phenomena—imagination, mood, or will.

The Mediation Issue: Conclusions

The hypothetical list of conditioned evoked potential mediators just reviewed may or may not include trivial mediators, and the triviality or nontriviality of the mediation may or may not be important depending upon the aims of the conditioners. What might these aims be?

Clinical

If the purpose of some convenient form of operant neural conditioning is to relieve a clinical condition and if the paradigm succeeds, there should be no concern about possible trivial mediation. One may, of course, be interested in the mediation. It could be learned, for example, that flash-evoked potential conditioning alleviates nearsightedness, and that the explicit changes in brain waves are secondarily mediated by a hypothetical relation between visual potentials and eye muscle activity. If the relation was not previously known, the finding is not trivial in any sense. If the relation was previously known, its roundabout rediscovery through neural conditioning would be trivial, but the demonstration could still have practical relevance. This would certainly be true if it were more convenient to condition visual-evoked potentials than eye muscles.

Identification of Novel Laws

To pursue the previous example from a different perspective, suppose a general relation between eye muscle state and photic-evoked potential amplitude were known, but details about the relation were not available. Any new law relating some descriptor of the eye musculature and photic-evoked potential amplitude would be of interest and, therefore, not trivial. How the neural conditioning process is suited to elucidating such conventional, translational codes has been discussed elsewhere (Rosenfeld & Rudell, in press). Briefly, a subject's being operantly conditioned for altering photic-evoked potential amplitudes might find (through standard, Thorndikian trial and error) that previously unsuspected combinations of eye muscle contractions mediate criterion-reaching evoked responses. The subject, in other words, writes the equation for the investigator through his behavior. Clearly, in this hypothetical example there is peripheral mediation of central events, but it is hardly trivial.

Identification of Novel Events

The major recent focus of much operant neural conditioning (including evoked potential conditioning) has been to rule out mediation of control through simple motor processes or through utilization of previously known relations. As will be reviewed in the next section of this chapter, the evidennce is now clear that operant conditioning of sensory-evoked potentials can occur in the proven simultaneous absence of orientation factors and cross-modality influences involving discrete voluntary movements. We have also, in this work, ruled out the direct contribution of a single or summating series of steady potentials (related to tonic or phasic motor events or to nonmotor events) by utilizing a prestimulus baseline-to-peak reinforcement contingency (see the first section in this chapter). Our aim in this research has been to show that operant control of evoked potentials involves a class of events that, even if mediated by other events, constitutes a previously undemonstrated set of phenomena with possibly new applications. To satisfy this aim, it has been necessary for us to rule out orientation and movement factors as potential mediators. For our purpose, in other words, mediation via orientation and discrete movement would have been trivial. Assuming the evidence that operant control of evoked potentials does not involve such trivial mediation, what events might, in fact, be involved and what are the implications in each case?

As noted briefly earlier, it remains possible that operant-conditioned evoked potentials represent, or are mediated by, motor processes (command or somatosensory) in some extremely complex and subtle way. It may be that a particular amplitude of a potential in visual cortex is a highly integrated representation of the tonic state of a large set of muscles. This set could be permanent or it might have a rotating membership. The integration could be direct or it could be a secondary result of the state of reticular activation associated with the particular muscular tonus.

If the representation is not too complex, it may be discoverable. In this case, the initial operant conditioning demonstration would have had the important function of originally suggesting the existence of the new phenomenon.[6] Obviously, the identification of a new neural event and the general nature of its representation of other physiological events is of potential importance. The implication in this case is that a new descriptor of a set of physiological processes would be available. It may be desirable to control these processes all at once. For example, suppose the motor processes are those occurring in head muscles associated with tension headache, or suppose they represent the eye musculature associated with some pathology in vision, as in the previous example. The identification of novel representation of such states invites clinical investigation. In addition, to the extent that evoked potentials represent sensory or perceptual events, their control through novel mechanisms may point to novel methods of changing perception. Rosenfeld and Rudell (in press) have discussed such an approach in a proposal for the neural biofeedback control of pain perception.

From a different point of view, revelation of new relationships is the foundation of the scientific method, whether or not the immediate practical consequences are obvious.

[6] It may be reasonably said that this situation involves finding new relations (laws) rather than new phenomena. This is a semantic issue. A neural event is considered a *novel event* to the extent that it can be shown to have a relation with some other phenomenon, and that the relation was previously unknown and unsuspected. If a general relation is known, the details of the relation remaining to be elucidated comprise potential *novel laws* as discussed in the previous section.

It is, of course, possible that the mediating motor processes could be so complexly related to the neural operant that the relationship might never be forthcoming. This possibility is not without application either. First, as we have detailed elsewhere (Rosenfeld & Rudell, in press), self-controlled neural activity of this kind could be developed as a new means of communication. Second, it can be fairly stated that, if the control of neural events can be learned and this learning is not a simple transformed representation of other learning, then new laws of learning may obtain from a new data base of neural operants. A similar notion is treated in depth by other discussions of the possibility that different behavior systems may be regulated by different laws (Seligman, 1970), and alone provides a good rationale for initiating a program of parametric studies of operant neural control. A third possible application, closely related to the second, has already been described in the preceding section—the successful attempt of Rose *et al.* (1974) to demonstrate learning in neonatal kittens. As already noted, to use evoked potentials as the only available operant with which to assess neonatal learning capacity, one need have no knowledge about the mediation, whether or not the nature of the mediation was ever forthcoming.

What uses are there for operant-controlled evoked potentials, unmediated by motor events of any kind? We have considered earlier the possibility that these could represent autonomic processes, emotional conditions, mental state, activity level, mood, imagery, and so on. The division of such novel representations into discoverable and complex (obscure) categories, as was suggested earlier regarding subtle motor mediation, leads to parallel implications.

If one can discover novel representations of internal autonomic and psychological events, then various clinical possibilities become obvious. In the case of purely mentalistic mediation, not only is there the possibility of direct control of mental states but, more fundamentally, there arises for the first time the possibility that physical manifestations of these events may be even observed.

If the representations of nonmotor, internal states in conditioned evoked potentials are never ultimately clarified, there are still the same applications of the phenomena as there were in the case of unclarified, subtle motor mediation. Thus, it may be still possible to use such phenomena as elements in a new communication method (Rosenfeld & Rudell, in press). It may also be possible to get at new laws of learning. These could be developmental (as in Rose *et al.*, 1974), anatomical (e.g., one could discover "placticity loci," as discussed by Rosenfeld and Rudell, in press), behavioral (e.g., pertaining to the effect of a partial reinforcement schedule), and so on.

Mixed Mediation

Finally, it is noted that in dealing with the various types of possible mediation (trivial and otherwise), this chapter may give the impression that these different mediators do not typically coexist. On the contrary, among the most difficult aspects of interepretation in operant conditioning of neural events is the logical possibility, and even likelihood, that different kinds of mediation can occur concurrently and/or consecutively. As the following review of recent work shows, a convincing demonstration of novel mediation demands the most stringent, multiple control procedures.

REVIEW OF RECENT STUDIES

In order to rule out mediation of evoked potential control via *(1)* orientation, *(2)* discrete movement with phasic consequences, and *(3)* steady potential processes, it is necessary to have a demonstration in which all possible contributors to the above mediating events are *simultaneously* obviated by experimental control. Such control would involve the following restrictions.

Receptor orientation is eliminated by preventing the subject from changing orientation relative to the evoking stimulus. As noted earlier, when it is desired that only a single evoked component change, steady potential additions into a record may be eliminated by applying the reinforcement contingency to the *difference* between an average segment of prestimulus baseline and the criterion segment of interest. Phasic macropotential effects due to discrete movements are eliminated by removing the timing cues necessary for subjects to timelock such events. In particular, the criterion segment latency must be less than reaction time (to the evoking stimulus) and, *simultaneously*, the interstimulus interval (intertrial interval) must be impossible for the subject to accurately predict. This can be accomplished by making it indefinitely long or, more conveniently, by making it random with mean, T, varying between limits T_{min} and T_{max} such that $T_{\text{max}} - T_{\text{min}}$ is very much longer than the duration of a suspected, phasic movement-evoked potential. If the "difference" contingency just described is simultaneously in effect, then $T_{\text{max}} - T_{\text{min}}$ may be as short as the latency of the criterion segment.

In studies published to date, some of these controls have been used yielding encouraging results, but until the unpublished work to be described below was done, there was no single study in which all necessary constraints were applied. In the earlier reports, the attempt to minimize orientation effects in the control of photic-evoked potentials consisted of using operant chambers with highly reflective white walls and a stroboscopic flash. It was typically observed that, with the reinforcement contingency applied to late components, the early components (more expected to reflect stimulus intensity effects) were not affected (Fox & Rudell, 1968, 1970; Rosenfeld & Owen, 1972; Rosenfeld *et al.*, 1974). Consistent with this finding was the typically observed independence of conditioned visual cortical and simultaneously recorded lateral geniculate responses (Rosenfeld and Owen, 1972; Rudell, 1970), although we have previously noted that these data are moot because the connections of the geniculate placements to the cortical sites were not adequately defined (Rosenfeld & Rudell, in press; Rosenfeld *et al.*, 1974). Rudell and Fox (1972) showed that several evoked components reflected independently manipulated light intensity in one situation, but only one prespecified component changed as required by the reinforcement contingency applied in a conditioning situation. This demonstration, however, is open to the criticism that the laws for intensity representation in evoked potentials may change from situation to situation. (This issue is discussed further in Rosenfeld and Rudell, in press.)

In other studies, orientation was directly controlled. Rudell (1970) and Rosenfeld *et al.* (1969) fixed the subjects' positions with respect to evoking stimuli without disrupting operant conditioning. Rosenfeld *et al.* (1974) explicitly manipulated stimulus intensity, and then later removed the control while explicitly monitoring orientation. These manipulations showed an absence of positive relations between intensity and reinforced component amplitude (see Figure 15.1). Rudell (described in Rosenfeld and Rudell, in press) conditioned visual potentials evoked by electrical stimulation of the optic radiations.

In all of the studies thus far described in this section, various control procedures were missing: Only Rosenfeld and Owen (1972) used a random interstimulus interval; only Rudell and Fox (1972) conditioned a component of short latency; only Rosenfeld *et al.* (1969) and Rudell and Fox (1972) used a "difference" contingency.

A doctoral thesis now in progress in our laboratory (Hetzler, 1977) is being devoted to a parametric study of evoked potential conditioning with all possible control procedures in effect. In particular, the stimulus is a .3-millisecond biphasic pulse to the optic chiasm and the rat is run in total darkness after having been dark-adapted for 12 hours. This manipulation rules out orientation factors. The evoked component in visual cortex having a peak at 70 milliseconds (SC = 55–85 milliseconds) is reinforced with lateral hypothalamic brain stimulation. A "difference" contingency is in effect such that successful re-

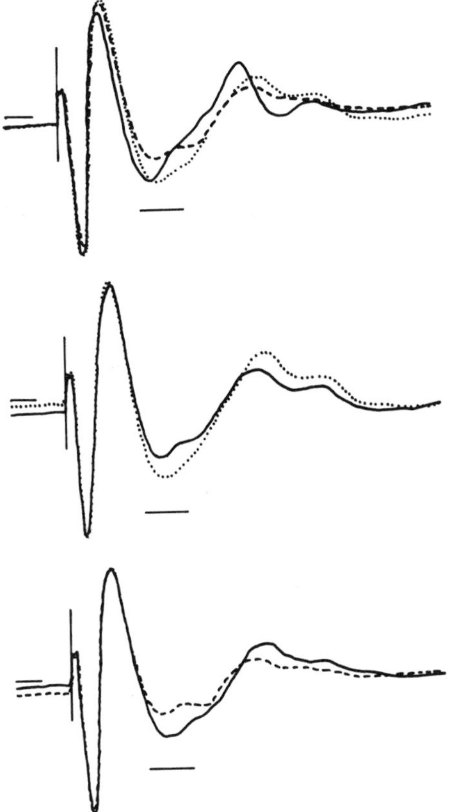

Figure 15.3 Average evoked potentials from rat whose performance is summarized in preceding figure. The horizontal lines at left of traces give DC level calibrations and represent 20 milliseconds. The horizontal lines under potentials show location of criterion segment from which the entire (40 milliseconds) prestimulus EEG level average is subtracted to yield the evaluated score. Vertical lines show location of .3-millisecond stimulus. Upper panel: superimposed averaged evoked potentials (all 500 trials of 1 representative day) from *baseline* (continuous line), increased amplitude *training* (dotted line), and *reversal training* (dashed line). Middle panel: superimposed successful (dotted line; N=252) and unsuccessful (continuous line; N = 248) averages from best day of *training* of increased amplitudes; (Day 1 of C, Figure 15.1). Bottom panel: superimposed successful (dashed line; N = 272) and unsuccessful (continuous line; N = 228) averages from best day of *reversal training;* (Day 2 of E, Figure 15.1). The operant changes are mostly confined to the later components.

sponses (of a priori probabilities = .35) are defined for the difference between the mean prestimulus EEG level (40 milliseconds) and the criterion segment. A random intertrial interval varying between 3500 and 4900 milliseconds is also utilized. To date, two rats have been successfully trained—one to increase the criterion differences and one to decrease them—with all of the above-described constraints in effect. One rat has additionally been given *reversal training* as shown in Figures 15.2 and 15.3.

It is noted that the recent report of Megirian, Buresova, and Bures (1974), showing that discrete movements evoke potentials in rat sensorimotor cortex but *not in rat visual cortex*, probably renders our random interval manipulation superfluous. Tonic motor effects on visual cortical potentials, however, were reported; these were quite gross. The specific localization of operant changes seen in Figure 15.3 (and usually reported by evoked potential conditioners) in conjunction with the conditioning effect's survival under simultaneous, multiple, stringent control procedures makes a persuasive case that operant control of evoked potentials is indeed a novel phenomenon.

REFERENCES

Black, A. H. The operant conditioning of central nervous system activity. In G. H. Bower (Ed.), *The psychology of learning and motivation.* New York: Academic Press, 1972.

Donald, M. W., & Goff, W. R. Contingent negative variation and sensory evoked responses. *Electroencephalography and Clinical Neurophysiology*, 1973, *33 (Suppl. 3)*, 109–117.

Fox, S. S. Evoked potential, coding, and behavior. In F. O. Schmitt (Ed.), *The neurosciences second study program.* New York: Rockefeller University Press, 1970.

Fox, S. S., & Rudell, A. P. Operant controlled neural event: Formal and systematic approach to electrical coding of behavior in brain. *Science*, 1968, *162*, 1299.

Fox, S. S., & Rudell, A. P. The operant controlled neural event: Functional independence in behavioral coding by early and late components of the visual cortical evoked response in cats. *Journal of Neurophysiology*, 1970, *33*, 548.

Hetzler, B. E. Instrumental conditioning of centrally evoked visual cortical macropotentials: A study of the influences on and significance of late component modification. Unpublished doctoral dissertation, Northwestern University, Evanston, Ill., 1977.

Megirian, D., Buresova, O., & Bures, J. Skilled forelimb movements and visually evoked potentials in rats. *Brain Research*, *66*, 103–112, 1974.

Megirian, D., Buresova, O., Bures, J., & Dimond, S. Electrophysiological correlates of discrete forelimb movements in rats. *Electroencephalography and Clinical Neurophysiology*, 1974, *36*, 131–139.

McAdam, D. W. Increases in CNS excitability during negative cortical slow potentials in man. *Electroencephalography and Clinical Neurophysiology*, 1969, *26*, 216–219.

Rose, G. H., Norman, R. J., Naifeh, K., & Collins, J. P. Placticity of visual evoked potentials in kittens demonstrated by operant conditioning, Manuscript submitted for publication, 1974.

Rosen, S. C., Loiselle, D. L., & Stamm, J. Operant conditioning of cortical steady potential shifts in monkeys. Paper read at 3rd Annual Meeting, Society for Neuroscience, San Diego, California, 1973.

Rosenfeld, J. P. Evoked potential conditioning in neuroscience research. In M. Chase (Ed.), *Operant conditioning of the electrical activity of the brain. Perspectives in the brain sciences,* Vol. 20 Los Angeles, Cal.: Brain Information Service, Brain Research Institute, UCLA, 1974.

Rosenfeld, J. P., & Fox, S. S. Operant control of a brain potential evoked by a behavior. *Physiology and Behavior,* 1971, *7,* 489–494.

Rosenfeld, J. P., & Fox, S. S. Movement-related macropotentials in cat cortex. *Electroencephalography and Clinical Neurophysiology,* 1972, *32,* 75–80. (a)

Rosenfeld, J. P., & Fox, S. S. Sequential representation of voluntary movement in cortical macropotential: Direct control of behavior by operant conditioning of wave amplitude. *Journal of Neurophysiology,* 1972, *35,* 879–891. (b)

Rosenfeld, J. P., & Hetzler, B. E. Discrimination versus conditioning of photic cortical potentials. *Physiology and Behavior,* 1973, *11,* 753–766. (a)

Rosenfeld, J. P., & Hetzler, B. E. Operant controlled evoked responses: Discrimination of conditioned and normally occurring components. *Science,* 1973, *181,* 767–770. (b)

Rosenfeld, J. P., Hetzler, B. E., & Kosnik, W. Operant photic evoked potential control unmediated by selective orientation. *Physiology and Behavior,* 1974, *13,* 479–482.

Rosenfeld, J. P., & Owen, R. L. Instrumental Conditioning of photic evoked potentials: Mechanisms and properties of late component modification. *Physiology and Behavior,* 1972, *9,* 851–858.

Rosenfeld, J. P., & Rudell, A. P. Mediation of operant controlled neural activity. In D. Mustovsky (Ed.), *Behavior control and modification of physiological activity.* New York: Appleton, in press.

Rosenfeld, J. P., Rudell, A. P., & Fox, S. S. Operant control of neural events in humans. *Science,* 1969, *165,* 821–823.

Rudell, A. P. The operant conditioning of primary and secondary components in the visual evoked potential with measurement of collateral neural and behavioral activity. Unpublished doctoral dissertation, University of Iowa, Iowa City, 1970.

Rudell, A. P., & Fox, S. S. Operant controlled neural event: Functional bioelectric coding in primary components of cortical evoked response in cat brain. *Journal of Neurophysiology,* 1972, *35,* 892–902.

Seligman, M. E. P. On the generality of the laws of learning. *Psychological Review,* 1970, *77,* 406–418.

Shapiro, D. Preface. In D. Shapiro, T. X. Barber, L. V. DiCara, J. Kamiya, N. E. Miller, & J. Stoyra (Eds.), *Biofeedback and self-control 1972.* Chicago: Aldine, 1973. Pp. v–xii.

Vaughan, H. G., Jr., Costa, L. D., & Ritter, W. Topography of the human motor potential. *Electroencephalography and Clinical Neurophysiology,* 1968, *25,* 1–10.

Walker, D. W. Signs of information processing in photic evoked potentials. Pp. 145–212, 1974. In M. Chase (Ed.), *Operant conditioning of the electrical activity of the brain. Perspectives in the brain sciences,* Vol. 2. Los Angeles, Cal.: Brain Information Service, Brain Research Institute, UCLA, 1974.

16

Clinical Implications of EEG Biofeedback Training: A Critical Appraisal*

M. B. STERMAN
Sepulveda VA Hospital
and Departments of Anatomy
and Psychiatry, UCLA

Studies of feedback training with EEG patterns some 10 or 15 years ago helped pioneer the field we today know as biofeedback. In spite of its primacy in the area, relatively little has been accomplished in developing the potential clinical applications of this feedback modality. This is not due to lack of efforts in this regard, but, indeed, reflects both the difficulty and haphazardness that have characterized the subsequent research onslaught. The opportunity to attempt a critical appraisal of this research elicits mixed feelings. One can easily attack this sometimes questionable literature; however, it is necessary also to appreciate the shortcomings of clinical research in general and to be tolerant of mistakes associated with the launchings of a new field of investigation. With this in mind, I shall attempt to draw upon appropriate exemplary studies from the literature. Also, I will refer to our own experience whenever the context is appropriate.

* The research reported by the author here was supported by NIH-NINDS Grant 5 R01 NS10726 and by the Veterans Administration. Bibliographic aid was provided by the UCLA Brain Information Service, Brain Research Institute Publications Office. Also, the author wishes to acknowledge the assistance in this effort of his able associates L. R. Macdonald and I. Berntsen.

At the beginning of 1975 when the review was initiated, there were, in fact, relatively few published studies examining clinical applications of EEG biofeedback. To make matters worse, many of these confounded any attempt at objective evaluation by utilizing several different behavioral or biofeedback modalities in tandem. Alpha rhythm training was combined with autogenic training and progressive relaxation, EMG feedback, skin temperature feedback, and even feedback of other EEG patterns. The assumption is, one would guess, that we know all about the process of alpha rhythm biofeedback and its clinical benefits. This is by no means true. Indeed, if investigators continue this practice we may never achieve that desirable goal. Excusing this approach as a patient-oriented method is not acceptable, since the patient will best be served by a comprehensive understanding of both the phenomenon and its clinical utility. Accordingly, these studies cannot contribute to the objectives of this chapter.

In considering what is left of this literature, a useful point of departure is provided by the review of clinical applications of biofeedback training by Blanchard and Young (1974). These authors focused upon experimental procedures as a means of evaluating the handful of EEG biofeedback studies that met their criteria for review. With regard to the more "popular" EEG rhythms, they concluded: "While the work on biofeedback training in producing high incidence of alpha activity in the EEG is relatively old and has received much publicity, the evidence for clinical efficacy of training to produce alpha or theta is very poor" (p. 586). There has been no study published since this review which would lead one to disagree with their conclusion.

This does not imply that clinical benefits cannot be derived from alpha or theta training. Clinical research is difficult because people do not live in cages and the world of man is not a shuttle box. Encephalization means more in this case than merely the addition of several billion neurons. Moreover, people become sick for many different reasons and can manifest illness in many different ways. For these reasons, it is necessary for research in this area to be most carefully conceived and executed. Yet, because of its potential relevance and the excitement a new approach always engenders, biofeedback has attracted the interest of investigators with diverse backgrounds for whom enthusiasm has often exceeded research judgment. We shall see later how this has affected the current literature. It should be pointed out, also, that alpha and theta frequencies are not the only significant spontaneous EEG patterns amenable to biofeedback study. In particular, higher frequency rhythmic activity from central cortex has also been studied extensively.

While Blanchard and Young dealt with research design, the broad nature of their review precluded a detailed evaluation of other factors affecting the validity of EEG biofeedback research. For example, methods of signal detection and criteria for reward were not considered. Additionally, their evaluation of clinical response was tabular, and did not deal with the critical question of correlation between these measurements and responses acquired through biofeedback training. These issues will be the focus of the sections that follow.

SIGNAL DETECTION AND CRITERIA FOR REWARD

Selective detection of covert physiological patterns is the initial component of any biofeedback study. It is this detection that provides the criterion for contingent information or reward and, thereby, the basis for altered control of physiological activity. Accordingly, the accuracy of detection as well as the functional relevance of the signal component utilized is of prime importance. With an easily detected process, such as the heart beat, one must exclude movement, muscle, and electronic artifacts before deciding whether to trigger feedback on heart rate, variability, or some other aspect of the EKG configuration. With the EEG, the problem is far more complex. The variety of artifacts and transients that can invade the low-voltage, highly amplified EEG signal are such as to require serious attention. Direct visulization of the trace on a polygraph is essential, at least in validating detection characteristics. Moreover, once the potential artifacts or other undesirable aspects of the signal are appreciated, the detection system must be equipped with circuits that automatically exclude them from the feedback loop. Without these safeguards, validity and reliability in signal detection cannot be assured.

Most studies to date have been concerned with the modification of rhythmic signals in the EEG, such as the alpha rhythm. These occur spontaneously as trains of electrical potential oscillations that fall in a particular frequency band, such as 8–13 Hz in the case of alpha. There are two basic methods for detecting these frequency trains. The time interval between waves, and therefore the frequency of the signal, can be measured by zero-crossing analysis. By determining a zero voltage level, the interval between crosses of this level for either positive or negative potential deviations can be measured to provide a digital representation of this analog signal. A second method utilizes tuned active band-pass filters. When properly designed, such filters are selectively activated by the occurrence of a particular frequency train in the EEG. Activation of such a filter can be used to operate a relay for providing reward. There may be very substantial differences in signal detection with these two methods, a fact that will be explored further below.

Functionally, the EEG trace can be considered in terms not only of frequency, but also amplitude, sequence, and topography. However, these components are not independent. For example, if one intends to study alpha activity, it is necessary to decide on the frequency band to be detected (that is, broad band, 8–13 Hz, or narrow band, e.g., 9–11 Hz), the amplitude at this frequency, the number of consecutive waveforms that constitute an appropriate train, and the brain area from which it will be recorded. Furthermore, it is desirable to know what the alpha feedback process is doing to other significant EEG components. Finally, to date, there is no basis for deciding upon the functional significance of any set of criteria chosen. Again, while these issues may appear to be highly technical, we shall never acquire the information necessary to efficiently apply EEG biofeedback in the clinical setting until they are dealt with scientifically.

Relatively few EEG biofeedback studies have seriously considered these issues in signal detection. Many investigators employ commercial biofeedback devices without the aid of concurrent polygraphic recording. Additionally, these devices are often designed without appreciation for the underlying physiology of the EEG and are, therefore, not equipped for evaluation of functional questions. Even when sophisticated equipment is utilized, the investigator may not be interested in, or familiar with, its functional characteristics. In a recent study of the treatment of headache with alpha feedback (McKenzie, Ehrisman, Montgomery, & Barnes, 1974), the detection and reward systems are described as follows:

> The two electrodes give us a single channel of information which is fed into an amplification system to increase the signal, to shape it, and to eliminate unwanted signals or noise. We then feed this signal into a filtering network which acts to divide the raw brain wave signal into four frequency bands. . . . These four channels are then fed into another "black box" which converts the signal into one suitable to drive a [visual] display [pp. 165–166].

A diagram provided shows two EEG leads, one apparently at the vertex and the other on the occipital area. Laterality is not specified. No mention is made of the filter frequency characteristics or of the amplitude and train duration criteria of alpha activity required for feedback. While these authors do record several EEG channels (locations unclear) and several frequencies other than alpha, mention is made only of occipital beta activity (13–25 Hz), which was negatively reinforced. Regardless of the outcome of this study, which will be discussed later, we have no precise idea of what EEG signal was being rewarded. Furthermore, any attempt to accurately replicate this study would require an elaborate letter to the authors.

One can contrast this with the report by O'Malley and Connors (1972) who studied the effect of unilateral alpha feedback training on visual-evoked potentials in dyslexia. The detection and reward system was described as follows:

> Grass gold disc electrodes were attached with active leads to the scalp at 01 and 02 with a ground at Fpz and referencing to bilateral mastoids (international 10–20 system). . . . For alpha conditioning experiments a NFI Neuro Analyzer Model 3001 was used containing three frequency analysis channels . . . with amplitudes of 6 db. The device also provided selective feedback logic controls for length of time alpha has to be present before feedback response was given (input duration), the minimum time between feedback responses (intertrial interval), and length of each feedback signal. For this set of experiments, input duration was set at 0.5 sec, intertrial interval at 2 sec, and length of feedback signal at approximately 0.5 sec. Input was from the Grass polygraph with the sensitivity set at 20μv/cm during conditioning trials. . . . The filters of the analyzers were set to read above 50% of maximum amplitudes. . . . A buzzer was used for feedback [p. 468].

In this case, we know clearly what was being rewarded and how to properly replicate the study. A significant increase in alpha time was obtained unilaterally, from the left (rewarded) hemisphere over a 5-day training period. Visual-evoked responses over this hemisphere were correspondingly increased, a finding consistent with the EEG asymmetry produced by the biofeedback regime. Unfortunately, this excellent experiment was carried out on one dyslexic adolescent, which indicates that the authors definitely should be the first to attempt replication.

Perhaps the most effective means of characterizing detection is to provide a diagram showing the response specifications of the system utilized. Several examples of such diagrams are shown in Figure 16.1 from Finley, Smith, and Etherton (1975) and Sterman, Macdonald, and Stone (1974), both of whom studied the effects of central cortical sensorimotor rhythm (SMR) training on epilepsy. The results of these and related studies will be discussed later.

If nothing else, it is hoped that this brief sample of problems in signal detection will draw the reader's attention to this important aspect of methodology. Before accepting any conclusions about the clin-

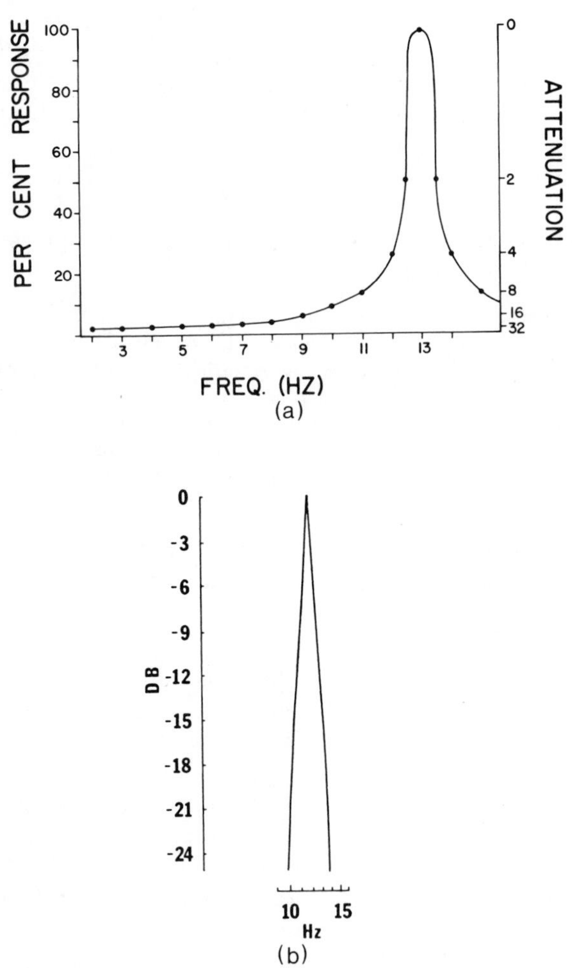

Figure 16.1 Frequency–response characteristics of two signal detection systems used in EEG biofeedback studies. The diagram at (a) shows symmetrical response curve of precision filter employed by Sterman *et al.*, (1974) to train central cortical 13-Hz activity in epileptics. The addition of an amplitude clipping circuit that rejected all signals above 40 μv exploited the inverse relationship between frequency and amplitude in the human EEG and assured limited rssponse in the 12–14-Hz band. A similar diagram is shown at (b) from Finley *et al.*, (1975). Here the effect of amplitude clipping on the sensorimotor rhythm filter is included and accounts for the extreme sharpness of the frequency–response curve.

ical implications of such studies, one should be sure that the author, at least, knew what signal was being rewarded.

RESPONSE ACQUISITION AND CLINICAL MANIFESTATIONS

The problem of response acquisition has been an area of controversy in EEG biofeedback research since its beginnings. Some of the problems mentioned above have definitely contributed to the confusion in this regard. While many studies claimed a trial-by-trial increase in alpha activity during feedback, similar to a learning curve, increases seldom exceed optimal baseline levels (Paskewitz & Orne, 1973), may be mediated by suppression of competing responses (Lynch *et al.*, 1974), and can be achieved, in some instances, with appropriate instructions in the absence of feedback (Beatty, 1972). This issue will be dealt with more thoroughly elsewhere in this text. For our part, we wish to point out that this is an unresolved area and that the controversy has developed primarily in laboratory studies utilizing blocks of consecutive training trials during one or, at most, several days of feedback sessions. Little has been written about acquisition with the long-term training model most appropriate in clinical applications of EEG feedback.

A typical treatment of this research parameter is provided by the previously mentioned study of alpha feedback and headache (McKenzie *et al.*, 1974). Data from seven tension headache subjects are presented as a series of 30-second pre–post samples of polygraphic tracings (Figure 16.2). Each figure is accompanied by a one-paragraph anecdotal case history and, for six of the seven, a sketchy review of the number of weekly headaches reported by the patient during a baseline week, at the end of training, and at several monthly intervals afterward. All of these patients are described as showing an increase in alpha rhythm activity after 10 feedback sessions, during a 5-week period, and all reported a marked and sustained reduction in headaches. These changes were sometimes associated with a decrease in the activity of frontalis and splenius capitis muscles. According to the authors, a control group of similar tension headache patients, who received taped instruction in relaxation exercise only, also showed a reduction in headaches. No data from these subjects are provided. However, the alpha feedback group was said to have earlier symptom reduction. Both of these treatments were more effective than any medication previously utilized in these cases (no data provided). One

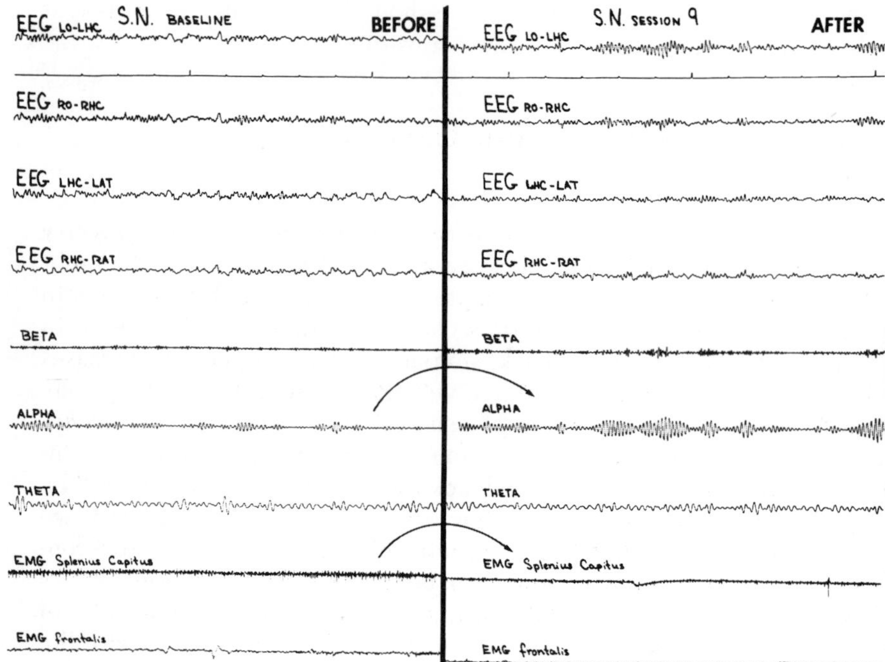

Figure 16.2 Data provided by McKenzie *et al.*, (1974) to demonstrate increase in alpha rhythm activity and decrease in EMG discharge resulting from nine alpha feedback sessions. The patient is described as a 31-year-old housewife whose headaches were reduced by this "treatment" from a baseline level of 55 hours per week to zero. No time or voltage calibrations are provided and the unusual EEG derivations utilized are not explained. Experience tells us that such a subject needs only to close her eyes (if that) to produce the "AFTER" pattern in the "BEFORE" recording. Such brief, unquantified samples of this labile EEG rhythm tell us nothing about the effects of EEG biofeedback training.

hopes that these patients did, indeed, benefit from the alpha feedback training, but since there are no adequate descriptive or quantitative data for the reader to evaluate objectively, we must take the authors' work on this count.

Several recent studies have explored the effects of EEG biofeedback training on sleep patterns in normal and insomniac subjects. Regestein, Buckland, and Pegram (1973) examined the effect of daytime alpha rhythm maintenance on subsequent sleep in normals. While the description and analysis of polygraphic sleep data are elaborate and sophisticated, perhaps reflecting the experience of the authors in this area, no methods or criteria for alpha rhythm detection or evaluation of response acquisition are provided. We are simply told that five subjects, who had previously demonstrated the ability to produce an average alpha percentage of 70 in another study, were provided with alpha and nonalpha (no other description given) EEG biofeedback practice on an experimental day during a week when their sleep was being monitored each night. On the night following the 12-hour day of alpha rhythm practice, a statistically significant decrease in total sleep time was obtained. No such effect was associated with the mysterious nonalpha practice or on the first night of sleep recording (a "first night effect" was indicated by a slight reduction in REM sleep time). The authors suggest that "production of high amounts of alpha rhythm does not appear to affect the discrete stages of sleep but may be associated with a slightly decreased sleep need." No EEG performance data are provided; however, it is stated that the amount of alpha produced per subject during the 12-hour experimental period did not correlate with total sleep time. While this is an interesting question and certainly worthy of study, reports such as this cannot provide meaningful answers.

In a preliminary report, Hauri (1976) compared the efficacy of EMG feedback, EMG plus EEG theta rhythm feedback, EEG sensorimotor rhythm (SMR) feedback, and standard medical procedures as treatment modalities in a large group of documented insomnia patients. Specific training criteria were established for each group involving a quantitative increase in the production of appropriate responses during a minimum of 10 laboratory training sessions. Effects on sleep were determined by pre–post comparisons of several measures derived from all-night sleep recording data and home sleep logs. This study is still in progress and, accordingly, detailed acquisition and clinical response characteristics are not yet available. It is clear, however, that the design of the study and methods of quantitative analysis utilized will yield interpretable results. The preliminary findings reported to date indicate that standard medical treatment (medications, advice, psychotherapy) produced no change in abnormal sleep patterns. EMG plus theta rhythm feedback gave very inconsistent results, apparently due to failure in theta acquisition, and was not recommended. Learned EMG control was not correlated with subjective or quantitative evidence of sleep improvement, but the author speculated that this approach might have utility for a restricted subgroup of insomniacs. Finally, SMR feedback was described as very promising, since quantitative improvements in sleep spindles were associated with significantly increased SMR during training sessions. Hauri reported that two out of five patients given SMR feedback showed no evidence of acquisition and no sleep improvement.

In several related studies completed earlier in our laboratory, similar findings were obtained with regard to SMR training and insomnia (Feinstein, Sterman, & Macdonald, 1974; Sterman, Feinstein, & Macdonald, 1975). Repeated, all-night sleep monitoring sessions provided for verification of sleep disturbance, and a prebiofeedback sleep baseline. Light and tone reward was given for production of central or occipital cortical EEG frequency trains of narrow band (±.5 Hz) 10, 13, or 15 Hz activity. Detection methods and reward criteria were specified. With the difficult requirements of such narrow band frequencies, it was found the 27% of our subjects had such low-voltage, unmodulated EEG characteristics as to be incapable of producing responses adequate for training. Of the subjects receiving 3 months of EEG biofeedback training (three 30-minute sessions per week), 50% did not demonstrate any significant acquisition of the rewarded EEG frequency. Those subjects who did demonstrate reliable increases showed several very different patterns of acquisition. Figure 16.3 shows changes in EEG activity both within and across training sessions in two insomniac subjects. One of these subjects showed a discrete and progressive increase in trained central cortical 13-Hz activity within, but not across, training sessions. The other showed minimal increase within each session, but a significant and progressive increase in the level of rewarded activity across the 3-month training period. It was noted, also, that subjects trained to produce 13-Hz activity showed a parallel increase in central 15-Hz rhythms and a decrease in central 10-Hz activity. Both subjects showed significant increase in spindle burst patterns during sleep in posttraining observations and both showed a significant improvement in sleep (Figure 16.4). Subjects who did not demonstrate any form of reliable increment showed no changes in either sleep EEG configuration or sleep patterning. Data from one such subject are shown in Figure 16.5. This insomniac patient was rewarded for occipital 10 Hz (alpha) and demonstrated a clear increase in this pattern within feedback sessions at the beginning of training. Thereafter, however, there was no further evidence of increment, and overall production was, in fact, decreased. Assumptions based exclusively on the initial response of this subject could have been very misleading.

This study demonstrated to us the importance of extended and careful assessment of EEG changes concurrent with training, and the utility of examining these in several different ways. The same extended evaluation of the clinical symptom under study, either progressively or through pre–post measurements, provides an essential basis for determining the significance of any observed clinical change.

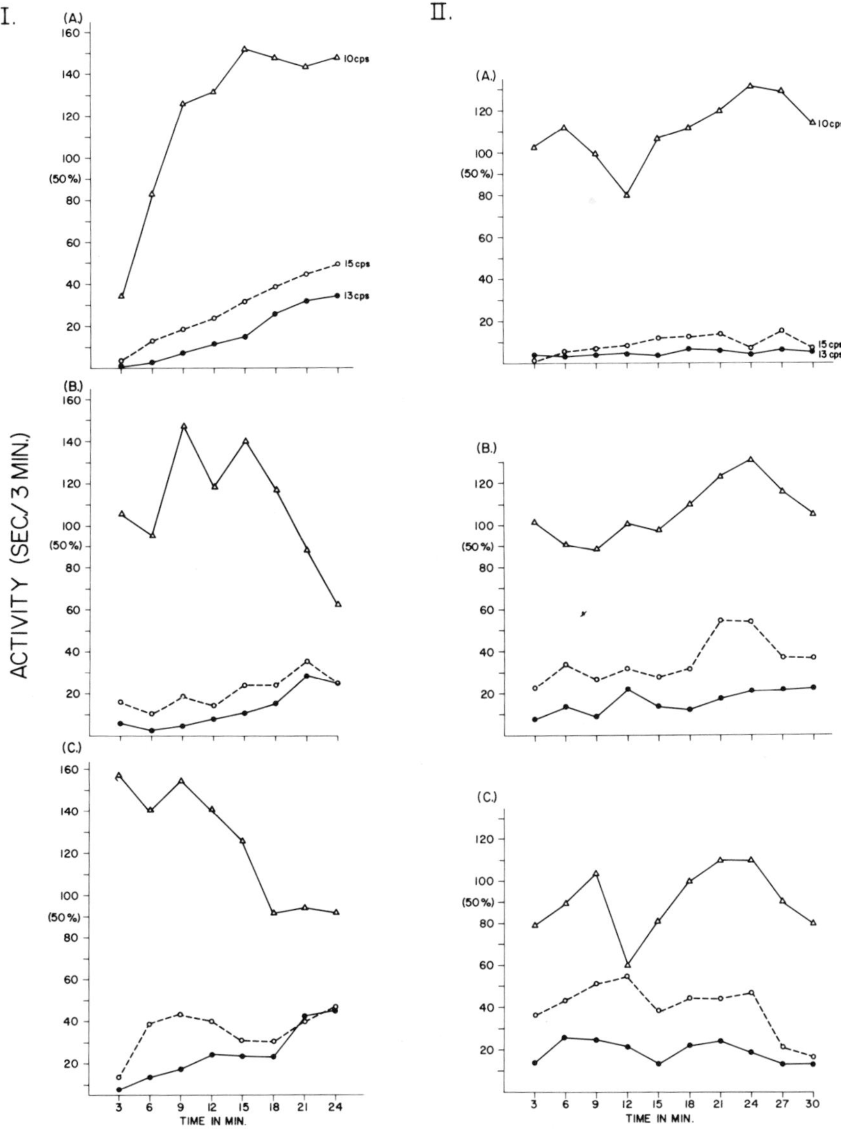

Figure 16.3 Two patterns of acquisition resulting from EEG biofeedback training of central cortical 13-Hz rhythmic activity (C3–T3). Both subjects were insomniacs provided with three 30-minute training sessions per week for 3 months. Graphs show rate of occurrence (percent time) of specified central 10, 13, and 15 Hz frequency trains in successive 3-minute epochs during the final training session of each month. The subject on the left (I) showed within-trial acquisition, but no increase in overall response level of 13 Hz across training sessions. Subject on right (II) showed different acquisition pattern with minimal increment within sessions but progressive increase in response level across sessions. Both subjects showed quantitative and qualitative improvement in sleep, but clinical effects were different. Note that training of central 13-Hz activity resulted in parallel increases in 15-Hz activity and concurrent decrease in 10-Hz activity.

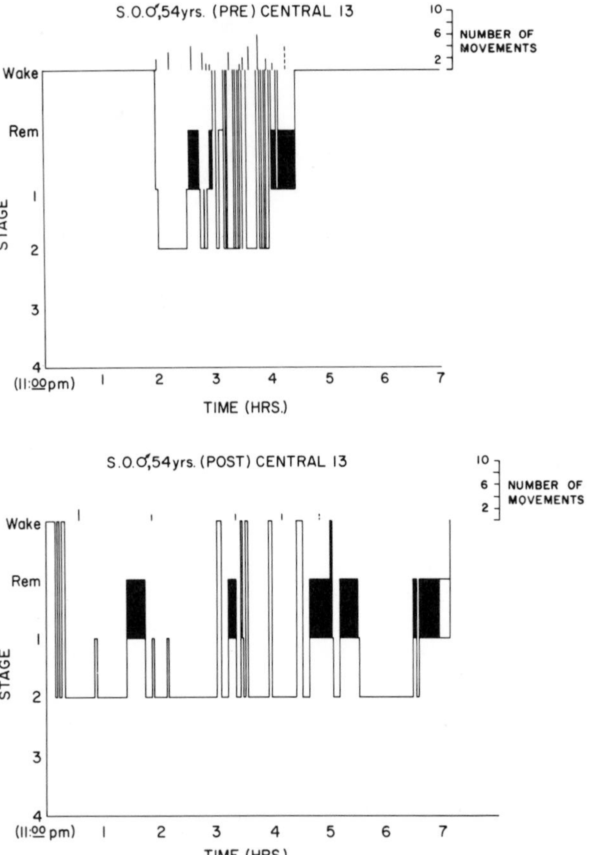

Figure 16.4 Sleep histograms derived from the third night of three consecutive laboratory monitoring sessions before (top) and after (bottom) 3 months of SMR biofeedback training in an insomniac. This subject showed acquisition of the rewarded EEG response (Figure 16.3-II). The posttraining sleep record showed marked improvement in sleep onset latency, total sleep time, and percent and sequencing of REM sleep. A reduction in movements during sleep was observed also.

The issue of response acquisition in EEG biofeedback studies is central to both theoretical and clinical considerations of this research area. In a recent and extensive review of the literature relating to this problem, Johnson (1976) concluded that there is no laboratory support for the notion that one can learn to produce more EEG alpha rhythm activity and that "alpha feedback has no unique recuperative or therapeutic powers" (p.18). With regard to theta activity, the evidence reviewed led him to suggest that "EEG theta activity is an

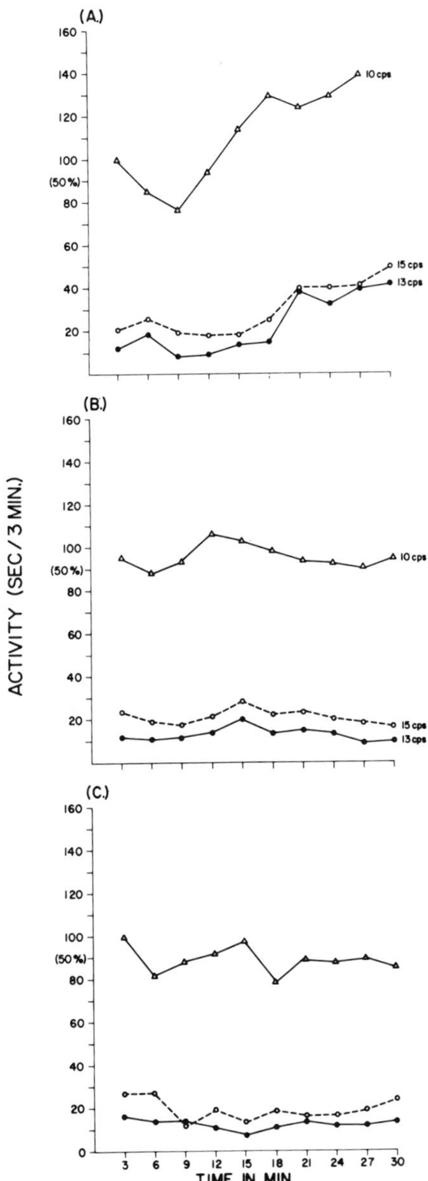

Figure 16.5 EEG biofeedback training data identical to those shown in Figure 16.3, except that they were obtained from an insomniac subject rewarded for occipital 10-Hz (alpha) rhythmic activity. Initial data from this subject suggested within-session acquisition (a) of the reinforced occipital activity. However, this pattern proved transient with continued training and was replaced by one of no change and even a slight reduction in response both within and across sessions. Activity at 13 and 15 Hz was also recorded from occipital cortex (P3–01). No improvement in posttraining sleep was observed in repeated, all-night sleep recordings.

epiphenomenon of a general lowering of arousal level" (p. 22). Accordingly, any physiological or clinical responses associated with theta feedback training are most parsimoniously attributed to changes in arousal level and not to feedback contingent alterations in theta activity. Based upon existing evidence this author must, at the present time, agree with Johnson's conclusions. However, our own experience with the sticky problems involved in the measurement of EEG response acquisition and clinical change suggest that such conclusions may be premature.

Our experience with EEG feedback training has resulted from a long history of investigation exploring this approach in the study and treatment of seizure disorders. The central nervous system origins of epilepsy and its *relatively* straightforward manifestations make this disease a good candidate for the biofeedback approach. Additionally, our work in this area developed out of neurophysiological investigations in the cat, which allowed us to draw upon known thalamocortical mechanisms for the patterns of interest, and to document not only behavioral correlates but electrophysiological ones as well.

In a continuing series of studies, we have evaluated the potential therapeutic benefits of training central cortical 12–16-Hz activity, a pattern we have termed the *sensorimotor rhythm* or *SMR*, first in cats, where it was discovered, and then in epileptics (Sterman, LoPresti, & Fairchild, 1969; Sterman, Wyrwicka, & Roth, 1969; Sterman & Friar, 1972; Sterman *et al.*, 1974; Sterman, 1976). In the cat, this rhythm appears prominently over sensorimotor cortex in relation to spontaneous and learned suppression of movement. Trained production of the SMR through operant conditioning was associated with specific changes in neuronal activity, suppression of somatic reflexes, and increased thresholds for drug induced seizures. These facts led to its study in epileptics.

Following our initial reports of reduction in EEG and clinical manifestations of epilepsy in a small group of previously uncontrolled epileptics (Sterman & Friar, 1972; Sterman *et al.*, 1974), a number of other laboratories joined the exploration of this approach to the treatment of epilepsy. In summary, some eight different studies have reported seizure reduction following central cortical EEG feedback training in severe epileptics (Finley, in press; Kaplan, 1975; Kuhlman & Allison, in press; Lubar & Bahler, 1976; Wyler, Lockard, Ward, & Finch, in press; Rundell, personal communication; Quy, personal communication). Questions raised initially about placebo effects, changes in drug-use compliance, and the lack of appropriate control groups or procedures have in part been resolved. It has now been established that noncontingent EEG feedback training does not produce seizure reductions (Kuhlman & Allison, in press; Wyler *et al.*, in press). In a study currently under way in our laboratory, the use of a crossover A–B–A–B design has shown clearly and consistently that prolonged training with reward for central cortical 6–9-Hz activity did not reduce seizures (Sterman, 1976). Moreover, Wyler (personal communication) is finding *increased* seizure manifestations in epileptic monkeys, with alumina cream implants, following reward for central cortical high frequency activity (24–28 Hz). Thus, it appears that EEG feedback training of central cortical activity between approximately 9 and 20 Hz can reduce seizures.

The long-term nature of training in these studies, together with the necessary collection of extensive EEG data, afford an excellent opportunity for the assessment of various methodologies. All published studies have utilized tuned active filters for initial band-pass selection of the rewarded central cortical EEG signal (Figure 16.6). The Sterman, Finley, Lubar, and Wyler studies had additional circuits for detection of artifacts, high-voltage slow waves and spikes, or other frequency bands, the occurence of which prevented feedback reward. This methodologic refinement may be of particular importance in studies of epileptics, since abnormal discharge and harmonics thereof can "ring" tuned filters or produce frequencies that invade the domain of interest in terms of feedback reward (Figure 16.7). The Kaplan and Kuhlman studies did not use these so-called "inhibit circuits." In

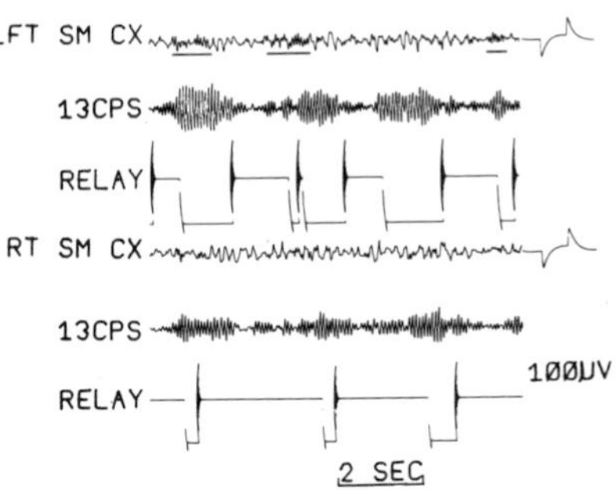

Figure 16.6 EEG traces from an epileptic subject after 9 months of SMR biofeedback training. Traces are from left and right sensorimotor cortex with corresponding 13-Hz detection filter and relay outputs. Underlined segments indicate SMR activity visible in the trace because of frequency stability and transient voltage increase. Note that filter response, which reflects frequency and not amplitude, still occurs during lower voltage bursts of SMR not visable in the EEG trace. The asymmetry of this EEG response may reflect the unilateral (left) training schedule utilized with this patient. [From Sterman *et al.*, 1974].

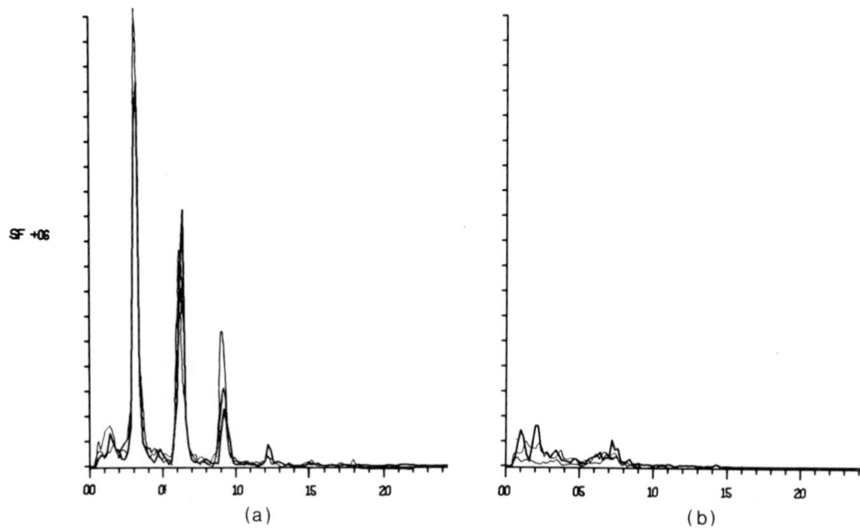

Figure 16.7 Power-spectral analysis of central cortical EEG activity (C_3–T_3) in an epileptic with generalized petit mal seizures. Plot at (a) shows isometric display of frequency distribution during a typical waking seizure in this patient, with three-per-second spike and wave EEG discharge. Each trace in this plot represents a 17-second epoch of EEG data; superimposed traces represent consecutive epochs during the seizure, which lasted slightly longer than 1 minute. Note that primary discharge at approximately three per second produced the dominant spectral peak. However, harmonics of this dominant frequency are apparent also at approximately 6, 9, and 12 Hz. Plot at (b) shows similar display in the absence of seizure discharge.

these studies, however, the filtered signal was passed to a second-stage digital processor set to detect the same frequency band through zero-crossing analysis. Signal amplitude criteria were also treated differently in these various studies. This aspect of the signal is as important as frequency, because the EEG patterns studied are often relatively low in amplitude under training conditions. The Sterman, Finley, and Lubar papers specified absolute amplitude requirements; the Wyler study employed a response "shaping" paradigm without reference to absolute amplitude criteria; and the Kaplan and Kuhlman experiments depended upon the resolution of the zero-crossing detection method.

It remains to be determined whether or not these discrepant signal detection methods result in significant differences in the EEG patterns rewarded by various investigators. In terms of observed seizure reduction, comparable results were obtained in all but the Kaplan study. She reported no effect in two patients following reward for 12–15-Hz central activity and a confounded but clear reduction in one of these and in two other patients rewarded for central 6–12-Hz activity. Since Kuhlman and Allison obtained significant seizure reductions in three of five epileptic patients following contingent reward for 9–14-Hz central activity using the same basic detection arrangement, we cannot attribute Kaplan's findings entirely to the detection parameter. Moreover, Kaplan did observe seizure reduction with reward for an overlapping 6–12-Hz band. It is possible that the filter characteristics and/or amplitude requirements prescribed by Kaplan's signal detection system were, in fact, different from those in Kuhlman's system, resulting in significantly different reward criteria. More likely is the possibility of a sampling effect, since only two subjects were studied at 12–14 Hz.

Our laboratory has obtained negative results in five patients, to date, following 6–9-Hz reward. These findings, together with those from other laboratories and the well-established fact that EEG abnormalities in epileptics include increased 4–8-Hz activity, suggest that Kaplan's positive results with reward for 6–12 Hz may have derived from manipulation of the 9–12-Hz component of this band. At any rate, on the basis of experience, this author would strongly advise against training of frequencies below 9 Hz in epileptics.

It has been noted by several investigators (Kuhlman & Allison, 1976; Sterman, 1976; Wyler *et al.*, in press) that control feedback conditions (ie., random or systematic noncontingent feedback, or feedback for low frequencies) must be tested prior to positive feedback conditions (reward for central cortical frequency trains between 9 and 20 Hz) in order to best document their negative effects. Once a patient has experienced training with positive frequencies and has responded with a reduction in seizures, it is difficult to reverse both EEG and clinical manifestations with control conditions. Thus, in our experience, after a patient has demonstrated a reduction in abnormal low-frequency central EEG activity and a corresponding decrease in seizures with positive reward for 12–15 Hz or 18–23 Hz and negative reward for 6–9 Hz, a reversal, with positive reward for 6–9 Hz, could at best only partially disrupt this improvement. Apparently, therefore, the patient's own internal reward system is not entirely subservient to our experimental trickery.

Response acquisition in these studies has been measured in two basic ways. One method has involved the tabulation of criterion responses (signal detection relays) over the period of training. Studies utilizing this method have uniformly reported quantitative increases in the rewarded response (Sterman & Friar, 1972; Sterman, 1974; Finley *et al.*, 1975; Lubar & Bahler, 1976; Wyler *et al.*, in press). These

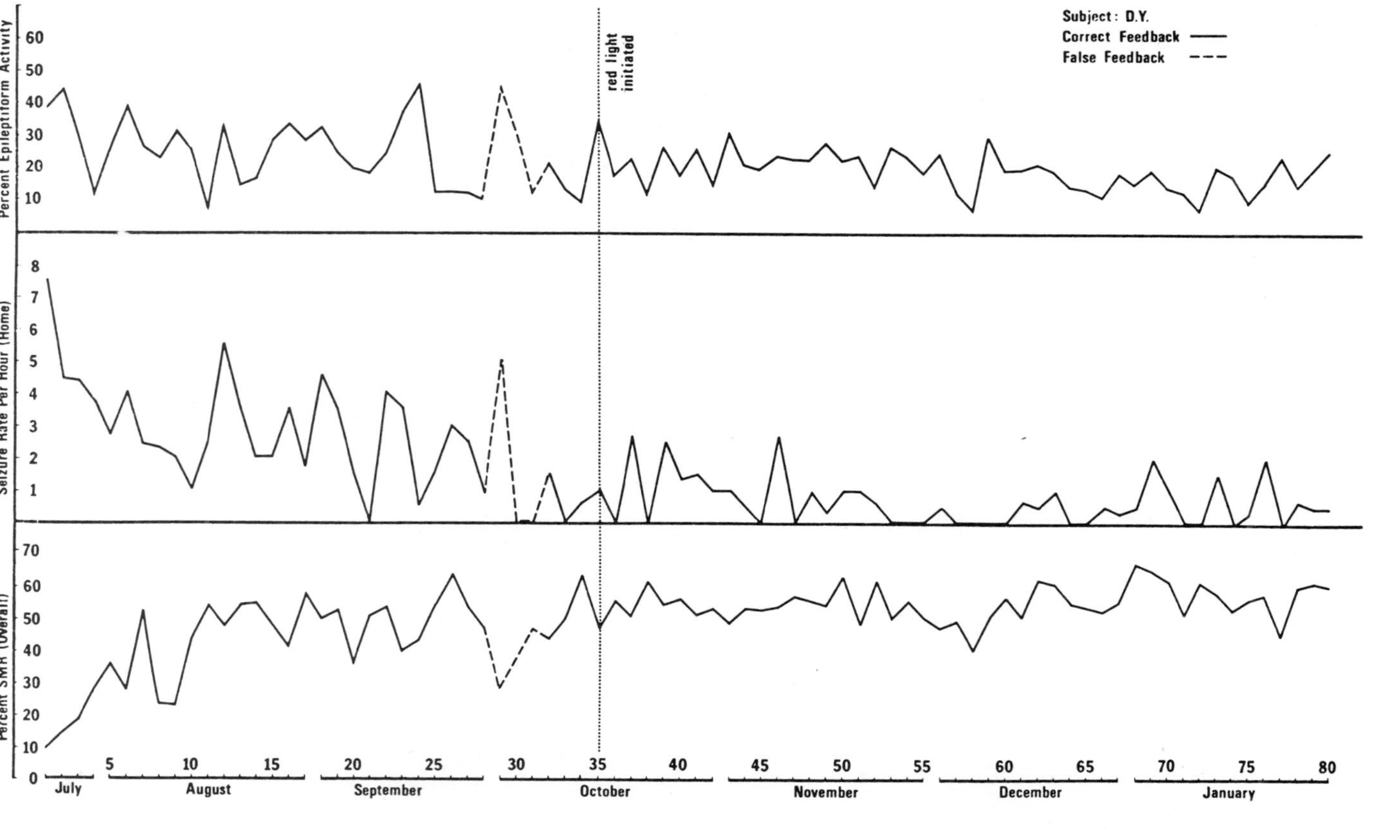

Subject: D.Y.
Correct Feedback
False Feedback
red light initiated
Percent Epileptiform Activity
Seizure Rate Per Hour (Home)
Percent SMR (Overall)
July
August
September
October
November
December
January
TRIALS

functions are usually irregular, and do not resemble typical learning curves, as noted previously in alpha training studies (Travis, Kondo, & Knott, 1974). This fact, together with the small number of patients studied to date, has made appropriate statistical analysis difficult. An early example was provided by Finley *et al.* (1975), who studied seizure rate in an adolescent akinetic epileptic by having the parents quantify his falling attacks during evening hours, throughout a 7-month period of three-per-week SMR biofeedback training sessions. Seizure rate per hour was compared with percent SMR during the 1-hour training sessions and with the percent of epileptiform activity recorded during these sessions. The results of these comparisons are shown in Figure 16.8. A significant negative correlation was obtained between seizure rate per hour and percent SMR. Furthermore, a significant negative correlation was found between percent epileptiform discharge in laboratory recordings and percent SMR. Thus, as SMR activity increased over trials, both seizure rate and EEG epileptiform activity decreased. Such single-case data cannot be considered as conclusive, however, and may not even justify attempts at statistical analysis.

A second method of acquisition analysis has utilized the digital computer for determination of power-spectral estimates from sampled EEG data. Power-spectral analysis provides a quantitative means for evaluating frequency–amplitude changes over time, and therefore offers a promising new method for EEG analysis. A number of studies have applied this method in the present context (Sterman *et al.*, 1974; Kaplan, 1975; Lubar & Bahler, 1976; Kuhlman & Allison, in press). Using this method, we have found that trained SMR responses in nonepileptics often emerged as variable spectral peaks between 10 and 15 Hz (Figure 16.9). To visualize these peaks, however, it was usually necessary to enhance voltage input and plotter scaling, due primarily to the characteristic low amplitude of trained SMR responses.

Both Kaplan (1975) and Kuhlman and Allison (in press) attempted

Figure 16.8 Seizure rate per hour and percent epileptiform activity as a function of percent recorded SMR across 6.5-month period of SMR biofeedback training in an adolescent akinetic epileptic. Seizure rate per hour was determined by parents who tabulated between 7:00 and 8:00 P.M. each evening. Percent SMR (overall) was determined by averaging percent SMR on pre- and postfeedback baselines and during the actual feedback period for each training trial. False feedback (noncontingent reinforcement) was instituted on Trials 29, 30, and 31 as indicated by the dashed lines. The vertical dotted line (Trial 35) depicts initiation of red light to inform the subject of occurrence of epileptiform activity. [From Finley *et al.*, 1975.]

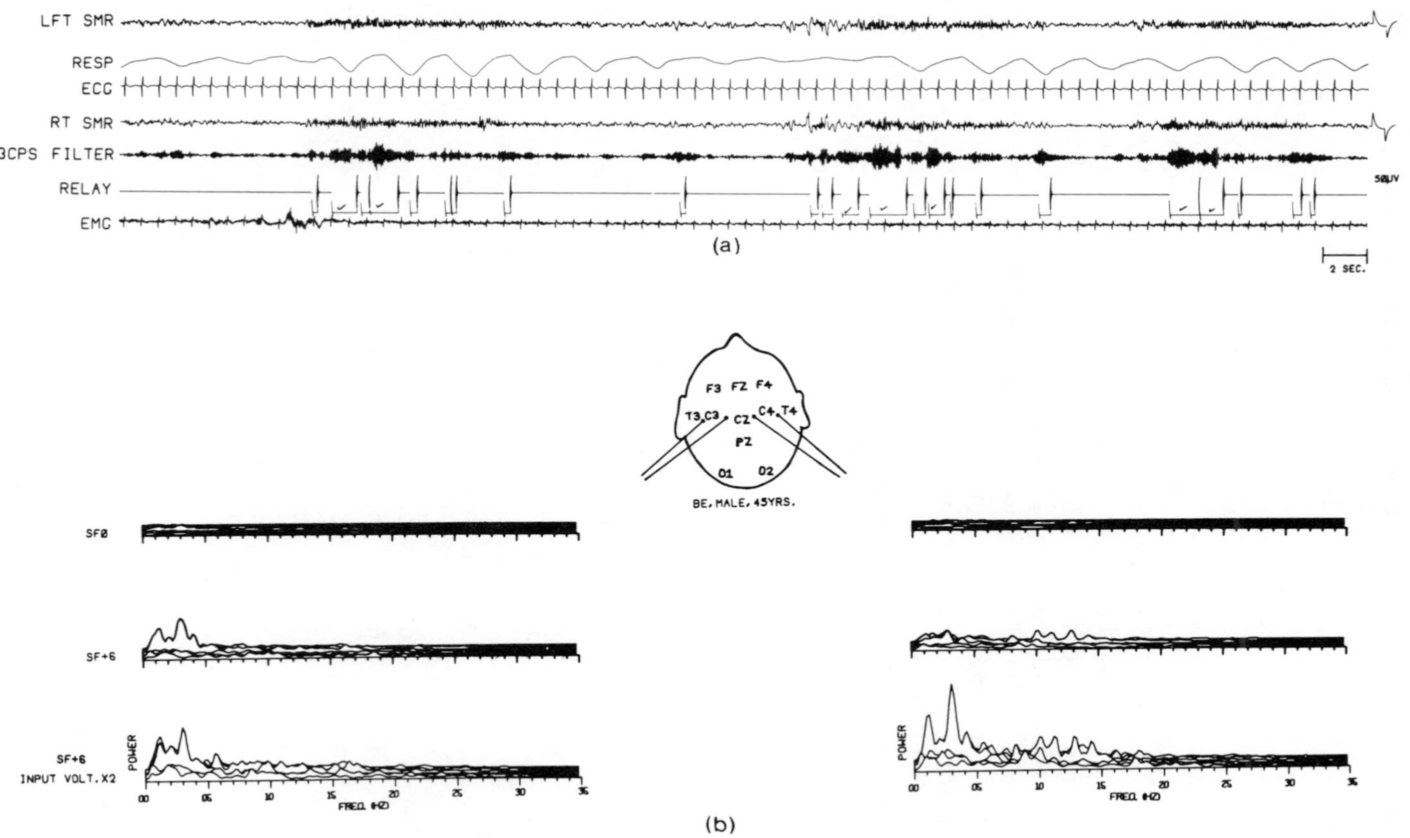
LFT SMR
RESP
ECG
RT SMR
13CPS FILTER
RELAY
EMG
50UV
2 SEC.
F3 FZ F4
T3 C3 CZ C4 T4
PZ
O1 O2
BE, MALE, 45YRS.
SFØ
SF+6
SF+6
INPUT VOLT.X2
POWER
FREQ (HZ)
00 05 10 15 20 25 30 35

(a)

(b)

this approach in their analysis of response acquisition following EEG biofeedback in epileptics. Kaplan found no systematic changes and Kuhlman and Allison found changes restricted to lower frequencies (8–10 Hz). However, the appropriate use of power-spectral analysis in epileptics is often thwarted by the extremely high voltage of abnormal patterns in the epileptic EEG. Since spectra are expressed as power functions, a 10-to-1 amplitude discrepancy between two frequency bands is transformed to 100-to-1 in spectral estimates. In the presence of the high amplitude, low frequencies common in the epileptic EEG, the extremely low amplitude, high frequency SMR may be masked. We are currently remedying this problem by performing log transformations of spectral values and developing other adjustment programs. Needless to say, this approach offers a number of technical problems. Moreover, the exact transformations accomplished upon the complex EEG signal by power-spectral analysis have not been thoroughly evaluated from a physiological standpoint. This is true because a combination of frequency and amplitude determines output in spectral analysis, and few of the assumptions upon which the method is based are met by the nonstationary quality of the EEG. Nevertheless, this method provides for a reliable, quantitative analysis of the EEG with potential utility in biofeedback applications.

CONCLUSIONS

This review has attempted to examine some of the many technical and interpretational issues that arise from the use of EEG biofeedback in clinical treatment. Aside from potential nonspecific influences, the comprehensive evaluation of clinical utility with this method depends upon its proper application. Accordingly, the focus here was primarily upon technical considerations in EEG signal detection and response

---

Figure 16.9 Polygraphic data (a) and corresponding power spectral analysis (b) sampled from recording obtained from a nonepileptic subject early in SMR biofeedback training. This subject was rewarded for criterion 13-Hz response from right central cortex (see head diagram for placement). Reward is indicated by check in relay activation display which, together with filter discharge, is shown only for right central (SMR) recording. Left central EEG, respiration, heart beat, and chin muscle activity are shown also. Spectral plots show consecutive 17-second epochs corresponding approximately to the same period of recording shown at (a). Spectral analysis of these data produced little or no reflection of obvious EEG responses unless digital scaling and voltage input were enhanced. This enhancement, however, also increased generalized lower frequencies and eyeblink artifacts.

acquisition and, to a lesser extent, upon the equally difficult problems of clinical evaluation.

Hopefully, this treatment has demonstrated the need for thoughtful consideration of these areas, and has discouraged casual entry into this field of investigation. Additionally, it is hoped that an equally casual and uninformed rejection of this research was discouraged also. Both exciting and promising results have been obtained during this period of scientific infancy in EEG feedback research, particularly in studies of less "popular" EEG components. Advancement of this field will require greater interaction between behaviorists, physiologists, and clinicians, and the development of a new body of knowledge in this interdisciplinary realm.

REFERENCES

Beatty, J. Similar effects of feedback signals and instructional information on EEG activity. *Physiology and Behavior,* 1972, *9,* 151–154.

Blanchard, E. B., & Young, L. D. Clinical applications of biofeedback training. *Archives of General Psychiatry,* 1974, *30,* 573–589.

Feinstein, B., Sterman, M. B., & Macdonald, L. R. Effects of sensorimotor rhythm biofeedback training on sleep. *Sleep Research,* 1974, *3,* 134. (Abstract)

Finley, W. W. Operant conditioning of the EEG in two patients with epilepsy: Methodologic and clinical considerations. *Pavlovian Journal of Biological Science,* in press.

Finley, W. W., Smith, H. A., & Etherton, M.D. Reduction of seizures and normalization of the EEG in a severe epileptic following sensorimotor feedback training: Preliminary study. *Biological Psychology.,* 1975, *2,* 189–203.

Hauri, P. The use of biofeedback in the treatment of "idiopathic" insomnia. Proceedings of the 16th Annual Meeting of the Association for the Psychophysiological Study of

Kaplan, B. J. Biofeedback in epileptics: Equivocal relationship of reinforced EEG frequency to seizure reduction. *Epilepsia,* 1975, *16,* 477–485.

Kuhlman, W. N., & Allison, T. EEG feedback training in the treatment of epilepsy: Some questions and some answers. *Pavlovian Journal of Biological Science,* in press.

Lubar, J. F., & Bahler, W. W. Behavioral management of epileptic seizures following EEG biofeedback training of the sensorimotor rhythm. *Journal of Biofeedback and Self-Regulation,* 1976, *1,* 77–104.

Lynch, J. J., & Paskewitz, D. A. On the mechanisms of the feedback control of human brain wave activity. *Journal of Nervous and Mental Disorders* 1971, *153*(3), 205–217.

Lynch, J. J., Paskewitz, D. A., and Orne, M. T. Some factors in the feedback control of human alpha rhythm. *Psychosomatic Medicine,* 1974, *36,* 399–410.
Sleep, Cincinnati, June 1976.

Johnson, L. C. Learned control of brain wave activity. In *Biofeedback and Behavior, Preliminary Proceedings of a NATO Symposium.* Max Planck Institute für Psychiatrie, München, 1976. Pp. 13–33.

McKenzie, R. E., Ehrisman, W. J., Montgomery, P. S., & Barnes, R. H. The treatment of headache by means of electroencephalographic biofeedback. *Headache,* 1974, *13,* 164–172.

O'Malley, J. E., & Conners, C. K. The effect of unilateral alpha training on visual evoked response in a dyslexic adolescent. *Psychophysiology*, 1972, 9(4), 467–470.

Paskewitz, D. A., & Orne, M. T. Visual effects on alpha feedback training. *Science*, 1973, *181*, 360–363.

Regestein, Q. R., Buckland, G. H., & Pegram, G. V. Effect of daytime alpha rhythm maintenance on subsequent sleep. *Biofeedback and Self-Control*, 1973, *4*, 384–387.

Sterman, M. B. Neurophysiological and clinical studies of sensorimotor EEG biofeedback training: Some effects on epilepsy. *Seminars in Psychiatry*, 1974, 5(4), 507–525.

Sterman, M. B. Effects of sensorimotor EEG feedback training on sleep and clinical manifestations of epilepsy. In *Biofeedback and Behavior, Preliminary Proceedings of a NATO Symposium*. Max Planc Institute fur Psychiatrie, München, 1976. Pp. 95–128.

Sterman, M. B., Feinstein, B., & Macdonald, L. R. Quantitative analysis of baseline and biofeedback training effects with central and occipital cortical frequencies in man. Presentation at Biofeedback Research Society Meeting, Monterey, Calif., 1975.

Sterman, M. B., & Friar, L. Suppression of seizures in an epileptic following sensorimotor EEG feedback training. *Electroencephalography and clinical Neurophysiology*, 1972, *33*, 89–95.

Sterman, M. B., LoPresti, R. W., & Fairchild, M. D. Electroencephalographic and behavioral studies of monomethyl hydrazine toxicity in the cat (Technical Report AMRL-TR-69-3). Wright–Patterson Air Force Base, Ohio: Air Systems Command, 1969.

Sterman, M. B., Macdonald, L. R., Stone, R. K. Biofeedback training of the sensorimotor EEG rhythm in man: Effects on epilepsy. *Epilepsia*, 1974, *15*, 395–416.

Sterman, M. B., Wyrwicka, W., & Roth, S. R. Electrophysiological correlates and neural substrates of alimentary behavior in the cat. In J. P. Morgane & M. Wayner (Eds.), *Neural regulation of food and water intake. Annals New York Academy of Science*, 1969, *157*, 723–739.

Travis, T. A., Kondo, C. Y., & Knott, J. R. Alpha conditioning: A controlled study. *Journal of Nervous and Mental Disorders* 1974, *158*(3), 163–173.

Wyler, A. R., Lockard, J. S., Ward, A. A., & Finch, C. A. Conditioned EEG desynchronization and seizure occurrence in patients. *Electroencephalography and Clinical Neurophysiology*, in press.

IV

THE SKELETAL MUSCULATURE

17

Learned Control of Single Motor Units

JOHN V. BASMAJIAN
Emory University
Atlanta, Georgia

INTRODUCTION

Historical Background

A seminal concept that grew rapidly into the modern uses of electromyography (EMG) biofeedback emerged in the early 1960s as single motor unit training (SMUT). Originally conceived as a methodology for neurophysiologic studies of motor control and learning, the EMG biofeedback approach to the training of single motoneurons was accepted immediately. Later it was transmuted to applied psychophysiologic studies of more gross muscle controls described elsewhere in this book. Thus, the present widespread application of muscle biofeedback for the treatment of various abnormal conditions depends on the existence of an exquisite cortical control system over individual spinal motoneurons—provided the subject has reliable electronic feedback.

The brevity of the part of this volume dedicated to biofeedback of skeletal muscle arises, to a large degree, from the relative lack of conjecture and confusion about EMG and muscle contraction. While the ultimate clinical applications of EMG biofeedback are still being explored, the basic understanding of the precise nature of the underlying phenomena and technologies has been well developed. In part, this is due to the greater ease with which the voluntary motor system can be examined and tested in man. In part, it is due to the relative clarity of the myopotential spikes that result—either individually or collectively—when a skeletal muscle contracts; this clarity is in sharp contrast with the scientific obscurity and diffuseness of other modes of biofeedback. Perhaps of more immediate interest, a major reason has been our deepening understanding of the exquisite nature of the voluntary control man can learn to exert on individual motoneurons.

Single motor unit training remains a useful tool for further explorations of the neurophysiologic and psychophysiologic bases of biofeedback. Its precise qualitative and quantitative nature and its relative freedom from equivocation—it is a clear on–off response—make it more than an historical step in the development of the biofeedback field.

When I introduced the ideas of systematically recruiting and training single motor units (hence, motoneurons) by displaying the EMG to patients in the early 1960s (Basmajian, 1963), my original purpose was to reveal the precision and accuracy of cortical control and inhibition. The first practical application, now in limbo, was to drive separate electric motors from a number of controlled individual motor unit discharges. Not only could subjects do this, but the speed with which they could learn to do tricks with the separate electric motors gave some promise of developing more complex integrated myoelectric limbs for the handicapped.

Financial limitations put that applied research on the shelf. Nevertheless, with my colleagues and students (Basmajian, Baeza, & Fabrigar, 1965), we continued to investigate the main factors that influence the conscious control of motoneurons as revealed by the EMG and made possible by feedback. In the early and mid-1960s, the gross control of whole muscles and their units with feedback was no mystery. We had known about it since EMG began (Adrian & Bronk, 1929). In clinical work from 1943 on, many physicians were aware that revealing the sight and sound of the EMG to patients helped to increase or decrease muscular contractions.

The new element was our introduction of single motor unit training (SMUT) which remained "basic science" until the biofeedback "movement" started. Our SMUT work owed its origins to the improvements in electromyography during the previous two decades. Although Smith (1934), Lindsley (1935), and Gilson and Mills (1940, 1941) had given accounts of man's ability to discharge single motor units (SMUs), electrophysiologists who had noted their isolated papers took this phenomenon for granted. Neither they nor psychologists performed systematic studies of it. Knowledge of the work of Harrison and Mortensen (1962), who would later report that subjects of kinesiologic studies on the tibialis anterior muscle could recruit a number of isolated motor units with surface electrodes, prompted my series of systematic studies of motor unit isolation and control (Basmajian, 1963; Basmajian *et al.*, 1965). Our coincidental development of a special fine-wire intramuscular electrode allowed rapid progress (Basmajian & Stecko, 1962).

Motor Units and Motor Unit Potentials

In many papers, reviews, and books (e.g., Basmajian, 1972, 1974), I have described the characteristics of this functional unit of contraction, the motor unit. Briefly, it includes only one motor neuron (motoneuron) in the spinal cord or, in the case of cranial nerves, in the brainstem. Thus, the activity of the motor unit is a reflection of the activity of the motoneuron. From the cell body of a motoneuron, a single axon runs in a nerve to a small group of striated muscle fibers. Collectively, the motoneuron (cell body and axon) plus the muscle fibers it supplies constitute the motor unit. A twitchlike contraction of the muscle fibers of the unit is detected by a recordable myoelectric potential and indicates an activation of the neuron, on a one-to-one basis. Immediately after each twitch, the fibers of the motor unit relax completely and they twitch again only when an impulse arrives along the nerve fiber. Individual muscles of the body consist of many hundreds of such motor units and it is their summated, but asynchronous, activity that develops the tension in the whole muscle.

The motor unit action potential has a brief duration (with a median of 9 milliseconds) and a total amplitude measured in microvolts or millivolts. Most SMU potentials recorded by conventional techniques (surface or needle electrodes) are sharp triphasic or biphasic spikes; but when fine-wire electrodes are used, the potentials are much more complex and so are recognizable by their shapes.

The motor units twitch repetitively and out of synchrony with their neighbors. It is this very random activity that causes the smooth tension of the whole muscle rather than a jerky one. The amount of external work or force produced by SMUs is quite small; in a living human being, it is usually insufficient to cause any external movement of a joint spanned by the whole muscle of which it is a part. There is, therefore, no external evidence of SMU twitches and, without artificial feedback, subjects are insensitive to SMU activity.

TECHNICAL CONSIDERATIONS

SMUT has now gained sufficient usage on a multidisciplinary and multinational basis to justify some standardization of basic techniques. Since its introduction, this methodology has been constantly modified by various investigators to fit the needs of specific research projects. A large element of "free wheeling" with no set constraints apparent in some of the studies has led us to develop a basic standard technique (Basmajian & Samson, 1973; Samson, 1971).

We have described a format for the conduction of these training sessions, which could be used to obtain results that allow better comparison between data obtained in different laboratories. Auditory feedback has proven to be more useful than visual feedback using a cathode ray oscilloscope. A visual feedback method under control of the experimenter has been developed, along with a work–rest schedule for experiments. Subject–experimenter interactions are minimized. The standard training procedure includes four different experimental tasks. The methodology is particularly adaptable to future computerized automation. A minimal configuration would include inexpensive commercial equipment designed for other general uses. A cheap single-channel assembly consisting of, for example, a Tektronix oscilloscope (Type 502), a Tektronix low-level preamplifier (Type 122), and a Heathkit audioamplifier (Type A-9C) with an ordinary loudspeaker is the minimal equipment requirement. Equivalent units of other manufacturers can be, and are, substituted.

Electrodes

For the excellent recordings required in SMUT, the difficulties arising from surface electrodes appear to be prohibitive (but see below). Moreover, inserted electrodes are no longer as forbidding as they once were. Our fine-wire electrodes (Basmajian & Stecko, 1962) are as easy to use and as easy to tolerate as are surface electrodes. They are *(1)* extremely fine and, therefore, painless, *(2)* easily injected and withdrawn, *(3)* as broad in pickup from a specific muscle as the best surface electrodes, and *(4)* give excellent sharp and unit-specific spikes with fidelity. With 1 mm of their tips exposed, such electrodes record the voltage from a muscle much better than surface electrodes (Sutton, 1962). Bipolar fine-wire electrodes isolate their pickup either to the whole muscle being studied or to fibrous boundaries of one part of any muscle that has parallel bellies or a pennate structure. Barriers of fibrous connective tissue within a muscle or around it act as insulation.

Thus, one can record all the activity as far as such a barrier without the interfering pickup from beyond the barrier (such as there always must be with surface electrodes, which are global in pickup).

There are circumstances in which any injection of an electrode must be avoided because of the inherent bias it may introduce in certain special types of psychophysiological experiments with SMUs (that is, where the covert nature of the phenomenon must be masked by the use of many dummy electrodes to mislead the subject). Basing his work on that of Bruno Davidowitz, and Hefferline (1970), Kahn (1971) has shown that when the surface-electrode response is recorded on magnetic tape at high speed and then played back at low speed through a standard EMG–EEG oscillograph, pen records of good resolution are obtainable. Of necessity, this technique relies upon the recording of obtrusive units which, of course, may be the requirement of a specific project, as in our study of SMUT in young children (Simard, Basmajian, & Janda, 1968).

The exclusive use of surface electrodes should be avoided except *(a)* where the experimental design demands them (e.g., where many dummy electrodes are placed on a subject and he is kept uninformed about the aim of an experiment either to study or to condition covert activity), and *(b)* where advanced computer technology is available for recognizing single units. Green, Walters, Green, and Murphy (1969) found alternate ways in which to minimize the problems inherent in the use of skin electrodes with standard polygraph equipment. They developed a rectifier circuit for detection of SMU firing with a feedback meter. Input through standoff capacitors allows the use of preamplifiers with high-voltage DC outputs. Green and his coworkers have used whatever combination of amplifiers was available.

Experimental Designs

Fundamentally the SMUT technique consists of providing human subjects with the best possible feedback of the activity of their motoneurons through the monitoring of EMG signals. The general experimental approach is not complex, and different laboratories have already devised their own routines (Basmajian & Samson, 1973; Lloyd & Leibrecht, 1971; Simard & Basmajian, 1967). For audio feedback, W. D. McLeod and R. V. Thysell (personal communication, 1974) substitute an electrically generated square-wave pulse which is triggered by a SMU firing. This feedback seems as effective as that from the MU itself. It has the advantage that the characteristics (for example, voltage and duration) of the pulse can be varied and specified precisely.

In his earlier reaction-time (RT) work, Thysell (1969) scrupulously trained subjects to a criterion of SMU control. (The criterion was the ability to fire a unit in a "once, twice, thrice" sequence for three consecutive trials without error.) Under this criterion, many subjects required 30–60 minutes or more of training before beginning RT trials. More recently, Thysell trained subjects for a maximum of only 20 minutes and then initiated RT testing regardless of whether the subject had reached criterion. Reaction-time performance in this experiment was superior to that in earlier experiments. Subjects performed with fewer errors and had faster mean reaction times (Thysell, personal communication, 1972).

Thysell believes that the frustration engendered by a long training period leads to poor RT performance. Minimizing the frustration by shortening the training period leads to better performance even though the subject has achieved a poorer level of control. Another possibility is that training subjects to a high level of proficiency on a specific criterion may actually be training in a pattern that later interferes with good RT performance.

A variation of the Thysell technique was described by Sutton and Kimm (1970). The subject faced a half-silvered mirror placed so that motor unit activity from a CRO display could be readily viewed, and through which a visual stimulus for the RT procedure could be presented, superimposed on the oscilloscope trace of motor activity. Thus, the subject could continuously observe his own activity as well as monitor the RT signals (light flash). Amplified electrical signals from the muscle were displayed both visually and aurally. The subject was instructed to use the visual and auditory signals as information to help him achieve voluntary control over the firing of a motor unit such that a single spike could be produced on command. When the subject reported he was able to produce a single spike voluntarily, a short practice run involving simple RT to a flash of light was begun. No warning signal was presented, and the interstimulus interval was 8 seconds. Termination of this practice session was followed immediately by the data collection period unless the subject had difficulty in controlling the unit during the practice run. In such cases, further practice was permitted and a rerun of the practice series was given.

Hefferline and Perera (1963), Bruno *et al.* (1970), and Hefferline, Bruno, and Davidowitz (1971) applied localized EMG to the discrimination of a covert operant. Their specific objective was to train a subject to report a covert twitch in a thumb muscle detectable only through EMG monitoring. The response in each study consisted of a ballistic deflection of a volt-meter needle or photorecorder beam which rose sharply above and then returned quickly to the resting tension level.

The basic process of training SMUs (i.e., consciously activating individual motoneurons while inhibiting surrounding motoneurons) remains virtually unchanged in spite of elaborate variations employing computers and automatic devices. After acquiring a good control of the first motor unit, a subject is asked to isolate a second with which he then learns the same tricks; then a third; and so on. His next task is to recruit, unerringly and in isolation, the several units over which he has gained the best control.

Many subjects then can be tested at greater length on any special skills revealed in the earlier part of their testing (for example, either an especially fine control of, or an ability to play tricks with, a single unit). Finally, the best performers are tested on their ability to maintain the activity of specific motor unit potentials in the absence of either one or both of the visual and auditory feedbacks. That is, the monitors are turned off and the subject must try to maintain or recall a well-learned unit without the artificial "proprioception" provided earlier.

Any skeletal muscle may be selected. The ones we have used most often are the abductor pollicis brevis, tibialis anterior, biceps brachii, and the extensors of the forearm. However, we have easily trained units in buccinator (Basmajian & Newton, 1973) and in back muscles; Sussman, Hanson, and MacNeilage (1972) have trained units in the larynx while Gray (1971) has trained them in the sphincter ani.

REVIEW OF EXPERIMENTAL RESULTS

Learning Paradigm

Lloyd and Leibrecht (1971) and Samson (1971) independently showed that the SMU training fulfills the requirements of the learning paradigm. The feedback methodology is not critical; thus, a highly artificial indication of successful training is satisfactory to a considerable degree. Leibrecht, Lloyd, and Pounder (1972) went on to show that direct EMG feedback substantially improved initial learning. The nature and amount of learning, including the ability to use proprioceptive cues in controlling an SMU, were not affected; neither was the retention of learning.

Ladd, Jonsson, and Lindegren (1972) investigated the learning process involved in the fine neuromotor control of single motor unit training which, of course, also embodies inhibition of motor activity. They employed trained units in five different muscles in 25 subjects. Voluntary inhibition, they found, is a conceptual type of response showing independence of the motor component; it generalizes and transfers positively from one muscle to another. However, the voluntary contractions of an individual unit is a specific perceptual motor type of response; the motor component of the response is essential and the learned response does not generalize or transfer from one muscle to another.

General Training

Ability to Isolate Motor Units

Almost all subjects are able to produce well-isolated contractions of at least one motor unit, turning it off and on without any interference from neighboring units. Only a few people fail completely to perform this basic trick. Analysis of poor and very poor performers reveals no common characteristic that separates them from better performers.

Most people are able to isolate and master one or two units readily; some can isolate and master three units, four units, and even six units or more. This last level of control is of the highest order, for the subject must be able to give an instant response to an order to produce contractions of a specified unit without the interfering activity of neighbors; he also must be able to turn the unit "off" and "on" at will. The ultimate ability of human subjects was demonstrated by Kato and Tanji (1972b), who found that within 30 minutes, their subjects could voluntarily isolate 73% of 286 motor units appearing on the oscilloscope during voluntary contractions.

Control of Firing Rates and Special Rhythms

Once a person has gained control of a spinal motor neuron, it is possible for him to learn to vary its rate of firing. This rate can be deliberately changed in immediate response to a command. The lowest limit of the range of frequencies is zero, that is, one can start from neuromuscular silence and then give single isolated contractions at regular rates as low as one per second and at increasingly faster rates. When the more able subjects are asked to produce special repetitive rhythms and imitations of drum beats, almost all are successful (some strikingly so) in producing subtle shades and coloring of internal rhythms. When tape-recorded and replayed, these rhythms provide striking proof of the fineness of the control.

Physiologic Constraints

Firing Rates of Motor Units

Units of low threshold have a wide (7- to 20-spike-per-second) firing frequency range and tend to be located deep in the muscle, according to Clamann (1970), who used human biceps brachii and bipolar fine-wire electrodes. The higher the tension threshold before a unit is recruited, the higher is the lowest firing frequency, the narrower is its frequency range, and the more superficially is it located. Approaching the threshold values in a slightly different way, Petajan and Philip (1969) reported intervals rather than frequencies. For limb muscles, the threshold intervals were 90 ± 19 milliseconds, but for the facial muscles, they were only 40 ± 16 milliseconds. These investigators also defined and recorded "onset intervals," the longest regular interval at minimal effort; in the limbs, it was 132 ± 32 milliseconds, and in the face, 86 ± 29 milliseconds with the distal limb muscles having the longest onset intervals.

Individual motor units appear to have upper limits to their rates beyond which they cannot be fired in isolation; that is, overflow occurs and neighbors are recruited. These maximum frequencies range from 9 to 25 per second (when the maximum rates are carefully recorded with an electronic digital spike-counter). Almost all lie in the range of 9 to 16 per second. However, one must not infer that individual motor units are restricted to these rates when many units are recruited. Indeed, the upper limit of 50 per second generally accepted for human muscle is probably correct, with perhaps some slightly higher rates in other species.

Reliance on Visual or Aural Feedback

Some persons can be trained to gain control of isolated motor units to a level where, with both visual and aural cues shut off, they can recall any one of three favorite units on command and in any sequence. They can keep such units firing without any conscious awareness other than the assurance (after the fact) that they have succeeded. In spite of considerable introspection, they cannot explain their success except to state they "thought about" a motor unit as they had seen and heard it previously. This type of training probably underlies ordinary motor skills.

Cerebral Mechanisms

Tanji and Kato (1971) found that cortical motor potentials related to the discharge of a single motor unit is about the same size as that related to the contraction of whole muscles (e.g., as in key pressing). This led to their obvious conclusion that cerebral mechanisms are involved in an important manner in conscious isolation of individual motor units; they later consolidated these views with more specific tests (Kato & Tanji, 1972a). However, my associates, McLeod and Thysell (1973), do not agree; their studies of evoked EEG potentials reveal no true response in the sensorimotor areas that can be related to single motor unit activity. Intensive research is in progress to resolve the question.

We find no personal characteristics that reveal reasons for the quality of performance (Basmajian *et al.*, 1965). The best performers are found at different ages, among both sexes, and among both the manually skilled and unskilled, the educated and uneducated, and the bright and the dull personalities. Some "nervous" persons do not perform well—but neither do some very calm persons.

Peripheral Mechanisms

Proprioception. Carlsöö and Edfeldt (1963) concluded that proprioception can be assisted greatly by exeroceptive auxiliary stimuli in achieving motor precision. Nevertheless, Wagman, Pierce, and Burger (1965), using both our techniques and a technique of recording devised by Pierce and Wagman (1964), emphasize the role of proprioception. They stress their finding that subjects believe that certain positions of a joint must be either held or imagined for success in activating desired motor units in isolation.

Over several years, we have conducted investigations of the various factors that affect motor unit training and control (Basmajian & Simard, 1967; Simard & Basmajian, 1967; Simard *et al.*, 1968). We find that repositioning a neighboring joint while a motor unit is firing is a distracting influence but most subjects can keep doing it in spite of the distraction. We tend to agree with Wagman and his colleagues, who believe that subjects require our form of motor unit training before they can fire isolated specific motor units with the limb or joints in varying positions. Their subjects reported that activation depended on recall of the original position and contraction effort necessary for activation. This apparently is a form of proprioceptive memory and almost certainly is integrated in the spinal cord.

Limb Movements (Kinesthetic Interference). Our observations were based on trained units in the tibialis anterior of 32 young adults, and showed that motor unit activity under conscious control can be easily maintained despite the distraction produced by voluntary movements elsewhere in the body (head and neck, upper limbs, and contralateral limb). The control of isolation and the control of the easiest and fastest frequencies of discharge of a single motor unit were not affected by those movements (Basmajian & Simard, 1967). Turning to the effect of movements of the same limb, we found that, in some persons, a motor unit can be trained to remain active in isolation at different positions of a "proximal" (i.e., hip or knee), "crossed" (ankle), and "distal" joints of a limb. This is a step beyond Wagman, Pierce, and Burger (1965), who observed that a small change in position brings different motor units into action. Consequently they noted the important influence of the sense of position on the motor response. Our continuing experience shows that, in order to maintain or recall a motor unit at different positions, the subject must keep the motor unit active during the performance of the movements. Therefore, preliminary training is undeniably necessary.

The control of the maintenance of a single motor unit activity during "proximal," "crossed," and "distal" joint movements in the same limb has been proved here to be possible providing that the technique of assistance offered by the trainer is adequate. The control over the discharge of a motor unit during proximal and distal joint movements requires a great concentration on the motor activity. But when one considers the same control during a "crossed" joint movement, there are even greater difficulties for obvious reasons.

The observation that trained motor units can be activated at different positions of a joint is related to the work of Boyd and Roberts (1953). They suggested that there are slowly adaptive end organs of proprioception that are active during movements of a limb. They observed that the common, sustained discharge of the end organs in movements lasted for several seconds after attainment of a new position. This might explain why a trained single motor unit's activity can be maintained during movements.

Sensory Isolation

Lloyd and Shurley (1976) studied the hypodynamic effects of sensory isolation on single motor units recorded through fine-wire electrodes in 40 normal subjects. A light panel indicated the trial onset, and correct and incorrect response. Isolation condition was produced by an air-fluidized, ceramic-bead bed in a light-and-sound-attenuating chamber. A relearning session followed the initial session after a 2-week interim rest. Subjects were randomly assigned to the isolation or nonisolation condition for both sessions. The hypodynamic effects of sensory isolation increased the speed of learning to isolate and control an SMU. The results suggested that subjects were better able to attend to the relatively weak proprioceptive information provided by the SMU through the reduction of the amount and/or variety of competing stimuli.

Level of Synergistic Activity

The problem of what happens to the synergistic muscles at the "hold" position or during movements of a limb has been taken into consideration only in a preliminary way. The level of activity appears to be individualistic. Active inhibition of synergists is learned only after training of the motor unit in the prime mover is well established. Basmajian and Simard (1967) and Smith, Basmajian, and Vanderstoep (1974) clearly demonstrated that as the subject focuses his attention on feedback from a single motor unit, the surrounding muscles and motor units in the same muscle become progressively relaxed to the point of complete silence when isolation of the SMU is complete. Only such motor units in a limb as are needed to maintain its particular posture are still active. The process of "active inhibition," probably the more dramatic element of motor unit training, is thus achieved.

Manual Skills

Although our earlier studies had failed to reveal any correlation between the abilities of subjects to isolate individual motor units and the variable of athletic or musical ability, a systematic study (Scully & Basmajian, 1969) cast some light on the matter. We used the base time required to train motor units in one of the hand muscles as the criterion. To our surprise, the time required to train most of the manually skilled subjects was above the median.

Henderson's (1952) work offers an explanation: The constant repetition of a specific motor skill increases the probability of its correct recurrence by the learning and consolidation of an optimal anticipatory tension. Perhaps this depends on an increase in the background activity of the gamma motoneurons regulating the sensitivity of the muscle spindles used in performing the skill. Wilkins, in 1964, postulated that the acquisition of a new motor skill leads to the learning of a certain "position memory" for it. If anticipatory tensions and position memory—or both—are learned, spinal mechanisms may be acting temporarily to block the initial learning of a new skill. Perhaps some neuromuscular pathways acquire a habit of responding in certain ways and then that habit must be broken so that a new skill may be learned. The "unstructured" nature of learning a motor unit skill would make this mechanism even more likely (Basmajian, 1972).

Age and Sex

Although the training of fine control of individual units is complicated when children are involved, we found it possible in children even below the age of 6 years (Fruhling, Basmajian, & Simard, 1969). Simard and Ladd (1969) and Simard (1969) have further documented the factors involved.

Zappalá (1970) found only minor sex differences in the ability to isolate SMUs; males showed some superiority. In a different type of experiment, Harrison and Koch (1972) found the opposite, but again the sex differences were not impressive.

Competing Stimuli

Electrical. Any changes in the action potentials of trained motor units as a result of electrical stimulation of the motor nerve supplying the whole muscle must reflect neurophysiologic changes of the single neuron supplying the motor unit. Therefore, we investigated the influence of causing strong contractions in a muscle to compete with a discrete SMU in it which was being driven consciously (Scully & Basmajian, 1969). Each of a series of subjects sat with his forearm resting comfortably on a table top. The stimulator cathode was applied to the region of the ulnar nerve above the elbow. The effective stimuli were .1-millisecond square-wave pulses of 70 to 100 volts, delivered at a frequency of 90 per minute. Because stimuli of this order are not maximal, all axons in the ulnar nerve were not shocked and slight variation must have existed in axons actually stimulated by each successive shock. Contrary to expectation, when the massive contraction of a muscle was superimposed on the contraction of only one of its motor units, the regular conscious firing of that motor unit was not significantly changed. Our experiments leave little if any doubt that well-trained motor units are not blocked in most persons. Even the coinciding of the motor unit potential with elements of the electrically induced massive contraction would not abolish the motor unit potential.

Cold. Brief cutaneous applications of ice over the biceps brachii in which an isolated motor unit had been trained elicited facilitation of both background activity and spontaneous activation of the trained SMUs (Clendenin & Szumski, 1971). Recently, Wolf and I (1972–1973, unpublished) were able to confirm this using a special electronic cooling device (Wolf & Basmajian, 1973).

Handedness and Retesting

When a large number of subjects were studied on two occasions using a different hand each time, Powers (1969) found that they always isolated a unit more quickly in the second hand. Isolation was twice as rapid when the second hand was the preferred (dominant) hand; it was almost five times as rapid when the second hand was the nonpreferred one. The time required to control a previously isolated unit was shortened significantly only when the preferred hand was the second hand. However, in a test–retest situation with many fewer subjects, Harrison and Koch (1972) found no significant improvement from test to test.

Reaction-Time Studies

A number of investigators have used trained single motor units for psychological testing of reaction times. Thus, Sutton and Kimm (1970) and Kimm and Sutton (1973) have shown stable differences in the RT in triceps and biceps brachii and a slowing of RT following the intake of alcohol. Generally, they concluded that single motor unit spike RTs were slower than gross EMG and lever-press RTs. But Thysell (1969) disagrees, finding them to be comparable and rather like those of Luschei, Saslow, and Glickstein (1967). Further, Vanderstoep (1971) questions the finding of inherent differences between muscles when the RT paradigm is used with triceps, biceps, the first dorsal interosseus, and the abductor pollicis brevis. Zernicke and Waterland (1972), on the other hand, have shown differences between the two heads of biceps brachii. The short head contains motor units that are easier to control than those in the long head. They relate this to various morphological and functional requirements of the two heads (e.g., the density of muscle spindles is greater in the short head). The willful fractionization of control between two heads of the same muscle, not entirely unexpected in view of the fineness of willful controls involved in single motor unit control, once more underlines the discrete nature of controls over the spinal motoneurons.

Effects of Internal States

At the time of writing, a number of laboratories are exploring the use of EMGs of localized or SMU contractions for studying covert responses to emotional states. Fundamentally, there is no training of units but rather the use of motor unit responses for externalizing internal events. Equipment and general methodology are similar except that there is no direct feedback for the subject. In one paradigm (S. D. Kahn, personal communication), the EMG response is processed electronically to manipulate visual displays offered to the subject as reinforcing or negative stimuli.

REFERENCES

Adrian, E. D., & Bronk, D. W. The discharge of impulses in motor nerve fibres. Part II. The frequency of discharge in reflex and voluntary contractions. *Journal of Physiology*, 1929, *67*, 119–151.

Basmajian, J. V. Control and training of individual motor units. *Science*, 1963, *20*, 662–664.

Basmajian, J. V. Electromyography comes of age. *Science*, 1972, *176*, 603–609.

Basmajian, J. V. *Muscles alive: Their functions revealed by electromyography.* Baltimore: Williams & Wilkins, 1974.

Basmajian, J. V., Baeza, M., & Fabrigar, C. Conscious control and training of individual spinal motor neurons in normal human subjects. *Journal of New Drugs*, 1965, *5*, 78–85.

Basmajian, J. V., & Newton, W. J. Feedback training of parts of buccinator muscle in man. *Psychophysiology*, 1973, *11*, 92.

Basmajian, J. V., & Samson, J. Standardization of methods in single motor unit training. *American Journal of Physical Medicine*, 1973, *52*, 250–256.

Basmajian, J. V., & Simard, T. G. Effects of distracting movements on the control of trained motor units. *American Journal of Physical Medicine*, 1967, *46*, 1427–1449.

Basmajian, J. V., & Stecko, G. A new bipolar indwelling electrode for electromyography. *Journal of Applied Physiology*, 1962, *17*, 849.

Boyd, I. A., & Roberts, T. D. M. Proprioceptive discharges from stretch-receptors in the knee-joint of the cat. *Journal of Physiology*, 1953, *122*, 38–58.

Bruno, L. J. J., Davidowitz, J., & Hefferline, R. F. EMG waveform duration: A validation method for the surface electromyogram. *Behavioral Research Methodology and Instrumentation*, 1970, *2*, 211–219.

Carlsöö, S., & Edfeldt, A. W. Attempts at muscle control with visual and auditory impulses as auxiliary stimuli. *Scandinavian Journal of Psychology*, 1963, *4*, 231–235.

Clamann, H. P. Activity of single motor units during isometric tension. *Neurology*, 1970, *20*, 254–260.

Clendenin, M. A., & Szumski, A. J. Influence of cutaneous ice application on single motor units in humans. *Journal of American Physical Therapy Association*, 1971, *51*, 166–175.

Fruhling, M., Basmajian, J. V., & Simard, T. G. A note on the conscious control of motor units by children under six. *Journal of Motor Behavior*, 1969, *1*, 65–68.

Gilson, A. S., & Mills, W. B. Single responses of motor units in consequence of volitional effort. *Proceedings of the Society of Experimental Biology and Medicine*, 1940, *45*, 650–652.

Gilson, A. S., & Mills, W. B. Activities of single motor units in man during slight voluntary efforts. *American Journal of Physiology*, 1941, *133*, 658–669.

Gray, E. R. Conscious control of motor units in a tonic muscle. *American Journal of Physical Medicine*, 1971, *50*, 34–40.

Green, E. E., Walters, E. D., Green, A. M., & Murphy, G. Feedback technique for deep relaxation. *Psychophysiology,* 1969, *6,* 371–377.

Harrison, V. F., & Koch, W. B. Voluntary control of single motor unit activity in the extensor digitorum muscle. *Physical Therapy,* 1972, *52,* 267–272.

Harrison, V. F., & Mortensen, O. A. Identification and voluntary control of single motor unit activity in the tibialis anterior muscle. *Anatomical Record,* 1962, *144,* 109–116.

Hefferline, R. F., Bruno, L. J. J., & Davidowitz, J. E. Feedback control of covert behavior. In K. J. Connolly (Ed.), *Mechanisms of motor skill development.* New York: Academic Press, 1971.

Hefferline, R. F., & Perera, T. B. Proprioceptive discrimination of a covert operant without its observation by the subject. *Science,* 1963, *139,* 834–935.

Henderson, R. L. Remote action potentials at the moment of response in a simple reaction-time situation. *Journal of Experimental Psychology,* 1952, *44,* 238–241.

Kahn, S. D. Comparative advantages of bipolar abraded skin surface electrodes over bipolar intramuscular electrodes for single motor unit recording in psychophysiological research. *Psychophysiology,* 1971, *8,* 635–647.

Kato, M., & Tanji, J. Cortical motor potentials accompanying volitionally controlled single motor unit discharges in human finger muscles. *Brain Research,* 1972, *47,* 103–111. (a)

Kato, M., & Tanji, J. Volitionally controlled single motor units in human finger muscles. *Brain Research,* 1972, *40,* 435–437. (b)

Kimm, J., & Sutton, D. Foreperiod effects on human single motor unit reaction times. *Physiology of Behavior,* 1973, *10,* 539–542.

Ladd, H., Jonsson, B., & Lindegren, U. The learning process for fine neuromuscular control in skeletal muscles of man. *Electromyography and Clinical Neurophysiology,* 1972, *12,* 213–223.

Leibrecht, B. E., Lloyd, A. J., & Pounder, S. Auditory feedback and conditioning of the single motor unit. *Psychophysiology,* 1972, *10,* 1–7.

Lindsley, D. B. Electrical activity of human motor units during voluntary contraction. *American Journal of Physiology,* 1935, *114,* 90–99.

Lloyd, A. J., & Leibrecht, B. C. Conditioning of a single motor unit. *Journal of Experimental Psychology,* 1971, *88,* 391–395.

Lloyd, A. J., & Shurley, J. T. Perceptual isolation on single motor unit conditioning. *Psychophysiology,* 1976, *13,* 340–344.

Luschei, E., Saslow, C. & Glickstein, M. Muscle potentials in reaction time. *Experimental Neurology,* 1967, *18,* 429–442.

McLeod, W. D., & Thysell, R. Cortically evoked potentials co-related with single motor units. Manuscript submitted for publication, 1973.

Petajan, J. H., & Philip, B. A. Frequency control of motor unit action potentials. *Electroencephalography and Clinical Neurophysiology,* 1969, *27,* 66–72.

Pierce, D. S., & Wagman, I. H. A method of recording from single muscle fibers or motor units in human skeletal muscle. *Journal of Applied Physiology,* 1964, *19,* 366–368.

Powers, W. R. Conscious control of single motor units in the preferred and non-preferred hand. Unpublished doctoral dissertation, Queen's University, Kingston, Ontario, Canada, 1969.

Samson, J. The acquisition, retention and transfer of single motor unit control. Unpublished doctoral dissertation, University of Illinois, Urbana–Champaign, 1971.

Scully, H. E., & Basmajian, J. V. Motor-unit training and influence of manual skill. *Psychophysiology,* 1969, *5,* 625–632.

Simard, T. G. Fine sensorimotor control in healthy children: An electromyographic study. *Pediatrics,* 1969, *43,* 1035–1041.

Simard, T. G., & Basmajian, J. V. Methods in training the conscious control of motor units. *Archives of Physical Medicine and Rehabilitation,* 1967, *48,* 12–19.

Simard, T. G., Basmajian, J. V., & Janda, V. Effect of ischemia on trained motor units. *American Journal of Physical Medicine,* 1968, *47,* 64–71.

Simard, T. G., & Ladd, H. W. Conscious control of motor units with thalidomide children: An electromyographic study. *Developmental Medicine and Child Neurology,* 1969, *11,* 743–748.

Smith, O. C. Action potentials from single motor units in voluntary contraction. *American Journal of Physiology,* 1934, *108,* 629–638.

Smith, H. M., Jr., Basmajian, J. V., & Vanderstoep, S. F. Inhibition of neighboring motoneurons in conscious control of single spinal motoneurons. *Science,* 1974, *183,* 975–976.

Sussman, H. M., Hanson, R. J., & MacNeilage, P. F. Studies of single motor units in the speech musculature: Methodology and preliminary findings. *Journal of Acoustical Society of America,* 1972, *51,* 1372–1374.

Sutton, D. L. Surface and needle electrodes in electromyography. *Dental Progress,* 1962, *2,* 127–131.

Sutton, D., & Kimm, J. Alcohol effects on human motor unit reaction time. *Physiology of Behavior,* 1970, *5,* 889–892.

Tanji, J., & Kato, M. Volitionally controlled single motor unit discharges and cortical motor potentials in human subjects. *Brain Research,* 1971, *29,* 243–346.

Thysell, R. V. Reaction time of single motor units. *Psychophysiology,* 1969, *6,* 174–185.

Vanderstoep, S. F. A comparison of the ability to control single motor units in selected human skeletal muscles. Unpublished doctoral dissertation, University of Southern California, 1971.

Wagman, I. H., Pierce, D. S., & Burger, R. E. Proprioceptive influence in volitional control of individual motor units. *Nature,* 1965, *207,* 957–958.

Wolf, S. L., & Basmajian, J. V. A rapid cooling device for controlled cutaneous stimulation. *American Physical Therapy Association Journal,* 1973, *53,* 25–27.

Zappalá, A. Influence of training and sex on the isolation of and control of single motor units. *American Journal of Physical Medicine,* 1970, *49,* 348–461.

Zernicke, R. F., & Waterland, J. C. Single motor unit control on m. biceps brachii. *Electromyography and Clinical Neurophysiology,* 1972, *12,* 225–241.

18

Clinical Implications of Electromyographic Training

THOMAS H. BUDZYNSKI
University of Colorado School of Medicine
and Biofeedback Institute of Denver, Colorado

In the psychological literature, there has been no lack of references to the condition commonly known as "tension" or "tenseness." The concept usually implies an excessive, chronic, or somehow maladaptive level of tonus in some or all of the skeletal muscles. In many cases, the label encompasses not only skeletal muscle tension but other correlates of heightened arousal such as cool, wet palms, rapid heart rate, unpleasant visceral sensations, and fast, uneven respiration. Younger people might refer to an individual with these characteristics as "uptight," a term that reflects the subjective state of tenseness.

Heightened muscle tension is a frequent, if not invariant, accompaniment of fear, anxiety, stress, and conflict. However, at times, it can be quite adaptive if in some way it aids us in taking physical action to reduce the fear or anxiety, or to resolve the conflict. Tension can be maladaptive if it increases to the point that our performance is decreased rather than increased or we are prevented from engaging in physical activity in the behavioral sense. Thus, the many restrictions of our fast-paced, overpopulated, red-tape society often prohibit the motor expression of what has been referred to as the "flight or fight" pattern (Cannon, 1932). The function of this pattern is to mobilize the body's resources for action. The heart rate is increased, muscle tension increases, stored sugar is released from the liver, the hands become damp and cool, as blood is shunted away from the periphery into the muscles, digestive processes slow, the blood's coagulation ability is increased, and hormones such as adrenaline and noradrenaline and certain stress substances are released into the bloodstream.

An increasing number of investigators believe that if this sympathetically mediated stress response is evoked frequently, or sustained too long, or if the completion of the pattern through vigorous physical activity is prevented, then disorders are likely to develop (Charvat, Dell, & Folkow, 1964; Folkow & Neil, 1971; Simeons, 1962; Wolff, 1968).

If these experts are correct, then this phenomenon (a maladaptive stress response) is widespread in our industrialized societies where there has been a dramatic shift in disease patterns from communicable to stress-related and degenerative disorders over the past 150 years. Most infectious diseases are now well controlled; however, cardiovascular disorders presently account for over 50% of all deaths in this country. High blood pressure, ulcers, colitis, back problems, insomnia, and the ubiquitous headache continue to plague millions.

Recently, two cardiologists, Friedman and Rosenman (1974), presented convincing evidence that the typical product of our culture—the aggressive, competitive, hard-driving individual (about one-half of all American males and a growing percentage of females)—is rendered very susceptible to heart disorders by virtue of his or her behavior pattern. The pattern involves an exaggerated sense of time urgency, an inability to relax, and a reluctance to let go of work-oriented thoughts even when engaging in recreation activities.

AUTONOMIC PATTERNS AND STRESS-RELATED DISORDERS

The behavioral pattern defined by Friedman and Rosenman rounds out the total picture of the individual whose life style, and to some extent his genetic makeup, predisposes him to fall prey to stress-related disorders. The physiological side of the picture appears to be one of a chronic, or frequently evoked, partial flight or fight response. More specifically, this individual manifests maladaptively high levels of muscle tension and a sympathetically dominated autonomic pattern.

The question of whether this physiological state of affairs actually precedes the onset of the stress-related disorder or is simply a result of the physiological deterioration, even in the early stages, is not entirely clear. However, a noted psychophysiologist has presented substantial evidence in support of the former view.

Wenger and Cullen (1972) studied the autonomic patterns of thousands of young, healthy Air Force cadets during World War II. He established an autonomic balance scoring system by which each individual was given an estimate of autonomic balance called the $\bar{A}$ *score*. This score was a composite of the values obtained on each of seven physiological variables reflecting autonomic function. Lower scores reflected apparent sympathetic nervous system (SNS) dominance. Higher scores reflected apparent parasympathetic nervous system (PNS) dominance. In the large group of cadets, Wenger found a wide distribution of $\bar{A}$ scores. Later, when measuring patients with different types of psychosomatic disorders, Wenger discovered that, almost without exception, the patients showed low $\bar{A}$ scores indicating an apparent sympathetic dominance.

It was not until some 15 years after the cadet study that Wenger sent out questionnaires to the former cadets. The questionnaire was designed to allow a determination of which disorders, including anxiety, had claimed the formerly normal, healthy cadets. Not surprisingly, those individuals who had been found to have low $\bar{A}$ scores (apparent sympathetic dominance) had, later on, produced the highest incidence of stress-linked disorders. In contrast, the incidence of these problems in the cadets who originally produced normal or high $\bar{A}$ scores was low. Thus, it would seem that those individuals who show an autonomic pattern characterized by sympathetic rather than parasympathetic functioning are more likely to suffer from stress-related disorders. Perhaps it can also be said that training in the direction of apparent parasympathetic dominance might be of value not only in alleviating certain stress-related disorders but in the prevention of them as well.

THE RELAXATION THERAPIES

Relaxation training in one form or another has been used in a number of therapies for dealing with anxiety and stress-related dysfunctions. The two most widely known techniques are Jacobson's Progressive Relaxation (Jacobson, 1938) and Schultz and Luthe's Autogenic Training (Luthe, 1969). In both of these techniques, the trainee is taught to relax voluntarily the main muscle groups; however, the autogenic training places greater emphasis on awareness of sensations associated with a decrease in sympathetic outflow and an increase in parasympathetic dominance.

Since both of these approaches are designed to teach the individual to produce voluntarily a low arousal, apparent parasympathetic pattern, they would seem to be tailor-made for application to stress-related disorders. In fact, this has been the focus of these techniques for almost half a century. The results, although reportedly good, have been obscured somewhat due to the scarcity of properly controlled studies and, in the case of autogenic training, the absence of English translations until recent years.

Although progressive relaxation and autogenic training can produce beneficial effects, the training is lengthy, and success is dependent upon the discrimination by the trainee of very subtle proprioceptive and interoceptive sensations. Discriminations of this sort seem to be particularly difficult for those individuals who most need the training, that is, those who suffer from stress-related disorders. Because their levels of arousal are frequently high, these individuals tend to become adapted to, and therefore lacking in awareness of, these sensations. Consequently, training effectiveness could be improved by the addition of a technique that would aid in the development of these fine discriminations.

BIOFEEDBACK TRAINING OF A "CULTIVATED LOW AROUSAL"

If, as a great deal of evidence would suggest, these relaxation therapies can result in the production of a physiological pattern (decreased sympathetic outflow—apparent parasympathetic dominance) that is opposite to that of the flight or fight pattern associated with stress-linked dysfunctions and anxiety, then a technique that could augment and refine such training would be of great value.

Biofeedback enhances discrimination of subtle physiological functioning because it produces an "effect" where before there was little or no effect signaling a change in such functioning. Sheffield (1965) has stated that an inherent feature of Thorndike's (1911) law of effect is that the *effect* of a response determines whether it is learned. That is, the effect of the response must in some way be detected by the organism or recorded in its nervous system. Somehow the organism's nervous system must detect the temporal contiguity of the response and its consequences. If a response has little or no sensory feedback, it is difficult to understand how the nervous system could take account of the fact that the response was executed. Perhaps this explains why the mastery of Zen or Yoga requires years of dedicated practice before voluntary control of certain autonomic responses is acquired, and why autogenic training and progressive relaxation demand such regular practice over a relatively long duration.

The "effect," or the feedback, of levels and changes in tonic skeletal muscle tonus is popularly known as EMG (electromyographic) biofeedback. It is one of the more useful forms of feedback for purposes of training low arousal patterns because it involves some voluntary as well as involuntary control, and thus learning accrues at a faster rate than with the training of completely involuntary responses. Moreover, the skeletal muscle system comprises a large percentage of the entire bodily mass and therefore a change in this system can, and usually does, produce changes in other systems such as the CNS (central nervous system) and the ANS (autonomic nervous system). In other words, voluntary control of the tonus of the skeletal muscle system gives one leverage in changing responses in the CNS and ANS.

Through the continuous feedback of the surface EMG, the bioelectric correlate of muscle tension, the trainee develops first an awareness of, and then control over, the level of that muscle tension (Budzynski, 1973). Eventually he is able to generalize that control to the other skeletal muscles and thereby affect, indirectly, autonomic and cortical functioning as well. Finally, he is trained to transfer that control to everyday life situations outside the clinic or laboratory.

In a series of experiments beginning in 1966, we were able to demonstrate that individuals could learn to relax the frontalis (forehead) muscle to a lower level of tension through EMG feedback than by relaxation alone, or by simply focusing their attention on a neutral stimulus (akin to certain meditation practices) (Budzynski & Stoyva, 1969). The series also included a study showing that subjects could learn to produce low masseter (jaw) tension levels in only one 20-minute session (Budzynski & Stoyva, 1973a). A third study demonstrated that the production of low frontalis levels through forehead feedback generalized to the forearm muscles; however, the reverse did not occur, that is, the production of low forearm extensor tension through arm feedback did not generalize to the forehead (Stoyva & Budzynski, 1974). However, another investigator, Alexander (1973), found that three sessions of frontalis feedback did not result in significant generalization to the forearm muscle. This may have been due to the fact that the forearm levels were quite low even before training was begun, and therefore, a "bottoming" effect may have occurred.

DOES EMG FEEDBACK-PRODUCED LOW TENSION GENERALIZE TO OTHER SYSTEMS?

Gellhorn (1958) had shown in a series of animal studies that the reduction of proprioception produces an apparent parasympathetic dominance in the autonomic system. Measures of the physiology of humans engaged in progressive relaxation and autogenic training also indicated a shift in autonomic balance toward the parasympathetic. In a later article, Gellhorn and Kiely (1972) have suggested that the mechanism of muscular relaxation leading to reduced proprioceptive input to the hypothalamus, in turn resulting in a dominance of the parasympathetic system, accounts for much of the similarity among progressive relaxation, autogenic training, and Wolpe's systematic desensitization technique (Wolpe, 1958).

Generalization to Cortical Regions

Support for the generalization of EMG feedback-produced low muscle tension to cortical regions was obtained from two studies in our laboratory. The first one demonstrated that two-flash threshold varied with frontalis and neck muscle tension (Budzynski, 1969). As the summed muscle activity of the neck and forehead decreased to low levels with biofeedback, subjects required longer intervals between flashes in order to report two distinct flashes. The study illustrated the definite decrease in cortical arousal resulting from greatly decreased muscle tension levels of the head and neck.

In a second study (Sittenfeld, Budzynski, & Stoyva, 1972), it was demonstrated that profound muscle relaxation was associated with the appearance of theta rhythms (4–7 Hz) in the electroencephalogram (EEG). In fact, we found that at the lower levels of frontalis muscle tension, there was an inverse relationship with EEG theta. As frontalis EMG decreased, theta increased. At higher frontalis levels, theta was minimal or absent. Not surprisingly, subjects with high frontalis EMG levels could not learn to increase theta even when provided with theta EEG feedback for eight 20-minute sessions. On the other hand, when subjects with high frontalis EMG were first given EMG feedback, they learned to decrease the muscle tension, thus increasing the level of theta. Following this, they were switched to theta EEG feedback. This sequence of two types of feedback enabled them to show increases in theta over a total of eight sessions.

The results of this last study provided support for the concept of using muscle relaxation as an initial stage in the biofeedback training of other, more specific responses. This procedure now constitutes an integral feature of our clinical approach to anxiety and stress-related disorders.

CLINICAL RESEARCH

Our early EMG feedback clinical research was targeted on anxiety disorders. Given Wolpe's assumption that successful desensitization of maladaptive fear or anxiety is contingent upon the production of a physiological pattern antagonistic to that produced by anxiety, it seemed that a technique that could enhance the production of such a pattern, and, in addition, provide objective evidence of that production, would be very useful. Thus, an EMG feedback system was designed which could be used to train the clients in muscle relaxation, and then function as a monitor of relaxation (or anxiety) during the systematic desensitization therapy that followed (Budzynski, 1969).

The procedure was applied initially to clients who were referred by therapists unable to train the clients to relax prior to desensitization. In this initial group of six clients, we found that the EMG indicator of anxiety was considerably more sensitive than the individual's verbal report (Budzynski & Stoyva, 1973b). In most instances, the subjective report of anxiety lagged the EMG indicator by 8 to 10 seconds.

Once the EMG feedback was found to be successful with these clients who had been refractory to other relaxation methods, we began to employ it as an integral part of the systematic desensitization process. A client would first be taught to produce thorough muscle relaxation with EMG feedback. The feedback (usually from the frontalis) was then used by the client to maintain relaxed levels during the desensitization itself. In most cases, these EMG procedures were sufficient to ensure a low arousal state; however, a few individuals showed evidence of autonomic arousal (high electrodermal activity), even though maintaining low EMG levels over the frontalis and forearm extensor muscles. When these clients proceeded through the desensitization hierarchy, it was necessary to monitor electrodermal activity (EDA) as well as EMG levels in order for the desensitization to be successful.

Le Boeuf (1974) found that chronic anxiety clients with predominantly muscular symptoms showed significant improvement in both specific symptoms and generalized anxiety as a result of EMG feedback (frontalis) training. On the other hand, Le Boeuf showed that, as a group, those clients with predominantly autonomic symptoms did not improve significantly as a result of this training. Raskin, Johnson, and Rondestvedt (1973) examined 10 chronically anxious clients who had not been helped by individual psychotherapy and medication for 2 years prior to the study. Training all 10 clients to a low EMG criterion (2.5 microvolts peak-to-peak average on the frontalis) they found beneficial effects on the anxiety of 4 of the 10. Of interest were the additional findings that 5 of the 6 clients who also had insomnia improved in this regard, as did headache conditions in 3 of 4.

From these studies, one might surmise that EMG feedback can be useful in certain types of anxiety disorders. Certainly, few of the relevant parameters have been defined experimentally; however, some tentative suggestions can be made at this point.

When is EMG Feedback Training Indicated in Cases of Anxiety?

Our research with generalized and specific anxiety disorders over a 5-year period (Budzynski & Stoyva, 1974), along with the results of the studies mentioned above, would suggest that EMG feedback is useful for anxiety problems when:

1. there is a notable skeletal muscle component to the anxiety pattern;
2. the client is unable to learn to relax with simpler, nonmachine relaxation procedures;
3. the client lacks awareness of his or her level of muscle tension;
4. the client believes strongly that EMG biofeedback will help him learn to relax;
5. the therapist is not sure that the client can or will provide an accurate subjective report of level of anxiety-relaxation during therapy.

Headache

Of all the clinical applications of biofeedback, that of EMG feedback for chronic tension headache would seem to be among the most successful (Blanchard & Young, 1974). Our research into this disorder was triggered by the observation that tension headache is usually associated with sustained high tension in the muscles of the neck, scalp, and forehead. A pilot study (Budzynski, Stoyva, & Adler, 1970), and a subsequent controlled group outcome study (Budzynski, Stoyva, Adler, & Mullaney, 1973) provided support for the use of frontalis EMG feedback for this common disorder. Without additional drug therapy, or psychotherapy, or instructed relaxation training (other than with EMG feedback), roughly 70% of the subjects in these studies showed clinically significant reductions in headaches. It should be noted that in both experiments the subjects were asked to practice relaxing at home, or at the office, twice each day for 20 minutes. Although they were told only to practice what they had learned during the feedback training, we felt that this home practice was necessary to effect a transfer of the skill from the laboratory to "real life." Raskin *et al.* (1973) also had their clients practicing twice daily at home; however, Wickramasekera (1972) obtained successful results with tension headache without home practice.

These research findings suggest that a "bare bones" EMG feedback procedure can be successful with chronic tension headache although the additional home practice appears to be of value. We have found that the motivation for home work is improved a good deal through the use of a cassette tape series that progresses the client through six stages of relaxation training. The tapes provide the client with basic relaxation skills which are then refined through the actual EMG feedback training.

Is EMG Biofeedback Necessary for Relaxation Training for Chronic Tension Headache?

Since the immediate pain of this disorder is usually brought about by sustained contraction of certain muscles about the head and neck, the specificity of the EMG feedback may be ideal. But then, not all tension headache clients show this elevated muscle tension, and in these cases, a more general nonbiofeedback relaxation program may be adequate. In one study, Haynes, Griffin, Mooney, and Parise (1975) showed that passive relaxation instructions produced a reduction in tension headaches equal to that resulting from EMG feedback. Hutchings and Reinking (1976) on the other hand, found that EMG feedback training reduced headaches to a greater degree than did progressive relaxation training.

In general, EMG biofeedback for tension headaches functions, as it does in all applications, not only as a training tool but as a motivator, allowing an objective, easily observable success experience for the client. If localized muscle tension is indicated by heightened EMG levels in the head or neck, biofeedback training will usually result in a rapid reduction of this tension. These factors may permit biofeedback to succeed in cases where other, nonmachine relaxation methods may fail. In combination with a structured home training regime, EMG feedback is very effective for chronic tension headache.

EMG Feedback: An Indirect Solution to Essential Hypertension?

The use of blood pressure cuff feedback procedures for essential hypertension has been well researched by a number of investigators, notably Schwartz (1973), Schwartz and Shapiro (1973), and Benson, Shapiro, Tursky, and Schwartz (1971). Less well known is the work of Montgomery, Love, and Moeller (1974), who had studied the relationship between relaxation training (progressive relaxation and autogenic training) and the reduction of blood pressure. These researchers then used an EMG frontalis feedback procedure sometimes augmented with a cassette tape series for home training. While the controls showed little change in pressures, the trained subjects ($N=32$) declined an average of 14.74 mm Hg systolic and 12.70 diastolic. At a follow-up session 1 year later, 23 of the original 32 trainees produced a mean decrease from the original baseline of 27.52 and 17.70 mm Hg systolic and diastolic, respectively. Thus, it appeared that a residual effect (change in life style?) continued after completion of training.

Additional support for a relaxation procedure for essential hypertension came from research reported by Russ (1974), who compared EMG feedback with an operant blood pressure feedback procedure. Although both regimes produced decreases in systolic pressures that were not significantly different, the EMG feedback group did show a greater reduction in diastolic pressures than did the operant procedure group.

Given that frequent daily relaxation will result in lower blood pressures, this indirect means of control may succeed where the more direct procedure may not, because of the proprioceptive cues (heaviness, warmth) associated with muscle relaxation. Once discriminated, these cues can serve to signal control in situations other than the training setting.

Other Applications of a Cultivated Low Arousal

If the arousal model for stress-related disorders is generally valid, then biofeedback training of voluntarily produced low arousal patterns should have wide applicability. Our research thus far indicates that this may be the case. Sleep-onset insomnia, for example, is a disorder usually associated with a tense musculature and an activated brain wave pattern. We have used a two-stage training program for clients with this problem. In this study, 11 clients were trained initially to lower tension levels through EMG feedback. A second stage of training consisted of theta (4–7 Hz) EEG feedback. The objective was to teach the clients to combat their insomnia by relaxing and then producing a drowsy brain rhythm. Of the 11 clients, 6 improved, 3 dramatically (Budzynski, 1973).

An interesting case study provided support for the potential use of low arousal training for certain forms of diabetes. Fowler, Budzynski, and VandenBergh (1976), working with one diabetic, obtained a 6-week baseline followed by a 9-week biofeedback relaxation training period. A follow-up began 1 year after the start of the baseline. Daily insulin requirements, which averaged 84 units during baseline, declined to 56 units during the last 6 weeks of training. During the 6-week follow-up 9 months after completing training, the average insulin requirement was 52 units. Training consisted of twice-daily 20-minute practice sessions with a cassette tape series and a portable PE-2 EMG feedback unit. The subject reported that, as a result of the training, she was able to maintain a relaxed, yet alert, state during stressful situations such as final examinations.

Although only a case study, the careful baseline and the follow-up results suggest that this sort of procedure may be effective for the type of diabetes condition that is generally exacerbated by stress.

MUSCLE REEDUCATION

While a "cultivated" relaxation or low arousal pattern involving all or most of the muscle system may be useful in dealing with a variety of stress-related disorders, the rehabilitation of muscles rendered dysfunctional through injury, stroke, or other disease has been implemented through the use of EMG feedback from quite specific areas. For example, Brudny, Grynbaum, and Korein (1973) and Cleeland (1973) used suface EMG feedback from neck muscles for successful alleviation of spasmodic torticollis.

Cleeland's approach involved a combination of EMG feedback and an aversive stimulus—a mild electric shock. The feedback was a tone that increased in frequency as the neck EMG increased. If the EMG rose above a certain level, the patient received a mild shock. This procedure resulted in a dramatic decrease in symptoms in 8 of 10 patients. A follow-up program at 19 months demonstrated that 6 patients still maintained marked improvement.

Brudny and his associates have trained their patients to reduce EMG through feedback from the muscle producing the torticollis, and then taught them to increase the tension in the atrophied contralateral muscle. Thus, the patients learned to equalize muscle levels on both sides of the neck. A home training program of isometric contractions of the atrophied muscle was encouraged.

In one of the better research studies in this area, John Basmajian and his associates compared biofeedback training with conventional physical therapy in treating adult hemiparetic patients with chronic foot drop (Basmajian, Kukulka, Narayan, & Takabe, 1975). Twenty patients were randomly assigned to two groups of 10 each. The first group received 15 sessions of 40 minutes each of therapeutic exercise. In the second group of 10 patients, the 40-minute session was divided into 20 minutes of therapeutic exercise followed by 20 minutes of EMG biofeedback. This biofeedback-trained group showed an increase in both strength and range of motion that was approximately twice as great as in the first group. Moreover, four of the patients in the biofeedback groups retained conscious control of the dorsiflexion, and three of them now walk without the use of the short leg brace.

Although biofeedback is usually thought of as a fairly recent phenomenon, the use of EMG feedback for muscle rehabilitation was explored by Marinacci and Horande (1960) some 14 years ago. More recently, Johnson and Garton (1973) have refined the technique for use with hemiplegia patients. After initial laboratory instruction, home training was accomplished by twice-daily use of a portable EMG feedback unit utilizing surface sensors. If sufficient surface EMG could not be generated, a monopolar needle electrode was used. Of 11 patients in this study thus far, the hemiplegia resulted from cerebrovascular accidents in 9 and from traumatic head injury in 2. Ten of the patients had been paralyzed for longer than 1 year and one patient had shown no functional return after 6 months of intensive physical therapy. The results look quite promising—only one patient did not improve, while 10 showed definite, positive change in motor function.

The dramatic results achieved with EMG feedback in muscle reeducation, particularly with patients whose paralysis had existed over a year's duration before training, would suggest that this procedure will meet with increasing acceptance.

Another variation of muscle reeducation through EMG feedback is the therapy used by Whatmore and Kohli (1968). These investigators and clinicians train individuals to correct maladaptive muscle bracing which Whatmore and Kohli often find associated with stress-related disorders. Patients are taught by means of verbal instruction and by watching recorders or meters and/or hearing the EMG activity through loudspeakers or headphones. Follow-ups as long as 20 years demonstrate the lasting results with this muscle therapy.

CONCLUDING REMARKS

Research involving biofeedback and clinical disorders generally has been focused on specific responses rather than on the developing of a physiological pattern that is incompatible with the "flight or fight" or defense–alarm pattern. However, clinical interest has recently shifted toward the use of a variety of biofeedback types within the same individual for the purpose of training a generalized "cultivated" relaxation. This use of several kinds of feedback sequentially and simultaneously represents the kind of systems approach that permits a structured, yet flexible, application (Budzynski, 1974). The use of EMG feedback in combination with a cassette tape home practice course is an excellent starting point for the training of cultivated relaxation. This initial training can be augmented by other feedback training such as peripheral temperature, electrodermal, or brain wave information if this is indicated. The relative effectiveness of the component parts of such multiple feedback programs is difficult to assess experimentally since, in this case, the whole somehow does seem to be greater than the sum of its parts.

The clinical picture is further clouded by the fact that biofeedback is seldom used "in a vacuum" in the clinical setting; that is, it is often combined with relaxation training, hypnosis, psychotherapy, behavior therapy, Gestalt therapy, or meditation. The skillful clinician uses biofeedback as one of the many tools at his disposal. However, it is possible that with the continued refinement of a structured systematic approach, a great deal of the biofeedback training could be carried out by a technician. This arrangement should result in less costly training and a greater availability of such training.

Stress Alleviation—A Preventive Approach?

There is the evidence that biofeedback can help alleviate or even eliminate certain stress-related disorders, but can it be used in a preventive program? Again, if it is granted that stress disorders arise as a result of sustained or frequently evoked hyperarousal, and that EMG biofeedback relaxation training can result in an incompatible set of physiological responses, then such training, along with the incorporation of the learning into everyday situations, should result in a decreased susceptibility. The research of Wenger and the results of some half-century of application of the relaxation procedures of Jacobson, Schultz, and Luthe suggest the possibilities of a refined, routinely administered biofeedback relaxation program.

REFERENCES

Alexander, A. B. Generalization to other muscles during EMG biofeedback training of the frontalis. Paper presented at the meeting of the Society for Psychophysiological Research, Galveston, Texas, October 1973.

Basmajian, J. V., Kukulka, C. G., Narayan, M. G., & Takabe, K. Biofeedback treatment of foot-drop after stroke compared with standard rehabilitation technique: Effects on voluntary control and strength. *Archives of Physical Medicine and Rehabilitation,* 1975, *56,* 231–236.

Benson, H., Shapiro, D., Tursky, B., & Schwartz, G. E. Decreased systolic blood pressure through operant conditioning techniques in patients with essential hypertension. *Science,* 1971, *173,* 740–742.

Blanchard, E. B., & Young, L. D. Clinical applications of biofeedback training: A review of evidence. *Archives of General Psychiatry,* 1974, *30,* 573–589.

Brudny, J., Grynbaum, B., & Korein, J. New therapeutic modality in the treatment of spasmodic torticollis. *Archives of Physical Medicine and Rehabilitation,* 1973, *54,* 575.

Budzynski, T. Feedback-induced muscle relaxation and activation level. Unpublished doctoral dissertation, University of Colorado, 1969.

Budzynski, T. Biofeedback procedures in the clinic. *Seminars in Psychiatry,* 1973, 5, 537–547.

Budzynski, T. A systems approach to some clinical applications of biofeedback. Paper presented at the American Orthopsychiatric Association meeting, San Francisco, California, April 1974.

Budzynski, T., & Stoyva, J. An instrument for producing deep muscle relaxation by means of analog information feedback. *Journal of Applied Behavior Analysis,* 1969, *2,* 231–237.

Budzynski, T., & Stoyva, J. An electromyographic feedback technique for teaching voluntary relaxation of the masseter. *Journal of Dental Research,* 1973, *52,* 116–119. (a)

Budzynski, T., & Stoyva, J. Biofeedback techniques in behavior therapy. In N. Birbaumer (Ed.), *Neuropsychologie der Angst. Reihe Fortschritte der Klinischen Psychologie.* Bd. 3. München, Berlin, Wien: Verlag Urban & Schwarzenberg, 1973. Pp. 248–270. (Republished in D. Shapiro *et al.,* (Eds.), *Biofeedback and self-control: 1972.* Chicago: Aldine, 1973.) (b)

Budzynski, T., & Stoyva, J. EMG biofeedback in generalized and specific anxiety disorders. In H. Legewie and L. Nusselt (Eds.), *Therapeutic applications of biofeedback methods.* Munich: Urban & Schwarzenberg, in press.

Budzynski, T., Stoyva, J., & Adler, C. S. Feedback-induced muscle relaxation: Application to tension headache. *Behavior Therapy and Experimental Psychiatry,* 1970, *1,* 205–211.

Budzynski, T., Stoyva, J., Adler, C. S., & Mullaney, D. J. EMG biofeedback and tension headache: A controlled outcome study. *Psychosomatic Medicine,* 1973, *35,* 484–496.

Cannon, W. B. *The wisdom of the body.* New York: Norton, 1932.

Charvat, S., Dell, P., & Folkow, B. Mental factors and cardiovascular disorders. *Cardiologia,* 1964, *44,* 124–141.

Cleeland, C. Behavioral techniques in the modification of spasmodic torticollis. *Neurology,* 1973, *23,* 1241–1247.

Folkow, B., & Neil, E. *Circulation.* New York: Oxford University Press, 1971.

Fowler, J., Budzynski, T., & VandenBergh, R. Effects of an EMG biofeedback relaxation program on the control of diabetes: A case study. *Biofeedback and Self-Regulation*, 1976, *1*, 105–112.

Friedman, M., & Rosenman, R. *Type A behavior and your heart*. New York: Knopf, 1974.

Gellhorn, E. The influence of curare on hypothalamic excitability and the electroencephalogram. *Electroencephalography and Clinical Neurophysiology*, 1958, *10*, 697–703.

Gellhorn, E., & Kiely, W. F. Mystical states of consciousness: Neurophysiological and clinical aspects. *Journal of Nervous and Mental Disease*, 1972, *154*, 399–405.

Haynes, S. N., Griffin, P., Mooney, D., & Parise, M. Electromyographic biofeedback and relaxation instructions in the treatment of muscle contraction headaches. *Behavior Therapy*, 1975, *6*, 672–678.

Hutchings, D. F., & Reinking, R. H. Tension headaches: What form of therapy is most effective? *Biofeedback and Self-Regulation*, 1976, *1*, 183–190.

Jacobson, E. *Progressive relaxation*. Chicago: University of Chicago Press, 1938.

Johnson, H. E., & Garton, W. H. Muscle re-education in hemiplegia by use of electromyographic device. *Archives of Physical Medicine and Rehabilitation*, 1973, *54*, 320–323.

Le Boeuf, A. The importance of individual differences in the treatment of chronic anxiety by EMG feedback techinque. Paper presented at the Biofeedback Research Society Annual Meeting, Colorado Springs, Colorado, February 1974.

Luthe, W. (Ed.). *Autogenic therapy*. Vols. 1–6, New York: Grune & Stratton, 1969.

Marinacci, A. A., & Horande, M. Electromyogram in neuromuscular re-education. *Bulletin of the Los Angeles Neurological Society*, 1960, *25*, 50–71.

Montgomery, D. D., Love, W. A., Jr., & Moeller, T. A. Effects of electromyographic feedback and relaxation training on blood pressure in essential hypertensives. Paper presented at the Biofeedback Research Society Annual Meeting, Colorado Springs, Colorado, February 1974.

Raskin, M., Johnson, G., & Rondestvedt, J. W. Chronic anxiety treated by feedback-induced muscle relaxation. *Archives of General Psychiatry*, 1973, *28*, 263–267.

Russ, K. L. Effect of two different feedback paradigms on blood pressure levels of patients with essential hypertension. Paper presented at the Biofeedback Research Society Annual Meeting, Colorado Springs, Colorado, February 1974.

Schwartz, G. E. Biofeedback as therapy: Some theoretical and practical issues. *American Psychologist*, 1973, *28*, 666–673.

Schwartz, G. E., & Shapiro, D. Biofeedback in essential hypertension: Current findings and theoretical concerns. In L. Birk (Ed.), *Biofeedback: Behavioral medicine*. New York: Grune & Stratton, 1973. Pp. 133–143.

Sheffield, F. D. Relation between classical conditioning and instrumental learning. In W. F. Prokasy (Ed.), *Classical conditioning*. New York: Appleton, 1965.

Simeons, A. *Man's presumptuous brain*. New York: E. P. Dutton, 1962.

Sittenfeld, P., Budzynski, T., & Stoyva, J. Feedback control of the EEG theta rhythm. Paper presented at the 1972 American Psychological Association meeting, Honolulu, Hawaii, 1972.

Stoyva, J., & Budzynski, T. Cultivated low arousal—an anti-stress response? In L. V. DiCara (Ed.), *Recent advances in limbic and autonomic nervous system research*. New York: Plenum, 1974.

Thorndike, E. L. *Animal intelligence*. New York: Macmillan, 1911.

Wenger, M. A., & Cullen, T. D. Studies of autonomic balance in children and adults. In

N. S. Greenfield & R. A. Sternbach (Eds.), *Handbook of psychophysiology.* New York: Holt, 1972. Pp. 535–569.

Whatmore, G., & Kohli, D. Dysponesis: A neurophysiologic factor in functional disorders. *Behavioral Sciences,* 1968, *13,* 102–123.

Wickramasekera, I. Electromyographic feedback training and tension headache: Preliminary observations. *American Journal of Clinical Hypnosis,* 1972, *15,* 83–85.

Wolff, H. G. In S. Wolf and H. Goodell (Eds.), *Harold G. Wolff's stress and disease.* (2nd ed.) Springfield, Ill.: Charles C. Thomas, 1968.

Wolpe, J. *Psychotherapy by reciprocal inhibition.* Stanford: Stanford University Press, 1958.

Author Index

H

I

M

S

Subject Index

C

D

E

F